ADAM S
ARN

C A S E S I N

MARKETING
MANAGEMENT
SECOND EDITION

CASES IN
MARKETING
MANAGEMENT

SECOND EDITION

LUIZ MOUTINHO

ADDISON-WESLEY
PUBLISHING
COMPANY

Wokingham, England · Reading, Massachusetts · Menlo Park, California
New York · Don Mills, Ontario · Amsterdam · Bonn . Sydney
Singapore · Tokyo · Madrid · San Juan · Milan · Paris · Mexico City · Seoul · Taipei

Many of the designations used by manufacturers and sellers to distinguish their products are
claimed as trademarks. Addison-Wesley has made every attempt to supply trademark information
about manufacturers and their products mentioned in this book.

Cover designed by Crayon Design of Henley-on-Thames
and printed by The Riverside Printing Co. (Reading) Ltd.
Typeset by Colset Pte Ltd, Singapore
and printed and bound by T. J. Press (Padstow) Ltd., Cornwall.

First printed 1995

ISBN 0-201-62744-2

British Library Cataloguing-in-Publication Data
A catalogue record for this book is available from the British Library.

Library of Congress Cataloging-in-Publication Data applied for

To my mother

Preface

One of the first laws of marketing management is that you must learn to adapt to a changing environment. With this in mind I have added a substantial number of new features to this edition to broaden the coverage of the casebook. Some of these new features highlight developments in international marketing, information technology, ethics in marketing, services marketing, the emphasis on marketing policy and strategy, legal implications in marketing, public sector marketing and marketing innovation. In addition, I have increased the emphasis on international cases in marketing management. The most important changes in the new edition are the following:

(1) Two-thirds of the cases included in the book are brand new.

(2) The remaining 10 cases, which were included in the first edition, have been updated, with the exception of MIT Tractors which now becomes one of the new 'computerized' cases.

(3) A computer software program is now available with the book which contains spreadsheet models related to 10 of the case studies.

(4) The inclusion of 11 international case studies from New Zealand, Canada, the USA, Mongolia, Sweden, Spain, Japan and Mexico. The remaining 17 cases are British-based.

(5) A number of well-respected academics were brought in as new contributors.

(6) The case studies cover a wide range of industries: public transport, financial services, power equipment, entertainment, medical research, drinks (brewery, wine and soft drinks), drugstores, radio stations, consulting services, car rental, motor racing, domestic catering services, carpets, foams, batteries, four-track vehicles, residential homes, videoconferencing, a football association, tourism and leisure, supermarkets and fitted windows.

(7) The 'Introduction to Case Analysis' section has been enhanced by including a full case study and respective teaching/learning notes.

The new cases have been added to expand coverage, and to provide analysis of significant developments in the marketplace and tackle new critical issues facing today's marketing managers. There are also longer cases to give students more data for analysis. Ten of the most popular cases from the first edition have been retained.

The layout of the casebook is different with an even split between cases on marketing policy and strategy and managing the marketing mix. This fact does not imply that the previous structure's content has been abandoned. Owing to the greater emphasis on international case studies, the area of international marketing is actually much better covered. Cases dealing with non-profit marketing are still present in the book but allocated in the table of contents according to their specific discussion issues. Part 2 still covers new product/service development, pricing policy, advertising management, distribution management and marketing mix strategies as well as many new areas like personal selling and customer management. Finally, the issues related to buyer behaviour, marketing information systems and market segmentation are still predominant in the discussion and analysis of many cases and are, therefore, embedded in several case studies.

Many of the cases are related to well-known organizations and companies (for example, Ever Ready/Duracell, Avis, London Underground, Asea-Brown Boveri, Team Lotus/Williams Grand Prix Engineering, Scottish Football Association, Fuji Bank, and so on), which will spur the involvement and motivation of students that dealing with the cases. The book gives many examples of marketing management practice, each case exploring specific aspects of marketing decision-making. All the cases are up to date so students will have the opportunity to analyse actual situations that have occurred recently. Most of the facts and figures presented in the cases are authentic; in some instances, names, locations or other information have been disguised. The types of decisions required and the process for making these decisions are unchanged, however, from what they were originally.

Some of the cases deal with small companies involving situations that students should find interesting and relevant.

I wish to express my gratitude to many people. First, I should like to thank all the past and current adopters of the book over the years for their support, constructive suggestions and feedback. Likewise, I wish to thank all the students who have used the casebook, and hope that they found it stimulating and challenging. Since I was able to test the case studies included in the new edition in my postgraduate classes, I should like to thank the students for their feedback. I should also like to express my appreciation to those contributors who made case materials available for the new edition. Very special thanks are due to my research associate Fiona Davies for her tremendous support during the last stage of preparation of this new edition. Other people to whom I wish to express my gratitude are: Christine Wilson for her continuous support and encouragement, Sergio Aguilar Bruce and Manuel Au-Yong Oliveira, former MBA students, for their efforts in data collection and three of my secretaries over these years of book preparation – Fran Godwin, Stacy Vallis and Karen Trigg. Finally, I wish to thank my editor Tim Pitts for his understanding, cooperation and valuable advice in the development of the manuscript. This new edition only became a reality with the outstanding contribution of all these individuals. Please accept this statement of gratitude.

I hope that you will find this new edition of *Cases in Marketing Management* a helpful teaching and learning tool. I sincerely hope you find it refreshing, mind-stretching, informative, challenging and thought provoking.

Luiz Moutinho
Cardiff, September 1994

Contents

Introduction to Case Analysis

A case enables you to bridge the gap between academia and the 'real business world'. Another benefit from case analysis is the further development of necessary marketing management skills. Case analysis requires you to examine a critical point in the life of a business. You are put in the position of the decision maker. In a real business situation, the key decision will have to be made logically, objectively and in a timely manner. In a case analysis, you will have to apply your analytical skills to identify and solve whatever problems appear in the case. Studying cases will help you to develop the experience to make these decisions.

An additional benefit should occur as you become involved in the operation of the interesting and different kinds of organizations presented in this book. Cases range from small retail stores to financial institutions, from a national orchestra and football league to some of the world's largest corporations; they will expose you to many different situations requiring many different types of decisions. You will become familiar with different organizational structures, different philosophies of business, and alternative techniques of marketing products, all of which should broaden your knowledge of business and marketing in particular.

The whole process involved in preparing a case analysis will benefit you in other ways. You will develop your communication skills as you write and present your final report. The cases will give you an opportunity to use your initiative, decide on a course of action and follow it through. If you work in groups, you will develop your ability to work with other people – a crucial skill in today's business world.

All the relevant information necessary to make critical decisions is there. You will learn by doing.

Format for Case Analysis

Analysing a business situation needs a formalized plan of action. In a marketing case analysis the goal of the process is the pursuit of knowledge. The case analyst tries to understand all elements in a particular business situation so that he or she can recommend action to improve that situation. The entire process must be systematic. In a marketing case analysis, there should be a systematic set of principles and procedures followed in examining a particular situation and making appropriate recommendations.

There are many ways for students to approach the analysis of business cases. Each instructor has his or her own ideas on the number and nature of the steps that are involved. A logical format should be used for analysing any business situation. The following four-step procedure is a practical way to begin:

(1) Define the problem.
(2) Formulate the alternatives.
(3) Analyse the alternatives.
(4) Recommend a solution.

The case method becomes an effective teaching device when students are encouraged to analyse the data presented and to formulate their own set of recommendations.

Case Overview

Suppose for a moment that you are a marketing consultant who has just been asked to analyse an organization and advise it on its marketing strategy. Where would you begin? First, you would acquaint yourself with the entire organization, including its products, processes, situation and any other relevant general factors. You would try to get a broad picture in your mind of the whole organization. With this overview, you would then be able to deal with specific elements of the situation.

Your first objective should be to get an overall feel for the case, an overview of what is going on. Do this by skimming over the case quickly, perusing its highlights. Try to answer these general types of questions: What kind of organization is it? What are some of the general factors at work in the case? What kinds of problems is the organization having?

After you have this overview of the case, go over it again, reading it carefully, underlining or identifying key statements in the case. During this in-depth reading, you should not only try to understand the case situation but also identify, at least on a preliminary basis, some of the problem areas. These problems will be formally delineated later. In writing up the first section of your case analysis, present a brief overview of the situation; this will set the stage for your analysis.

Pre-case Analysis

Most students jump to recommendations and conclusions for cases almost before they have finished reading them for the first time. This section describes a way of forcing marketing students to do more analysis before preparing a formal case report.

Although marketing cases can be used in a number of different ways, most marketing instructors use them, frequently with text material, to get students to apply principles and to develop decision-making abilities. This is supposed to provide an involvement which builds analytical skills and accelerates learning and understanding rather than rote memory. But experience with this method – both as a student and a teacher – suggests that something is missing.

In case analysis many students find it difficult to sift the data for useful information. But case analysis offers a new dimension. Sometimes crucial information is missing. Then the student has the opportunity to make assumptions, for example, about dealers' willingness to cooperate with the present marketing mix, about the quality of the product in the eyes of potential consumers, and so on.

Practice in making assumptions is extremely valuable, since business executives regularly have to make 'educated guesses'. But this may be one of the weaknesses of the case method for instruction purposes. The student may avoid careful analysis of the given data by making a strong assumption which overwhelms all other considerations. In other words, lack of structure in case analysis may be both an asset and a liability.

Structuring the Analysis

The rather discouraging conclusion here was that the majority of students do not even know where to begin when given the 'raw material', that is, the judgements or assumptions which instructors usually expect students to create for themselves! This result certainly makes more understandable the frequent class experience of dominated unstructured case discussion by students with strong unsupported conclusions.

In other words, in the normal unstructured case analysis, many students are just guessing. Less extensively, treatment of a few other cases has led to similarly discouraging results. Average students give superficial analyses, and may completely miss the underlying difficulties of which the current problem is only a symptom.

Sizing Up the Situation

A special exercise can be developed to force students back one step in their thinking. Students are required to submit a one-page paper entitled 'Sizing Up the Situation'. They are expected to describe (using marketing terminology) the situation in the case, including the underlying situation which gives rise to the present problems and which will affect their solution. They are not permitted to solve any problems or make any recommendations at this stage.

Basically, the students are asked to put on paper the essential facts and the logical, basic assumptions which they feel they can make on the basis of the material presented in the case. In the usual case analysis, student are expected to select the key facts. Here more is required. There are certain fundamental, logical assumptions about the nature of the situation which can be developed from the case material. Other less fundamental assumptions can be brought out later in the formal report. These modifying assumptions may determine the conclusion.

When pressed in this way, it is surprising how many new students differ about the fundamental considerations, for example about the nature of the company's product, probable target markets, and even the nature of the market situation. When first starting out, some students even call obvious monopolistic competition situations pure competition (and then are willing to develop policies accordingly!).

Steps in Sizing Up the Situation

Before writing the paper, the students are encouraged to go through the following mental steps.

(1) Look at the product or products now being produced or contemplated and provide a tentative classification into categories such as convenience goods, shopping goods, accessories, and so on, and specify the apparent target market of the company. Something about the company's product policy and overall strategy might be noted. The type of market situation (pure competition, monopolistic competition, and so on) and the stage of the product in its life cycle should also be considered. Further, some thought should be given to the degree of brand preference achieved or sought.

(2) Develop a 'reasonable' marketing mix on the basis of the preliminary judgements in Step 1. This should be merely a quickly developed 'ideal' based primarily on the product classification.

(3) Look at the way the product is actually being handled by the company in the case.

(4) Rethink the nature of the product and the target market(s) before condemning the company's procedure if it differs from the student's 'ideal'. The student should try to give the company management the benefit of the doubt, but should not accept everything as 'right'.

(5) Size up the situation, including the strengths and weaknesses of various elements of the marketing mix.

The One-page Report

The thinking in Step 5 is then incorporated into the one-page report. Here students should present the essential facts and any logical, basic assumptions which seem in order. They should include any major considerations which they feel will have a bearing on the direction of the case analysis or which they may need in the later analysis. Specific facts, however, such as 'They are selling pianos', should be avoided in favour of generalized facts or assumptions using marketing terminology, for example: 'They are selling shopping goods'. Recommendations and conclusions should be avoided.

This report then becomes the base on which a formal case analysis can be built. In many cases, if the 'Sizing Up the Situation' exercise is well done, the statement of the problem is clear and the rest of the analysis is greatly simplified. It still requires imagination and logic, but it is not a vague guessing game.

An Illustration

The following example illustrates the kind of paper a student might write for a 'Sizing Up the Situation' assignment.

A Student Report 'Sizing Up the Situation'

A manufacturer of a shopping good is selling through its own salespeople directly to retailers. It is now contemplating the possibility of switching a large part of this year's (relatively small) advertising expenditure to in-store promotion. This shopping good is in the market growth or market maturity stage and is faced with competition from similar products (monopolistic competition). The company has been advertising its brand in national magazines like *Better Homes and Gardens* but the advertising manager does not believe it is possible to develop an effective brand awareness for porch furniture.

The sales manager feels that the company can afford to slow down national advertising for the remainder of the year because customers will compare his products, in the store, on price and quality anyway (that is, they are shopping goods). He feels point-of-purchase promotion will yield better results. Apparently he has not been tying into national advertising.

Significant judgements and observations made by student

(1) Products – shopping goods.
(2) Advertising expenditure relatively small.
(3) Products in market growth or market maturity stage.
(4) Monopolistic competition situation (thus covering similarity in products, prices, margins and promotional push).

(5) Brand recognition difficult to achieve.
(6) Sales manager's view compatible with shopping goods classification.
(7) Possibility of national advertising, but no effort to 'tie in' made.

Situation Analysis

After having understood the case and identified the key problem areas, you should break the case down into parts so you can evaluate critically all aspects of the organization. Look closely at all details of the case, then try to pull this information together into a more manageable form. The situation analysis stage involves analysing four general areas: the organization, the customer, the competition and the environment. Although these four areas of study are important, the most extensive analysis will be of the internal operation of the organization. Here is an outline to help you organize your situation analysis:

Company Analysis

(1) Financial situation

(a) Balance sheet/income statement analysis
You should analyse the financial statements both vertically and horizontally. *Vertical analysis* involves the calculation of meaningful figures from the financial statements of one year. For the balance sheet, each item may be expressed as a percentage of total assets. For the income statement, each item may be expressed as a percentage of sales. These figures can then be compared with industry figures, competitors, or other divisions of the same company.

Horizontal analysis consists of comparing items on the financial statements, or calculations derived from the vertical analysis, with the same items in other time periods. A comparison of key items over a five-year period can be especially enlightening. For example, you might analyse sales trends over the past five years, calculating the percentage change from one year to the next. You might do the same for other key items such as cost of goods sold or net income. Not only can these figures be compared between years, but they may also be compared with industry trends, those of competitors, or other divisions of the same company.

(b) Ratio analysis
To obtain an accurate measure of a firm's financial position, it is best to calculate several financial ratios. Some of the more frequently used financial ratios are shown in Exhibit I.1, and Exhibit I.2 shows a summary of profit measures. These ratios might be calculated for two or more years to uncover any significant trend in the company's financial performance.

Exhibit I.1 Selected Financial Ratios

Ratio	How calculated	What it measures
(1) *Liquidity Ratios*		
(a) Current ratio	Current assets / Current liabilities	Measures the ability of the firm to meet short-term debt. The rule-of-thumb for this ratio is 2.
(b) Quick (acid test) ratio	Current assets − Inventory / Current liabilities	A more accurate measure of a firm's ability to pay off immediately its short-term debt.
(c) Inventory to working capital	Inventory / Current assets − Current liabilities	Measures the extent to which the firm's working capital is tied up in inventory.
(2) *Profitability Ratios*		
(a) Return on net worth (return on equity)	Profit after taxes / Net worth	Measures the rate of return on stockholders' equity.
(b) Return on assets (return on investment)	Profit after taxes / Total assets	Measures the return on total investment in the firm.
(c) Net profit margin (return on sales)	Profit after taxes / Sales	Indicates return on sales.
(3) *Leverage Ratios*		
(a) Debt to assets ratio	Total liabilities / Current assets	Measures the extent to which borrowed funds have been used to finance the operation of the business.
(b) Debt to equity ratio	Total liabilities / Stockholders' equity	Provides a comparison of the equity of the owners with the funds provided by the creditors.
(c) Times interest earned	Profit before taxes & interest charges / Interest charges	Measures the risk that a company might not be able to meet its interest payments.
(4) *Activity Ratios*		
(a) Inventory turnover	Sales / Inventory	Measures the number of times the average inventory is turned over in the year.
(b) Fixed assets turnover	Sales / Fixed assets	Measures the sales productivity and utilization of plant and equipment.
(c) Total assets turnover	Sales / Total assets	Measures the sales productivity and utilization of all the firm's assets.
(d) Average collection period	Accounts receivable / Total sales ÷ 365	Measures the average collection period for accounts receivable.

Exhibit I.2　Summary of Profit Measures

Method	Definition	Computation
Payback period	Number of years until investment is recouped	If rate of flow is constant, Payback = $\dfrac{\text{Investment Net}}{\text{Cash Flow}}$ otherwise, the payback is determined by adding up the expected cash inflows until the total equals the initial investment
Accounting (or Unadjusted) rate of return	Ratio of average annual income after depreciation to the average book value of the investment	$\dfrac{\text{Average Annual} - \text{Average Annual}}{\text{Cash Flow}\qquad\text{Depreciation}}$ over $\text{Half Initial Investment}$
Net present value (NPV)	Difference between cash inflows and outflows discounted to the present at a given interest rate	$\text{NPV} = \displaystyle\sum_{t=1}^{T} \dfrac{F_t}{(1+i)^t}$ where F_t = net cash flow at time period t i = discount rate T = planning horizon
ROI (Rate of Return of the investment or Internal Rate of Return)	Discount rate which makes the net present value of inflows and outflows equal to zero	The ROIs is determined by solving the equation $\displaystyle\sum_{t=1}^{T} \dfrac{F_t}{(1+i)^t} = 0$ where i is the rate of return of the investment

(c)　Other quantitative analyses

Depending on the information provided in the case, you may be able to carry out other quantitative analyses. For example, *break-even analysis* is a helpful technique for analysing the relationship among fixed costs, variable costs and revenue. *Marketing profitability analysis* examines the profitability of various segments of the company or of various market segments served by the company. You should evaluate carefully all of the quantitative information you are given in a case and ask yourself, 'What can I do with this data to make it more meaningful?'

(d)　Overall financial assessment

After you have scrutinized all of the financial information in the case, you should be able to make some general statements regarding the financial position of the firm. For example, you may have determined from your ratio analysis that the firm is in a precarious position relative to its liquidity. You should draw attention to this, since it limits what the company is able to do in the short run and, thus, what you are able to recommend. It is imperative that you state concisely the firm's financial position since it directly impacts on future marketing strategy.

(2) Organization structure

Examine all aspects of the organization structure: the various components, the formal lines of authority and responsibility, the communication flow, as well as the management style and capabilities.

(3) Marketing system

Evaluate critically all elements of the marketing system: product(s); marketing channel(s); physical distribution; pricing strategy; and promotion strategy.

(4) Other aspects

Examine other relevant aspects of the company: corporate philosophy; mission or purpose; attitudes in the company; key individuals, etc.

Customer (Market) Analysis

Since the customer should be the focal point of the business, take a careful look at the market for the company's products: Who are the customers? Why do they buy the product? When or how frequently do they buy? Has the organization segmented the market properly and clearly defined its target market? Ask yourself questions like these to get some feel for the type of people who are likely customers for the company. You can then evaluate whether the company is reaching this market. Also carefully analyse what changes are taking place in the market and how the market of the future will be different from today's.

Competitive Analysis

It is important to understand the competitive structure of the industry. Where does the company stand relative to the competition? Is the company a leader, a follower, or a 'nicher' (that is, after a special market segment)? What are the organization's strengths and weaknesses relative to the competition? What changes are occurring in the industry?

Environmental Analysis

In addition to the company, customers and competition, evaluate the external environment. Are there any changes taking place, or expected to take place, in the political, legal, technological, or economic environment that may affect the organization? Look for environmental *threats* as well as environmental *opportunities*; realize, however, that what at first may appear to be a threat may actually be a great opportunity for the firm.

The student must add to the facts by making reasonable assumptions regarding many aspects of the situation. Business decision-making is rarely based on perfect information. What is required in these situations is the making of reasonable assumptions and learning to make decisions under uncertainty. The ability to make decisions based on well-reasoned assumptions is a skill that must be developed for a manager to be truly effective.

You should always ensure that a logical analysis is given.

Problem Identification

Now that you understand the case and have critically evaluated all of its key elements, you are ready to formalize the problems existing in the organization. Not only is this normally the most difficult part of the case analysis, it is also the most crucial. Since the remainder of the case analysis revolves around solving the problems defined at this stage, it is important to consider the problem areas very carefully.

A good way to start is to define all of the problem areas you see in the case. Then go over each of these, and try to sort out the symptoms of problems from the actual problems themselves. You may have to search to find the problem behind the symptoms. A company may be having problems with increasing inventory costs, declining profitability and declining customer services quality. After examining all aspects of the situation, you may conclude that the company's major problem is poor product management, particularly the lack of a formal product elimination strategy. As you carry out this process, you may find that there is more than one problem in the case. In this situation you need to prioritize the problems into major and minor. Focus your case analysis around what you define as the one major problem. On occasion, you may identify two major problems. If so, treat them separately: solve one completely, then solve the other. In most situations, try to pick out the one problem that is more immediate than any other and focus your analysis on it. However, you should not disregard the minor problems; deal with them fully at the end of the case analysis.

In writing up this section of your case analysis, define concisely the major problem (or, occasionally, problems). Also list the appropriate symptoms. Following this statement of the major problem, list all of the minor problems, along with the corresponding symptoms.

Problem definition is also a matter of delineating a suitable framework within which to deal with what may be posed in the case as an immediate question. The problem scope should not be unrealistically and unmanageably broad. Good problem definition names the immediate problems and defines them in a way that calls for action-oriented answers.

Statement and Evaluation of Alternatives

Now that you have identified the major problem, you are ready to solve it. Develop as many possible solutions as you can, and then screen out those ideas that are illogical until you have a set of realistic alternatives. You can then examine the advantages and disadvantages of these remaining alternatives to reach a solution.

The initial process of alternative generation is similar to idea generation in the creative process. The objective is to generate as many alternative courses of action as possible. The next step involves mentally making a pass over each of these to eliminate any that are not feasible. This process should leave you with some realistic alternatives to be assessed more critically.

In writing up your case analysis, list these realistic alternatives, making sure that each relates to the major problem you defined. Each alternative should be a potential solution to the major problem in the case; the alternatives should be completely different ways of solving the problem, independent of one another and mutually exclusive. Then list the specific advantages and disadvantages of carrying out each alternative. You may even wish to construct a 'T-account' for each alternative, listing the pros on one side and the cons on the other. If you stated more than one major problem, you should follow the same procedure for each. In a poor analysis there is no explicit discussion of the pros and cons of each alternative. Problem and opportunity statements serve as the basis of your pro (opportunities) and con (problems) discussion. Different ones relate to specific alternatives.

Recommended Solution and Justification

After following this logical approach to identifying potential solutions to the major problem and evaluating the alternatives, you should be in a position to recommend a course of action. In this section of your case analysis, state the alternative you selected and explain why. In cases where you defined more than one major problem and set of realistic alternatives, select and justify an alternative for each problem. Remember that, ideally, no more than one alternative should be selected. If you could select more than one, it is probably because (1) the alternatives in that set were not really independent and mutually exclusive, or (2) your major problem statement is too general and should be more specific. Recommend the solution you think is most suitable, offering reasons for your decision. In your recommendations and implementation, beware of constraints on the organization. Some important constraints include strength of competition, company resources, production capacity, budgets, and philosophies and capabilities of top management. You must reach a clear decision. Part of the skill of decision-making is to be forced to reach a decision under ambiguous circumstances and then be prepared to defend this decision. A good analysis reaches a decision that is logically consistent with the situation analysis that was done. This is the ultimate test of an analysis.

Implementation

You may feel that after you have recommended a solution the case analysis is finished. However, in many respects the important decisions have yet to be made. All you have accomplished so far is to decide on a specific course of action for the future. Now you must answer such questions as:

- How will it be accomplished?
- When will it be accomplished (short term, long term)?
- Who will do it?
- Where will it be done?
- How much will it cost?
- How much is the projected revenue?
- How much is the projected contribution?

A good proportion of your written analysis will be devoted to your plans for implementation. In addition, you may have a technical appendix at the end of your paper in which you specify each part of your plan, along with the corresponding cost and revenue projections. In your recommendations for the organization, also consider how these plans will impact on the minor problems you identified earlier in the case analysis. Address each of these minor problems and make appropriate recommendations for their solution as well.

The final paragraph should attempt to tie a bow around your analysis. Briefly summarize how your recommendations will solve the major and minor problems faced by the organization. Suggest what the organization should do in the future and how it will be better off because of it.

Writing the Report

Students who prepare written reports do a better job of analysing business problems. Writing a good report takes a certain skill.

When instructors read reports, they check to see whether students fully understand the situation and whether their interpretations of the facts are reasonable. They also like to see papers that are objective, balanced, consistent and decisive. Perhaps the most common error made by students in writing case reports is to repeat the facts that have been provided. Instead of analysing the data in the light of the alternatives, students frequently repeat statements that appear in the cases, with no clear objective in mind. Another deficiency often observed in writing reports is a lack of organization. The end result is a paper that has no beginning and no end, and often consists of one long paragraph. To avoid this problem, some instructors require that reports be presented in outline form. The condensed nature of such reports sometimes makes them hard to follow, and the more readable narrative approach is preferred.

One system of organization that has proved effective divides the report into three sections. The sections are designated and arranged in the following order:

- Problem statement
- Analysis containing subheadings
- Recommendations

The problem statement should be brief. The analysis section makes up the bulk of the report and should include a number of subheadings. The first subheading might be a statement of the possible alternatives. Other subheadings might include evaluations of the data or discussions of the influence of the data on the various alternatives. Some of the topics that might be considered in the analysis section are the following:

(1) Customer demand
(2) Competitive structure and reactions
(3) Product characteristics
(4) Price analysis
(5) Advertising and promotional efforts
(6) Distribution channels
(7) Effects on organization sales, costs and profits

The recommendations section should be relatively short and concise.

There is no optimum length for a written case analysis. It depends on the amount of data provided, the preference of the instructor and the number of cases turned in by the student during the course. The report should be long enough to cover adequately the subject but not so long as to bore the instructor and the class. It is fairly obvious that written reports must be neat, legible and free of grammatical and spelling errors. Instructors expect certain minimum standards of performance in written expression. Their standards for written work are reflections of what the business community expects from college graduates.

Final Suggestions

How do you know when you have done a good analysis? As you develop your analyses of the cases, keep the following points in mind:

(1) *Place yourself in the role of a marketing consultant or a particular decision maker in the organization, and address your comments to the appropriate company executive.*

(2) *As with any report sent to an executive, you should keep it as concise as possible* Do not rehash all the information contained in the case. Stick with a critical evaluation of the facts.

(3) *Remember to operate within the time frame of the case* Do not spend your time trying to find out what the organization actually did and then recommend that as your solution. This destroys the whole purpose of the case analysis. And just because the organization did something does not

mean it was right. A solution you come up with may be better than what the organization actually did.

(4) *Do not use the expression 'I need more information'* The information provided for you in each case is sufficient for making a decision. Marketing managers would always like to have more data, but cost and time limitations prevent this. Assume you have all the possible information and make a decision based on it.

(5) *Be complete* It is imperative that the case analysis be complete. Each area of the situation analysis must be discussed, problems and opportunities must be identified, alternatives must be presented and evaluated using the situation analysis and the relevant financial analysis, and a decision must be made. Each area above must be covered in good depth and with insight.

(6) *Avoid rehashing case facts* A good analysis uses facts that are relevant to the situation at hand to make summary points of analysis. A poor analysis just restates or rehashes these facts without making relevant summary comments.

(7) *Make reasonable assumptions* Every case is incomplete in terms of some piece of information that you would like to have. Incomplete information is an accurate reflection of the real world. All marketing decisions are made on the basis of incomplete information. A good case analysis must make realistic assumptions to fill in the gaps of information in the case. It is better to make your assumptions explicit and incorporate them in your analysis than to use them implicitly or not make them at all. If we make explicit assumptions we can later come back and see if our assumptions were correct or not.

(8) *Do not confuse symptoms with problems* For example, you might list one problem as decreasing sales volume. This would not be correct. This is a symptom. The real problem is identified by answering the question:
    Why are sales down? For example, sales volume may be low due to inadequate salesforce training. But this may not yet be the root problem. You still need to ask: Why is sales training inadequate? It may be due to poor sales management policies. What you do is keep asking 'why' until you are satisfied that you have identified the root problem.

(9) *Do not confuse opportunities with taking action* One can recognize a market opportunity but not take any action related to it. A company may decide not to compete in this market due to lack of resources or skills or the existence of strong competition. Decisions involve the complex trading-off of many problems and opportunities.

(10) *Recognize alternatives* A good analysis explicitly recognizes and discusses alternative action plans. You must do your situation analysis and recognize alternatives before evaluating them and reaching a decision.

(11) *Make effective use of financial and other quantitative information* Financial data (break-even points and so on) and information derived from other quantitative analyses can add a great deal to a good case analysis. Totally ignoring these aspects or handling them improperly results in a poor case analysis.

The cases give you the opportunity to relate the theoretical content of your marketing course to the business world, and will be helpful in developing your marketing skills. You will find that your case study technique will improve with practice.

Remember to take a logical approach to identifying and solving problems. Exhibit I.3, a flow chart of the recommended case analysis process, will aid your efforts.

Perhaps the greatest pedagogical benefit of the case method is that it generates a high degree of involvement in the learning process. Much of the challenge and satisfaction of case teaching comes from the interaction between students and instructors. The author hopes that you enjoy tackling these case studies and find the approach to be a stimulating learning experience.

Example Case

A short case study follows, with assigned questions and case analysis. This will give you some idea of the points an instructor would expect to be covered in this case.

Bartels Paperbacks

Introduction

In late August of 1978, armed with 200 cinder blocks, 500 board feet of shelving and 2000 paperbacks, Peter Jones moved to Bradford, West Yorkshire, to start a business: thus began Bartels Paperbacks. Peter got the idea for a paperback exchange from a friend who had opened one a few years before. At the time, he was in graduate school for journalism. He worked at the store during the day, attended classes in the evening, and slept on the couch at night. Peter thought he would make a million pounds.

Although Peter has not yet made a million pounds, Bartels Paperbacks has grown to be one of the largest used paperback chains in the Yorkshire area. There are currently two locations: Emm Lane and Jacob's Well near the city centre. Another store in Huddersfield was sold in 1979, shortly after opening the Emm Lane store. Bartels carries more than 50,000 used books.

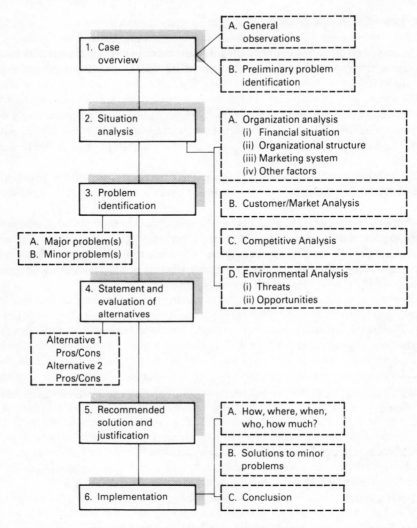

Exhibit I.3 *Flow chart of case analysis.*

The Emm Lane Store

The Emm Lane store opened in August of 1979 with 4000 books. Today, the same 400 square foot space contains 20,000 books with new trades coming in at a rate of nearly 100 per day. Since only about 1000 books are sold every month, the Emm Lane store is practically doubling its stock each month.

The Jacob's Well Store

The Jacob's Well store originally opened in November of 1982 in an upstairs location. Since moving to a storefront location with 1000 square feet of space in August of 1984, sales have increased 300%. The store contains a little more than 30,000 books with new trades coming in at a rate of around 60 per day. Since about 1500 books are sold every month, it appears that growth is minimal. Yet, the overflow of books coming into the Emm Lane store provides nearly 500 new books for Jacob's Well each month.

The Trade Concept

Bartels buys, sells and trades almost any paperback which is in good physical shape: recent fiction, mysteries, children's books, romances, science fiction, classics, biographies and non-fiction. Paperbacks are typically priced at one-half the cover price + 25 pence (for example a £4.95 new book would be £2.48 + 25 pence = £2.73 if bought used at Bartels Paperbacks).

The most unique concept that Bartels brings to the market is the idea of trading used paperbacks. Although the concept is essentially that of a two for one swap, Bartels has provided some refinements: Bartels gives credit in exchange for paperbacks. The customer receives 25% of the cover price in trade for paperbacks listed over £2.00; 20% of the cover price in trade for romance paperbacks; and 10% of the cover price in trade for all other paperbacks. The customer receives a credit slip when he or she brings in paperbacks to trade. Each time a paperback is selected, one-half of the cover price will be deducted from the credit slip. All the customer pays is 25 pence in cash for each paperback chosen, up to the limit of the credit. One caveat: science fiction paperbacks may only be bought with cash or with science fiction trade. However, science fiction is the only type of paperback for which cash will be given: science fiction books may receive either 25% of the cover in trade, or 10% of the cover in cash.

Bartels was founded on a simple philosophy: provide people with an opportunity to trade their used books and to purchase books at a reasonable price, and the business will take care of itself.

Although this philosophy provided for great growth, it did little to provide for a steady revenue stream and profit picture. Thus, this marketing analysis is designed to provide a means to improve that profit picture.

Marketing Overview

Marketing has been a neglected aspect of Bartels' business. The company has no cohesive marketing strategy. It does not provide any cohesive plan, control or organization to market its business. The single marketing strategy employed is: when the company has sufficient cash flow, then money is spend on marketing.

Although no unified marketing plan is in place, Bartels uses a committee approach to spend its few marketing pounds. The responsibility for determining where the money is to go is shared between the owner and the two divisional managers. The owner makes the final decision as to money spent to benefit both stores, but each manager has some discretion as to money spend in local support.

The Market

The company image possessed by Bartels is a 'small-town mum-and-dad shop' image. Bartels is not a 'high-tech' or 'glossy-slick' company with high power sales tactics. It is a low-key approach, with a comfortable atmosphere and little, if any, sales pressure. The company is concerned with customer satisfaction rather than pressure sales tactics.

Customer service is the most important component of Bartels. The employees of the company are continually assisting the customers in finding the books they need, reserving books for customers, and even referring customers to competitors who may have a special book. Bartels have even bought books from competitors and resold them at no profit to satisfy customers.

The two divisions have a relatively different clientele. The Emm Lane store consists of approximately 50% women, 25% men and 25% children. Also, the clientele of the Emm Lane store is typically affluent individuals with more than a passing interest in reading. The Jacob's Well store customer base consists of approximately 50% young adults, 25% older adults and 25% children. Repeat customers represent a majority of the business at both divisions.

Bartels offers customers a wide selection of books at a very reasonable price. Of the 50,000 books offered between the two locations, the selection is wide: children's books, classics, mystery, romance, science fiction, out-of-print paperbacks, recent fiction, biographies, non-fiction and poetry. This product mix is essential to the company because it offers a wide selection of books for its customers' varied interests. This also assists in maintaining the company's major goal of customer satisfaction.

Further, Bartels offers its products at very low prices because the company wanted to offer a reasonable price to its customers that would also provide the company with some revenue stream to continue its operations. The books are priced at one-half the cover price plus 25 pence. With the trade policy, as explained above, customers only pay 25 pence cash for each book they take out. This trading system provides two important functions: (1) it continually builds up the company's inventory; and (2) it provides cash by charging 25 pence for each book taken out. This pricing strategy and trading system is extremely important to the company because the low prices and trading system are the major factors in bringing in new customers and generating repeat sales.

Thus, Bartels has an excellent relationship with its suppliers because its suppliers are its customers. All inventory is built up by the trading system and the company's inventory has grown tremendously over the years.

Marketing Goals

Bartels' marketing goals are:

(1) To double the company's business by reaching more customers through generating more repeat sales, and by acquiring more new customers.

(2) To diversify the company's product line into used records, tapes, videos and books on tape.

(3) To continue to provide superior customer service and satisfaction.

The major factors in bringing in repeat customers are:

- low prices,
- unique trading system,
- excellent customer service, and
- convenience due to good location.

New customers are more difficult to find. Bartels does not have any assistance in promotions from any outside sources such as advertising agencies. However, advertisements are sometimes generated from other sources, such as the organizers of poetry readings held monthly at the Jacob's Well store.

Nor does Bartels use any marketing research. This lack of marketing research could be detrimental to the company because it is impossible to gauge the success of the current marketing policy. To develop a marketing strategy, it is critical to know the number of potential customers and the market mind share in order to implement the correct strategy.

Marketing Strategies

Customers The target markets of Bartels are mainly women and young adults (college students) since these markets represent the majority of the company's business.

Price Bartels keeps its prices very low to keep customers and provide for new customers and it also provides a trading system to offer its customers a different alternative for purchases.

Location The Emm Lane division's location in the city provides easy access for its customers. This division also enjoys a quality reputation in the city. The Jacob's Well division also offers an excellent location for its customers because it is on a main street and has excellent walking traffic. It is also near some colleges and a few years ago, the division moved from an upstairs location to the downstairs and this move provided an immediate increase in revenue of three times its previous business. Also, Bartels takes great advantage of its shelf utilization. It is extremely important for the customers to be able to get the books they need conveniently. All books are organized by category and by author in each category and the high-margin books get a full-cover display to catch the attention of the customer.

Promotion Bartels does not provide any cohesive, well-thought-out plan for promotions. A written facsimile of the trading policy is given to each customer. This provides an opportunity to understand better the policy, and serves as a reminder that Bartels takes in trades. The poetry readings which occur once a month at the Jacob's Well store are another avenue of generating good public relations. The poets put together their own leaflets and post them. The *Telegraph and Argus* has also mentioned Bartels as a place to listen to poetry in a number of articles. Further, the *Telegraph and Argus* contains a listing of happenings around town which also mention the poetry readings. Bartels also gives away gift certificates to local benefits, auctions and proms.

Advertising The company uses mostly leaflets that are posted at local establishments such as small retail shops and restaurants. They are also posted at only one of the nearby colleges (University of Bradford). The company also runs a once a month ad. in a local newspaper (the *Target*). An advertisement is run very infrequently in the University of Bradford newspaper. Also, Bartels runs a classified ad. every week in the *Telegraph and Argus* and in the *Yorkshire Post* in the Leeds area.

Product selection With 50,000 books, Bartels provides a wide range of books to satisfy all its customers' needs.

Product mix Having a single product line, used books, hampers Bartels' ability to provide a broader product mix to interest new customers and keep old customers. Exhibit I.4 shows the BCG (Boston Consulting Group) portfolio matrix as applied to Bartels' product mix.

Finally, adjustments are made to the marketing programme as the need occurs since there is a lack of an organized marketing plan and no stringent rules that must be followed. There is no measurement of the effectiveness of the marketing plan nor are there policies to evaluate performance, standards, or the monitoring of the marketing plan.

Competition The competition facing Bartels consists mainly of used book stores, convenient-type stores, and major book store chains. In the convenience stores, impulse buying at the check-out counter accounts for the greatest competition for recent fiction. There are many major book chain outlets which also provide for competition in the recent fiction category. However, few have the breadth of product in the science fiction area. Further, out-of-print books and non-bestsellers are all but impossible to find at the major chains. Thus, the competition for older fiction is greatest among other used book stores. However, used book stores are few and far between.

Financials The Emm Lane store contains 20,000 books. New trades are coming in at a rate of nearly 100 per day. Since only about 1000 books are sold every month, the Emm Lane store is practically doubling its stock each month.

Sales have been growing at nearly 15% annually, but profits have continued to lag due to an increase in expenses of nearly 20% annually. Much of this is due to a new landlord who raised rents almost 50%.

Relative Competitive Position

	High		Low
High	Science fiction books		Recent fiction
		Self-help / How-to-books	
	Ecletic books	Classics	
	'STARS'	'QUESTION MARKS'	
	Poetry books		
Business growth rate	Romances	Older fiction 'Text' books	
	'CASH COW'	'DOGS'	
	Mysteries		
Low	Children's books		

Exhibit I.4 *BCG portfolio matrix.*

The Jacob's Well store, since moving to a storefront location, has experienced a 300% increase in revenue. The store contains a little more than 30,000 books with new trades coming in at a rate of around 60 per day. Since about 1500 books are sold every month, it appears that growth is minimal. Yet, the overflow of books coming into the Emm Lane store provides nearly 500 new books for Jacob's Well each month.

Overall, Bartels is not a great profit operation as can be seen in Exhibit I.5. The Emm Lane store is showing a loss mainly due to the 150% increase in rent. The only cost of goods borne by the company is from the science fiction books, since these are the only books purchased outright.

The trading system used by the company does not provide a sufficient amount of revenue and, due to the trading system, the company only averages £1.17 per book. Also, Bartels must bear a large amount of fixed costs and the company must sell at least £34,596 to break even. Owing to the small amount of revenues generated by each book, Bartels must overcome its barrier of high fixed costs by generating enough revenue to cover its fixed costs and provide profits.

SWOT Analysis: The SWOT analysis is an assessment of both the internal and external environments of the company. The strengths and weaknesses of the company are analysed in the internal environment and the opportunities and threats

Exhibit I.5   Income Statement for Bartels

	Emm Lane (£)	Jacob's Well (£)	Total (£)
Revenues	16,200	19,020	35,220
Cost of goods sold	300	900	1,200
Gross profit	15,900	18,120	34,020
Operating expenses:			
Rent	6,000	4,800	10,800
Administrative & general	2,100	2,520	4,620
Selling	8,400	9,600	18,000
Total expenses	16,500	16,920	33,420
Pre-tax income	(600)	1,200	600
Number of books sold/year	12,000	18,000	30,000
Average revenues/book (£)	1.35	1.06	1.17
Break-even (£)	16,500/0.982	16,920/0.953	33,420/0.966
	16,802	17,755	34,596

of the company are analysed in the external environment. Exhibit I.6 shows the SWOT analysis for Bartels.

Peter Jones was hoping that a turnaround strategy would bring a brighter future for Bartels.

Exhibit I.6   *SWOT analysis.*

Questions

(1) How could you assess Bartels' marketing capability? Develop a framework of analysis which would help Bartels to scan the environment and assess market opportunities.

(2) Based on the assessment of the BCG matrix, develop product portfolio strategies to help Bartels take advantage of the opportunities offered.

(3) Bartels need to monitor customer needs, market trends and shifts in book preferences through a consistent and systematic gathering process of market information. Develop a marketing research plan for Bartels emphasizing the sampling approach and procedures to be used, the most suitable data collection methods, as well as considerations involved in questionnaire design.

(4) Design a product mix policy and strategy for the company.

(5) Develop a promotional strategy and plan for Bartels.

Case Analysis

Question 1

How could you assess Bartels' marketing capability? Develop a framework of analysis which would help Bartels to scan the environment and assess market opportunities.

The following checklist of seven questions provides a quick test that could be used as a rough measure of Bartels' marketing capability:

- Has the company carefully segmented the various segments of the consumer market that it serves?

- Does the company routinely measure the profitability of its key products in each of these consumer market segments?

- Does Bartels use market research on a systematic basis to monitor the needs, preferences and buying habits of consumers in each segment?

- Has the company identified the key buying factors in each segment and does it know how Bartels compares with its competitors on these factors?

- Is the impact of environmental trends (demographic, competitive, life style, etc.) on Bartels' business carefully gauged?

- Does the company prepare and use an annual marketing plan?

- Does Bartels 'talk' marketing?

Environmental scanning and market opportunity assessment could be carried out by Bartels through the utilization of a framework of analysis similar to the one shown in Exhibit I.7.

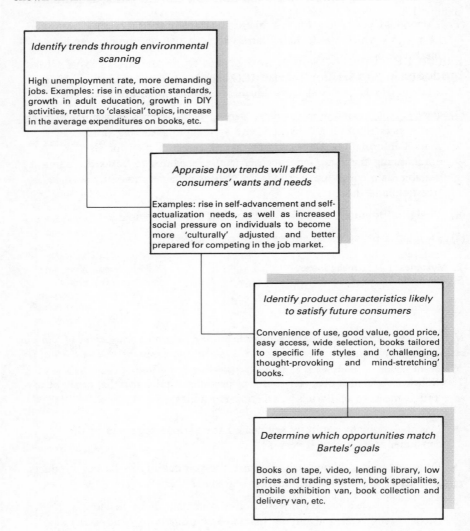

Identify trends through environmental scanning

High unemployment rate, more demanding jobs. Examples: rise in education standards, growth in adult education, growth in DIY activities, return to 'classical' topics, increase in the average expenditures on books, etc.

Appraise how trends will affect consumers' wants and needs

Examples: rise in self-advancement and self-actualization needs, as well as increased social pressure on individuals to become more 'culturally' adjusted and better prepared for competing in the job market.

Identify product characteristics likely to satisfy future consumers

Convenience of use, good value, good price, easy access, wide selection, books tailored to specific life styles and 'challenging, thought-provoking and mind-stretching' books.

Determine which opportunities match Bartels' goals

Books on tape, video, lending library, low prices and trading system, book specialities, mobile exhibition van, book collection and delivery van, etc.

Exhibit I.7   *Environmental scanning and opportunity assessment for Bartels.*

Question 2

Based on the assessment of the BCG matrix, develop product portfolio strategies to help Bartels take advantage of the opportunities offered.

Bartels can take advantage of the opportunities offered to it by analysing the strategy implications of products in the strategy quadrants, in terms of investment policy, earning characteristics and cash-flow characteristics, as indicated in Exhibit I.8.

Exhibit I.8 Characteristics and strategy implications of Bartels' products in the BCG strategy quadrants

Quadrant	Investment policy	Earning characteristics	Cash-flow characteristics	Strategy implication
Stars				
1. Science fiction books 2. Eclectic books 3. Poetry books	Continual expenditures for capacity expansion	1. High 2. Low to high 3. Low to high	Negative cash flow (net cash user)	Continue to increase market share. If necessary, at the expense of short-term earnings.
Cash Cows				
1. Romances 2. Mysteries 3. Children's books	Capacity maintenance expenditures	High	Positive cash flow (net cash contributors)	Maintain share and cost leadership until further investment becomes marginal
Question marks				
1. Recent fiction 2. Self-help/How-to books 3. Classics	High initial capacity expenditures	1. Negative to low 2. Low 3. Low	Negative cash flow (net cash user)	Assess chances of dominating the segments. If good, go after share. If bad, redefine product policy or withdraw
Dogs				
1. Older fiction 2. 'Text' books	Gradually deplete stock capacity	High to low	Positive cash flow (net cash contributors)	Plan an orderly stock reduction or withdrawal so as to maximize cash flow

Question 3

Bartels needs to monitor customer needs, market trends and shifts in book preferences through a consistent and systematic gathering process of market information. Develop a marketing research plan for Bartels, emphasizing the sampling approach and procedures to be used, the most suitable data collection methods, as well as the considerations involved in questionnaire design.

Since primary data are needed, the first task is to pick the sample to be interviewed. The sample selected should be representative of the customer population to which the results are to be projected.

An initial step in designing the sample is to define the parameters of the sample:

Sample Size

This could vary from 200 to 500 respondents, according to the objectives of the research survey.

Sampling Units

This should represent the individual elements of the customer population to be sampled. For example:

- young adults
- female customers
- male customers
- children
- heavy users of books
- heads of households
- etc.

- upper- and middle-income customers
- older customers
- students
- local residents
- non-local residents
- individuals with professional occupations

Sampling Frame

This is based on the lists, indices, maps, or other sources from which the sample will be selected. Bartels could use customer files, telephone books, association membership rosters, etc.

Sampling Method

The sampling method is related to the specific means by which the sampling units will be selected from the sampling frame.

Bartels should use a probability method (either random or stratified sampling), although non-probability methods (convenience or judgement sampling) could also be utilized.

Foot traffic surveys based on random sampling could also be carried out within a one-mile radius from each location of both Bartels' stores.

The data collection method to be used can have a significant effect on the type of sampling used. Two very important constraints for Bartels when doing marketing research are money and time. Since sampling and data collection approaches have different costs, it is important to compare their costs and time requirements with their advantages and disadvantages. Personal interviews (or in-house questionnaires given to current customers) carried out inside both stores can be somewhat time consuming but not that costly. Mail samples are not very expensive to select and contact, but take more time and have lower response rates.

Bartels needs to prepare a data collection form which will maximize the usefulness of the information collected. The development of a good questionnaire requires care in planning and testing. The questionnaire format should be as simple and concise as possible and yet be complete enough to provide the necessary data. Unnecessary questions should be avoided unless they help to increase recall or response rates. The specific question topics, question wording, placement and means of answering the questions, all have an effect on the response rate and response error of the survey.

Bartels could effectively use questionnaires based on a fill-out postcard-size format in order to maximize the response rate. The survey instrument should only include a few factual or topical questions developed according to the different marketing research objectives set up by the company.

'Early-bird' inducements to reward the customer for filling out the questionnaire, prompt response or just the return of the questionnaire, such as 50-pence off coupons, or any other discount coupons, free booklets, tickets for special events or exhibitions, and so on, could also be used when conducting mail surveys.

Marketing research that does not meet the test of applicability, does not represent a good use of money. A well-planned and well-executed marketing research study should help Bartels with marketing decision making.

Question 4

Design a product mix policy and strategy for the company.

Based upon the current knowledge of the business at Bartels Paperbacks, it is important to implement an economically feasible marketing plan that may be accomplished within a one-year time frame.

Product strategies specify the market needs that may be served by offering different products. Product strategies deal with such matters as number and diversity of products, product innovations and product scope.

The *product-scope* strategy deals with the perspectives of the product mix of the company (that is, the number of product lines and items in each line that Bartels may offer). The product-scope strategy must be finalized after a careful review of all facets of the business since it involves a long-term commitment.

Additionally, the strategy must be reviewed from time to time to make any changes called for because of shifts in the environment.

Product-line expansion is an effective alternative product mix strategy available to Bartels. The company could promote high-margin point-of-purchase (POP) items, such as:

- bookmarks
- bookbags
- bookends
- cards
- booklights
- highlighter, pens and pencils
- stationery

Bartels should utilize attractive displays in order to push the sales of these point-of-purchase product items.

New product development is an essential activity for companies seeking growth. By adopting the new-product strategy as its posture, Bartels will be better able to sustain competitive pressures on its existing products and make headway.

A firm may diversify when *diversification* opportunities promise greater profitability than expansion opportunities. Diversification strategies might include internal development of new products or markets. Essentially, there is one form of diversification that Bartels may pursue: horizontal diversification.

Horizontal diversification refers to new products that technologically are unrelated to a company's existing products, but can be sold to the same group of customer to whom existing products are sold.

Bartels' horizontal diversification strategy could be based on the following product lines:

- records
- tapes
- video
- books on tape
- lending library of hard-cover bestsellers

Other things being equal in a competitive environment, the horizontal diversification strategy is more desirable if the present customers are favourably disposed towards the company and if one can expect this loyalty to continue for the new products. Loyalty can help initially in successfully introducing the products; in the long run, however, the new product must stand on its own. Stated differently, horizontal diversification tends to increase the company's dependence on a few market segments.

Diversification strategies respond to the desire for growth when some current products have reached maturity and stability by spreading the risks of fluctuations in earnings. In order to reduce the risks inherent in a diversification strategy, Bartels should provide the products introduced with adequate support and forecast the effects of diversification on the existing lines of products. The expected results of this strategy would be an increase in sales and greater profitability and flexibility.

Bartels could develop a set of marketing operations that would introduce, within the business, products new to its previous line of products and, on the market, products that would provide new types of satisfaction.

Question 5

Develop a promotional strategy and plan for Bartels.

Bartel can achieve positive results by organizing advertising's seven key decision areas as a sequential process.

Specific Goals

Specific goals serve as focal points around which the budget may be formulated and also provide a means of evaluating performance.

The advertising goal should be specific about both the time involved and audience cognitions. Bartels could set up several possible concrete advertising goals:

- An increase of 50% in company awareness in 12 months.

- A 10% shift in the proportion of target customers having a preference for Bartels by the end of the current year.

- A reduction of 20% in all target customers who do not know that Bartels' books and services cost less than those of its competitors in the same area by the end of the current year.

Besides attainability, an important criterion for assessing the reasonableness of the advertising goals is their compatibility with the company's overall promotion objective. It may be necessary for Bartels to change its advertising goals over time as strategies or environments change.

Target Audience

This stage is critical to developing successful advertising programmes. The process parallels that of defining the target market, as the members of the target and audience are generally one and the same.

Bartels should target its advertising campaign for young adults (predominantly female consumers) and affluent individuals (high- or middle-income households, residential areas and occupational status) with much more than a passing interest in reading (heavy- and medium-users of books).

The definition of the target audience will help to develop better messages and to select the most appropriate advertising vehicles to reach the intended audience.

Budget

The promotional budget could be set up by using the percentage of sales method (approximately 10%, taking into account the sales growth rate), or to base the decision upon the amount of funds available.

The use of cooperative advertising – where Bartels and some publishers or any other related companies, or even media organizations, could combine their promotional efforts – is an important way to stretch a promotional budget. Most cooperative advertising or promotion takes place among companies vertically related in a distribution channel. The idea is to get the entire channel supporting the promotional effort. Besides stretching the budget, cooperative advertising or promotion offers the advantages of obtaining favourable media rate structures for advertisements placed by a local firm. This combination of efforts can also have a favourable synergistic impact on Bartels' sales.

Message Development

Message development involves making decisions about an advertisement's three basic components:

(1) *Theme* (the overall information to be conveyed)
  (a) Rational appeals:
    (i) Low prices and trading system
    (ii) Wide selection of books
    (iii) Information on new products (records, tapes, videos, and books on tapes)
    (iv) Push recent fiction, self-help/how-to, classics, science fiction, eclectic and poetry books
    (v) Information on special events
    (vi) Information on book specialities
  (b) Emotional appeals:
    (i) Portrayal of the target market's lifestyles
    (ii) 'Mind-stretching' and acquisition of knowledge
    (iii) Leisure-activity approach – social needs and gregarious approach
    (iv) Self-esteem needs
    (v) Pleasant store atmosphere

(2) *Copy* The advertisement's pictures, words and symbols should be designed to fit the presentation of specific themes.

(3) *Format* The layout specifications, including specific colours to use, the length of a TV or radio spot, the space for print, type sizes, and so on, should also be defined in accordance with the theme and copy approaches. Larger than usual advertisements could be recommended.

Creative copy and presentation can greatly increase an advertisement's impact. Effective advertising stimulates interest in both the advertisement and the product. The advertisements should also generate desire among the audience to try the product. Finally, the ultimate test of a message's effectiveness is whether or not it affects the action desired. Effective advertising messages capture an audience's attention, develop interest in buying the product and stimulate sales.

Media Selection

Two types of decisions are needed at this stage: (1) how much to spend on various media types and (2) what specific media to use.

Conceptually, an advertising budget should be allocated to various media in proportion to their potential for effectively conveying the intended message.

The objectives to be accomplished through advertising are key when evaluating specific media and instrumental in choosing specific media vehicles. Media cost is another important criterion in choosing particular media. One measure is total cost. This is one of the reasons why smaller companies often use low-cost media, such as local radio and newspapers.

Another cost factor to consider is the 'cost per person' of reaching the target audience. This is typically measured in 'cost per thousand' (CPM), which is calculated as follows:

$$\text{Cost per thousand (CPM)} = \frac{\text{Price of a single message}}{\text{Circulation size}} \frac{\text{(space or time insertion)}}{\text{(in thousands)}}$$

Finally, the character of the media chosen should be compatible with the advertising message. For example, if Bartels' objective is to convey detailed information about its trading system or specifications about the available product mix, then a print medium would probably be better suited. A suggested media plan for Bartels could be designed and specified as shown in Exhibit I.9.

Timing Selection

Bartels need to determine when the advertisements should be placed. An intermittent, unevenly spaced pattern could be used, due to the characteristics of the target audience, product mix, message strategy (containing diversified themes), selected media plan, varied promotional tools, as well as budget constraints. Some advertising 'flights' or 'waves' within some concentrated periods of the year (the 'burst' approach) would seem appropriate to certain promotional messages. Ideally, Bartels should space advertisements in such a way as to help ward off attitude inroads made by competitor advertisements.

This pulsing schedule tactic could help increase the impact of Bartels' advertising and reduce total expenditure. These fewer advertisements need to be effectively placed in order to have the same impact as continuous advertising.

Evaluation

Bartels also needs to evaluate the effectiveness of its advertising campaigns. One might think that simply measuring the change in sales after the advertising would be the only good test, but this is not so. Many factors affect sales – not just advertising. Further, advertising tends to have a long-run cumulative impact.

Exhibit I.9   Bartels' media plan

Percentage of promotional budget to be spent on each medium

Media type

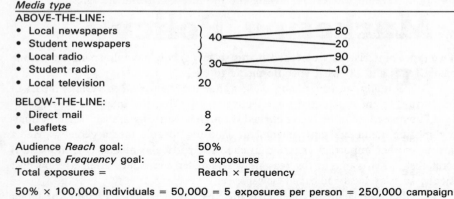

ABOVE-THE-LINE:
- Local newspapers } 40 ⟨ ═══ 80
- Student newspapers   ─20
- Local radio } 30 ⟨ ─── 90
- Student radio   ─10
- Local television   20

BELOW-THE-LINE:
- Direct mail   8
- Leaflets   2

Audience *Reach* goal: 50%
Audience *Frequency* goal: 5 exposures
Total exposures =   Reach × Frequency

50% × 100,000 individuals = 50,000 = 5 exposures per person = 250,000 campaign exposures

Bartels should consider the utilization of message research, which involves determining if the audience perceives, comprehends and remembers its advertisements.

Post-tests could be used for some campaigns in order to estimate how well the audience has received the advertisements after they have been run. Examples of these post-tests include: recall tests, recognition tests and attitude tests.

Some firms run their advertisements and then compare sales before and after in an informal manner. However, this practice should be avoided because it does not isolate advertising's effects.

Other Promotional Activities

Bartels could explore some new avenues and opportunities to promote the company and its products and service mix. For example:

- Book-of-the-month club
- Bartels' newsletter
- Bring a friend, get a discount scheme
- Exploit poetry reading opportunities
- Event creation with guest speakers, presentations and demonstrations related to specific product lines (that is, clowns/circus atmosphere – children's books; gardening expert – how-to books; DIY expert – self-help books; dating company specialist – romance books; criminologist – mystery books, etc.) and the subsequent generation of publicity stories
- Sciences fiction conventions and meetings
- Participation in well-known flea markets and book fairs
- Mobile exhibition van and book collection and delivery van painted with the logo and colours of the company, as well as displaying updated promotional messages (through the use of side panels)

PART 1
Marketing Policy and Strategy

Strategic Marketing

In its strategic role, marketing focuses on a business's intentions in a market and the means and timing of realizing those intentions. This is quite different from marketing management, which deals with developing, implementing and directing programmes to achieve designated intentions.

The marketing function plays different roles at different levels in the organization. At the corporate level, marketing inputs (for example, competitive analysis, market dynamics, environmental shifts) are essential to formulate a corporate strategic plan. Marketing represents the boundary between the marketplace and the company, and knowledge of current and emerging trends in the marketplace is extremely important in any strategic planning exercise. At the other end of the scale, marketing management deals with formulation and implementation of marketing programmes to support the marketing strategy. Marketing strategy is developed at the business unit level.

Essentially, within a given environment, marketing strategy deals with the interplay of three forces, known as 'the strategic 3 Cs: the customer, the competition and the corporation. Marketing strategies should devise ways in which the corporation can differentiate itself effectively from its competitors, capitalizing on its distinctive strengths to deliver better value to its customers. A good marketing strategy should be characterized by: (a) a clear market definition; (b) a good match between corporate strengths and the needs of the market and (c) superior performance, relative to the competition, in the key success factors of the business.

Put together, the strategic 3 Cs form the marketing strategy triangle. The matching of needs between the customer and the corporation must be not only positive, but also better or stronger than between the customer and the competitor. Marketing strategy is thus an endeavour by a corporation to differentiate itself positively from its competitors, using its relative corporate strengths to better satisfy customer needs, in a given environmental setting.

Importance of Strategic Marketing

Strategic planning deals with the relationship of the organization to its environment and thus relates to all areas of a business. Among all the areas of a business, however, marketing is the most susceptible to outside influences. Thus marketing concerns become pivotal in strategic planning and the strategic perspective of the marketing side of the business assumes significance in defining a company's purpose.

Characteristics of Strategic Marketing

Strategic marketing has a different perspective from that of marketing management. Its salient features are as follows.

Emphasis on Long-Term Implications

Strategic marketing decisions usually have far-reaching implications. In the words of a marketing strategist, strategic marketing is a commitment, not an act.

The long-term orientation of strategic marketing requires greater concern for the environment as environmental changes are more probable in the long run than in the short run, and proper monitoring of the environment requires strategic intelligence inputs. Strategic intelligence differs from traditional marketing research in requiring much deeper probing. For example, simply knowing that a competitor has a cost advantage is not enough. Strategically, it is necessary to find out how much flexibility the competitor has in further reducing the price.

Corporate Inputs

Strategic marketing decisions require inputs from three corporate aspects: corporate culture, corporate publics and corporate resources. The corporate perspectives set the degree of freedom a marketing strategist has in deciding which market to enter, which business to divest, which business to invest in, and so on. The use of corporate-wide inputs in formulating marketing strategy also helps to maximize overall benefits for the organization.

Varying Roles for Different Products/Markets

Traditionally it had been held that all products exert effort to maximize profitability. Strategic marketing starts from the premise that different businesses have varying roles for the company.

The practice of strategic marketing seeks first to examine each product/market before determining its appropriate role. Further, different products/markets are synergistically related to maximize total marketing effort. Finally, each product/market is paired with a manager who has the proper background and experience to manage it.

Organizational Level

Strategic marketing is conducted primarily at the business unit level in the organization.

Relationship to Finance

Strategic marketing decision-making is closely related to the finance function. The importance of maintaining a close relationship between marketing and finance, and for that matter with other functional areas of a business, is not new. But in recent years, frameworks have been developed that make it convenient to relate marketing to finance simultaneously when making strategic decisions.

Exhibit P1.1 summarizes the differences between strategic marketing and marketing management. Strategic marketing differs from marketing management in many respects: orientation, philosophy, approach, relationship with the environment and other parts of the organization, and the management style required. Strategic marketing deals with the business to be in, while marketing management stresses running a delineated business.

In marketing management the question is: Given the array of environmental forces affecting my business, the past and the projected performance of the industry and/or market, and my current position in it, which kind of investments am I justified in making in this business? In strategic marketing, on the other hand, the question is rather: What are my options for upsetting the equilibrium of the marketplace and re-establishing it in my favour? Marketing management takes market projections and competitive position as given, and seeks to optimize within these constraints. Strategic marketing, by contrast, seeks to throw off these constraints wherever possible. Marketing management is deterministic. Strategic marketing is opportunistic. Marketing management is deductive and analytical, while strategic marketing is inductive and intuitive.

Strategic decisions are characterized by the following distinctions:

(1) They are likely to effect a significant departure from the established product market mix.

Exhibit P1.1   Major differences between strategic marketing and marketing management

Point of difference	Strategic marketing	Marketing management
Timeframe	Long range; i.e. decisions have long-term implications	Day-to-day; i.e. decisions have relevance in a given financial year
Orientation	Inductive and intuitive	Deductive and analytical
Decision process	Primarily bottom-up	Mainly top-down
Relationship with environment	Environment considered ever-changing and dynamic	Environment considered constant with occasional disturbances
Opportunity sensitivity	Ongoing to seek new opportunities	*Ad hoc* search for a new opportunity
Organizational behaviour	Achieve synergy between different components of the organization, both horizontally and vertically	Pursue interests of the decentralized unit
Nature of job	Requires high degree of creativity and originality	Requires maturity, experience, and control orientation
Leadership style	Requires proactive perspective	Requires reactive perspective
Mission	Deals with what business to emphasize	Deals with running a delineated business

(2) They are likely to hold provisions for undertaking programmes with an unusually high degree of risk relative to previous experience.

(3) They are likely to include a wide range of available alternatives to cope with a major competitive problem, the scope of these alternatives providing for significant differences in both the results and resources required.

(4) They are likely to involve important timing options, both for starting development work and for decisions about when to make the actual market commitment.

(5) They are likely to call for major changes in the competitive 'equilibrium', creating a new operating and customer acceptance pattern.

(6) They are likely to resolve the choice of either leading or following certain market or competitive advances, based on a

trade-off between the costs and risks of innovating and the timing vulnerability of letting others pioneer (in the expectation of catching up and moving ahead at a later date on the strength of a superior marketing force).

Future of Strategic Marketing

A variety of factors point to an increasingly important role for strategic marketing in the future. First, the battle for market share is intensifying in many industries as a result of declining growth rates. Faced with insignificant growth, companies have no choice but to seek out new weapons to use in the fight to increase their share. Strategic marketing could provide extra leverage in share battles. Second, deregulation in many industries has increased competition and is mandating a move to strategic marketing. Third, many packaged-goods companies are acquiring companies in hitherto non-marketing-oriented industries and are attempting to gain market share through strategic marketing.

Competition from overseas companies is intensifying. More and more countries around the world are developing the capacity to compete aggressively in world markets. Business people in both developed and developing countries are aware of world market trends and are confident that they can reach new markets. Eager to improve their economic conditions and their living standards, they are willing to learn, adapt and innovate. Today competition from Europe, Japan and elsewhere is becoming insurmountable. To cope with worldwide competition, renewed emphasis on marketing strategy achieves significance.

Strategic Marketing Cases

The cases in this book cover a wide range of situations and circumstances in which strategic marketing decisions have to be made. The *Arhi Pivnii Kombinat* case focuses on a large Mongolian company facing numerous changes in its operating environment, as Mongolia moves from a planned economy to a market economy. The company is totally production-oriented with no marketing orientation. The case explores issues such as environmental analysis, marketing organization, market opportunity analysis, marketing mix strategies and strategic marketing planning.

The *Plaswin* case deals with a small and fairly new Welsh

company in the highly competitive industry of door and window supply and fitting. In an industry where many small firms go out of business less than three years after starting up, Plaswin is determined to be one of the successful ones. The case highlights the marketing and financial issues to be considered in a small company with limited resources.

The *Battle for Portable Power: Ever Ready versus Duracell* case follows the fluctuating fortunes of Ever Ready, which once dominated the UK portable battery market but was then challenged by Duracell, an aggressive, market-led competitor. Now Ever Ready is faced with the challenge of managing change in a hostile global market where market share has been increasingly difficult to gain and retain. The case is designed to demonstrate the danger of marketing myopia and the importance of a marketing orientation, and gives students the opportunity to formulate an offensive marketing strategy and a marketing plan.

In the *Dawson & Company Limited* case students should be examining the strategic choices open to a company in corporate and marketing terms. The case requires the application of financial and market opportunity analyses in order to allow for the generation and evaluation of strategic options. The critical issues include the development of a mission statement, strengths, weaknesses, opportunities and threats (SWOT) analysis, market segmentation plan, and selection of corporate and marketing strategies, as well as the use of the portfolio analysis concept.

The *Scottish Foam Limited* case examines the marketing approach of a small company to see whether marketing at 'the sharp end' follows the same basic principles as those which apply in large companies. The case is designed to introduce students to a pragmatic application of strategic marketing in the context of a small business, and helps to develop decision-making skills. Students will gain experience in critical evaluation of alternative marketing strategies and of the strategy and courses of action actually followed by Scottish Foam (described in the update).

The *Fuji Bank* case concerns a major Japanese and international bank, and in particular its one UK branch. The changing financial climate brought about by factors such as lower interest rates, trends towards deregulation and the recent recession in both the United Kingdom and Japan, has had an effect on both the bank's performance and its attitude to its overseas operations. The case explores issues such as competitiveness, marketing orientation, and the relationship between profitability and market share.

The *Lysander's Wine Cellars* case outlines a situation faced by the proprietor of a company with no other employees. Although his goals are well defined, the company is in trouble, and he has several options to consider. It is primarily designed as an exercise in small company strategic marketing, and puts the student in a similar situation to that of a marketing consultant called in to help a company of this type.

The *Great Western Brewing Company Limited* case describes the progress and success of a Canadian beer company through the initial stages of the product life cycle. However, the company's sales and market share have dropped, due to economic recession in Canada and removal of interprovincial trade barriers. The case demonstrates the necessity of adjusting marketing strategy as products move through their life cycle, and examines ways in which markets can be penetrated or expanded and growth maintained.

In the *PPP* case, students have the opportunity to develop a critical analysis of strategy development in a difficult service industry. PPP is a New Zealand recruitment company about to embark on a programme of vigorous growth. The case examines issues of market information, buying behaviour, market segmentation and positioning strategy.

The three cases grouped under the title of *Grand Prix Motor Racing Innovation* show how coalitions of organizations were formed in the evolution of Grand Prix motor racing to ensure that financial, technological, economic and sporting objectives could be met. Marketing issues revolve around technical and economic competition, attracting and keeping sponsors, and satisfying several publics, while strategic issues revolve around the forces that compel constructor/sponsor alliances, keep them together and, on occasion, lead to their breakdown. Linking marketing and strategic issues is the question of technological innovation and its evolution in a competitive environment.

The *Cifra* case deals with the leading retail company in Mexico, which runs various store chains targeting different market segments. Cifra is an aggressive and pioneering company, very highly regarded by market analysts, which has for many years been the dominant influence on the Mexican retail industry. The case lets students analyse the strategy of a market leader, looking at strategic alliances, segmentation, targeting, positioning, differentiation from competitors, promotional activities and use of new technology.

The *Asea-Brown Boveri* case looks at a pan-European electrical engineering firm wishing to expand internationally. Students will be able to study ABB's objectives and the current and potential problems facing the company, and analyse the internal and external influences on it, in order to formulate a marketing strategy.

In the *Medical Research Incorporated* case, the focus is on the interplay between a multinational corporation and a small firm. The case highlights the aggressive nature of multinationals and how they can keep small companies out of 'their' markets through patent litigation. Medical Research Inc., however, was in a position to defend its interests, and the case examines the expensive and lengthy process of litigation and illustrates the importance of market protection.

Finally, *The Scottish National Orchestra* case looks at an organization which has created a new post of marketing manager to help maintain its international reputation at a time of change, competition and limited funding. The case demonstrates the need for a non-profit-making organization, as much as a commercial one, to maintain efficient and effective marketing management control, and the importance of a formal and detailed marketing strategy. It also illustrates the difficulties associated with the introduction of marketing disciplines, and with implementing marketing ideas and concepts when it is not possible to define the product or consumer in clear terms.

References

Jain Subhash C. (1985). *Marketing Planning and Strategy*. Cincinatti, OH: South Western Publishing Co.

CASE 1
Arhi Pivnii Kombinat
Strategic Marketing

Luiz Moutinho
Cardiff Business School, University of Wales College of Cardiff

The Company and the Market

Arhi Pivnii Kombinat is the largest brewery, spirits distillery and soft-drinks factory in Mongolia and is based in Ulaanbaatar, the capital city. It has four factories – two for soft drinks, one for vodka and a brewery – in different premises which cover a wide area. The largest building is occupied by the brewery.

The factory was built in 1975 under a project financed by the former Soviet Union and has since undergone four stages of modernization in 1983, 1986, 1991 and 1992. The second soft-drinks factory was built in 1988 to replace a spirits factory which the government had decided to close down.

Not all the buildings and facilities of the plant have been fully modernized. For example, it still uses a very old system of refrigeration, mostly for its brewing activities. In contrast, there is a large modern warehousing unit used to store wheat containing a waste recovery system whose end product is used for animal feed. The company is also involved in the export of wheat which has been supplied by two large Mongolian farms since 1983.

The company was a nationalized organization with 507 employees. It was privatized in 1992, with 51% of the shares going to the government and 33% to private shareholders. The remaining 16% were distributed among the employees who also became shareholders.

The paramount corporate goal is to maintain profits. The company's two main strategies are related to the renewal of its technological base and the implementation of a foreign licensing agreement for bottling Coca-Cola. Its two key competitive advantages are the availability of raw materials and the 'uniqueness' of the technology used by the company.

The company is contemplating the organizational breakdown of the factory into three new strategic business units (SBUs): vodka, brewery and soft-drinks operations.

Competition

There are no major direct competitors but the company is expecting some to emerge in the future. At present potential competitors are too small in terms of production capacity and corporate resources. They are scattered throughout the 18 different *aimak*. (These are the regional districts of Mongolia. Each *aimak* is subdivided into around 300 smaller geographically units called *sumons*.) This geographical segmentation coupled with poor accessibility (due to the rugged terrain, infrastructure, constraints on physical distribution and logistics, such as transportation delays, fuel and spare parts shortages, and so on) make it almost impossible to cover the national market. Consequently there is no competitive structure in any of the three consumer markets where Arhi Pivnii Kombinat is developing its business. The company is now concentrating its efforts on marketing its products only in the capital city, Ulaanbaatar.

The Market

The capital city market represents only 25% of the total national market (the population of Mongolia is 2.1 million people), so the untapped market potential is quite considerable. However, the lack of information on consumer drinking habits, product usage rates or market share information makes it difficult to estimate exactly what that potential is.

Exports in 1991 accounted for 2.5 million tugriks (in 1992 $1 = 200 tugriks) or 1.4% of the company's total sales revenue of 175 million tugriks. The exported vodka products went primarily to former socialist countries like Hungary and Bulgaria as well as to Japan and Italy.

Marginal cost-pricing was used for the exported vodka products. The export price was 7.20 tugriks a litre to wholesalers compared with the retail selling price of 78 tugriks in the domestic market. Export profits were all channelled to the state. The exported products were marketed abroad through two foreign trade corporations, Mongolexport and Mongolimpex. The promotional material was published by the Mongolia People's Republic (MPR) Chamber of Commerce.

In 1991 the company stopped exporting mainly because of a shortage of bottles. Only 10% of the bottles came from an old bottling company in Mongolia, whereas 90% came from Russia. Since 1991 there has been no supply of bottles from Russia. The company plans to develop a backward integration strategy which will involve the building of a new bottling plant as well as the control of some of its key raw materials.

The Product Mix

Vodka

There are 11 product lines within this category. The 'flagship' vodka product is 'Chinggis Khan' Mongolian Arkhi (40° proof in bottles of 70 centilitres). This is a product of specialized technology, distilled from genuine spirit of selected wheat cultivated in the native land of Chinggis Khan, the founder of the Mongolian Empire. It is blended with Mongolian mountain spring water.

Mongolian Vodka 'Arkhi' (38° proof in bottles of 50 and 75 centilitres) is distilled from selected wheat grain and blended with pure spring water. Mongolian Vodka is a 100% grain neutral spirit.

The superb quality of Arkhi was repeatedly acknowledged at both domestic and international fairs and exhibitions where it was awarded gold medals and diplomas.

Other prominent vodka product lines include the following:

- 'Altan Tal' Mongol Balzam – a spirit infusion of 24 herbs found in the Mongolian countryside, containing various biologically active substances.

- 'Mongolian Vodka' – 42° proof bottles of 50 and 75 centilitres.

- 'Bolor' – 40° proof in bottles of 50 centilitres.

- 'Altan Turuu' – 40° proof in bottles of 75 centilitres.

The total production of vodka in 1992 was 3.7 million litres. The machinery in the vodka factory was imported from Russia in 1981 and the plant also has some new manufacturing equipment imported from Germany in 1988.

The production target for vodka is 3 million litres a year which is solely for the domestic market. Up to 1991 (when the company stopped exporting vodka for the reasons stated above) there was a separate production department which was set up to deal with the exported vodka product lines.

The vodka factory employs 66 people. The production operations range from a satisfactory three-stage visual quality control system involving four workers, to the manual application of aluminium lids to the bottles, which seems to be an old-fashioned method and, surely, not a very safe device for the consumer when opening the product.

Soft Drinks

The two soft-drinks factories are operating with old machinery imported from Russia. They were last modernized in 1976. The total production per year for both factories is 15 million litres: 8.5 million litres for 0.5 litre bottles and 6.5 million litres for 0.33 litre bottles. The two soft-drinks factories employ 80 people who work in two shifts (16 hours) during the winter and three shifts (24 hours) during the summer. The raw materials come from China and Russia. The company markets 12 lines of soft drinks. Consumers rate the company's soft drinks as a good quality product.

Beer

The brewery operates with equipment installed in 1986 and imported from Russia. New bottling machinery imported from Germany was added in 1990 and 1991, and a new German production line in 1992. The brewing operations are based on two production lines with a total capacity of 10 million litres a year.

At present only one production line is in operation (with a capacity of 5 million litres a year) because the flour, sugar and other necessary raw materials are imported from Russia and their delivery has been unreliable. The organizational structure of the brewery also includes quality control laboratories.

The product mix is based on six lines of beer, 'Niislel' being the most famous brand name. The beer has on average a strength level of 12° (in terms of wheat concentration) and between 3% and 4% alcohol content. Currently the brewery employs 100 workers.

Financial Analysis and Key Indicators

The company's sales revenue in 1992 totalled 1,234 million tugriks. The total profit was 181.6 million tugriks and the total cost 205.8 million tugriks. The company contributed 805.3 million tugriks to the state budget and allocated 41.3 million tugriks for new investment. The last substantial investment in the factory was made in 1988 and represented 2.9% of total sales. The amount allocated in 1992 represented 3.3% of total sales.

The company had a 41% return on investment in 1992, mainly because it substantially increased prices – 200% for beer and 400% for soft drinks – due to the increase in the cost of raw materials.

Earnings per employee were 375,000 tugriks in 1992 and total productivity was 84,509 tugriks per worker. Exhibit 1.1 shows the company productivity levels achieved in 1991 and 1992.

Exhibit 1.1   *Company productivity levels (1991–92)*

	1991 *(tugriks per worker)*	*1992* *(tugriks per worker)*	*Change year on year (%)*
Vodka	55,600	56,300	1.26
Soft drinks	68,500	72,600	6
Beer	21,800	49,000	125

Exhibit 1.2 compares prices per litre in 1988 and 1992.

Exhibit 1.3 compares variable costs per litre in 1988 and 1992.

There are two stock warehouses on the factory premises, one for storage of finished products and the other for storage of empty bottles.

The company uses the 'just-in-time' approach for its inventory management. Stocks are kept at a level which represent around 15% of the total production capacity. The normal stock levels of each product category are as follows: vodka 60,000 litres; soft drinks 110,000 litres; and beer 80,000 litres.

Exhibit 1.2 *Comparison of prices per litre† (1988 and 1992)*

	1988 (tugriks)	1992 (tugriks)
Vodka	68.00	230.00‡
Soft drinks	2.10	16.00
Beer	6.00	30.36

† The wholesale price can be calculated from these prices taking into account that the company markets its products in 0.5 litrebottles.

‡ Out of this selling price of 230 tugriks, 206 tugriks are allocated to the state budget in taxes.

Exhibit 1.3 *Comparison of variable costs per litre (1988 and 1992)*

	1988 (tugriks)	1992 (tugriks)
Vodka	6.00	17.59
Soft drinks	1.10	10.03
Beer	1.40	7.37

The Marketing Function

The company is totally production-oriented and there is no formal marketing function (except for sales). Marketing is the responsibility of the department of procurement (purchasing) and sales. This department has a manager and two specialists – one responsible for procurement and the other in charge of sales.

The company has never undertaken an analysis of consumer behaviour through market research nor has it utilized market segmentation, targeting or product positioning approaches.

The product mix policy is based on the availability of raw materials. The sales manager decides about the introduction of new products and on changes to be made with regard to the company's product mix. The company uses a multi-brand strategy for its different product lines. The product labels are designed in a simple format which does not do justice to the product.

The branding, labelling and packaging decisions are usually made by technologists (research and development specialists). The initiator/creator of the new product is allowed to select a brand name, label and package strategy, although the so-called product committee has the final say.

All the company's product lines are profitable.

The pricing policy is totally cost-oriented. The company used to give a 10% discount to wholesalers but it has decided to discontinue this practice.

The company only uses promotion when launching new products. The media plan for the introduction of new products comprises newspaper and television advertising and the organization of launch shows and displays at retail stores. The company does not develop any sales promotion programmes.

Arhi Pivnii Kombinat does not have a sales force which would allow it to sell its product lines to both wholesalers and retailers. The original distribution policy was based on selling all the product lines to wholesalers, who would then sell on to retailers with a price mark-up of 15%. The new distribution strategy being implemented by the company is based on selling all the product lines directly to retailers. The price mark-ups used by the different retail stores vary between 5% and 8%.

Physical distribution is carried out by a fleet of 40 rented delivery trucks which distribute the products to retailers located within the company's primary geographic market, the capital city Ulaanbaatar. Each of the four factories has its own loading bay to facilitate the transportation and delivery of the products to the customer. The delivery trucks only distribute products to 60% of the company's customers. The remaining 40% buy directly from the factory.

Arhi Pivnii Kombinat has never had a marketing plan with a clearly designed marketing strategy, an effectively allocated marketing budget and the proper marketing control mechanisms, nor has it developed an international marketing strategy. The current marketing budget process relies on specific requests for financial appropriations which are submitted to the general manager on a pro-gramme-by-programme basis.

Questions

(1) Develop a SWOT (strengths, weaknesses, opportunities and threats) analysis as well as a financial analysis of the company and present some concluding remarks.

(2) How would you improve the organization of the marketing function within the organizational chart of the company?

(3) What recommendations can you make in the areas of market opportunity analysis (MOA), the analysis of consumer behaviour, the use of marketing research and the implementation of a market segmentation, targeting and product positioning strategy?

(4) How would you relate the production technology issue with the development of an effective product mix policy?

(5) Make recommendations on a suitable pricing policy and price strategies that could be developed by the company.

(6) Design a potentially effective marketing communication strategy (including sales management efforts) which could help the company expand its future business.

(7) What are the critical problem areas facing the company in the context of a distribution channel policy and physical distribution management? Make your own recommendations.

(8) Design a pragmatic strategic marketing plan which would assist the company in achieving sustainable competitive advantages in the future.

CASE 2
Plaswin Group
Strategic Marketing

Fiona Davies and Luiz Moutinho

Cardiff Business School, University of Wales College of Cardiff

Company History

The Plaswin Group, based in Gwent, South Wales, is a supplier of windows, doors, patio doors, fire screens and conservatories. Plaswin started as a maker of PVC window kits to fit DIY sheds. As cheaper ready-made products became available for this purpose, Plaswin's directors decided to enter the more profitable commercial sector. For this purpose Plaswin became qualified to supply NHBC guaranteed builders, and obtained a British Board of *Agrément* (BBA) Certificate and Local Authority Window Assessment Panel (LAWAP) approval. In 1992 Plaswin obtained Quality Assessment BS 5750 and a subsidiary company, Steelwin, was formed to supply the fire screen and steel window market.

Group Policy

The policy of the two companies has been stated by the Managing Director, Philip McCarthy, as 'to market only products of a quality that will merit and earn customer satisfaction by performing all functions reliably and effectively and which are discernibly better than those provided by the competition'. Management are committed to ensuring that the quality of all products satisfies the specific contractual obligations of the customer, as well as all relevant British Standards. The emphasis on quality extends to Plaswin's service. All the company's installers are skilled craftsmen with many years' experience in the industry. They work quickly and cleanly and many installations are completed in one day. All company personnel are aware of the Quality policy, which is laid down in a Quality manual and associated Quality Procedures.

Market and Industry Background

The doors and windows industry can be divided into three sectors according to construction material. In terms of manufacturer sales the largest sector is timber, followed by plastics (mainly uPVC), and aluminium and steel. Their percentage shares are shown in Exhibit 2.1. In recent years timber doors and windows have lost market share. Aluminium has also lost a large part of its market share, mainly to uPVC. It is now little used in the housing sector, but is still used in the commercial sector, particularly in shopfittings where new coatings in attractive colours and finishes are suited to new styles of shop design. Steel, which has held its market share, is also used in shopfittings and in replacing older steel units. Plastics, mostly as uPVC, have seen a rapid growth in market share.

Exhibit 2.2 shows the size distribution (by turnover) of firms in all three sectors. There are many franchising organizations and subcontractors are also often

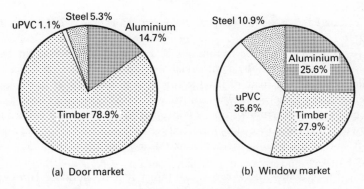

(a) Door market   (b) Window market

Exhibit 2.1 *UK door and window markets.*
Source: Industry estimates.

Exhibit 2.2 Size distribution by turnover (1989)

Turnover (£'000)	Builders' carpentry and joinery	Metal window and door manufacturers	Plastic building products manufacturers
		(Number of legal units)	
22–50	721	134	56
51–100	405	103	41
101–250	484	137	67
251–500	289	84	71
501–1,000	188	72	75
1,001–5,000	219	90	103
5,000+	45	26	35
Total	2,351	646	448

used, particularly for installation. Most firms manufacturing, supplying and installing doors and windows are small organizations, in terms of both employee numbers and turnover. The larger firms generally belong to a holding company or group. The intense competition between small local firms means that less than 50% of them survive for more than three years.

The manufacture of doors and windows has developed into a highly mechanized industry using sophisticated computer controlled machine tools. This has increased the cost of entry to the industry.

The UK market for windows and doors is worth about £2 billion (1992), with the split approximately 70% for windows/window frames and 30% for doors/door frames. It is extremely fragmented and a complex mixture of direct sales (mainly for replacement windows and doors) and builder/merchant sales (mainly for new buildings). Direct sales are estimated to account for 67% of window sales but only 20% of total door sales. Imports account for more than 13% of UK sales as home manufacturers are unable to supply all the demands of the UK market.

It is estimated that about 40% of the total doors and windows market is accounted for by new buildings, and the remaining 60% by the replacement market. New buildings may be commissioned by the public sector, for example schools and hospitals, or built by commercial developers, for example office blocks. The public sector, in the form of local authorities, also plays a major role in the replacement market. Local authorities control 6–7 million dwellings, and the financial burden of replacing windows on these properties has led many councils to set up their own uPVC window production facilities. Private home-owners, replacing their doors and windows for various reasons, are also major customers in the replacement market.

During the recession there was a downturn in new building construction. This decline bottomed out in 1992 but, despite present low interest rates, there is as yet no sign of recovery. Local authorities are currently restricting expenditure due to the recession, but the demand for more public expenditure on housing development, maintenance and improvement is growing. Expenditure on housing and house maintenance is eventually expected to pick up as the economy recovers. Demand in the repair and maintenance markets will be stimulated by lower interest rates.

Plaswin and Steelwin Products

Plaswin manufactures high standard uPVC windows and doors, which have passed rigorous tests in accordance with BS 5368/6375 for air permeability and water-tightness. uPVC products are extremely durable, do not warp, crack, split or rot, and never need painting. They are tailored precisely to the requirements of each building.

Steelwin manufactures steel windows and doors, entrances, and fire screens and doors. The architectural steel systems have the benefits of:

- smooth surface finish
- narrow sight lines even on large openings
- sophisticated weather stripping
- excellent thermal properties
- light weight
- multi-point locking mechanisms
- fire resistance
- excellent value for money.

These products conform to BS 6375 standards for performance, watertightness and wind resistance, and BS 476 for fire resistance. They are available in galvanized steel, aluminium, bronzofinestra (a copper/zinc alloy) and stainless steel. They come in seven colours and carry a 10-year warranty covering paintwork and corrosion.

Product Lines

(1) Casement windows – 70% of products manufactured, available in 64 different shapes, measuring up to 3 metres in height or width.

(2) Tilt and turn windows – for ease of cleaning, also for fire escapes.

(3) Residential doors – available in 20 different styles, with a variety of glass and infill panels.

(4) Conservatories – combination of windows and doors as above, with a roof added.

(5) Fire check screens – mainly for schools and hospitals.

(6) Steel windows – mainly for schools and universities, high security windows made for secure hospitals.

(7) Bronzofinestra (bronze windows and doors) – a unique range used by banks, museums, churches and the National Trust.

(8) Stainless steel – a variety of applications, usually entrances to busy public places.

Plaswin's Marketing Strategy

Plaswin differentiates itself from competitors by its high-quality image. This is apparent to specifiers and customers on presentation of the unique range of bronze and stainless steel products. Many specifiers would not need such prestige products, but they enhance Plaswin's image. Moreover, as previously stated, all Plaswin and Steelwin products conform to British Standards and their quality satisfies the public utilities sector which demands the highest standards.

Plaswin also believes in being totally customer orientated. The company's intention from the outset was to gain a major share of commercial business in its locality, and to that end it supplies a high-quality uPVC product, meeting the high specifications of local and health authorities, which is up to 17 mm wider and therefore stronger (and more expensive) than that used by the mass market. Recently, however, Plaswin decided to expand into the trade market, which demands a cheaper window, so a new economy product range (Index) has been introduced to offer to this market. Plaswin's intention, as stated by Philip McCarthy, is to 'follow a market-led strategy advancement introducing new products and services as they become viable opportunities for growth'.

The Marketing Department and its Budget

The marketing department is staffed by four sales people and two marketing assistants who report to the Marketing Manager. The department's budget is based on up to 18% of revenue, out of which is paid salaries (5%), sales commission (3%), advertising (2%) and direct mail (1%), leaving a balance of up to 7% of revenue which is used to discount orders, based on the value of the production schedule. Sales commission is based on more than 50% of salary, and can be up to 10% of the value on some orders. An additional 1% of revenue is spent on paying incentives (10% of total salary).

Marketing Activities

The company uses a sophisticated database which keeps track of all existing and prospective customers, tender applications and mailings. It uses search facilities, weighting discounts, strength of customer contact and contract specification to produce a weekly 'hot list' of opportunities for sales staff. Plaswin also uses the Barbour Index to contact specifiers, particularly in the niche market of Steelwin. Apart from personal contact, most marketing activity is direct mail based. Incentives are given to marketing assistants based on number of replies to direct mail, and conversion rates of replies to opportunities/tenders and opportunities/tenders to revenue. For market research purposes, a questionnaire is sent with new contracts.

Pricing

The company's price list is based on cost plus 100%. Discounts are allowed up to a maximum of 25% (this maximum for 'Crown Financed' customers only). Commercial orders are won by tender. Tender applications are cost plus a percentage determined by the order book and coupled with a judgement taken on customer/debtor security. When bidding for orders from public utilities, no provision is made for bad debt. Trade customers are offered discounts based on order size, and customer loyalty is encouraged by offering larger discounts on subsequent orders. Additional discounts are given to prompt payers.

Recent contracts have ranged in value from £35,000 to over £200,000. The most common cause of tenders being lost has been that Plaswin has been more expensive than its competitor(s).

Competition

Plaswin has identified three competitors: New England, Westleigh and New Guide. New England, regarded as the most serious competitor, is a subsidiary of a large conglomerate, and its products sell at prices up to 15% less than Plaswin's. However, Plaswin's better quality product, earlier delivery dates and higher standard of installation mean that it regularly wins orders from New England. Westleigh's quality, on the other hand, is almost as high as Plaswin's, but its main area of operation is outside Plaswin's locality. New Guide is regarded as more of a nuisance than a true competitor, as it seems to have no pricing policy and is thus an unknown quantity when bidding for work.

Company Goals

Plaswin wishes to expand into new markets and to expand its customer base in existing markets by customer networking. It feels the key to growth will be the appointment of directors with a proven track record, who will be offered shares in the company. Increasing the volume of business will allow the company to buy in greater volume, thus enabling it to give lower tenders in cost-plus situations. It also aims to move to a larger production facility, and to seek investors in the company to strengthen the balance sheet. A long-term aim of the directors is to groom managers to become directors and adopt a more hands-off stance by the year 2000.

Financial Information

Exhibit 2.3 shows the profit and loss account for the year February 1992 to January 1993.

Acknowledgement

The author would like to thank Philip McCarthy and Victor Smith for providing the necessary information and allowing it to be used as a case study.

Exhibit 2.3   Plaswin uPVC Ltd   Profit and Loss Budget

	FEB	*MAR*	*APR*	*MAY*
SALES COMMERCIAL	135,000	130,000	120,000	105,000
SALES TRADE	0	0	0	0
	135,000	130,000	120,000	105,000
Sales Invoiced	135,000	130,000	120,000	105,000
Materials	64,125	61,750	57,000	49,875
Carriage	405	390	360	315
Sub Contractors	13,500	13,000	12,000	10,500
Consumables	675	650	600	525
Commission	6,750	6,500	6,000	5,250
Factory Wages	11,475	11,050	10,200	8,925
Gross Profit	38,070	36,660	33,840	29,610
Gross Profit %	28.20%	28.20%	28.20%	28.20%
Director's Salaries	5,450	5,450	5,450	5,450
Admin Salaries	6,450	6,450	6,450	6,450
Marketing-Trade/Commercial	2,000	500	500	500
Marketing-Retail	0	0	0	0
Rent	1,825	1,825	1,825	1,825
Rates	375	375	375	375
Light & Heat	500	500	500	500
Repairs & Maintenance	250	250	250	250
Cleaning	150	150	150	150
Motor Expenses	3,500	3,500	3,500	3,500
Travel & Entertainment	750	750	750	750
Professional Fees	1,000	1,000	1,000	1,000
Insurance	1,100	1,100	1,100	1,100
Postage & Printing	300	300	300	300
Office Supplies	400	400	400	400
Telephone/Fax	1,000	1,000	1,000	1,000
Bank Charges	250	250	250	250
Trade Memberships	250	250	250	250
Misc. Expenses	250	250	250	250
Discounts given	200	200	200	200
Contingency	1,250	1,250	1,250	1,250
Depreciation	2,800	2,800	2,800	2,800
Total Fixed Costs	30,050	28,550	28,550	28,550
Profit before Interest	8,020	8,110	5,290	1,060
Bank & Other Interest	1,000	1,000	1,000	1,000
HP Interest	750	750	750	750
Other Income	(750)	(750)	(750)	(750)
Discounts Received	(250)	(250)	(250)	(250)
Profit before Tax	7,270	7,360	4,540	310
Provision for Tax	1,818	1,840	1,135	78
Profit after Tax	5,453	5,520	3,405	233
Cumulative Profit	5,453	10,973	14,378	14,610

Exhibit 2.3 *Continued*

JUN	JUL	AUG	SEP	OCT	NOV
100,000	90,000	95,000	115,000	130,000	140,000
0	0	5,000	10,000	15,000	15,000
100,000	90,000	100,000	125,000	145,000	155,000
100,000	90,000	100,000	125,000	145,000	155,000
47,500	42,750	47,500	59,375	68,875	73,625
300	270	300	375	435	465
10,000	9,000	10,000	12,500	14,500	15,500
500	450	500	625	725	775
5,000	4,500	5,000	6,250	7,250	7,750
8,500	7,650	8,500	10,625	12,325	13,175
28,200	25,380	28,200	35,250	40,890	43,710
28.20%	28.20%	28.20%	28.20%	28.20%	28.20%
5,450	5,450	5,450	5,450	5,450	5,450
6,450	6,450	6,450	6,450	6,450	6,450
500	500	500	500	500	500
0	0	0	0	0	0
1,825	1,825	1,825	1,825	1,825	1,825
375	375	375	375	375	375
500	500	500	500	500	500
250	250	250	250	250	250
150	150	150	150	150	150
3,500	3,500	3,500	3,500	3,500	3,500
750	750	750	750	750	750
1,000	1,000	1,000	1,000	1,000	1,000
1,100	1,100	1,100	1,100	1,100	1,100
300	300	300	300	300	300
400	400	400	400	400	400
1,000	1,000	1,000	1,000	1,000	1,000
250	250	250	250	250	250
250	250	250	250	250	250
250	250	250	250	250	250
200	200	200	200	200	200
1,250	1,250	1,250	1,250	1,250	1,250
2,800	2,800	2,800	2,800	2,800	2,800
28,550	28,550	28,550	28,550	28,550	28,550
(350)	(3,170)	(350)	6,700	12,340	15,160
1,000	1,000	1,000	1,000	1,000	1,000
750	750	750	750	750	750
(750)	(750)	(750)	(750)	(750)	(750)
(250)	(250)	(250)	(250)	(250)	(250)
(1,100)	(3,920)	(1,100)	5,950	11,590	14,410
(275)	(980)	(275)	1,488	2,898	3,603
(825)	(2,940)	(825)	4,463	8,691	10,808
13,785	10,845	10,020	14,483	23,175	33,983

Exhibit 2.3   *Continued*   **12/02/93**

DEC	JAN	TOTAL
110,000	120,000	1,390,000
5,000	15,000	65,000
115,000	135,000	1,455,000
115,000	135,000	1,455,000
54,625	64,125	691,125
345	405	4,365
11,500	13,500	145,500
575	675	7,275
5,750	6,750	72,750
9,775	11,475	123,675
32,430	38,070	410,310
28.20%	28.20%	28.20%
5,450	5,450	65,400
6,450	6,450	77,400
500	500	7,500
0	0	0
1,825	1,825	21,900
375	375	4,500
500	500	6,000
250	250	3,000
150	150	1,800
3,500	3,500	42,000
750	750	9,000
1,000	1,000	12,000
1,100	1,100	13,200
300	300	3,600
400	400	4,800
1,000	1,000	12,000
250	250	3,000
250	250	3,000
250	250	3,000
200	200	2,400
1,250	1,250	15,000
2,800	2,800	33,600
28,550	28,550	344,100
3,880	9,520	66,210
1,000	1,000	12,000
750	750	9,000
(750)	(750)	(9,000)
(250)	(250)	(3,000)
3,130	8,770	57,210
783	2,193	14,303
2,348	6,578	42,908
36,330	42,908	

Questions

(1) Develop a SWOT analysis for Plaswin.

(2) For the year 1992/93 (see Exhibit 2.3), calculate the following financial ratios, given that the total assets of Plaswin at 31 January 1993 totalled £500,000:
   - Net profit margin
   - Marketing expenses to sales
   - Return on assets

(3) Develop a marketing plan for Plaswin to help the company to achieve its goals.

(4) Plaswin is considering its tender for the installation of doors and windows in a new development of 16 houses. The cost price has been calculated as £1,250 per house. Based on previous information, such as results of tenders against the other firms tendering for the contract, Plaswin has calculated the probability of winning the tender with different bids, as below:

Bid (£'000)	Probability of winning tender
24	0.9
25	0.81
26	0.7
27	0.62
28	0.5
29	0.35
30	0.2
31	0.1
32	0.05

Calculate the expected profit for each bid level. What would you advise Plaswin to bid for this tender?

(5) What are the advantages and disadvantages of Plaswin's commission policy?

CASE 3

The Battle for Portable Power: Ever Ready versus Duracell[†]

Strategic Marketing

Douglas Brownlie
University of Stirling

Sandra Connor
University of Paisley

Norma Macedo
Glasgow Caledonian University

Introduction

Take a walk down any high street these days and you will be amazed by the array of portable electronic gadgetry that people adorn themselves with. There is every chance that you will pass someone wearing a personal hi-fi; someone sporting a cellular telephone or pager; someone hungrily capturing memories with a camera or camcorder; and the occasional wheeler-dealer zealously consulting an electronic organizer, or with a small case containing a laptop computer, casually slung just off-the-shoulder. Then fast forward to the home where you may very well have remote controls for the hi-fi, television and video; hand-held video games and other electronic toys for the children, including portable keyboards; smoke alarms, watches, clocks, portable power tools, bicycle lights, calculators, typewriters, personal computers, hand-held TVs, torches, shavers, ghetto-blasters and all sorts of electronic gizmos. They all draw their electricity from some form of portable power source, even if many of them languish in a corner somewhere for the want of replacement batteries and a bit of interest.

[†] This case study is based on publicly available information and does not necessarily reflect the opinions of Duracell or Ever Ready.

It seems that these and other portable consumer electronic products are no longer luxury items, mere trifles to pamper or distract yourself with, but the necesssary pillars of modern living. Many of them look set to become the fashion accessories of the late 1990s, as new designs and styling make them ever lighter, more compact and visually appealing. However, few of us, least of all the manufacturers, can overlook the annoyance of having to constantly renew the portable power source that makes these devices operable. Indeed, in the United Kingdom alone, annual sales of such power sources are estimated to be worth around £380 m at retail value. As you might guess, the battle for market share in this territory is very intense with two major players, Ever Ready and Duracell, slugging it out from their various vantage points of market dominance. Their combined strength currently accounts for around 60% of sales in the UK battery market, but this position is being threatened by new entrants.

Yet it is only around two centuries since the Italian Count Alessandro Volta invented the first battery using the idea of a contained chemical reaction through which electricity is generated as electrons flow from one material to another. The technology, if not the scientific principle, has moved on considerably since then, but not as fast as that of microchip technology which drives product development in consumer electronics. Indeed, during the last decade the fraction of the total weight of portable electronic products which is taken by the battery has grown from around 10% to 30%, largely because of the miniaturisation of electronic circuitry. Battery technology looks likely to continue to develop as manufacturers of consumer electronic goods look for lighter, smaller and longer-lasting ways of powering their ever-increasing range of portable appliances.

The Sun Rises Over Ever Ready

Ever Ready was established in Manchester in 1908 as a manufacturer of portable sources of low-voltage electric power. In 1914 the American and British operations of Ever Ready were de-merged and since then they have operated as independent companies with different owners. Since the 1920s, Ever Ready in the United Kingdom has been a leading innovator in the field of zinc–carbon cell technology, successfully developing a range of small, low-voltage batteries for a variety of intermittent-use applications.

Until the late 1970s Ever Ready held a very strong competitive position in the UK battery market, largely as a result of its early and sustained investment in a sound product-technology base and in a system of direct retail distribution. Over the years it has built up its own fleet of delivery vehicles which provide it with extensive coverage of the available retail outlets. In the 1960s 70% of all battery sales were made through what was then a highly fragmented body of *specialist* high street retailers and convenience stores (see Exhibit 3.1). The fleet has been rationalized in recent years. However, the company still employs van salespeople to deliver its products, fill racks and arrange other merchandizing activities such as in-store display racks and point-of-sale materials.

Exhibit 3.1   *Distribution outlets*

Outlet type	Number (1988, approx.)	Retail sales (% of value)			
		1971	*1981*	*1989*	*1991*
Chemists, photographic	14,200	40	20	7	6
Electrical goods shops	18,600	20	18	13	11
Supermarkets	35,000	5	22	30	26
Mixed retail stores†	10,000	8	15	20	21
CTNs‡	52,000	8	5	7	11
Hardware/DIY/garages	24,000	4	5	6	8
Others	8,000	15	15	17	17

† Including Boots and Woolworths.
‡ Confectioners, tobacconists, newsagents and convenience stores.

Although Ever Ready's version of the standard zinc–carbon battery has been with us for around 70 years, it was not until the 1950s that volume growth really started to take off. During the consumer boom of the 1960s sales of transistor radios and other small electrical appliances grew rapidly. Ever Ready was quick to seize this opportunity and as a result established itself as the clear market leader, so that in the early 1970s it was supplying some 60–70% of all batteries sold in the United Kingdom. Indeed, by the mid-1970s three out of every four zinc–carbon batteries that were bought were Ever Ready products (see Exhibit 3.2) with such labels as HP2, HP7, HP16, HP11 and PP3.

The rise to dominance of Ever Ready was engineered by a strong, driving management team. Over the years, it had implemented a policy of responding to most technological innovations in electrical and electronic goods that required battery power of 1.5 volts, or combinations thereof. In this way, the firm evolved a very wide range of zinc–carbon batteries which were particularly suited to low-drainage and intermittent applications, such as transistor radios, torches, toys, calculators and shavers. Of the 14 batteries in its 1981 product range, the HP2, HP7 and PP3 generated some 60% of the company's sales turnover.

Exhibit 3.2   *Historical sales trends (£m)*

	1976	*1983*	*1985*	*1987*	*1989*	*1991*	*1992*
Total sales (m units)	280	410	430	420	455	460	465
Total sales (£m)	100	175	200	260	300	360	380
Ever Ready	67	70	98	94	100	108	110
Duracell	—	35	56	81	99	115	120
Vidor	n/a	n/a	n/a	13	12	14	14
Varta	n/a	n/a	n/a	6	12	14	15
Kodak	n/a	n/a	n/a	5	9	14	15
Panasonic	n/a	n/a	n/a	n/a	3	7	8
Own label	—	5	10	20	30	40	50
Other brands	—	15	20	41	35	48	48

Source: Adapted by the authors from Mintel, Market Intelligence, 1992.

By virtue of a large equity stake in a small independent alkaline battery manufacturer, Ever Ready had also been involved, since the 1940s, in the low-volume manufacture of alkaline manganese button-cells, which were designed for specialist high-power applications where small size is important, such as hearing aids, cameras and watches. But, in the wake of a Monopolies Commission investigation of the battery industry, Ever Ready divested itself of this equity in 1977. In 1979 the board rejected an approach by a major supermarket chain to supply it with batteries it would market as its own-label product. The board was then of the opinion that this supply deal would not be consistent with its policy of evolving and maintaining a long-term competitive advantage based on a strongly branded product range.

Until the early 1980s the company's research and development effort had been exclusively spent in three major areas: first, in improving quality control, labour productivity and working practices; second, in examining the problem of leakage from its zinc–carbon batteries; and third, in looking for possible ways to improve the average life of these batteries, particularly for applications where continuous use is to be expected. The problem of chemical failure was one the company had wrestled with for some years since it not only restricted battery *not-in-use* life, but also made the product unsuitable for long continuous use applications.

Round 1: Enter the Competition, Stage Centre

The growth in the demand for low voltage batteries has been driven by the proliferation of innovative consumer electronic products, such as portable cassette players, personal stereos and hand-held games and toys (see Exhibits 3.3 and 3.4).

Exhibit 3.3 *Estimated value of UK market for selected electrical goods (£m)*

	1984	1986	1988	1990	1992
Colour TV	515	580	975	806	800
Video	525	562	644	563	530
TV/video games	150	110	24	67	72
Hand-held games	56	34	35	36	62
Hi-fi	800	1,060	810	652	643
Radio	76	95	18	23	25
Portable radio-cassette	125	155	151	130	118
Personal stereo	50	90	106	124	155
Home computer	35	549	834	115	100
Torches	9	32	34	33	28
Calculator	52	58	50	60	55
CD player	n/a	100	90	113	128
Camcorder	n/a	n/a	134	287	324
Smoke alarm	n/a	n/a	30	72	84
Portable keyboard	n/a	n/a	60	81	92
Radio-controlled toys	n/a	n/a	24	16	20
Electric shaver	47	46	67	58	56

Exhibit 3.4   *Estimated UK household penetration of selected battery-powered goods (%)*

	1986	1991
Watch	57	84
Camera	43	70
Radio-cassette	36	67
Personal stereo	21	39
Shaver	21	36
Children's games/toys	25	27
Bicycle lights	17	22
Musical instruments	n/a	17
Electronic games (e.g. Nintendo, Sega)	n/a	13
Other household items (e.g. remote control, smoke alarm)	n/a	77

Source: BMRB/Mintel, 1992.

Clearly the 60% growth in personal disposable income which occurred during the 1980s has driven the soaring demand for those products. Since the consumer boom of the 1960s the average number of battery-powered appliances owned in each UK household has risen from a mere handful to around 11.

Ever Ready was the first to capitalize on this growth. But with the rapid diffusion of high-drainage applicances, such as personal stereos and portable radio-cassettes, latent consumer demand for a longer-lasting battery soon became apparent. The opportunity to meet this emerging demand was seized by Duracell, a wholly owned subsidiary of the major US battery manufacturer, Duracell Inc.

Early in 1977 Duracell laid plans to establish a UK manufacturing and whole-saling base in Crawley, Sussex. The parent company specialized in the manufacture of alkaline–manganese batteries, sales of which at the time accounted for over 60% of the total US battery market, a figure that has since risen to over 75%.

At the heart of Duracell's strategic planning was the assumption that the long-term patterns of battery sales in the United States and United Kingdom were very similar, with the UK market lagging the US by some six or seven years. In the mid-1970s, sales of alkaline–manganese batteries in the the United States had suddenly rocketed with the rapid development of the markets for portable high-power radio-cassettes and personal stereos. It also coincided with the growing presence of the large grocery chains as distribution outlets. Duracell expected this pattern of market development to begin to take off in the United Kingdom during the early 1980s. Although its alkaline batteries were more difficult to manufacture than their zinc–carbon counterparts, they made use of chemical properties that imparted high performance characteristics. This made them very well suited to high-drainage applications, particularly of the motorized variety where continuous use is to be expected.

Duracell's marketing strategy took advantage of what it found to be surprisingly fluid purchase habits and customer attitudes to the product. Although the price of Duracell batteries was almost twice that of their zinc–carbon counterparts, the claim that they lasted up to six times longer in continuous use (and had a longer not-in-use life) was seen to be a sufficiently strong selling point to persuade many customers to trade up from the brands they were familiar with. Its simple proposition of longer life succeeded in encouraging existing consumers to switch from zinc–carbon batteries to longer-lasting alkaline–manganese batteries, and in the process to pay a premium price. It also attracted new customers into the market, particularly young people who were then at the vanguard of the ghetto blaster/personal stereo culture. As a result, unit sales of alkaline batteries rose in the 1980s at annual rates of around 20%, while total unit sales grew by as much as 5% per year (see Exhibits 3.5, 3.6 and 3.7). In value terms market growth was often more dramatic as consumers switched to the premium priced alkaline cells which offer a significant cost saving on the basis of per unit power delivered.

Exhibit 3.5 *Volume sales by battery type (m units)*

	1976	1983	1985	1987	1989	1991	1992	1993 (est.)
Zinc	272	346	288	238	235	207	195	187
Alkaline	2	50	108	161	198	229	244	260
Rechargeable†	4	7	9	10	9	11	12	13
Others‡	2	7	10	11	13	13	14	15
Total	280	410	430	420	455	460	465	475

† Nickel–cadmium rechargeable.
‡ Lithium cells and button-cells.

Exhibit 3.6 *Sales value by battery type (£m)*

	1985	1987	1989	1991	1992	1993 (est.)
Zinc	100	110	105	107	110	113
Alkaline	68	116	156	207	220	230
Rechargeable†	16	18	23	28	30	31
Others‡	16	16	16	18	20	21
Total	200	260	300	360	380	395

† Nickel–cadmium rechargeable.
‡ Lithium cells and button-cells.

Exhibit 3.7 *Alkaline cells: year-on-year growth by volume (%)*

1983	1984	1985	1986	1987	1988	1989	1990	1991	1992	1993 (est)
20	30	18	24	25	14	14	10	2	2	3

Since launching its UK product range in 1978, Duracell has implemented a strategy of building market share which has increased its sales from around £4 million in 1978, to over £120 million in 1992. The growth in the volume of UK sales of alkaline–manganese batteries from 2 million in 1976, to 244 million in 1992 is largely attributed to the early marketing activity of Duracell and Ever Ready's response in late 1982 with the launch of its own alkaline battery range, Gold Seal.

The early success of Duracell's differentiated marketing approach is attributed to its avoidance of direct competition in the traditional stronghold of Ever Ready's zinc–carbon batteries. Its product range consisted of five battery sizes (see Exhibit 3.8) which it claimed was conceived to serve 90% of applications. Vindication of

Exhibit 3.8   *Battery nomenclature and sizes*

Duracell	Description	Ever Ready
R6	Slim, pencil-like for personal stereos, cameras, shavers	HP7
R03	Slimmer, pencil-like, for remote controls, cameras, calculators	HP16
R14	Short, barrel-like for torches, radio-cassettes, toys	HP11
R20	Larger, barrel-like for radio cassettes, toys	HP2
PP3	9 volts square battery for remote controls, smoke alarms, radios	PP3

this product policy decision came in 1985, when it was reported that these five battery sizes accounted for 88% of all battery sales.

In the first half of the 1980s, an average spend of around 4% of sales on above-the-line activity enabled Duracell to develop consumer awareness and thus to stimulate the trial purchases it needed to establish repeat buying patterns. *No ordinary battery looks like it or lasts like it* was the simple and consistent promotional message that was used to convey the longer life and higher performance of Duracell's alkaline batteries in specific applications, such as cassettes and electronic toys. The longer-life proposition was powerfully communicated in its TV ads which carried a clever demonstration, featuring a motorized bunny drummer, showing that Duracell's alkaline batteries lasted up to six times longer than standard zinc batteries in such applications. This activity was concentrated in the period leading up to the Christmas spending spree on battery-operated gifts, especially toys and games. Indeed, around 35% of annual sales volume is moved between November and January, with the remainder being spread evenly over the year.

The success of Duracell's marketing strategy also depended on winning listings in selected distribution outlets, especially the large grocery retailers, where the quality of in-store displays and shelf space would become vital marketing weapons. It introduced point-of-sale material, as well as packaging and product design features that would make it easy for the consumer to spot and identify its batteries and to associate them with specific applications. Only in this way could it build up the coverage, as well as the rate of sale of its 'copper-topped' products. In its fight for shelf space Duracell also undertook to extend its merchandising policy to confectioners, tobacconists and newsagents, as well as other convenience stores, including garage forecourts, which because of their long opening hours were well placed to capitalize on impulse or distress purchases. The large supermarkets such as Tesco, Asda, Sainsbury, Safeway and Gateway were attracted by the comparatively high trade margins provided and this issue has since further stoked their interest in own-label batteries, largely supplied these days by Philips and Vidor. By opting to distribute its products through the wholesaler route, Duracell also came under pressure from these retailers to provide special discounts as well as free merchandising units to obtain the coverage it needed.

Round 2: Ever Ready's Response

By the late 1970s Ever Ready was quickly becoming sensitive to the view that some of Duracell's success could be attributed to its own defensive response to the new entrant's aggressive intrusion into the market. An offensive response was felt at the time to have at its core the development of Ever Ready's own alkaline battery. However, in 1979 the mood of the firm was against new product development, since it would have meant heavy investment and a subsequent decline in short-term performance, in addition to the prospect of cannibalizing the sales of its existing range of zinc–carbon batteries. By early 1981, it was becoming clear that strong measures needed to be taken against Duracell, since Ever Ready was finding itself with a large share of a declining market and no presence in the growth areas. After much heartsearching, the management of Ever Ready decided to move on several fronts. In laying its plans the findings of an externally commissioned market research study were taken into account (see Exhibit 3.9).

Around this time Ever Ready in the United Kingdom was acquired by the Hanson Corporation for £95 million. One of the first steps taken by the new owner was to sell the company's European operations to Duracell Inc. for £54 million. Hanson's analysis of Ever Ready's operations led to other disposals, as well as a keen focus on cash flow and profit centre accountability. This strengthened the balance sheet while throwing the strategic spotlight on consolidating the position of the cash cows among its existing zinc brands, HP7, HP11, HP2 and PP3.

One of the first steps Ever Ready took was to launch, with a new livery, its own version of the alkaline battery under the *Gold Seal* name. The following year it relaunched its existing range of zinc batteries under the same family name and livery. The original standard type of zinc–carbon battery was relaunched under the *Blue Seal* brand. It also launched an improved, medium-life zinc–chloride battery under the *Silver Seal* brand. In addition, the range of batteries available within each brand was rationalized to focus on the five main types that were emerging (see Exhibit 3.10).

Bearing in mind the need to avoid compromising the position of its major profit base, that is its existing zinc brands, Ever Ready devised a marketing platform that attempted to avoid the 'me too' trap for the Gold Seal brand. Despite increasing pressure on margins, this entailed heavy promotional expenditure of around 5% of sales on above-the-line activity, with much of its advertising weight being put behind the Gold Seal brand. In 1983 20% of its overall promotional budget supported below-the-line activity, which tended then to be concentrated around the Christmas period. But, because of the need to protect the position of its zinc brands, Ever Ready could not afford to be as direct as Duracell in its advertising proposition for the long-life alkaline brand. Gold Seal advertising employed the message *The Heart of a Machine* with a storyline that featured a weedy British teenage character, later to become Forever Eddy, scaring the rednecks in an American bar with the power of his ghetto blaster batteries. Industry observers felt that this approach tended to dissipate Ever Ready's long-life message.

Other elements of the relaunch strategy included a more clearly focused

Exhibit 3.9   UK Battery Market: Independent Research Study (1982)

Summary Findings

Brand awareness:	Ever Ready	72%
	Duracell	46%
Advertising awareness:	Ever Ready	47%
	Duracell	60%
Market penetration:	Ever Ready	70%
(% retail outlets	Duracell	56%
stocking products)		

Consumer confusion over the very wide range of battery sizes and types, and the applications for which they are suited.

Fifty-six per cent of purchases were made by **women**, up to the age of 44, compared with 46% in 1978.

Younger purchasers tended to buy alkaline batteries to a greater extent, with 60% of the sales of these batteries being made to people under the age of 45.

Over 67% of consumers held strongly **negative attitudes** to the generic standard products' performance reflected in the commonly held belief that *'batteries never last long enough'*. This is often a distress purchase where convenience and availability are important.

Growth areas: high-powered portable radios and cassette players, personal hi-fi and electronic toys and games where continuous use for periods of up to 2 hours or more is expected.

Perceived benefits: mobility, convenience, reliability, image-status enhancement.

Important product attribute: durability; value for money; ease of use; suitability for application; weight; ease of identification.

High rates of recognition of Duracell products and unprompted recall of its positioning statement. This was attributable not only to a high rate of TV, press and poster advertising exposure, but also to its simple application information and clear positioning as technically superior and better value for money for high-drainage applications.

Source: Mintel, May 1992.

Exhibit 3.10   *Total volume sales by five most popular battery sizes (%)*

	1989		1991	
	Zinc	*Alkaline*	*Zinc*	*Alkaline*
LR6	20	30	23	32
LR03	1	5	2	6
LR14	11	8	10	6
LR20	10	7	9	6
PP3	3	3	2	2

Source: As Exhibit 3.9.

merchandising effort to improve the in-store positioning of the new product range; streamlining of the management structure; and rationalization of the distribution fleet.

During the course of the 1980s, advertising support was maintained at significant levels (see Exhibit 3.11) with Ever Ready and Duracell accounting for almost all of the measured advertising expenditure. However, below-the-line activity, including point-of-sale support, sponsorship and on-pack promotions, grew in importance as all the main brands chased market share gains through strengthening brand loyalty, widening their distribution coverage and increasing their rate of sale per outlet. Given that many of the supermarket chains were increasingly prepared to make do with one of the major brands, often Duracell, plus their own brand, the battle for listings and quality shelf space began to take on major proportions. Clearly, the battle for growth increasingly depended on being competitive on the shelf.

Exhibit 3.11 *Advertising support for all brands at rate card cost (£m)*

1985	1986	1987	1988	1989	1990	1991	1992
7.37	6.16	9.63	8.06	6.71	4.18	4.23	5.60

Source: Adapted by the authors from Mintel, May 1992.

By the early 1990s, Ever Ready had gained a 17% share in the alkaline market, compared with Duracell's 56%, while maintaining its dominance of the zinc sector (see Exhibit 3.12). However, in the meantime own-label products have been gaining market share, especially in the major grocery chains, but also through variety stores such as Woolworths and Boots. While many own-label purchases are made on impulse, there is a suspicion that, in the case of the supermarkets at least, battery purchase has become yet another item in the weekly shopping trip of a growing number of shoppers. Indeed it has been estimated that 80% of battery purchases in supermarkets are made by women. Smaller players, including Varta, Vidor, Kodak and Panasonic, have also gained share at the expense of the major players, largely through focusing their promotional effort on below-the-line activity and gaining distribution coverage in convenience stores where emergency or distress purchase needs are met. All this has contributed to the importance of improving the quality of in-store displays and point-of-sale material, especially in the large supermarket chains which now tend to devote prominent shelf space to their own brands and where rate of sale is such an important factor in winning and keeping a listing.

Exhibit 3.12 *Brand share of zinc and alkaline batteries by volume (1991)*

	Zinc		Alkaline	
	m	*%*	*m*	*%*
Ever Ready	109	53	39	17
Duracell	—	—	129	56
Vidor	12	12	7	3
Varta	12	12	7	3
Others†/own label‡	74	35	47	20

† Brands include Kodak and Hitachi as well as a number of budget brands produced in the Far East.
‡ The major own-brand suppliers are Philips, Vidor and Saft.
Source: Mintel, Market Intelligence, May 1992.

During this time both Duracell and Ever Ready began to seek out links with the appliance manufacturers. They also started to market, under their own label, complementary product lines, especially torches, which come with batteries supplied.

In a surprise move, Duracell closed its Crawley plant early in 1992, transferring its component manufacturing and warehousing operations from the United Kingdom to Belgium.

As the battle arena moved into the 1990s, it was clear that despite its valiant efforts, Ever Ready had largely failed to make significant inroads into Duracell's heartland with its Gold Seal brand. Indeed, research showed that where Gold Seal was displayed alongside Duracell equivalents, the latter outsold the former by more than three to one. Out of the top five grocery chains, only Sainsbury stocked Gold Seal, the others stocking Duracell products. Research also showed that consumers persistently expressed an overwhelming preference for Duracell's alkaline brands and that when many of them thought of long-life batteries, they thought of Duracell.

Yet it was clear that with the continued development and diffusion of novel and ever smaller portable, high-drainage electronic devices, a major market opportunity still existed in the alkaline sector. Indeed, in the recessionary period of the last few years, the battery market has still performed well, partly because of the product development activity of appliance manufacturers. This may have fuelled the optimism of a recent Mintel (1992) forecast that predicted 8% volume growth (13% by value) in battery sales between 1993 and 1996, with the lion's share of this growth coming from the continued expansion of the alkaline sector. Independent market research studies had already highlighted this and other issues (see Exhibits 3.13–3.16).

Round 3: The Battle Intensifies

If the battle for market share in the United Kingdom had been fiercely contested, then the battle in the United States was just as fiercely contested by the American counterparts of Duracell and Ever Ready. During the 1980s, the American Ever Ready had successfully mounted a concerted attack on Duracell's overwhelming presence in the alkaline sector of the US market, where it discovered how difficult it is to defend a market share position of over 50%. The centrepiece of Ever Ready's strategy was the *Energizer* brand, the advertising for which talked in a witty and contemporary American way about an alternative brand that clearly delivered the key proposition in the alkaline market, that of long life. Within three years of its launch, this new brand had snatched pole position from Duracell, with American consumers expressing a strong preference for the zappy upstart, Energizer.

Exhibit 3.13 Issues Raised by Independent Research Studies

Increased Penetration of Household Battery Powered Products
Between 1990 and 1996, the number of households owning items such as smoke alarms, shavers, portable power tools, personal stereos, cameras, radio-cassettes, electronic musical instruments and electronic games will continue to increase significantly, with consumers becoming more sophisticated in their purchasing.

Brand Awareness
Gold Seal has an unprompted awareness level of around 60%. Consumers associate it with the other Seal brands, Silver Seal and Blue Seal, viewing it as the top of the Ever Ready range, but with some reservations about its quality.

Demographic Analysis of Purchasers
The data provided in Exhibits 3.14, 3.15 and 3.16 are drawn from a BMRB/Mintel study (1992). They plot the changing demographic profile of purchasers. Among other things, they show that the ownership of battery-powered products is greater among men in the ABC1 socio-economic group. There is also a growing bias towards younger age groups and to adults in the 35–44 age group who are most likely to have children at home. Although men dominate purchasing where battery use is heavy or medium, woman who are non-users are twice as likely to make purchases than men, especially where there are children in the household.

Environmental Concerns
In the near future more stringent limits are likely to be imposed on the amount of heavy metals such as mercury and cadmium that batteries can contain. So far, this has mainly affected producers of alkaline cells. Further pressure to reduce those levels may force manufacturers to raise prices. Although no legislation covering the disposal and recycling of batteries has yet been announced by bodies such as the EU, it is possible that manufacturers will be required to recycle their products, or develop collection schemes so that they can be disposed of safely. In areas where such schemes are already operating, a significant educational effort has been required to overcome consumer resistance. There is also the possibility that the introduction of recycling schemes could boost the popularity of rechargeable batteries, which have yet to achieve any significant market presence.

Varta, the UK subsidiary of Varta Batteries AG, claims to be the first manufacturer to produce an environmentally friendly zinc–carbon battery which has mercury-free cells. It launched this product into the UK market in 1989. Since then it has been heavily criticized by other manufacturers who dispute its green claims. Philips also claims to have developed a range of 'green' batteries. It produces a mercury- and cadmium-free alkaline range, as well as mercury-free zinc–carbon batteries.

Rechargeable Battery Technology
NiCad batteries are still the main type of rechargeable, although other technologies are being developed by US and Japanese consortiums. They are widely used in laptop computers and camcorders. Until 1991, soaring sales of these devices made the NiCad battery the industry's fastest growing product. Output in Japan has almost tripled during the last few years and now has an annual value of over $1 billion. Sales of disposable lithium cells are also growing rapidly, but they account for only around 7% of the total battery market.

Exhibit 3.13   *continued*

	Average energy output (watt-hours/kg)	*Energy density (watt-hours/space)*	*Average voltage*	*Cost per watt-hour*
NiCad	30–50	150	1.2	46p
Nickel–hydride	55–60	200	1.2	78p
Lithium	80–200	250	3.6	90p

In recent years serious environmental concerns have been raised over the use of the toxic metal cadmium in NiCads. This metal can leach into groundwater when discarded in landfill sites. Pressure is growing either to ban their use, or to find safer ways of disposal. Improvements to NiCad technology are reaching their limit. Alternatives are being developed that are not only safer, but lighter, cheaper to make, longer-lasting and quicker to recharge. At present the nickel–hydride technology is the focus of development efforts. It can deliver the same voltage as NiCad, but can store nearly twice as much power in terms of watt-hours. A recent industry report stated that when charged for an hour, a nickel–hydride battery could power a camcorder for 90 minutes, compared with a NiCad's 50 minutes. Between them, Sanyo, Matsushita and Toshiba are currently producing around 10 million nickel–hydride units a year. Duracell has formed an alliance with Varta and Toshiba to make nickel–hydride batteries in Japan to be marketed in Japan, the United States and Europe. Rechargeable lithium cells are also being developed for large-scale manufacture by a number of US and Japanese firms.

Exhibit 3.14   Demographic Breakdown of Household Ownership of the Main Battery–Powered Items, 1991 (%)
Base: 1,081 adults

	Radio radio/ cassette	*Home office items†*	*Personal stereo*	*Shavers*	*Hand-held electronic games*
All	67	53	39	36	13
Men	71	62	43	37	15
Women	63	45	36	35	11
15–19	83	75	79	53	23
20–24	69	69	54	48	17
25–34	66	54	41	40	13
35–44	75	66	57	36	25
45–54	64	61	37	38	15
55–64	65	42	21	31	3
65 +	57	24	9	19	1
AB	83	65	47	43	16
C1	71	61	47	39	12
C2	65	54	36	40	16
D	60	49	39	29	13
E	55	30	24	25	5
London/TVS	70	59	46	34	12
Anglia/Central	70	56	40	33	14
Harlech/TSW	64	51	38	32	12

Exhibit 3.14 *continued*

	Radio radio/ cassette	Home office items†	Personal stereo	Shavers	Hand-held electronic games
Yorkshire/Tyne Tees	64	51	36	38	15
Granada	68	50	38	40	9
Scotland	55	42	37	39	12
Working	70	64	47	43	17
Not working	63	46	39	30	12
Retired	67	36	16	28	4
Children	75	65	57	41	26
No children	63	47	30	33	6

† Includes calculators, portable computers, portable telephones and typewriters.
Source: BMRB/Mintel.

Exhibit 3.15 Demographic Analysis of Battery Purchasers, 1985 and 1991 (%)

	1985	*1991*
TGI annual survey sample (number)	24,651	25,604
All	86.8	86.5
Men	90.8	91.0
Women	83.2	82.4
15–24	82.1	83.0
25–34	90.4	90.0
35–44	91.7	90.4
45–54	89.3	88.3
55–64	88.1	86.4
65+	81.5	81.7
AB	91.8	90.9
C1	89.1	89.3
C2	87.2	87.5
D	85.0	84.5
E	79.2	75.7
London/TVS	88.6	88.4
Anglia/Central	87.8	87.4
Harlech/TSW	86.7	86.2
Yorkshire/Tyne Tees	85.3	85.6
Granada	84.2	83.5
Scotland	85.9	85.6
Own/buying home	88.6	88.1
Renting home	83.6	82.4
No children	85.4	85.2
Child(ren) under 1 year	87.3	90.5
Child(ren) 1–4 years	90.3	90.7
Child(ren) 5–9 years	91.2	89.7
Child(ren) 10–15 years	88.4	88.2

Source: TGI, BMRB 1985–91/Mintel.

Exhibit 3.16   Demographic Analysis of Battery Purchasers by Level of Purchasing, 1991 (%)[†]

	Heavy users	Medium users	Light users	Non-users
All	15.1	18.3	53.2	13.5
Men	18.9	20.9	51.3	9.0
Women	11.6	15.9	54.9	17.5
15–24	15.4	15.9	51.7	17.0
25–34	18.9	22.2	49.0	10.0
35–44	21.3	20.4	48.7	9.6
45–54	16.8	20.5	51.0	11.7
55–64	11.7	17.9	56.8	13.6
65+	6.6	13.5	61.6	18.3
AB	19.7	22.1	49.1	9.1
C1	15.9	19.9	53.6	10.7
C2	15.4	17.7	54.3	12.5
D	13.3	17.8	53.4	15.5
E	8.6	11.9	55.1	24.3
London/TVS	18.4	19.9	50.1	11.6
Anglia/Central	15.2	18.3	53.9	12.6
Harlech/TSW	12.6	18.6	55.0	13.8
Yorkshire/Tyne Tees	12.8	15.6	57.2	14.4
Granada	13.8	17.9	51.8	16.5
Scotland	14.1	17.1	54.3	14.5
Own/buying home	15.9	19.3	53.0	11.9
Renting home	12.8	15.7	53.9	17.6
No children	12.1	16.9	56.3	14.8
Child(ren) under 1	17.1	22.0	51.3	9.5
Child(ren) 1–4 yrs	22.0	22.2	46.5	9.3
Child(ren) 5–9 yrs	24.7	22.4	42.6	10.3
Child(ren) 10–15 yrs	20.7	20.4	47.0	11.8

† Taken from TGI annual survey of 25,604 adults.
Source: TGI, BMRB 1991/Mintel.

In 1991 Hanson attempted to acquire the patent company of the American Ever Ready, Ralston Energy Systems. However, the parties could not reach agreement on the terms of the sale and in June 1992, in a surprise turn of events, Ralston ended up buying the British Ever Ready from Hanson for £132 million. Thus, with one timely stroke, Ever Ready in the United Kingdom found itself moving from the periphery of Hanson's strategic activities to the core of Ralston's global ambitions for the Energizer brand. What goes around comes around. Early in the new marriage the strategic decision was taken to launch Energizer into the UK market. The stage was also set for importing the American company's experience with the brand in the US market to the situation facing its newly acquired UK operations.

Questions

(1) What factors contributed to Ever Ready's competitive position before 1983?

(2) How could a company minimize the chances of these difficulties reoccurring in the future?

(3) What conclusions would you draw from the 1983 market research study about the direction and strength of the trends in the marketplace?

(4) What impact do you think the market trends might have on Ever Ready's competitive position?

(5) What impact do you think the market trends might have on Duracell's competitive position?

(6) Which of Ever Ready's current strengths would you say it should build on in formulating an offensive marketing strategy?

(7) Which of Ever Ready's current weaknesses would you say are most likely to undermine its ability to fend off Duracell's competitive inroads?

(8) Critically analyse Ever Ready's current marketing mix and suggest possible areas where the company could gain a comparative advantage.

(9) Draft a proposal for launching Energizer in the rest of Europe. What information do you think you might need prior to the launch of Energizer in Europe?

(10) Devise a detailed plan for improving Ever Ready's merchandising effort in the light of Duracell's dominance in the major multiples within the context of its relationship marketing efforts.

CASE 4
Dawson & Company Limited
Strategic Marketing

Peter Coyne
British Waterways Board

Company History

Because of the particularly good quality of the spring water in Birton, beer has been brewed there since the Middle Ages. Ewan Dawson established his brewery at Birton in 1830 on the site of the spring still sourced by the company today. When the brewery was rebuilt in 1850 ownership passed to the Wallace family. Wallace McNiall died in 1958 and death duty liabilities resulted in the disposal of the majority of the company's managed houses.

The Company's Products

The company produces seven types of beer: 60/-, 70/-, 80/- and porter real ales plus Light, Special and Export keg ales. In addition, the company factors a full range of other beers, wines and spirits. So as to provide a one-stop shop for the licensed on trade, glasses, bar accessories, stationery and catering can be provided together with stocktaking and audit services.

Sales of Dawson's ales have been dropping by about 2% in real terms per annum since the early 1970s. It has been necessary to carry a full range of products in order to maintain the interest of the free trade and even to supply other ales which compete directly with the company's own products. The only way that the company has been able to keep the rate of decline as low as 2% has been to expand the managed house portfolio to its current level of eight pubs and one hotel and to secure sales convenants with freetraders by way of property purchase finance arrangements.

The Commercial Manager recognizes not the consumer but the retailer as his customer. There are many good standard beers on the market and most consumers do not select between retail establishments on the basis of the beer available. As the retailer is interested in trading profitably and securely, it is his needs for financial and product supply service that the company is seeking to satisfy. The retailer is prepared to put Dawson's ales on his counter if the package deal with the company is satisfactory. However, often the retailer expresses concern that Dawson's ales are relatively unknown to consumers and may not be recognized as a good standard beer. Consequently he negotiates on the premise that the company must also supply competitors' products. 1986 turnover breaks between products are shown in Exhibit 4.1.

Exhibit 4.1 *Turnover breakdown figures for Dawson's products (1986)*

Turnover (%)	Product	Turnover (£'000)	Mean gross margin (%)	Gross profit (£'000)
3	Dawson's real ale	215	35	75
12	Dawson's keg ale	862	35	301.5
28	Factored keg lager	2,011	16.5	331
7	Factored keg ales	502	16	80
33	Wines and spirits	2,370	5	118.5
7	Factored bottled beer	503	15	75
5	Factored canned beer	360	3	11
5	Minerals, etc.	360	22	79
100	Brewing and whole-sale	7,183	15	1,071

Production of Beer Products

The technology employed is traditional and uncomplicated. Although the company has the capacity to malt and mill its own barley, this raw material is now bought in from one of a handful of suppliers to the industry on a three-year advance purchase agreement.

The barley is brewed in open vats then boiled and mashed in closed copper vats in a process that lasts about five days. At this time the production may be split between real or keg and both products are then processed within a further five to ten days. Unit production costs are similar for each of the range of beers.

An average production run is currently about 40% of capacity and the most efficient level of capacity utilization is estimated at 80% by the Director of Production. In 1986 31,700 kegs of Dawsons keg and real ale were produced.

There are 26 employees, including management, engaged in production, one less than in previous years and it is felt that this number could handle a doubling of output with overtime in the short term. One or two additional employees might be necessary in the longer term in such circumstances.

Although the company has no bottling facility it has provisionally negotiated the subcontracting of this to another firm. As a means of utilizing the production slack, the sales potential of bottled Dawson's ales is being tested. The feasibility of launching a new bottled premium beer, aimed at the export market, is also under consideration. The Commercial Manager feels that this could successfully become a status product in North America and parts of Europe.

Consideration is being given to the introduction of large plastic non-returnable ale packs for the off trade.

Over the last 20 years the trend has been away from dark ales and towards lagers. At present the company sells twice as much factored lager as its own beers and the Director of Production has indicated that the existing plant is capable of producing lager along with ale in an integrated batch production system.

Culture and Resources

The company is privately owned and there are 11 separate shareholdings. United Kingdom Brewers holds 20% of shares through historical accident, former directors and their families own another 25% or thereabouts, while the majority of shares are held by Wallace & McGrigor (Holdings) Limited, which was established at the time of Wallace McNiall's intestate death and in which the venture capitalists Investors In Industry have a major interest.

The Commercial Manager describes the company as 'small, fiercely independent, Scottish, traditional and conservative – a low profile real ale brewer which has responded to the demand for keg beer'.

There is almost a 'family' culture in the company with many long-serving employees, low staff turnover and a tendency to promote from within. The company directors are mainly full-time, long-serving employees and tasks tend to be managed with fairly loose functional demarcation.

Reporting to the Managing Director are the Production Director, the Company Secretary, the Commercial Manager and the Retail Manager. The Production Director controls 25 production staff including a biologist research assistant, and 20 draymen. Some 19 administrative staff report to the Secretary, and the Commercial Manager is responsible for three salesmen. The Retail Manager controls 122 full-time and part-time staff employed in the managed pubs and hotel.

Training has traditionally meant learning the job and the company has not perceived any need for management or marketing skills training in staff, nor has the company ever required to engage consultants or market researchers. Much of the company's market information is fed from the salesforce as it encounters demand 'at the sharp end'. However, PR consultants have recently been appointed 'to raise the profile of the company'.

Financially, the company does not feel that there is a problem. (Full details of accounts are shown in Exhibit 4.2.) As the Commercial Manager commented '... we are extremely sound at the moment, but I wonder where we will be in ten years time'.

Exhibit 4.2 Company Accounts and Notes

Profit and Loss Account for the Year ended 30th September 1986

	Notes	1986 (£)	1985 (£)
Turnover	2	7,967,940	7,139,711
Cost of sales		6,750,821	5,996,911
Gross profit		1,217,119	1,142,800
Net operating expenses	3	844,770	750,920
Operating profit	4	372,349	391,880
Income from other fixed asset investments		48,168	41,900
Other interest receivable and similar income		20,363	19,022
Interest payable and similar charges		–	(15)
		440,880	452,787
Exceptional item	5	78,008	–
Profit before taxation		518,888	452,787
Tax on profit on ordinary activities	8	239,109	236,749
Profit on ordinary activities after taxation		279,779	216,038
Dividends paid and proposed	9	99,498	77,188
Retained profit for the year		£180,281	£138,850

Statement of Retained Profit

Retained profits at 1st October 1985	1,396,221	1,257,371
Retained profits for the year	180,281	138,850
Retained profits at 30th September 1986	£1,576,502	£1,396,221

Balance Sheet – 30th September 1986

	Notes	1986 (£)	(£)	1985 (£)	(£)
Fixed Assets					
Tangible assets	10		2,935,256		2,914,047
Investments:					
Loans to group companies	11	–		2,000	
Other investments other than loans	11	3,075		3,075	
Other loans	11	900,839		772,181	
Current Assets			903,914		777,256
Stocks	12	383,430		433,897	
Debtors	13	1,084,267		1,035,549	
Cash at bank and in hand		286,215		299,215	
		1,753,912		1,768,661	
Creditors – amounts falling due within one year	14	1,104,147		1,111,764	
Net Current Assets			649,765		656,897
Total assets less current liabilities			4,488,935		4,348,200
Less: Non-current liabilities					
Creditors – amount falling due after more than one year	15	199,401		207,019	

Exhibit 4.2 *continued*

	Notes	1986 (£)	1986 (£)	1985 (£)	1985 (£)
Provisions for Liabilities and Charges					
Deferred Taxation	16	62,672		67,166	
			262,073		274,185
			£4,226,862		£4,074,015
Capital and Reserves					
Called up share capital	17		1,410,000		1,410,000
Revaluation reserve	18		1,240,360		1,267,794
Profit and loss account			1,576,502		1,396,221
			£4,226,862		£4,074,015

These accounts were approved by the board on 14 November 1986.

Directors

Notes to the Accounts – 30th September 1986 (continued)

1. Principal Accounting Policies (continued)

(d) *Turnover*
Turnover which excludes value added tax represents the value of sales invoiced during the year.

(e) *Taxation*
The charge for taxation is based on the profit for the year as adjusted for disallowable items. Tax deferred or accelerated is accounted for in respect of all material timing differences to the extent that it is probable that a liability or asset will crystallize. Timing differences arise from the inclusion of items of income and expenditure in tax computations in periods different from those in which they are included in the accounts. Provision is made at the rate which is expected to be applied when the liability or asset is expected to crystallize. Where this is not known the latest estimate of the long term tax rate applicable has been adopted. The amount of unprovided deferred tax is calculated at the best estimate of corporation tax rates in the longer term and is analysed into its major components.

Exhibit 4.2 *continued*

2. Turnover
The contributions of the various activities of the company to turnover and profit before taxation, are set out below:

	1986		1985	
	Turnover	*Profit before taxation*	*Turnover*	*Profit before taxation*
Principal activities	*(£)*	*(£)*	*(£)*	*(£)*
The brewing of beers and the wholesaling of beer and spirits	7,183,256	371,934	6,344,201	257,190
Ownership and management of public houses and hotels	784,684	146,954	795,510	195,597
	£7,967,940	£518,888	£7,139,711	£452,787

During the year the company changed its method of categorizing turnover between principal activities.
Accordingly the 1985 figures have been stated.
The company's entire operation is based in Scotland.

3. Net Operating Expenses
Net operating expenses are made up as follows:

	1986 *(£)*	1985 *(£)*
Distribution costs	157,250	160,489
Administrative expenses	687,520	590,431
	£844,770	£750,920

4. Operating Profit
Operating profit is stated after charging:

	Notes	1986 £	1985 £
Depreciation	10	190,304	147,905
Directors' emoluments:	6		
As directors		900	1,100
For management		93,811	137,579
		£94,711	£138,679
Auditor's remuneration		£6,900	£8,600
and after crediting:			
Gain/(loss) on sale of fixed assets		£16,842	£(3,317)
Net revenue from property		£68,311	£59,274

Exhibit 4.2 *continued*

5. Exceptional Item
A repayment of £78,008 was received from the company pension scheme during the year in respect of overfunding.

6. Directors' Emoluments
Particulars of the emoluments of the directors of the company, excluding pension contributions, disclosed in accordance with Sections 22–34,Schedule 5 Part V of the Companies Act 1985, are as follows:

	1986	1985
Emoluments of the Chairman	£8,230	£7,449
Emoluments of the highest paid director	£25,953	£26,238
Number of other directors whose emoluments were within the ranges:		
£Nil – £5,000	2	1
£5,001 – £10,000	1	–
£20,001 – £25,000	1	2

Notes to the Accounts – 30th September 1984 (continued)

1. Principal Accounting Policies (continued)

(d) *Turnover*
Turnover which excludes value added tax represents the value of sales invoiced during the year.

(e) *Taxation*
The charge for taxation is based on the profit for the year as adjusted for disallowable items, and for timing differences, to the extent that they are unlikely to result in an actual tax liability in the foreseeable future.

Timing differences arise from the recognition for tax purposes of certain items of income and expenses in a different accounting period from that in which they are recognized in the accounts. The tax effect of other timing differences as reduced by the tax benefit of any accumulated losses is treated as a deferred tax liability.

Exhibit 4.2 *continued*

2. Turnover

The contributions of the various activities of the company to turnover and profit before taxation, are set out below:

	1984		1983	
	Turnover	Profit before taxation	Turnover	Profit before taxation
Principal activities	*(£)*	*(£)*	*(£)*	*(£)*
The brewing of beers and the wholesaling of beer and spirits	5,388,942	231,697	5,321,479	338,808
Ownership and management of public houses and hotels	781,528	168,676	757,962	94,968
	£6,170,470	£400,373	£6,079,441	£433,776

The company's entire operation is based in Scotland.

3. Net Operating Expenses

Net operating expenses are made up as follows:

	1984 *(£)*	1983 *(£)*
Distribution costs	156,727	148,667
Administrative expenses	529,012	510,510
	£685,739	£659,177

Balance Sheet – 30th September 1984

	Notes	1984 *(£)*	1984 *(£)*	1983 *(£)*	1983 *(£)*
Fixed Assets					
Tangible assets	10		1,849,438		1,918,236
Investments:					
Loans to group companies	11	2,000		2,000	
Other investments other than loans	11	3,075		3,075	
Other loans	11	678,802		581,199	
			683,877		586,274
Current Assets					
Stocks	12	405,857		362,561	
Debtors	13	1.032,926		1,023,377	
Cash at bank and in hand		371,215		174,215	
		1,809,998		1,560,153	

Exhibit 4.2 *continued*

	Notes	1984 (£)	(£)	1983 (£)	(£)
Creditors – amounts falling due within one year	14	1,125,319		925,694	
Net Current Assets			684,679		634,459
Total assets less current liabilities			3,217,994		3,138,969
Less: Non-current liabilities					
Creditors – amounts falling due after more than one year	15	200,454		207,645	
Provisions for Liabilities and Charges	16	77,956		135,830	
			278,410		343,475
			£2,939,584		£2,795,494
Capital and Reserves					
Called up share capital	17		1,410,000		1,410,000
Revaluation reserve	18		272,213		272,213
Profit and loss account			1,257,371		1,113,281
			£2,939,584		£2,795,494

These accounts were approved by the board on 15 November 1984.

⎫
⎬ Directors
⎭

Notes to the Accounts – 30th September 1982 (continued)

4. Principal Accounting Policies (continued)

(d) *Turnover*
Turnover which excluded value added tax represents the value of sales invoiced during the year.

(e) *Taxation*
The charge for taxation is based on the profit for the year as adjusted for disallowable items, and for timing differences, to the extent that they are unlikely to result in an actual tax liability in the foreseeable future. Timing differences arise from the recognition for tax purposes of certain items of income and expenses in a different accounting period from that in which they are recognized in the accounts. The tax effect of other timing differences as reduced by the tax benefit of any accumulated losses is treated as a deferred tax liability.

Exhibit 4.2 *continued*

5. Turnover

The contributions of the various activities of the company to turnover and profit before taxation, are set out below:

	1982		1981	
	Turnover *(£)*	Profit before taxation *(£)*	Turnover *(£)*	Profit before taxation *(£)*
The brewing of beers and the wholesaling of beer and spirits	4,949,262	239,539	4,570,057	236,820
Ownership and management of public houses and hotels	722,617	39,154	723,490	33,577
	£5,671,879	£278,693	£5,293,547	£270,397

The company's entire operation is based in Scotland.

3. Net Operating Expenses

Net operating expenses are made up as follows:

	1982 *(£)*	1981 *(£)*
Distribution costs	136,359	132,311
Administrative expenses	497,079	459,001
	£633,438	£591,312

Balance Sheet – 30th September 1982

	Notes	1982 *(£)*	*(£)*	1981 *(£)*	*(£)*
Fixed Assets					
Tangible assets	11		1,971,096		2,012,879
Investments:					
Shares in group companies	12	–		1,850	
Loans to group companies	12	2,000		–	
Other investments other than loans	12	3,075		3,075	
Other loans	12	573,394		444,700	
			578,469		449,625
Current Assets					
Stocks	13	343,412		411,654	
Debtors	14	936,869		744,871	
Cash at bank and in hand		55,215		69,900	
		1,335,496		1,226,425	

Exhibit 4.2 *continued*

	Notes	1982 (£)	(£)	1981 (£)	(£)
Creditors – amounts falling due within one year	15	910,870		781,404	
Net Current Assets			424,626		445,021
Total assets less current liabilities			2,974,191		2,907,525
Less: Non-current liabilities					
Creditors – amounts falling due after more than one year	16	170,198		166,972	
Provisions for Liabilities and Charges Taxation, including deferred taxation	17	125,369		143,178	
			295,567		310,150
			£2,678,624		£2,597,375
Capital and Reserves					
Called up share capital	18		1,410,000		1,410,000
Revaluation reserve	19		273,053		273,053
Other reserves	20		–		4,760
Profit and loss account			995,571		909,562
			£2,678,624		£2,597,375

} Directors

Sales Management

The salesmen mainly service existing accounts and there is very little cold calling. Most new business is by referral by existing clients to acquaintances and 50% of these calls are successful.

The three salesmen each have about 12 years of experience on the job. They are all on fixed incomes and there is no formal performance measurement. Sales are generally expressed at retail prices less discount and the salesmen have discretion to negotiate discount according to guidelines. *Ad hoc* sales meetings are held from time to time to exchange information on prices and products. There have been no sales promotions as such but occasionally discounting incentives are made to push one particular product, usually in response to a general trade promotion of a factored product. Generally prices are set at the market rate.

The annual advertising budget is £43,000 (4% of own product sales).

The Market

The Brewers' Society publishes production statistics for the principal brewers in the United Kingdom. From this and from other informal sources the company estimates its market share to be between 1% and 1.5% in Scotland and between 0.10% and 0.015% in the United Kingdom. UK and Scottish brewers are considered to control almost 85% of the Scottish market between them.

Because the free trade is largely indifferent to which beer it stocks, market share is gained by getting freetraders tied to the product by capital financing arrangements or by competing on trade service provision. But the most secure way to capture market share is to expand the managed estate and that is the main thrust of many of the brewers now. The company is aiming to expand its portfolio by a minimum of one unit each year into higher quality, higher yielding units.

In order to compete on the capital financing of retail units the company has introduced, as a first on the market, a unit-linked endowment scheme whereby the retailer is bound only to stock Dawson's ales, although other beers may be stocked so long as display, maintenance and availability are not unfavourable to Dawson's. By this means the company plans to expand the tied estate to 50 units from the current 29 in the medium term.

While the company's sales are almost entirely within the free trade, recent discussions have been held with major brewers on the subject of bulk brewing real ale on a contract arrangement for distribution as a product item on the major's range. These discussions have been productive, if as yet inconclusive, and there is now a good possibility of increasing production towards capacity over the next few years.

The Monopolies and Mergers Commission is reviewing the trade at this time and it seems likely that legislation will follow to allow loan tied traders to select and stock a 'guest' beer to which they are not otherwise committed in their loan contract. This is aimed at breaking up the big brewers' grip on the market.

The Future

The Commercial Manager, in considering the company's strategic position, wishes to secure long-term growth and profitability. He asks himself whether this is inevitably attained as a factor or contract brewer or whether the company can grow as a traditional independent branded brewer.

Questions

(1) Analyse the company's financial position, calculating key ratios and trends. Analyse contribution to profits from beer production.

(2) What is the purpose and the mission of the company?

(3) Develop a SWOT analysis of the company.

(4) Identify the critical strategic problems faced by the company.

(5) Analyse the market segmentation.

(6) Propose alternative corporate and management strategies.

(7) Describe the company in the terms of the Boston Consulting Group Matrix. Explain your conclusions.

CASE 5
Scottish Foam Limited
Strategic Marketing

Martin Davidson
Glasgow Development Agency

Company History

Scottish Foam Limited is a small Scottish company which was formed in 1983 to service the Scottish Electronics Industry. The company is located in a recently built factory in Clydebank Enterprise Zone.

The founding members of the company, now the Managing, Marketing, Sales and Production Directors, were, until 1983, employed by the Scottish branch of Kay Metzler, an international packaging company.

In the early 1980s Alistair Nicol, a director of Kay Metzler, was aware that the impact on Kay Metzler of rising oil prices and the recession might well lead to the closure of its branch plant in Scotland. Together with colleagues he investigated two ways forward:

- A management buy-out of the foam converting operation of Kay Metzler.
- Going it alone and forming a new company.

Even though foam converting is neither a technically sophisticated nor capital intensive industry, should it be necessary to form a new company, such a company would have to compete in a market which, at that time, was occupied by only two companies, each of which was a subsidiary of a major foam manufacturer.

Kay Metzler would not agree to a management buy-out and Mr Nicol and his colleagues decided to form a new company and to trade on their own account.

A business plan had already been prepared and after a number of meetings in England and Scotland Scottish financial support was obtained.

A shelf company was bought in May 1983 and a new company, with three employees, began trading on 1 July 1983.

The company name, Scottish Foam Limited, was seen as an important promotional tool, Scottish Foam being the only wholly Scottish company in that market segment. The name proved difficult to get from the registrar since a company using Scottish or English in its title would normally have to occupy a prominent position in its market – something a newly formed company could hardly be expected to do. Nevertheless, the company's solicitor persevered and Scottish Foam Limited began trading on 1 September 1983. The five shareholders were those who had originally agreed to leave Kay Metzler.

Since 1 September 1983 the company's results have exceeded those predicted in the original business plan:

Year	Target turnover	Actual turnover
1983	£400,000	£600,000
1984	£600,000	£1,100,000
1985	£800,000	£1,000,000 (estimated)

In 1986 the company had a total workforce of 32.

Company Objectives

The main company objectives are long-term survival and growth by the following methods:

- Increasing market share at competitors' expense. This is necessary since the market is only growing at an estimated 5% to 10% per annum.

- Broadening the customer base and thus placing less reliance on one or two major customers such as IBM.

- Replacing other similar products such as rubber with the company's foam products.

- Introducing new forms of specific packaging applications.

- Introducing higher performance foams.

- Introducing new foams and new techniques such as polystyrene moulding.

- Manufacturing consumer products which are new to the company, for example pot scourers, insulation lagging for pipes. Both of these can be sold through the same wholesale outlets.

- Extending the services the company provides to cover film wrapping, inspection, packaging and part assembly.

- Horizontal integration by buying a cardboard box manufacturer so that Scottish Foam can provide the complete packaging service.

Certain of these items may be done by more aggressive selling and better customer service to increase market share, while others are extensions of the company's existing product/service line.

Some, like the purchasing of new foam, will follow their being made available by the foam manufacturers but diversifications such as cardboard box making and polystyrene foam moulding will require substantial capital investment by the company.

A clearer picture of the company can be provided by analysing its strengths, weaknesses, opportunities and threats as shown below.

SWOT Analysis

Company Strengths

- A competent, aggressive and well-motivated management with excellent knowledge of the cushion packaging industry.
- Local control in the hands of a few people which allows decisions to be taken quickly.
- Well-established company name.
- Good financial relationships with banks, suppliers and customers.
- Efficient credit control.
- Flexible plant and workforce with low overheads.
- Good return on capital.
- A quick build-up in market share showing good relationships/service to customers.

Company Weaknesses

- Although flexible, the manufacturing process is limited and requires substantial capital investment to develop. This would commit the company to achieving high volume to get a satisfactory return on investment.
- Too much time may be being spent on small one-off products such as pot scourers, and so on, thus taking effort away from developing the company's main strategy.
- The company is still too dependent on one or two major customers.
- The foam product is not a stand-alone product. Tenders usually have to be made with a cardboard box supplier.
- Market position is weakened by the lack of a total package (that is, including the carton) and by lack of polystyrene moulding facilities.

- Technical knowledge in the company tends to be restricted to foam conversion.

- Financial resources are limited compared with national competitors.

- Company success is very dependent on high quality personal service which is expensive and may be difficult to sustain over a long period.

Opportunities

- Packaging is a very large market in which the company has undoubted expertise and contacts.

- The need for high quality and personal service in packaging could be extended to other parts of the packaging industry.

- There may be opportunities for the company to use its flexible plant to move into consumer goods.

- The company may well be in a good position to diversify into other areas of packaging.

- There is demand in the packaging industry for an integrated cardboard box/cushion packaging product/service.

Threats

- The market in which Scottish Foam operates has a low-cost entry point which is perhaps one of the reasons Scottish Foam has made such quick penetration.

- There may be a danger of being squeezed out by a big foam manufacturer whose main concern is turnover and who can dump foam on the market.

- With a material cost of 58% of finished product cost this is a possibility.

- The size of goods being packaged, especially electronics goods, is getting smaller, a system of mark-up on cost will therefore result in reduced turnover and hence reduced profits.

- Many goods, particularly electronics, are imported. Package buying decisions may increasingly be made in London and abroad.

- Most company headquarters are in London, hence buying decisions will be made there.

- The carton manufacturers may get more easily into foam than foam converters into cardboard manufacture owing to the low entry cost.

Products and Services

Scottish Foam Limited operates within the UK packaging market – which is extremely wide and varied – from high-volume card and paper packaging to low-volume specialist packaging. Scottish Foam Limited operates at the low volume/specialist end of the market, having segmented its market by identifying customers requiring polyurethane and polyethylene foam cushioning as part of their packaging requirements and by concentrating on Scottish companies.

The company attempts to differentiate itself and its product by promoting itself as the only wholly Scottish company in this particular market segment and by providing quickly, specific designs to each customer's requirements together with fast reliable delivery and a high degree of after-sales service.

In addition to general packaging the company also provides:

- contract seating, furniture and bedding foams;

- leisure and sports products such as caravan and boat bedding, judo mats, and so on;

- industrial foams for insulation, filters and sponges;

- contract packing including shrink wrapping, glass repacking, assembly, inspection, storage and distribution.

At present these services represent only 7% to 10% of turnover.

Scottish Foam Limited does not manufacture the various foams required. These are imported from manufacturers in England. Scottish Foam's expertise is in designing, cutting and forming the raw material into specialist shapes, sometimes in association with other packaging media, such as corrugated cardboard, to suit each client's requirements. In this sense the company is a service industry. The service it sells is the ability to design, cut and reform foam to each customer's requirements.

The flexibility of the material and the company's manufacturing processes give the company a wide product line curtailed only by the specifications inherent on the raw material and its ability to meet the client's requirements.

The average breakdown of finished product costs is as follows:

Labour	12%	
Material	58%	(this includes polyurethane and polyethylene foam and various cardboards)
Distribution	5%	
Margin	25%	(overheads are absorbed in this margin)

The low level of capital employed in the business in machinery and stocks (only two and a half weeks' supply are kept on hand) and the low level of fixed costs compared with the high level of variable costs mean that the company's return on capital employed is potentially very good.

The product is low value/high volume which means that companies tend to serve local markets – the high freight cost and varying order size mediating against wider distribution and hence a wider geographical spread of customers.

The product is also a throw-away part of a large and more expensive item, for example an electronic component. As a filler to packaging the product is normally used in conjunction with another product, for example an outer casing or carton.

Suppliers

There are nine UK suppliers of the raw foam material which the company converts into packaging cushioning. All are located in England and are part of large industrial companies such as ICI and Dow Chemicals. The constituents of foam are the by-products of the oil refining industry. It is estimated that there is presently three to four times overcapacity in foam manufacturing.

Scottish Foam Limited obtains foam from three or four suppliers at present and, although the manufacturing companies are quick to pass on any price increases, there appears to be no price advantage in attempting to play one manufacturer off against another. New types of foam come on the market from time to time but this is very much in the hands of the manufacturers.

Scottish Foam's sources of supply look secure for the foreseeable future.

Because the company's products are generally used along with other packaging products the company has reciprocal trade arrangements with other packaging companies. Where Scottish Foam and a cardboard box manufacturer compete for the same contract, each may have previously agreed to use the other's product if it wins the contract.

Pricing

Scottish Foam Limited is primarily in the industrial buying/selling market and therefore has to provide prices in three main circumstances:

- as a competitive quotation;
- as a repeat order;
- as a small one-off batch.

Where the job is sufficiently large, price is arrived at by a full allocation of costs plus a 10% margin. This can easily be replicated, with adjustment as necessary, for repeat orders. Given that the company's two competitors in the market are divisions of much larger companies with higher fixed costs, this may give Scottish Foam a competitive edge.

Where contracts are small they are priced on a materials plus 40/50% margin.

The cost plus method of pricing is probably quite reasonable in a situation where material and labour costs are fairly well known and where a small number of companies compete on design ability, speed of response, reliability and after-sales service.

Where the company is involved in the consumer market, for example selling pot scourers, price is determined by reference to the current market/quality price – the company first ensuring that it can make the product at a cost that will allow it to be sold at a reasonable profit.

The company intends to computerize its costing system. This will enable it to control cost allocation and pricing more easily.

The Market

The company's generic market is the UK foam conversion market. This it has segmented by product – the cushion packaging market – because of the company's expertise in polyurethane and polyethylene foam, and by location – Central Scotland – because of high transport costs (although the company does a small amount of business in other areas of Scotland and England).

The company has also dabbled in other markets such as shrink wrapping, inspection, storage and delivery.

Market Size/Share and Competitors

The value of the Scottish polyurethane/polyethylene foam conversion market has been estimated at 3 million to 4 million and this is divided among three companies as follows:

> Scottish Foam Limited 40%
> Kay Metzler Limited 40% (down from 60% over the last three years)
> Vitafoam 30%

The market is thought to be growing at about 5% to 10% per annum which means that to increase market share Scottish Foam must take it from one or both of its competitors, Kay Metzler or Vitafoam, both of which are part of much larger foam manufacturing companies.

Given the closed nature of the market and the low component value of the product, companies compete on design, delivery and service rather than on price.

Seasonality

Demand is not truly seasonal. The only fluctuations in demand occur around the summer holiday period.

Customers

The main customers in the market are the major electronic companies – IBM had 40% to 60% of the market in 1984 – Hewlett Packard, Wang, Honeywell, National Semiconductor, Burroughs and their many subcontractors. This can lead to an over-reliance on IBM and, as happened in 1985, when that company's requirements fell dramatically, there can be serious knock-on effects on suppliers such as Scottish Foam.

Product Range

A specific standard product range, other than cushion packaging, is hard to identify – each order requiring individual design and make-up. On the other hand the specific products manufactured run into hundreds and new ones are being continuously created. However, there is a need for one company to offer a complete packaging service which would integrate card/carton manufacturing and the foam/cushioning element.

Geographical Location of Market

Scottish Foam's market is found in Central Scotland where the users of its product are located. Selling is direct to the companies who use the product or to intermediaries such as carton makers. The costs of distribution are high relative to product value and Central Scotland will probably remain the company's main market for some time to come. The personalized service required by customers also suggests a local market.

Marketing Strategy

The company's marketing strategy comprises the following:

- Increasing the cushion packaging market share by broadening the customer base. This would be done by targeting customers with known packaging requirements, for example electronic subcontractors, by expanding the salesforce, by aggressive selling, better design and after-sales service and competitive pricing.

- Increasing the penetration of the packaging market by introducing new but related products such as 'Jiffy Bags', shrink wrapping.

- Increasing the company's wholesale market share of foam-related products such as sponges and foam pipe lagging.

- Long-term entry to complete packaging systems comprising the existing foams, polystyrene moulding and cardboard box manufacture.

- Continuing to provide high quality, personal before-/after-sales service.

- Introducing computerized pricing to ensure competitiveness and protect margins.

- Introducing a wider range of polyurethane and polyethylene foams and their applications to a broader customer base.

Marketing Orientation

Scottish Foam clearly has a marketing orientation rather than a product or selling orientation. This derives in part from the need for close ties with customers to design specific packagings and in part from company policy. Nevertheless, in the move towards the use of existing plant and equipment to manufacture small consumer items such as pot scourers, one senses the need to create turnover by putting machinery to work and then trying to sell the goods produced rather than a response to consumer demand.

Marketing Budget

The marketing budget is set on a yearly basis as follows:

- Agreeing sales estimates
- Deducting
- – material costs
- – labour costs
- – distribution costs
- – overheads
- Arriving at profit

A view is then taken on what the company can afford to spend on marketing.

In reality this is the advertising and promotion budget. Marketing activities such as intelligence gathering, research, product development and agreement on marketing strategy are done by the directors as part of their normal workload. What proportion of their time is spent on these activities is very difficult to estimate.

The marketing budget for 1985 was £10,000 and was spent in four areas:

- Design and reproduction of brochures (copy enclosed)
- Advertising in trade journals, Yellow Pages
- Mail shots
- Seasonal gifts of whisky, calendars, Christmas cards, etc.

The main objectives of this form of advertising are to introduce and reinforce the company name in the minds of existing and possible future customers. The company attempts to evaluate the worth of some of the advertising by asking the customers to identify the sources from which they heard about the company, but one suspects that given the nature and size of the market most new customers would come through personal contacts and recommendation in the trade and the efforts of the three-man sales team.

Marketing Activities

Market Intelligence and Market Research

The size, type and geographical location of the company's present market suggest that trade journals, regular business contacts and the activities of the salesforce are adequate to provide sufficient market intelligence for the company's needs, even if this is collected in an informal manner. Close contacts among managers will ensure that important information is quickly disseminated.

Market research, although once again informal and to some extent unstructured, is close to its customers. The company works closely with potential customers to develop new ideas and applications and these are clearly transferable from customer to customer. The company feels that useful market research would be difficult and therefore costly.

New Product Development

New product development in cushion packaging comes from the close contact with customers outlined above and has so far proved successful. Other products and services appear to be added in a slightly haphazard way on the basis of 'What else can we do to make money?' rather than a strategic development of the firm's objectives.

However, the firm does innovate at all levels and this creates an exciting atmosphere of change and development rather than a more bureaucratic and ritualized atmosphere which might exist in larger companies.

Selling

About 95% of the company's products are sold to other manufacturers through a third party on tenders obtained by the company's salesforce. This comprises three people, two of whom are directors (the Sales and Marketing Directors). IBM is dealt with personally by the Managing Director.

Sales targets are set by the salesforce and agreed by the board. They are based on:

- Turnover
- New accounts

The Managing Director has a policy of always setting targets 5%–10% above possible.

Remuneration is by salary – there is no commission.

On joining the company, new salesmen spend four weeks on product training and two weeks on selling training.

Taking into account all the elements presented in this marketing audit (Exhibit 5.1), the managers of Scottish Foam Limited are confronted now with a difficult decision-making process with regard to the development of an effective marketing strategy. Should the company adopt a diversification strategy? Should it develop new uses for the existing product? Should it fight for market share? Should the company introduce new products? Should it extend its product range and launch complementary products? Many strategic marketing routes are now open to the company. The problem lies in finding the total value (by weighting its benefits and drawbacks) of each alternative strategy.

Exhibit 5.1 *Financial information (see Appendix 5.1 for accounts).*

	1985	1984
Operating ratios		
Return on capital employed	67%	—
Gross profit margin	42.8%	37%
Trading profit/sales	6.6%	—
New profit/sales	4.5%	—
Trade debts/sales – collection time	64 days	80 days
Stock/sales	4.6%	6.7%
Financial ratios		
Gearing: Debt as percentage of capital employed	47.4%	76%
Liquidity: Current ratio	1.33%	1.6%
Quick ratio	1.05%	0.8%

Appendix 5.1   Scottish Foam Limited Financial Statements 31 December 1985

Exhibit 5.2 *Directors' Report*

The Directors submit their report together with the financial statements for the year to 31 December 1985.

Principal Activities

The company is principally engaged in polyurethene foam conversion.

Appendix 5.1 *continued*

Review of the Business and Future Developments

The profit for the year after taxation amounted to £48,747. The directors do not recommend payment of a dividend and the profit has therefore been retained.

The Directors have continued to develop the business of the company in the light of prevailing trading conditions and the position at 31 December 1985 is reflected in the audited financial statements for the period ended on that date. The present intention is to continue the development of the existing business of the company.

Post Balance Sheet Event

Since 31 December 1985 the company has agreed to become a 75% subsidiary of Beaverco plc, a company registered in England. In addition the company is disposing of its investment in Scottish Foam (Transport) Limited at par.

Directors and their Interests

The interests of the directors in the ordinary share capital of the company are as set out below. All served on the Board throughout the year.

	31 December 1985	31 December 1984
A.M. Nicol	9,200	9,200
J.W. Craig	3,400	3,400
J.W. Shaw	2,000	2,000
Z. Lipka	2,400	2,400

In accordance with the article of association, J.W. Craig retires by rotation and being eligible offers himself for re-election.

Tangible Fixed Assets

Details of movements in tangible fixed assets are shown in note 6 to the financial statements.

Auditors

Grant Thornton (formerly Thornton Baker) offer themselves for re-appointment as auditors in accordance with Section 384(1) of the Companies Act 1985.

By Order of the Board,

M. Milne
Secretary.

27 March 1986

Group Accounts

The company does not prepare consolidated financial statements for the group. The activities of its trading subsidiary, Scottish Foam (Transport) Ltd. are dissimilar from that of the holding company and in view of the insignificant amounts involved, it is not considered consolidated accounts would be of value to the members of the company.

Exhibit 5.3 *Profit and Loss Account 12 Months to 31 December 1985*

	Notes	12 months to 31 December 1985		16 months to 31 December 1984	
		(£)	(£)	(£)	(£)
Turnover	1		1,072,883		682,167
Cost of sales			751,538		496,738
Gross profit			321,345		185,429
Distribution & selling costs		73,900		58,794	
Administrative expenses		176,864		135,340	
			250,764		194,134
Operating profit/(loss)	2		70,581		(8,705)
Interest	3		8,238		9,391
Profit/(loss) on ordinary activities before taxation			62,343		(18,096)
Taxation charge	4		13,596		–
Profit/(loss) for period after taxation			48,747		(18,096)
Statement of retained profits:					
Deficit on reserves as 1 January 1985			(18,096)		–
Profit/(loss) for period			48,747		(18,096)
Retained profits at 31 December 1985			30,651		(18,096)

Exhibit 5.4 **Balance Sheet 31 December 1985**

	Notes	31 December 1985		31 December 1984	
		(£)	(£)	(£)	(£)
Fixed Assets					
Tangible fixed assets	6		34,658		37,826
Investment	7		4,000		4,000
Current Assets					
Stock	8	49,652		46,056	
Debtors	9	187,925		151,359	
Cash at bank and in hand		314		198	
		237,891		197,613	
Creditors: amounts falling due within one year	10a	177,859		186,741	
Net Current Assets			60,032		10,872

Appendix 5.1   *continued*

	Notes	31 December 1985		31 December 1984	
		(£)	(£)	(£)	(£)
Total Assets Less Current Liabilities			98,690		52,698
Creditors: amounts falling due after					
more than one year	10b		33,465		43,822
			65,225		8,876
Deferred Income					
Regional Development Grants	11		5,756		6,972
Provisions for Liabilities and Charges					
Deferred taxation	12		8,818		—
			50,651		1,904
Capital and Reserves					
Called-up share capital	16		20,000		20,000
Profit and loss account			30,651		(18,096)
			50,651		1,904

27 March 1986   Date of Approval

A.M. Nicol   Director

J.W. Craig   Director

	12 months to		16 months to	
	31 December 1985		31 December 1984	
	(£)	(£)	(£)	(£)
Working capital:				
Stocks		3,596		46,056
Debtors		36,566		150,539
Creditors		4,536		(165,759)
		44,698		30,836
Movement in net liquid funds:				
Cash and bank balances		11,240		(11,926)
		55,938		18,910

Exhibit 5.5 *Notes to the Financial Statements 12 Months to 31 December 1985*

1. **Turnover**
   Turnover comprises sales invoiced to customers net of value added tax. All turnover was earned within the United Kingdom.

Appendix 5.1 *continued*

2. **Operating Profit/(Loss)** The operating profit/(loss) is stated after charging:	*12 months to* *31 December 1985* (£)	*16 months to* *31 December 1984* (£)
Leasing charges	16,506	15,422
Depreciation	8,341	8,469
Auditor's remuneration	1,625	1,500
and crediting:		
Grant release	1,216	1,216

3. **Interest**	*12 months to* *31 December 1985* (£)	*16 months to* *31 December 1984* (£)
Bank overdraft interest	1,762	3,542
Interest payable on loans repayable within 5 years	2,572	2,300
Interest payable on loans repayable in more than 5 years	3,904	3,263
Other interest	—	286
	8,238	9,391

4. **Taxation** The taxation charge based on the results for the period is made up as follows:	*1985* (£)	*1984* (£)
Corporation tax at 30%	4,073	—
Payment in respect of group relief	705	—
Deferred taxation	8,818	—
	13,596	—

5. **Directors' and Employees' Remuneration** Staff costs during the period:	*12 months to* *31 December 1985* (£)	*16 months to* *31 December 1984* (£)
Wages and salaries	212,748	162,116
Social security costs	19,771	16,205
Pension costs	8,965	1,485
	241,484	179,806

The average number of persons employed during the period was 25. All employees were engaged in polyurethane foam conversion.

Staff costs include numeration in respect of directors, as follows:

	12 months to *31 December 1985* (£)	*16 months to* *31 December 1984* (£)
Management remuneration (including pension contributions)	68,528	68,490

Appendix 5.1   *continued*

6. Tangible Fixed Assets	Leasehold Property Improvements (£)	Plant and Machinery (£)	Office Fittings (£)	Motor Vehicles (£)	Total (£)
Cost					
At 1 January 1985	3,710	40,760	550	1,275	46,295
Additions	1,892	2,355	926	–	5,173
At 31 December 1985	5,602	43,115	1,476	1,275	51,468
Depreciation					
At 1 January 1985	618	6,466	110	1,275	8,469
Charge for year	1,120	6,925	296	–	8,341
At 31 December 1985	1,738	13,391	406	1,275	16,810
Net Book Value					
At 31 December 1985	3,864	29,724	1,070	–	34,658
At 31 December 1984	3,092	34,294	440	–	37,826

7. **Investment**
This represents 80% of the issued share capital of Scottish Foam (Transport) Ltd, a company registered in Scotland. This company did not start to trade until 1 January 1985.

8. Stocks	1985 (£)	1984 (£)
Raw materials	37,399	41,278
Work in Progress	814	791
Finished Goods	11,439	3,987
	49,652	46,056

There were no significant differences between the replacement cost and the values disclosed for stock.

9. Debtors	1985 (£)	1984 (£)
Amounts falling due within one year:		
Trade debtors	163,565	145,245
Amount owed by subsidiary	8,000	–
Other debtors	820	820
Prepayments	15,540	5,294
	187,925	151,359

10a Creditors – Amounts falling due within one year:	1985 (£)	1984 (£)
Trade creditors	136,096	137,864
Amount owed to subsidiary	1,981	–
Bank overdraft	1,000	12,124
Loans	8,000	6,000
	1985 (£)	**1984 (£)**
Clydebank Enterprise Fund loan	2,857	2,857
Social security and other taxes	8,921	15,616
Sundry creditors and accruals	14,931	12,280
Corporation tax	4,073	–
	177,859	186,741

Appendix 5.1 *continued*

10b	Creditors – Amounts falling due after more than one year	1985 (£)	1984 (£)
	Loans	22,751	30,250
	Clydebank Enterprise Fund loan	10,714	13,572
		33,465	43,822

The loan from the Clydebank Enterprise Fund bears interest at a rate of 5% per annum and is repayable in 28 quarterly instalments of £714.29 from November 1983, the last instalment being due in August 1990.

The loans represent two loans received under the Department of Industry Small Firms Loan Guarantee Scheme.

The first loan for £15,000 was received in September 1983. Capital repayment of £250 per month commenced in November 1985, the last instalment being due in October 1990.

The second loan for £25,000 was received in March 1984. Capital repayments of £416.66 per month commenced in April 1984, the last instalment being due in March 1989.

These loans bear interest at 3% per annum over the bank's base rate. The company's bankers hold a bond and floating charge and personal guarantees by the directors as security for the bank overdraft and the element of the small firm loans not secured by the Deparment of Industry.

11. Deferred Income	1985 (£)	1984 (£)
Regional Development Grants		
Grants receivable on tangible fixed asset additions	6,972	8,188
Released to profit and loss account	(1,216)	(1,216)
	5,756	6,972

12. Deferred Taxation

The following shows the total potential liability for deferred taxation at 30% in respect of timing differences:

	1985 (£)	1984 (£)
Accelerated capital allowances	8,818	10,400
Trading losses	—	(10,400)
	8,818	—

13. Future Capital Expenditure	1985 (£)	1984 (£)
Items authorized but not contracted for	Nil	Nil
Items contracted for but not invoiced	Nil	Nil

14. Pension Commitments

Individual contributory pension schemes are in force for the directors and certain senior employees funded on a money purchase basis. There are no other pension commitments.

Appendix 5.1 *continued*

15. **Leasing Commitments**
The company has commitments in respect of operating and finance leases as follows:

	1985 (£)	1984 (£)
Payable in next financial year	17,056	13,441
Payable between two and five years	7,556	11,695

16. **Called-up Share Capital**	1985	1984
Authorized:	(£)	£)
100,000 ordinary shares of £1 each	100,000	100,000
Allotted, called-up and fully paid:		
20,000 ordinary shares of £1 each	20,000	20,000

Question

(1) Define and evaluate in a critical and comprehensive manner the alternative marketing strategies open to Scottish Foam Limited.

Scottish Foam – Case Study Update

In 1986 the company operated in only one market: packaging. It produced low volume specialist packaging for customers requiring polyurethane and polyethylene foam cushioning as part of their packaging requirements.

The company still operates in the packaging market but has added two further divisions:

- In 1986 Scottish Foam set up a Case Division by acquiring for £5,000 an existing business making musical instrument cases. This division produces large material handling cases for the transportation of components from one plant to another in the electronics industry. Some of these components are very fragile and wastage rates are high. Scottish Foam's cases have substantially reduced these rates. This division has a £250,000 turnover and 10 employees.

- In 1988 the company created from new a Plastics Division. This division specializes in injection moulding complex plastic components such as computer keyboards and light fittings. It also produces low value items such as coat hangers (for Marks & Spencer) and Hoover carpet cleaner parts.

The Plastics Division required a capital investment of £2.25 million. The company is still trying to prove itself in this market.

The markets for both of these diversifications were initially based on Scottish Foam's packaging customer base in the electronics industry. The company has made considerable efforts to broaden this customer base and has moved into the consumer industry, for example Marks & Spencer, and into plastic bottle packs and plastic printing for the whisky industry.

The company now sees growth in injection moulding and expansion in the case division as its future targets. Packaging, its cash cow, is unlikely to expand significantly.

Gross margins in the case division and in injection moulding are 35% to 40%. The reasons for the company moving in the chosen directions were:

- Falling turnover in packaging, especially in 1989/90:

    1986   £1 million
    1987   £1.6 million
    1988   £2.3 million
    1989   £1.7 million
    1990   £1.4 million
    1991   £2.2 million (with three divisions)
    1992   £3.7 million (with three divisions)

- The need to give the company a 'technical edge' over its competitors.

- In 1988 a major market report (by the Scottish Development Agency) identified areas for expansion in companies servicing the electronics industry:
  (1) metal fabrication
  (2) injection moulding
  (3) tool making
  Item (2), where the company's interest lay, indicated a £65 million market with only £15 million currently supplied in Scotland.

- Value of sales in the packaging market, based on a 'cost plus' formula, was shrinking since components and consequently packaging have become smaller.

Company Objectives

The following objectives have been abandoned:

- Replacing other similar products such as rubber with the company's foam products – too difficult a market to break into, and margins too low.

- Introducing new foams – no market.

- Manufacturing consumer products – the company would have to give too much of a margin to wholesalers/retailers, so margins would be too low.

- Horizontal integration by buying a cardboard box manufacturer. There are already too many players, and so it is easier to buy in.

Comments on SWOT Analysis

Strengths

Company strengths are as before, with improvements as follows:

- Company name – even stronger.
- Even more efficient credit control – now 49 days.

Weaknesses

- Flexible manufacturing has been challenged by injection moulding. Injection moulding has high overheads.

- High capital investment in injection moulding has left the company with a high level of debt which requires a high turnover to repay.

The company has improved with regard to some of its previous weaknesses. It no longer makes small, one-off products such as pot scourers, and technical knowledge is not now restricted to foam. The company is still too dependent on one or two major customers but is managing gradually to broaden its customer base.

Opportunities

The most valuable opportunity has proved to be the use of the company's existing customer base, as an initial market for its diversification into cases and injection moulding. The possibilities of moving into consumer goods, other areas of packaging, or an integrated cardboard box/cushion packaging product/service have been investigated, and abandoned as unlikely to prove profitable.

Threats

Many likely threats have not materialized. There is less danger of being squeezed out by a big foam manufacturer, due to the amalgamation of Kay Metzler and Vita Foam which leaves only one major competitor for Scottish Foam. The material cost element in the finished product has fallen to 48%. Buying decisions being made in London headquarters mainly happen with consumer goods, a market Scottish Foam has decided against moving into. Carton manufacturers have not moved into the foam business, and are unlikely to in the medium term. The foam market still has a low-cost entry point, but injection moulding, where Scottish Foam envisages its growth will be, requires high capital investment.

Products and Services

- Cases and injection moulding are now included.

- The company still relies heavily on personal selling and good after-sales service.

- Foam products are still as stated apart from contract packaging, which has been abandoned.

- The average breakdown of costs for packaging is now:

Labour	12%
Materials	48%
Distribution	5%
Gross margin	35%

- At one time the product was 'thrown away'. The company has now to address the 'green' revolution by trying to make the product reusable.

Suppliers

At the time of the case study the cost of the raw material, foam, could not be 'bargained' downwards. Now, with the collapse of the British Furniture industry, there is overcapacity and margins may be improved by bargaining for supplies.

Pricing

Pricing is still done on a cost plus basis. The company has computerized and improved its cost allocation procedure, and is improving margins by more accurately allocating overheads to specific products.

Market Size

The value of the market in foam has not grown although it is now between £5 million and £6 million in real terms.
This is shared as follows:

Scottish Foam	40%
Kay Metzler/Vita Foam	40%
Others	20%

There has been little real market growth over the last 5 years and none is predicted, but the markets for casing and for injection moulding should show growth over the next 10 years.

Customers

Scottish Foam's list of clients has grown by active selling. New players such as Mitsubishi of Japan have also come to the market.

Market Location

The company's market has spread from Central Scotland to the whole of Scotland.

Marketing Strategy

- Long-term entry into packaging systems has been abandoned.

- The case and plastics divisions have been added as part of the firm's diversification strategy.

Marketing Budget and Marketing Intelligence

The marketing function has grown considerably from being the provision of inducements to purchasers to being a vital resource of information gathering on the company's potential markets.

The marketing budget has risen from £10,000 in 1985 to £100,000 now, and it is spent mainly on intelligence gathering and market research through outside consultants, rather than on gifts and inducements.

The company has ceased to rely on informal intelligence gathering.

Question

(1) Has Scottish Foam taken the right courses of action? Critically appraise its actions and current position.

CASE 6
Fuji Bank
Strategic Marketing

Fiona Davies and Luiz Moutinho
Cardiff Business School, University of Wales College of Cardiff

Company History

The Fuji Bank, established in 1880, is one of the leading commercial banks in Japan, and indeed the world, with total assets of £351 billion, 35% of which are overseas. It has 367 offices in Japan, plus 18 overseas branches and agencies, 25 representatives and 19 subsidiaries throughout the rest of the world. Exhibit 6.1 shows the 50 largest commercial banking companies for 1992, with Fuji Bank lying second. In its international business, Fuji Bank is primarily concerned with the corporate market of Japanese international companies, and an expanding group of multinational and local companies.

In Japan, Fuji Bank's policy has been to foster connections with large Japanese companies. Currently it is the main bank of the Fuyo group, which consists of major Japanese companies including Nissan, Hitachi and Canon.

Fuji Bank's first overseas branch was opened in London in 1953 with the aid of the Midland Bank. This is still the only UK branch, although there is now a representative office in Manchester. Subsequently other overseas branches were opened. In 1992 the bank established the European Advisory Board, which enables it to incorporate the recommendations of some of the world's leading experts into its global strategies and European merger and acquisition activities.

Fuji Bank's Mission Statement

The bank has the following fundamental values:

- To be conscious of the public role of the bank and its responsibilities in society.
- To put the customer first.

Exhibit 6.1 *The 50 largest commercial banking companies*

1992	1991	Companies ranked by assets		Assets [1] $ millions	% change from 1991
1	1	Dai-Ichi Kangyo Bank [4]	Japan	493,434.0	3.7
2	3	Fuji Bank [4]	Japan	493,363.0	8.3
3	2	Sumimoto Bank [4]	Japan	490,934.0	5.8
4	5	Sanwa Bank [4]	Japan	485,032.1	9.0
5	4	Sakura Bank [4]	Japan	470,814.9	5.0
6	6	Mitsubishi Bank [4]	Japan	460,820.6	6.6
7	8	Norinchukin Bank [4,5]	Japan	379,060.0	21.9
8	7	Industrial Bank of Japan [4]	Japan	370,026.4	11.0
9	10	Crèdit Lyonnais [G]	France	350,675.8	14.8
10	11	Deutsche Bank [6]	Germany	306,586.1	3.8
11	9	Crèdit Agricole	France	298,094.5	(2.7)
12	14	Mitsubishi Trust & Banking [4,5]	Japan	293,334.0	12.1
13	13	Tokai Bank [4]	Japan	291,961.9	7.7
14	16	Long-term Credit Bank of Japan [4]	Japan	290,407.9	13.6
15	12	Banque Nationale de Paris [G]	France	283,712.6	3.1
16	19	Sumitomo Trust & Banking [4]	Japan	280,748.9	19.5
17	22	Bank of China [G]	China	279,364.3	21.8
18	24	Mitsui Trust & Banking [4,5]	Japan	265,322.5	17.1
19	32	HSBC Holdings [7]	Britain	257,890.8	61.1
20	20	Sociètè Gènèrale	France	256,881.9	9.7
21	17	Bank of Tokyo [4]	Japan	254,753.3	3.1
22	18	ABN AMRO Holding	Netherlands	253,055.0	4.4
23	23	Asahi Bank [4,8]	Japan	251,904.4	10.8
24	41	Daiwa Bank [4,5]	Japan	224,194.3	14.6
25	15	Barclays Bank	Britain	222,680.3	(13.6)
26	21	National Westminster Bank	Britain	216,685.8	(5.3)
27	25	Citicorp	U.S.	213,701.0	(1.5)
28	29	Yasuda Trust & Banking [4,5]	Japan	208,851.0	15.2
29	27	Dresdner Bank [6]	Germany	203,459.9	4.9
30	26	CIE Financière de Paribas	France	203,125.4	2.0
31	28	Union Bank of Switzerland	Switzerland	181,959.8	(0.6)
32	34	Toyo Trust & Banking [4,5]	Japan	181,841.6	18.4
33	51	Bankamerica Corp. [9]	U.S.	180,646.0	56.4
34	36	Westdeutsche Landesbank [6]	Germany	169,604.2	11.9
35	30	Istituto Banc. San Paolo di Torino	Italy	161,487.1	(9.4)
36	31	Groupe des Caisses D'Épargne	France	161,262.9	(5.8)
37	37	Monte dei Paschi di Siena	Italy	160,939.3	7.0
38	39	Bayerische Vereinsbank [6]	Germany	155,427.4	4.2
39	43	Nippon Credit Bank [4]	Japan	152,752.8	11.7
40	38	Commerzbank [6]	Germany	143,688.3	(3.6)
41	50	Shoko Chukin Bank [G,4]	Japan	141,155.9	21.2
42	42	Chemical Banking Corp.	U.S.	139,655.0	0.5
43	35	Swiss Bank Corp.	Switzerland	137,040.2	(9.8)
44	47	Bayerische Hypotheken & Wechsel [6]	Ger.	136,138.6	7.2
45	48	Bayerische Landesbank [6]	Germany	132,190.0	8.5
46	33	Rabobank	Netherlands	127,926.9	0.9
47	44	Deutsche Genossenschaftsbank [6]	Ger.	127,669.3	(5.6)
48	61	Zenshinren Bank [4,5]	Japan	122,395.5	25.3
49	52	Nationsbank Corp.	U.S.	118,059.3	7.0
50	53	Crèdit Suisse	Switzerland	118,033.4	3.3

Source: FORTUNE. AUGUST. 1993

G Government owned
1 As of 31 December 1992, unless otherwise noted. All companies on the list must have more than 80% of their assets in commercial banking institutions. Daiwa, Mitsubishi Trust, Mitsui Trust, Sumitomo Trust, Toyo Trust, Chuo Trust, and Yasuda Trust include holdings of major trusts in their assets.
2 Figures for German banks include their own bonds; so do figures for Bank of Tokyo, Industrial Bank of Japan, Long-term Credit Bank of Japan, Norinchukin Bank, and Shoko Chukin Bank.
3 Figures include lease financing and call loans and are net of loan-loss reserves.
4 Figures are for fiscal year ended March 31, 1993.
5 Figures are unconsolidated.
6 Figures exclude some subsidiaries more than 50% owned.

Exhibit 6.1 *continued*

Deposits[2]		Loans[3]		Profits		% change from	Stock-holders' equity	
$ millions	Rank	$ millions		$ millions	Rank	1991	$ millions	Rank
399,919.5	2	323,496.0	2	372.6	36	(40.6)	17,552.2	3
401,702.6	1	302,561.6	5	466.9	33	(32.7)	17,414.3	4
396,569.9	4	317,440.8	4	168.9	58	(80.7)	19,641.4	1
399,850.2	3	320,235.3	3	762.7	15	(5.0)	17,588.7	2
393,353.4	5	327,276.8	1	462.6	34	(23.7)	15,156.6	8
379.459.6	6	291,454.3	6	503.1	32	8.1	15,789.7	5
345,440.1	7	156,826.1	15	344.5	39	13.3	2,814.1	83
298,645.7	8	223,203.1	8	328.0	42	(25.6)	12,244.3	12
147,387.0	29	175,541.0	14	(349.0)	96	(162.2)	15,383.9	7
269,728.4	9	249,587.2	7	1,148.5	7	37.6	13,860.6	10
189,064.6	22	182,974.0	12	995.0	10	9.8	14,534.8	9
223,918.7	15	130,109.4	25	128.8	68	(40.9)	7,111.4	31
235,359.4	13	185,092.9	10	202.6	53	(47.2)	9,618.4	20
239,554.8	11	181,442.4	13	186.2	54	(60.6)	9,662.9	19
138,876.6	32	150,162.5	18	450.7	35	(25.7)	10,249.1	16
259,045.6	10	124,343.0	27	149.8	63	(34.6)	6,881.7	36
127,405.4	38	98,420.4	40	2,249.0	1	23.8	11,785.0	14
238,148.4	12	113,179.6	32	92.3	74	(52.0)	5,668.9	45
229,674.9	14	136,952.2	21	2,155.1	2	108.0	12,120.6	13
194,511.1	17	110,284.4	33	617.1	21	3.3	7,257.8	30
189,642.8	21	133,384.4	24	303.2	45	0.0	8,833.4	24
191,900.5	19	145,824.6	19	957.3	11	16.5	8,836.7	23
211,792.8	16	183,154.0	11	289.1	46	1.7	9,352.7	21
191,991.0	18	106,739.2	34	135.1	66	(44.0)	5,070.7	49
176,837.9	25	154,782.9	17	(605.4)	99	(241.5)	7,987.1	27
190,976.9	20	191,603.3	9	370.6	37	191.1	8,382.0	26
144,175.0	30	135,851.0	22	722.0	17	—	11,181.0	15
187,092.6	23	90,681.7	43	70.8	79	(56.2)	4,510.8	58
186,102.7	24	155,737.2	16	607.0	23	59.3	6,369.6	39
36,422.7	94	82,085.8	45	167.3	60	—	9,741.5	18
150,536.2	27	145,398.4	20	954.2	12	12.5	12,260.6	11
162,280.5	26	76,825.5	50	59.4	85	(49.1)	3,862.5	69
137,883.0	33	120,602.0	28	1,492.0	3	32.7	15,488.0	6
149,153.4	28	118,510.6	29	145.7	65	6.2	7,071.5	32
122,841.2	40	93,763.0	42	110.7	72	(81.7)	5,067.8	50
132,911.2	36	50,750.9	71	364.6	38	(17.8)	9,227.4	22
77,795.6	57	59,056.9	60	7.0	95	(97.4)	3,903.6	67
143,766.9	31	133,559.7	23	273.0	49	85.6	3,990.7	66
133,939.9	34	100,398.9	37	147.3	64	(52.3)	4,916.2	52
133,572.2	35	118,246.8	30	536.2	29	64.0	6,010.6	43
130,376.3	37	102,749.0	36	154.1	62	(26.0)	3,812.8	70
94,173.0	47	82,010.0	46	1,086.0	9	605.2	9,851.0	17
94,980.2	46	125,712.8	26	714.7	18	(0.6)	8,437.2	25
125,425.7	39	113,200.4	31	234.5	52	10.2	4,329.9	60
113,256.3	42	103,385.3	35	280.1	48	59.1	3,177.6	76
75,636.1	59	73,010.4	52	579.8	24	7.1	7,739.4	29
118,315.9	41	99,681.3	39	30.0	90	(82.3)	2,929.6	80
101,246.7	44	56,969.7	63	118.9	70	14.0	2,184.0	91
82,726.5	54	72,714.0	53	1,145.2	8	466.9	7,813.7	28
102,931.8	43	100,255.1	38	608.9	22	3.0	6,636.4	37

7 Figures reflect acquisition of Midland Bank (1991 Global Service rank: B51), July 1992.
8 Name changed from Kyama Saitamo.
9 Figures reflect acquisition of Security Pacific Corp. (1991 Global Service rank: A77), April 1992.
10 Figures are for fiscal year ended 31 October 1992.
11 Figures are for fiscal year ended 30 September 1992.
12 Figures are for fiscal year ended 30 June 1992.

- To act sincerely and justly.
- To contribute to and cooperate with society.
- To respect individuals' thoughts, values and beliefs.

Company Goals

Fuji Bank aims to expand its customer base by acting in accordance with the high principles set out in its mission statement. It will continue, as it always has, to try to provide its customers with traditional, reliable and on-time financial services.

Products and Services

In the domestic Japanese market, Fuji Bank's operations include both retail and wholesale banking, covering current and savings accounts, loans, credit cards, home banking, investment management, business information services, leasing, factoring, consulting, dealing in gold and bonds, and other services. However, the London branch deals only with wholesale handling services, mainly focusing on:

- Trade finance
- Aircraft finance
- Project finance
- Loan arrangement
- Agency services

Fuji International Finance plc, a subsidiary of the bank in London, assists Japanese investors with international investments and also helps non-Japanese institutions such as UK local government pension funds. It uses highly quantitative investment techniques to achieve the highest possible returns at controlled risk levels.

The bank works with many other organizations to monitor current trends and develop specialized advisory services. It helps customers with mergers and acquisitions, capital participations, strategic alliances and technological licensing. The Fuji Capital Markets group in London provides high-quality services related to secondary markets. Customer transactions are backed up by in-depth investment information services, including market surveys and analysis, tailored to the needs of individual customers. Special emphasis is placed on the development of strategy recommendations, which are based on advanced portfolio management and risk management techniques.

The bank's Financial Engineering Division is always developing and proposing a variety of sophisticated and innovative financial products and schemes to meet customer needs. A very wide range of information can be supplied; for instance, customers involved in mergers, acquisitions, capital participations and strategic alliances are given high-quality advice based on accumulated expertise and information gathered through the bank's extensive worldwide network.

Competition

The initial objective of Japanese banks expanding overseas was successful penetration of the market, that is gaining a high market share, even at the expense of profits. Recently, however, with the downturn in the Japanese economy, the pursuit of profit has become more important. In the United Kingdom, Fuji Bank's competitors can be categorized into two groups.

First, for business with Japanese companies overseas, the main rivals are other Japanese banks with UK branches. These number over 50, but true competitors are those of a similar size to Fuji Bank, that is:

* Dai-Ichi Kangyo Bank
* Sumitomo Bank
* Sanwa Bank
* Sakura Bank
* Mitsubishi Bank

This competition is carried overseas from Japan, because of the strong company–bank relationships which exist there. For example, Fuji Bank's close relationship with Nissan in Japan is carried over to Nissan in the United Kingdom.

The second category of competition relates to Fuji Bank's business with non-Japanese companies. Here, in addition to other Japanese banks, competition includes the major UK banks, which have the great advantage of being established and well known in the UK marketplace. Fuji Bank's strategy, like that of many other foreign banks, is to find market niches and to use personal contacts to gain business, rather than the high profile promotion strategies of most UK banks. For instance, Fuji Bank's European Advisory Board consists of prominent economic figures who have great influence with different companies.

For comparison, Exhibits 6.2, 6.3 and 6.4 show the rankings of the top six Japanese banks, Japanese bank results at September 1993, and details of strength, jobs and employee performance for the top four Japanese and top four British banks.

Marketing Orientation and Strategy

Fuji Bank wishes to maintain a high reputation for reliability, responsiveness to customer needs and social responsibility. It emphasizes its strategy of strengthening relationships with individual customers and smaller companies. It also stresses the promotion of its international and securities business, based on rigorous risk management policies.

The bank wants to grow and expand worldwide, while remaining financially secure, close to its customers, and competitive in its product and service offerings. The bank emphasizes continual new product/service development to ensure products and services are tailored to customer needs, and exploits new technology to the full to maintain the highest quality standards of production, delivery and

Exhibit 6.2   *Top six Japanese banks*

Ranking Latest Prev[1]	Strength Tier-1 Capital		Size			Soundness Capital assets ratio			
	$m	%ch[2]	Assets $m	rank	%ch[2]	% latest	% prev.	rank latest	rank prev.
1 1 Sumimoto Bank Osaka, Japan (31/3/93)	19,524	1.0	448,934	3	−8.2	4.35	3.95	718	697
2 2 Dai-Ichi Kangyo Bank Tokyo, Japan (31/3/93)	17,377	−5.1	456,484	1	−10.5	3.81	3.59	810	765
3 4 Sanwa Bank Osaka, Japan (31/3/93)	17,155	0.9	445,918	4	−5.4	3.85	3.61	803	762
4 3 Fuji Bank Tokyo, Japan (31/3/93)	17,045	−1.9	454,747	2	−5.2	3.75	3.62	819	760
5 8 Mitsubishi Bank Tokyo, Japan (31/3/93)	15,982	6.6	424,348	6	−4.6	3.77	3.37	817	799
6 6 Sakura Bank Tokyo, Japan (31/3/93)	15,608	1.0	437,952	5	−9.0	3.56	3.21	855	814

1. Previous ranking refers to last year's Top 1000. Figures used to calculate % changes have been adjusted over the year in some cases.
2. All % changes are calculated using local currency.

service. Fuji Bank has developed a three-year medium-term business plan for commercial customers. This aims to maximize operating profit by expansion of a quality customer base, and to establish superiority in quality of products and services offered in the target markets by always being one step ahead of the competition in understanding and responding to customer needs. The bank aims to maximize efficiency by getting the best results from its staff, developing them into highly skilled professionals through educational programmes and enhanced on-the-job training.

Market research is continuous at Fuji Bank. The bank aims to be constantly in touch with what customers want, what its competitors are doing, and how the market is changing. It aims to oppose competitors not only on the basis of its strength in traditional banking, but also on modernization of delivery of financial services using new technology. Internally, the bank aims to create a corporate culture that is open, enthusiastic and full of vitality, with all staff feeling able to communicate their ideas and suggestions for improvement.

Marketing Budget

The total (Japanese and international) marketing budget of Fuji Bank was estimated at £1,521 million (1991/92) and £1,571 million (1992/93). Advertising and promotion accounts for 40% to 60% of the total.

Exhibit 6.2 *continued*

Pre-tax profit $m	profit %ch[2]	Real profits growth % latest	Real profits growth % prev.	rank latest	rank prev.	Profits on capital % latest	Profits on capital % prev.	rank latest	rank prev.	Return on assets %	rank	BIS Capital Ratio %	F.T. Comp. Credit Rating
669	−67.4	−67.9	−15.7	775	583	3.4	10.8	809	542	0.15	841	9.37	3.0
1,026	−36.9	−37.9	−14.5	718	575	5.8	9.0	761	617	0.22	788	9.36	3.0
1,649	−7.9	−9.4	−11.5	571	550	9.7	10.9	609	539	0.37	672	9.43	2.8
900	−41.4	−42.3	−12.8	727	561	5.2	9.2	775	608	0.20	812	9.26	5.0
1,135	−33.2	−34.2	−14.5	699	574	7.3	11.5	691	517	0.27	759	9.12	2.6
965	−25.5	−26.7	−12.1	666	555	6.2	8.6	738	630	0.22	792	8.96	4.4

Source: The Banker, July 1993.

Advertising and Promotion

In Japan Fuji Bank advertises on radio and TV, in newspapers and magazines, and by direct mail. Gifts such as calendars, pocketbooks and savings boxes are given to customers. However, overseas advertising and promotion is on a much smaller scale, with the only media advertising being in magazines such as *Banking World*. Annual reports and Christmas cards are sent to customers. Other promotion of the bank is by personal contact, for example by members of the European Advisory Board.

Problems for Fuji Bank in the United Kingdom

Although the rise of the yen against the dollar has strengthened the position of Japanese banks, Fuji Bank has had some difficulties with its UK operation. In 1992 the total income of the Fuji Bank Group decreased by about 25%, mainly due to a decrease in interest received and paid as a result of the lowering of market interest rates. In the past, Fuji Bank overseas has sometimes spent in excess of its resources in the pursuit of market share; now it cannot afford to do this. In addition, the bank has a lot of bad debts. Financial deregulation has increased competition in the UK market, and Japanese banks also have to comply with the standards for financial performance required by the Bank for International Settlements (BIS) in addition to their own legislation. Japanese banks are falling back in the syndicated

Exhibit 6.3   Japanese Bank Results, 30 September 1993 (¥ bn)

	Total assets Sept 1993	% change from March 1993	Net income Sept 1993	% change on Sept 1992
City Banks				
Dai-Ichi Kangyo	50,181	−1.47	16.2	−44.3
Sakura	49,697	−1.44	17.5	−37.5
Sumitomo	50,268	−0.73	30.3	−19.8
Fuji	48,370	−3.37	25.9	−0.4
Mitsubishi	44,877	−6.56	26.9	−17.7
Sanwa	47,648	−2.63	39.9	−1.0
Tokai	29,706	−1.88	11.4	−15.6
Bank of Tokyo	21,245	−2.85	30.2	28.0
Asahi	26,720	−0.74	10.1	−11.4
Daiwa	17,660	51.57	8.5	15.0
Hokkaido	10,298	−0.43	4.5	−27.4
Long-Term Credit Banks				
IBJ	36,995	−1.64	15.4	−27.0
LTCB	28.950	−0.67	113.0	−27.7
Nippon Credit	16,529	0.56	6.6	−51.5
Trust Banks				
Mitsubishi Trust	22,929	−4.36	8.7	−24.4
Sumitomo Trust	21,889	−3.07	8.5	−43.7
Mitsui Trust	23,094	7.40	5.7	−40.0
Yasuda Trust	15,665	−0.19	4.6	−38.7
Tovo Trust	14,337	−2.12	3.7	−32.7
Chuo Trust	7,332	0.55	1.7	46.9
Nippon Trust	2,737	−1.76	0.8	−33.3
	107,983	−0.46	33.7	−37.0

† Net unrealized profits/losses on listed securities.
‡ Level of Nikkei at which hidden reserves wiped out.
Source: IBCA Limited.

loans market; the percentage of issues in London involving at least one Japanese bank in the syndication fell from 84.5% in 1989 to 66.6% in 1992.

Finally, as an overseas commercial bank which does little advertising, Fuji Bank has low customer awareness, and there may be difficulties in communications with customers due to language problems.

Personnel

Few Japanese banks have non-Japanese top-level staff. The Fuji Bank in London has a Japanese director and general manager, and five joint general managers, who until 1993 had always been Japanese. However, a big step forward was made in 1993 by the appointment of Michael Clarke, a former Lloyds Bank executive, as one of the joint general managers. This is part of a 'localization' programme to involve senior local staff in the management of Fuji's branches outside Japan.

Exhibit 6.3 *continued*

Non-performance loans Sept 1993	Hidden reserves† Sept 1993	Capital Ratios % Tier One	Total	Nikkei level‡
1,386	1,726	5.0	9.8	11,689
1,463	2,204	4.53	9.05	11,329
1,162	1,502	5.45	8.91	11,912
1,256	1,437	5.12	9.82	12,680
595	1,961	4.91	9.81	10,213
908	1,712	5.18	10.20	11,311
859	1,140	4.64	9.27	12,009
346	634	5.44	10.42	10,172
554	1,175	4.99	9.93	13,752
320	834	4.66	9.32	11,941
401	349	4.59	9.19	11,428
559	2,350	4.63	9.25	9,980
731	1,639	4.63	9.25	10,689
609	722	4.55	9.10	11,957
569	1,055	6.50	10.98	11,499
460	890	6.67	11.00	11,033
571	1,102	5.78	1.71	10,181
424	508	6.42	11.05	13,549
299	443	6.39	10.64	12,738
178	148	5.74	10.75	15,642
86	65	8.50	11.51	13,200
2,587	4,211	6.36	10.90	11,878

Exhibit 6.4 *Strength, jobs and employee performance*

	Capital ($ m)	No. of staff	Profits/ employee ($'000)	Capital/ employee ($'000)	Assets/ employee ($'000)
Japan					
Sumitomo	19,524	17,710	37.78	1,102.43	25,349.18
Dai-Ichi Kangyo	17,377	18,849	54.43	921.91	24,217.94
Sanwa Bank	17,155	14,517	113.59	1,181.72	30,716.95
Fuji Bank	17,045	15,953	56.42	1,068.45	28,505.42
United Kingdom					
HSBC Holdings	11,798	99,148	26.07	118.10	2,599.26
Barclays Bank	9,014	105,000	−3.49	85.85	2,147.22
National Westminster	8,428	85,900	7.12	98.11	2,520.78
Abbey National	4,814	17,760	48.03	271.06	6,113.51

Source: The Banker, January 1994.

Collective decision-making is a characteristic of Japanese banks. Many formal and informal meetings are held, to which all staff are encouraged to contribute. Any plan of action needs to be drawn up in writing and submitted for approval, first to the planner's senior executives (in ascending order of seniority), and then to officers in related departments, before a final executive decision is reached. This is known as the '*Ringi*' system. In addition, informal get-togethers, perhaps over a drink after work, are very much a part of the Japanese culture.

The organizational structure of the bank is typical of a Japanese city bank, being composed of several divisions, each hierarchical in structure and fulfilling specific tasks.

Current Financial Situation

The bank's net business profit, which demonstrates the performance of its core business, rose 40.7% between 1991/92 and 1992/93 to the highest level in the bank's history (£1,956 million). Net income on a consolidated basis saw a reduction of 36.9% to £363 million. However, total stockholders' equity on a consolidated basis rose by 1.6% to £12,413 million. These strong results were mainly attributable to broad-based management efforts to increase lending to a wider range of customers, strengthen credit controls and streamline overseas operations. The bank in 1992/93 made substantial provision against non-performing assets arising from the continuing slump in the real estate market, and consequently net income on a non-consolidated basis remained at £194 million. The bank's capital to assets ratio was 9.26% (well above the 8% required by the BIS).

Economic Background

In 1993 economic growth in developed economies averaged only 1%. Japan was an area of particular weakness, where the economy actually went into recession, recording its first fall in output for almost 20 years. Some experts predict the situation in Japan will get worse before it gets better, while others forecast an upturn in Japan's economy in 1994.

In 1993 Japanese banks reported much lower profits, mainly due to a very large volume of non-performing loans. The Ministry of Finance encouraged the setting up of the Co-operative Credit Purchasing Company (CCPC), jointly owned by the banks, to buy the bad loans. But many bankers believe that the full extent of bad debt in Japan has still not been revealed, and analysts predict that the majority of operating profits until March 1996 will go towards absorbing loan losses. Financial deregulation is also beginning to take place in Japan, with divisions between banks and securities houses being broken down. However, the Japanese international banks all managed to satisfy the BIS requirement of a minimum capital to assets ratio of 8% by March 1993.

In the United Kingdom, the major banks improved their capital to assets ratios in 1993. In previous years heavy provision had been required for bad or doubtful debts, but such provisions are beginning to decrease. The major banks are seeking new sources of income, as much of their profit has come from trading in volatile markets and very little from branch banking. There is a trend for large corporations to seek finance outside the banking sector, and banks may be better off looking for business among small and medium-sized corporations.

Generally, wholesale banking markets are becoming more global as multinational companies focus and organize globally. The banking industry is already a intensive user of information technology and this will increase in the future.

SWOT Analysis

Company Strengths

- One of Japan's oldest commmercial banks. A leading bank with a well established position in the market.

- One of the world's largest banks, with total assets of 56.2 trillion yen (£351 billion).

- Reputation for reliability and quality.

- Places emphasis on fairness of transactions in capital markets.

- High level of customer satisfaction.

- Many highly regarded companies worldwide are clients of Fuji Bank.

- Competent, aggressive and highly motivated management – highly skilled professionals with excellent knowledge of the banking industry.

- Management flexibility in adapting to environmental changes and possible risks.

- Open organization where all staff are encouraged to communicate and make suggestions for improvement.

- Constantly entering new markets and developing innovative financial services.

- Using and continually developing sophisticated new technology.

- Steady expansion in Europe.

- The European Advisory Board – the first such advisory board established by a Japanese corporation.

- Rise of the yen against the dollar.

Company Weaknesses

- Low customer awareness in the United Kingdom.

- Communication difficult with UK companies due to language problems and training difficulties.

- Unwise expenditure in the past in pursuit of market share overseas, and bad publicity associated with this.

- Trends towards financial deregulation and internalization indicate a need for methods to avoid marketing risk.

- 25% fall in income of Fuji Bank group from 1991 to 1992, mainly due to decrease in interest received and paid as a result of lowering of interest rates.

- Large number of bad debts.

- Value of security houses has fallen.

- Decreasing involvement by Japanese banks in the syndicated loans market.

- Difficulty in complying with BIS requirements.

Opportunities

- Banks now allowed to participate in securities and trust business through subsidiaries.

- Liberalization of financial system is an opportunity to introduce new services.

- Expansion of activities.

- Economic recovery in the United States will allow Fuji Bank's US branch to develop more business.

- Single European market will allow Fuji Bank to build stronger relationships with European companies.

- Opportunities to capitalize on advantages as an Asian bank, as Asian countries are growing economically stronger and attracting more US and European companies.

Threats

- Poor economic situation at home and abroad.

- Drop in housing investment, together with a slowdown in the growth of both consumer spending and capital investment.

- Stock prices sluggish due to slump in corporate performance.

- Lowering of market interest rates, changing exchange rates, and risks of further interest rate fluctuations.

- Continuing trend towards financial liberalization has increased complexity of banking operation and led to a proliferation of risk factors.

- Disagreement in European Union over monetary policy.

- Increased complexity of the business environment due to developments in Europe, the break-up of the Soviet Union and financial deregulation.

- Deregulation has led to more direct competition from both financial and non-financial institutions, and now securities companies and Trust banks are allowed to go into commercial banking.

- Some large companies are issuing their own bonds rather than borrowing from banks.

- Indirect competition in personal credit market, for instance from finance houses, hire purchase companies and department stores offering their own credit facilities.

- Increased movement of customers between banks.

- Continuing rapid technological changes.

Acknowledgement

The author would like to thank Koichi Igarashi, Nickolaos Parisakis, Azmat Abbas Shah and Sapna Vyas for providing the necessary information and allowing it to be used as a case study.

Questions

(1) Analyse the competitive position of Fuji Bank.

(2) (i) How does the marketing approach used by Fuji Bank in the United Kingdom differ from that which would be used by (a) a retail bank? (b) a UK commercial bank?
   (ii) What competitive advantages and disadvantages are there to this marketing orientation?

(3) Calculate the following ratios for the year ended 31 March 1993:

- Current ratio
- Return on assets

- Debt to assets
- Debt to equity

(4) Is it possible for Fuji Bank in the United Kingdom to continue to increase its market share, bearing in mind the requirement to contribute to overall profits and to satisfy the BIS capital to assets ratio requirement? Why/why not?

(5) Develop a promotional plan and budget for Fuji Bank in the United Kingdom.

CASE 7
Lysander's Wine Cellars[†]
Strategic Marketing

R. P. Hamlin
University of Otago, New Zealand

Introduction

Most cases that business students are asked to deal with illustrate the problems that may be faced by large or medium-sized companies. As a rule these cases resemble a Cecil B. De Mille movie with a cast of thousands and a budget of millions.

All large companies were small once. Invariably only a few companies survive their early years to become giants with names known throughout the world. Many perish before they become known outside their own local environment.

During this crucial period, decisions are made which will affect the nature and even the survival of a company. Normally these decisions involve a single person, who has extremely limited resources and very little time in which to make a decision. As a result, small company decision-making is not the logical and well funded process that is described in most business courses. It frequently involves large assumptions, and even outright guesses based on the information available.

This case outlines a situation faced by the proprietor of a company with no other employees. Although his goals are well defined, the company is in trouble, and he has several options to consider.

[†]Ted Proctor, Lysander's Wine Cellars and the town of Terence do not exist. The case is based on information and experiences derived from a variety of sources. However, it has been written with great care and in such a way that any general information that is given in the case or exists elsewhere concerning the production and consumption of wine both in the State of Indiana and the United States will be both accurate and relevant.

Any resemblance of characters and situations in this case to real individuals and their activities is purely accidental.

Ted Proctor

Late in 1989 Ted Proctor sat in his winery shop and pondered both his own future, and that of his company. Ted lived and worked in Terence, Indiana, a small town in the American Midwest. He had been in business for about eight years. After an encouraging start his sales had flattened off, and had been erratic over the previous three years. Although the company showed a profit, it was not enough to support both himself and his wife. Ted wanted to start a family, but at present the business could not support his wife working on a part time basis while she looked after the children. The net income of the business was about $2,200 a month.

A decision had to be made. If the company could not be expanded to provide a living for two, he would sell up and take a job that would. Ted loved his company, and the lifestyle that it offered him. He would save it if he could. Once again, he picked up the pile of papers in front of him.

History of the Indiana Wine Industry (before 1972)

The Indiana wine industry was founded in the early 1800s by Swiss settlers. They enjoyed considerable success during the first half of the century in the Ohio Valley region of Southern Indiana before black rot destroyed the vines. After this disaster the settlers turned to other crops, and the focus of the US wine industry moved west to the Missouri Valley in Southern Missouri. Production in Indiana continued, but it lost its pre-eminence in the field.

The rise of the California wine industry towards the end of the nineteenth century led to the decline of Midwest wine production in general. Still, in 1919, Missouri boasted the third largest winery in the country with some 30,000 acres of vines.

Prohibition halted wine production throughout the United States. After the repeal of prohibition in 1931, the Midwestern wineries did not recover. Even in California, the recovery was a slow drawn-out affair. Although the American public resumed the consumption of alcohol, their drinking habits and the industry that served them had been profoundly changed by the years of enforced abstinence. One large winery operated in the Indianapolis area for several years after the repeal, but when this concern failed, wine production in Indiana ceased.

One of the legacies of prohibition was that all legislation concerning the production and sale of wine was left to the individual states. This led to large discrepancies in the state-by-state treatment of wineries. Indiana state law from 1931 to 1972 prohibited direct sales to the public by wineries. All sales had to be to retail outlets via a licensed wholesaler. This had the effect of suppressing start-up ventures in Indiana, and worked very much for the benefit of the large, established California and foreign wine producers.

The Small Wineries Act (1972)

Throughout the 1960s restrictive alcohol production and sale legislation was repealed in many Eastern states. These changes were forced through in the teeth of opposition from established wine producers. Repeal legislation was sponsored in Indiana by a group of wealthy and influential prospective winery owners.

In 1972 their recommendations were adopted, and became the Small Wineries Act. Its purpose was to encourage the expansion of wineries, and through them the grape growers of Indiana. The farming sector was very depressed at this time, and the desire to help the state's agricultural sector was the main motivation for the bill.

The act covered a range of issues. Three clauses were relevant to wineries.

Section 7.1–3–12–4

This dealt with the definition of a small winery. It stated that if a company was to be considered a small winery it must produce wines from grapes and fruits grown in the state, and must produce less than 100,000 gallons of wine a year.

Section 7.1–3–12–5

This allowed the manufacture and bottling of wine at the winery. It also permitted the establishment of tasting rooms at the winery, and permitted sales direct to the public and retailers.

Section 7.1–3–10–13

This allowed tastings to be conducted at retail outlets other than the winery, although only during regular business hours. Samples were not allowed to exceed one ounce, and could not be charged for.

History of the Indiana Wine Industry (after 1972)

The small wineries act transformed the situation in Indiana. Small wineries were given privileges that allowed them to compete head to head with the large out of state concerns at a local level. The act achieved its objectives. The production of wine in Indiana rose rapidly.

The surge in production was led by Ohio Valley Winery, which specialized in the production of fruit wines in its early years. These were a great deal sweeter than most wines produced from grapes. Sales of Ohio Valley Fruit Wines rose rapidly in the years following the introduction of the act.

In the late 1970s several factors combined to sharply suppress Indiana wine production. A succession of hard winters decimated the grape and soft fruit harvests, and a number of tax advantages for wineries included in the initial act were withdrawn. These events put the new wineries under a great deal of financial stress. The depression of the early Reagan years and the general move away from fortified and sweetened wines such as fruit wines and mead forced many of these already distressed wineries into bankruptcy.

As the economy boomed in the mid-1980s the industry recovered, and a second surge in production occurred. This was encouraged by a modification to the Small Wineries Act that gave small wineries the right to sell liquor for consumption off the premises on a Sunday. No other type of liquor outlet was allowed to do this.

By 1989 wine production in the region was rising rapidly, but had still not recovered to its previous peak. Ohio Valley Winery had survived, and was now one of 11 wineries in Southern Indiana. Lysander's Wine Cellars was one of the new generation of smaller wineries that had stated up in the early years of the decade.

Unlike wine production, local grape growing had not recovered from its previous setbacks. However, over the previous two years the acreage of grapes had finally stabilized, and was expected to rise in response to the increased demand from the expanding wineries.

State Aid

In order to encourage the recovery of grape production and wine-making in general, the Indiana Department of Commerce was planning an advertising and promotion drive to support local wine. The details of the scheme were still unclear, but the outline below had been proposed, and was likely to be implemented in the near future.

Value: $300,000 per year
Employees: 2–3, including marketing professional
Distribution: Vineyards   c. 25%
                Wineries   c. 25%
                (This aid in research, consulting etc.)
                Promotions   c. 50%

Quality of Indiana Wines

The wine and general press had not paid too much attention to Indiana over the years. However, there had been a contest for wines across the country in Indianapolis earlier in the summer. The wine correspondent from the *Indianapolis News* had run an article on the event:

'The overall impression from the judging was a respect and confidence in our local wine industry. (Since only two years ago), the quality has gone up considerably. Mediocre wines ... have been replaced by solid well made wines with character and flavour. Indiana stacks up pretty well, and makes as good French hybrids as are produced anywhere.'

One entry, a sparkling wine made from French hybrid grapes, got one of the two highest scores ... it was extremely well made, and could hold its own against most first class sparklers from California.'

Lysander's Wine Cellars

The Owner

Ted Proctor was in his mid-30s. He received his first degree in engineering from Penn State University. This was followed by a Master's degree in Limnology from the University of California at Davis.

Although his original ambition had been to become an aircraft engineer, his interest in the wine business had been aroused by amateur wine-making, and the presence of large numbers of wine-making books in the local library. The wine industry also offered him an opportunity to own and run his own agricultural concern. He came from a farming background, but the farm had been bequeathed to his elder brother.

After graduating from Davis in 1977, he took a job with a Sonoma Valley boutique producer as a wine technician. He stayed there for two years before being appointed head wine-maker by a smaller Napa Valley vineyard. He worked with this employer for a further three years before returning to the Midwest.

His decision to return to the Midwest and start on his own was largely due to his being unhappy with the direction that his employer started to take, and the presence of a son in the business meant that he was in a dead-end job. The California industry offered good experience, but it did not offer any independent opportunities because of its maturity and large cash requirement. Indiana was more suited to his ambitions, as it was close to his home state of Pennsylvania, and offered a young industry and a pioneering environment.

The land around Terence appeared ideal for wine-making. He decided to found a winery in the town. A bequest from his father's estate allowed him to buy an old town house and to turn it into a small winery. The very small debt that he had incurred in the process had been paid off in the first five years of operations. He and his wife lived in a flat above the winery.

The Wines

Ted considered that it was possible to produce a high quality and distinctive wine from local Indiana grapes. Indeed, he considered producing an individual style of wine from local varieties to be essential for the long-term integrity and survival of the industry. He particularly disliked the concept of producing wine from imported California grape juice. In his opinion this would just lead to an inferior locally labelled California wine.

Indiana does not have the ideal climate for the better known varieties such

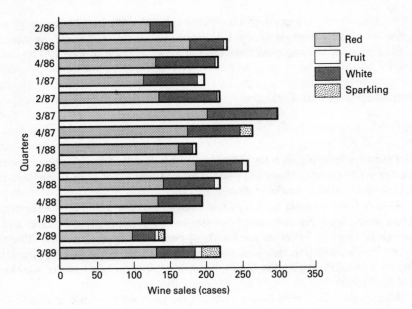

Exhibit 7.1   *Lysander's Wine Cellars, wine sales by type.*

as Zinfandel, Chablis and Reisling. The high humidity and sustained high temperatures at night during the summer make it very difficult to produce a high quality and consistent harvest from these varieties.

Ted turned to hybrids that could cope with these conditions. These included the French-style varieties, Aurora and Chelois, and the Reisling-like Vidal and Seyval. Wines produced from these varieties tended not to have the tannin that allows wine to keep. Indiana varietals[†], and blends thereof, had to be consumed within four years of purchase, and ideally within two.

Ted did not grow his own grapes. He had not had the money to buy a good winery site with a contiguous vineyard site in a good growing and selling area. The capital requirement for planting vines was high, and the return on them delayed and uncertain. With his restricted capital base, Ted had been unable to acquire the bank backing required to set up an integrated operation.

Lysander's Wine Cellars was based on one of the main streets of Terence, and the grapes were shipped in unpressed from local vineyards. Grapes were purchased on forward contract. All the stages of wine production subsequent to harvest were performed by Ted on his own in the cellar.

Over the years he had built up a portfolio of about a dozen wines that covered almost the entire range of wine types. In blind taste tests they had dose well against

---

[†] A varietal wine is made from one, or sometimes two, major grape varieties. Examples are Cabernet Sauvignon and Cabernet Sauvignon/Merlot blends. Non-varietal wines can contain a very wide range of grapes used by the wine maker to maintain consistency of character from year to year.

comparably priced California and Eastern Seaboard wines that were based on the traditional grape varieties.

Ted's total wine sales in 1988 amounted to about 900 cases. He had production capacity for about twice this, and had been stockpiling wine for two years in anticipation of a major sales push. In 1989 he had about 4,000 cases in the cellar. The major types were available in rough proportion to the sales of the last two years.

Production was evenly spread among the types of wine in the catalogue. His production had been rather haphazard, and availability of all of the wines on the list was by no means guaranteed. At this time Lysander's Ruby was on the verge of being sold out which would reader it unavailable until at least autumn 1990. Lysander's Diamonds was his latest project. One other grower produced a sparkling wine in Indiana, and Ted had been impressed by this product. His experimental run some two years previously had been somewhat ordinary, but had sold out almost immediately. He had now started to produce a sparkling wine that he was happier with, and this was also selling well. On a recent trip to the United Kingdom he had come across the higher quality British apple ciders, and he was keen to produce one of the 'Pomagnes' for the local market.

Exhibit 7.2 shows Ted's one-page wine catalogue as it was in 1989.

Exhibit 7.2
LYSANDER'S WINE CELLARS
WINE LIST 1989

Lysander's Diamonds (Retail $14.00)
This is one of only two champagnes produced in Indiana. It is fully bottle fermented to produce the French brut style known and loved around the world. The local grapes enhance this classic flavour with a full bodied taste that is wholly Indiana. Supplies of this classic are limited so buy early for Christmas.

Lysander's Special Reserve – White (Retail $7.30)
Bleeded and produced in the same manner as our special reserve red wine, this wine incorporates some of the finest grapes grown in Indiana to produce our top white wine. A very dry wine, it is excellent with appetizers and with poultry. A connoisseur's sipping wine.

Lysander's Special Reserve – Red (Retail $6.40)
Our top red wine. Blended in a manner familiar to the master wine-makers of the best French chateaux. The mixture of local grapes combine to produce a dinner wine unmatched this side of Athens.

Lysander's Reisling (Retail $6.25)
An extremely fragrant and fruity wine produced from locally grown Reisling grapes. A relatively dry example of its type, it is probably one of the state's best wines to accompany fish.

Lysander's Seyval (Retail $6.25)
A dessert wine. The noticeably sweet flavour of this wine makes it suitable for drinking on its own, or for rounding off that special dinner occasion. Serve well chilled.

Exhibit 7.2 *continued*

Lysander's Aurora (Retail $4.80)
Our most popular white wine. A finely balanced, dry yet smooth wine that almost any guest will like. Also very good for drinking on its own, or with a light snack.

Lysander's Ruby (Retail $4.80)
A sweeter wine than our special reserve. Its light and flowery nature makes it an ideal spring and summer drink.

Hellenic (Retail $3.70)
A light refreshing wine made entirely from apple cider [t]. Very delicate apple taste. A very dry example of its type. Good with fish and light cheeses. Its low alcohol content makes it an ideal entertaining drink.

[t] American cider is unfermented apple juice.

Ted used traditional clear or green Burgundy bottles to present his product. The labels on all the still wines had a cream base. The symbol of the winery, a shield bearing a cross with bunches of grapes and Greek urns, was printed on this base. The label was surrounded by a plain gold band. The intention was to replicate the rather austere labelling of the top California wineries. The cap that protected the cork was always made from dark green plastic.

The label also carried the health and sulphite content labelling required by state law. Recently these requirements had been changed, and the warning box had increased considerably in size and visual impact. Because of this, Ted was seriously considering a complete redesign of his labels.

As state law required the warning to be carried on the main label, no back label was employed. There was no other information on the bottle.

The exception to this rule was Lysander's Diamonds. As the winery's premier product, this Methode Champenois wine had its own form of presentation. The champagne foil on Sparkling Nights was dark red, and the bottle was very dark green. Both front and back labels were employed. The back label gave a brief history of the wine, and stressed its uniqueness. The front label was oval and carried a picture of a Grecian urn on a deep red background. The name ran around the edge of the label. The state health warning box was carried on a separate oval label on the front.

The Customer Base

Tourists

Indiana wines accounted for 1% of all US wine production in 1989. Ted accounted for about 2% of this. His customer base was restricted to individuals who were in Terence or Crawford County as either tourists, students or residents.

Terence was situated in a major tourist area. The Hoosier National Forest stretched away to the north west, and Lake Patoka and its associated resort town of Patoka were close by. Tourists coming from Louisville and other points in Kentucky frequently passed through Terence on the way to these attractions. There was a weaker flow of tourists coming south from Indianapolis and the major tourist-trap in the Brown County/Bloomington area. Tourism into the area was highly seasonal, peaking in the autumn when the leaves in the Hoosier National Forest turned.

Typically, tourism accounted for between 20% and 80% of sales from Indiana wineries. Ted had kept records of tourist purchases, and had found that he was towards the high end of this range, with about 50% of total sales coming from tourists. A couple of years previously, Ted had conducted an informal sales survey to find out his most important tourist 'source'. In order of volume he had found that the top five home addresses were:

Louisville	54%	Other Indiana	6%
Other Kentucky	15%	Cincinnati	4%
Indianapolis	8%	Other	13%

There were almost no repeat sales from tourists. Their knowledge of wines varied widely. The Californians tended to be the most knowledgeable and impressed with his wines. There was a tendency for tourists to arrive in groups with not all of the members interested. About 35% of visits led to a sale, and the average sale per individual/group was about $17. He had tried to reach tourists by distributing leaflets on the State Route (SR)62 running past the town. In 1988 he had distributed about 25,000 of these leaflets, and had plans to increase this to 100,000. The leaflets cost 8–10 cents each. He had also tried billboards on the SR62, but had thought that these were not very effective.

Local Market

Ted divided his local customer base into four groups: single purchasers, repeat bottle buyers, repeat case buyers and trade.

Single/irregulars

People in this group tended to buy for novelty or sentimental reasons, or because they had an emergency on a Sunday. They were very difficult to assign to any particular social type. Students and blue- and white-collar groups seemed to be represented in almost equal numbers. Irregular customers could be almost any age. Ted thought that these sales accounted for about 20% of his volume.

Regular bottle buyers

Regular bottle buyers were the least important group of local customers in terms of volume. They might come in four or five times a year and buy a couple of bottles. His inquiries had led him to believe that this group tended to buy the wine when they were entertaining guests from outside the state. Students, white-collar townspeople, university staff and military personnel from the Crane Naval Weapons Base accounted for the majority of this segment. Ted estimated that about 10% of his sales went to this group, which contained a much higher proportion of women than the other two.

Regular case buyers

Regulars were small in number, but important in terms of sales. Ted thought that they accounted for about 15% of his volume. Individuals in this segment bought one or two cases a year. Again, Ted thought that the wine was being used primarily for entertainment purposes. Individuals in this segment were almost exclusively university staff and businessmen from the town. They also tended to be older than regular bottle buyers.

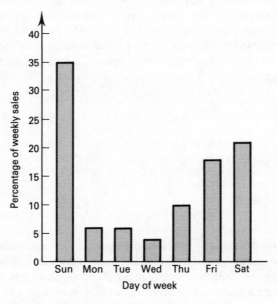

Exhibit 7.3 *Wine sales by day of the week.*

Trade

Ted had made some efforts to get his product into the retail liquor stores in the town. He had found that the first sale was easy, but repeat sales were very difficult to come by. The trade outlets in the town could be divided into four main types:

(1) *Independent liquor stores*

There were two major chains in the town, Nelson Liquors and Liquor King. Each chain had about five outlets. Both catered primarily to student and blue-collar customer bases. However, the nature of the customer base depended almost entirely on where the store was situated in the town. In one or two of the stores the clientele had a sizeable staff/white-collar element. They all carried extensive ranges of domestic wine. The shelves were dominated by the major Californian producers such as Gallo.

(2) *Supermarket liquor departments*

The Terence grocery trade was dominated by Cost Cutters which had a large supermarket at either end of town. The two markets catered for different customer bases. The larger of the two on the north side of the town had a customer base consisting of students and academic staff. This store was modern, and was part of an extensive mall system, which had virtually displaced the downtown area as the retailing centre of Crawford and Perry Counties. The store on the west side catered for townspeople of all types. It stood alone in an area of houses, factories and warehouses.

(3) *Bars*

The majority of bars catered for students, and beer sales formed the basis of their business. A few of the more upmarket bars in the centre of town served food of reasonable quality, and a limited range of low priced or carafe wines. There were no wine bars in the town or anything resembling one. Only one bar, the Scots Pine, sold a reasonable range of wines. Ted thought that two or three others could be persuaded to carry more wine.

(4) *Restaurants*

Restaurants could be divided into several categories. The majority catered primarily for students, and served only beer. Many in the fast-food sector served no alcohol at all in view of the strict under-age drinking laws.

A small number of the more upmarket restaurants did serve wine. They were either associated with the better motels on the peripheral roads, or were situated downtown.

The motel restaurants catered for travellers, residents and for special occasions in the town or university. They relied very heavily upon activities associated with the university for their business, as there was no major interstate highway running round the town. Most served restricted ranges of California and house wines.

Most of the downtown restaurants that served wine were 'ethnic'. A large number of high quality Chinese restaurants operated in the area. Greek, German, Italian, Tibetan, Russian, Mexican, Thai and vegetarian/Californian eateries could also be found in the area. The wine lists in these restaurants were extensive, and included a range of domestic and 'ethnic' wines. The clientele was dominated by university staff and students. There was also a fair representation of the dynamic and wealthy town residents.

Alcohol Laws

The local laws that were relevant to Ted were:

(1) Alcohol was not to be served to an individual under the age of 21. (Undergraduates enrolled at 18 and stayed for four years.)

(2) Alcohol was not to be available on university premises. This law was absolute, and covered staff entertainment and functions. Parties, functions and receptions had to be held off campus.

(3) No alcohol was to be served for consumption off the licensed premises on a Sunday. (Ted's was the only outlet in town not subject to this law.)

(4) The drink/drive limit was equivalent to 1.5 pints of beer or three glasses of wine.

As Terence possessed no fewer than four separate police forces, these rules were strictly enforced.

Ted's Marketing Efforts

Ted's attempts to reach his tourist base have been described. His efforts on the domestic front were rather more restricted. There were no signs for the winery other than the one on the facade of the building. This was painted in a dark red with white letters. Some three years previously he had briefly set up a booth in University Mall next to the larger of the two Cost Cutter supermarkets. He also tried to keep in touch with his repeat case buyers by enrolling them in a club, and sending them a quarterly four-page news letter.

He took a stand at the Indiana festival, an annual weekend festival held in the autumn. Stands were set up in the town square, and discos and other events were held in the surrounding streets.

His only other retail outlet was one of the Nelson Liquor stores. Nelson stocked Lysander's along with the other domestic wines. It was to be found among the cheaper large-scale wine offerings from California. Lysander's Diamonds was stacked in its cardboard cases among the lower priced wines in the middle of the store. This particular store was close to the winery, and catered almost exclusively for students.

Premises and Location

Lysander's Wine Cellars was based in a small town house on the north side of one of the two main east/west roads leading through the town. The centre of Terence and the main commercial centre of the area lay about three-quarters of a mile to the south. The winery was in a relatively quiet residential area. The university lay directly to the east, and quite a large number of students lived around the winery. There was street parking in front of the building, and a pay parking lot some way up the street.

Ted lived in the top floor of the building, and made and stored his wine in the cellar, which had been enlarged to include the entire area under the house.

Business was conducted on the ground floor, which consisted of four main areas:

(1) *The wine tasting counter.* A large counter, with wine racked both in front and behind it. This was located to the rear of the store in front of the office. Opened bottles of wine were kept in pails of ice on the bar, and tasting was done with standard glasses.

(2) *The wine tasting room.* About half the original house had been opened up to accommodate a wine tasting room, a pleasant wooden floored area with oak chairs and tables. The room was well decorated in a restrained manner, and was bright and airy. Ted sold wines by the glass and bottle to groups who used this area, almost invariably tourists.

(3) *The shop.* Although wine was his main interest it was not his only business. In the shop he had three major lines:
- Wine books, accessories and home wine-making equipment
- Beer books, accessories and beer-making equipment
- Cheese

Ted spent little time with these items, and they took up only a small amount of his floor space, but he knew that they made his business viable at that point in time. In particular, the home brew kits and the cheese sold well. The cheese was the only traditional style cheese available in the area, and once tried had a high repeat purchase ratio. It was supplied by a local farmhouse producer who was keen to increase his sales and product range. At present two types of Cheddar and a Cheshire were available. The producer had no other outlets in town. Ted thought that repeats on cheese could be as high as 60% whenever it was bought by the locals, which was not very often.

Beer kits were a good source of regular customers, as the sale of a beer-making kit increased the likelihood of reorders for ingredients and spares. There were a couple of other sources for beer kits in the town, and one dedicated outlet. In 1989 the income from these other activities was about half that of the winery, and produced a higher margin. The split between cheeses and beer was about even, with accessories contributing another 10%. The margin on these items was about 30% higher than on his wine.

(4) *The garden*. There was also a tasting garden accessible through French windows at the rear of the tasting room. Although large, it had a rather scruffy appearance with lank grass, and bent white plastic chairs. The walls which sheltered the garden were of attractive red brick, as was the winery itself.

Terence and Southern Indiana

Terence

Terence was a medium-sized university town based in a rural and none-too-wealthy part of the United States. The town population was about 60,000. A large number of residents were employed by industry based on the west and north side of town. The major employers were two large plants manufacturing air conditioners and hospital equipment. The residential areas of the south and west were heavily concentrated around the town, and were hemmed in by the river.

The north and east sides of town were dominated by the university. Terence was the main campus of Saint Paul's University, and had an undergraduate population of about 20,000. The academic and ancillary staff numbered about 6,000. On the north and west sides of town there were large areas of low-density, high-cost residential development leading out towards the Hoosier National Forest. These areas were heavily populated by staff. Students lived exclusively on the north and east sides of town. The majority lived in university property of one sort or another.

There were two main commercial areas, the centre of town and University Mall on the north side. University Mall contained about 300 stores including most of the major national multiples. There were also several minor centres on the west side. The mall on the east side catered exclusively for students.

Printed news came via two local papers, the *Saint Paul's Student Post*, and the *Crawford County Herald*. There were three town radio stations. WFSP was a classical and current affairs station run by the university. The other two were independent commercial stations that carried advertising. 97.2FM played current hits and WYTF played golden oldies. WFSP carried no commercials, but used corporate sponsorship of programmes to fund its activities. There was one local TV station for Southern Indiana, and several that covered the Louisville area for the national networks. The town also supported a large number of free advertising sheets.

Southern Indiana

Southern Indiana was a poor and sparsely populated area. The nearest major concentration of white-collar worker was in Louisville 40 miles to the east. With the exception of Evansville there were no other sizeable towns within 100 miles. The other local town, Patoka, was a tourist centre and, as a result, was not really typical of the state as a whole.

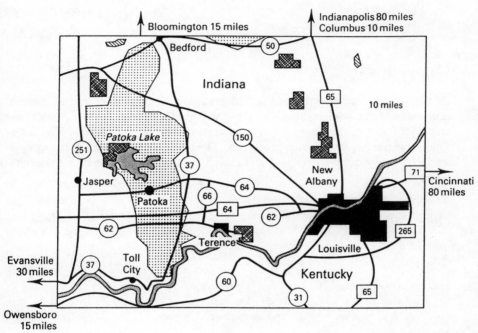

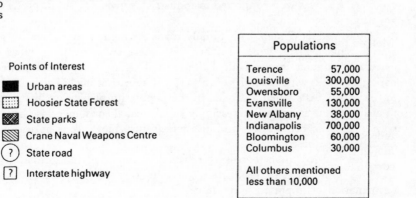

Points of Interest

■ Urban areas
▦ Hoosier State Forest
▧ State parks
▨ Crane Naval Weapons Centre
(?) State road
[?] Interstate highway

Populations	
Terence	57,000
Louisville	300,000
Owensboro	55,000
Evansville	130,000
New Albany	38,000
Indianapolis	700,000
Bloomington	60,000
Columbus	30,000

All others mentioned
less than 10,000

Exhibit 7.4 *Map of Terence and surrounding area.*

Patoka had a population of about 5,000 and lived exclusively off the summer tourist trade into the Hoosier National Forest and Lake Patoka. The town's shops were devoted almost entirely to tourist services and souvenirs. Most tourists came into the area from Evansville, Louisville and Cincinnati. Around 35% of all visitors were thought to originate in Louisville. About the same number came from Cincinnati, Indianapolis and Evansville combined. Estimates varied, but the Patoka/Southern Hoosier National Forest complex was thought to process nearly 300,000 tourists annually. Total tourism expenditure was not known. Although not widely known, the County Route Four (C4) was a very quick way to reach Patoka from Terence.

The residents of most other small towns in the area had below average incomes and were extremely conservative.

Competitors

Of the 11 small wineries located in Indiana, most were situated in the historical centre of Indiana wine-making, the Ohio Valley. Three were in Ted's immediate vicinity. Ted did not perceive any of these wineries as competitors. The major threat was the large California producers. The small Indiana wineries had cooperated with one another in the past, and even had connections further east with producers in Ohio and New York states.

Ohio Valley Winery

The Ohio Valley Winery was the oldest and largest winery in the area. Ted thought that the capacity of the winery was now about 15,000 cases per year. Mark Lafranchi was nearly 70, and was beginning to leave the day-to-day running of the business to his son. However, he still took a considerable interest in proceedings, and was well connected in industrial, university, legal, professional and government communities.

Ohio Valley Winery had initially made its name and money by producing a wide range of fruit wines. In the 1970s these sweet fortified wines had been extremely popular in the United States, and Ohio Valley had followed Gallo's national success with examples of this type of wine. Lafranchi had run into trouble in the early 1980s when a decline in the popularity of his flagship products due to changing tastes and an increasingly sophisticated consumer base had coincided with a series of bad winters and disasters in his vineyards as he was developing his new grape-based wines.

This had led to an increasing reliance on imported Californian grape juice. By 1989 Ohio Winery production was almost exclusively based on the local fermentation of imported grape juice.

The Ohio Valley Winery product range was about the same size as Ted's, and consisted primarily of the better known varietals such as Chardonnay. Typically, the wines cost from $6 to $9 a bottle. Most were drinkable but totally unexceptional, a couple were poor or downright bad. In a blind taste test it was extremely difficult to tell the difference between Ohio Valley Winery wines and California carafe varieties which retailed at about $3.50 a bottle. No Ohio Valley Winery wine had won a competition for years. A wide range of bottles and colourful boutique labels was used. Fruit wine was still produced and sold in small quantities. Lafranchi had tried a champagne, but it had been a failure.

Ohio Valley Winery made a great deal of money, and a fair amount of this profit was spent on promoting the wines that it produced. The company operated on a landscaped site just off the SR62 about 4 miles to the north of the town. The decor of the winery and grounds could be described as 'twee', with a wood lined tasting room filled with old wine-making equipment and sales assistants. The landscaped grounds included a lake and picnic area. Extensive parking was provided, and the winery was signposted for 8 miles in either direction. It was also clearly visible from the road.

Produce was also sold through independent liquor chains, and both branches of Cost Cutters. Every store was provided with a display stand, which was made of wood and stood about 4 feet high. The free-standing display normally found its way into the middle of the store, or the end of one of the aisles. The name and location of the winery was clearly visible, and was at chest level. The wine racks were serviced at least once a week, and representatives would come out to restock specially if called.

Considerable effort was expended in gaining exposure for the winery. The company had its own hot air balloon which was lent out for charity and other events. The media were well covered, and were heavily sponsored in the case of WFSP. Ohio Valley Winery booths could be found at every sizeable event.

Chipmunk's Jump

Chipmunk's Jump Winery was small and located in isolated country beyond Lake Patoka. Superficially this winery resembled Lysander's closely, having broadly similar products, sales volume and customer base. However, Bill Henry, the proprietor, was on the verge of retiring, and, without a successor, the winery was closing down. Although they were produced from local grapes, Bill's wines were also frequently so distinctive as to be almost undrinkable!

Patoka Winery

Patoka Winery was also very small. It produced slightly more wine than Lysander's, and much more than Chipmunk's Jump. However, the wines were unremarkable. Ted suspected that some Californian juice was finding its way into the wine, and would continue to do so in increasing quantities if local grape prices recovered to any great extent. Given the location of the winery in a prime tourist area, wines did not need to be all that good anyway. Their promotion was no better than his was, and local awareness of the enterprise was almost non-existent. Ted did not have much time for the winery, and thought that any major setbacks would encourage it to turn to other methods of relieving tourists of their money.

Trade Opinions

Over the previous few days, Ted had sent one of his friends to see a few of his colleagues in the liquor industry. He wanted to talk to more people, but had no time to do so. He reviewed the notes from the interviews that lay in front of him (see Exhibits 7.5, 7.6, 7.7 and 7.8).

Exhibit 7.5   Trade Opinions (1)

Dan (Manager of the Liquor King – North)
Liquor King – North was situated on the north side of the University campus.

Product Quality
Dan admitted to being not too well versed in Indiana wines. He knew that Indiana had once been the major producer of wines in the United States. He was aware of Lysander's Wine Cellars, but said that Ohio Valley Winery had done a much better job of increasing its visibility. It had been so successful that it had almost identified Indiana wine with its product. As its wines tended to be very sweet, and were based on imported grapes, this did not bode well for the other wineries and vineyards in Indiana which were trying to produce a quality local product. He had heard good things about Lysander's Wine Cellars, but complained of a lack of visibility, and of weak attempts to increase public awareness and interest.

Retail Markets
The market for wine in the state is increasing rapidly at the expense of beer and spirits as people drink less, but better quality. The majority of the local market consists of the 'yuppie' sector. These people are prepared to pay $15–20 for a bottle of wine. The market changes over the last five years as observed by Dan could be summarized as follows:

- Higher volumes of quality wine.

- Increased knowledge. This is connected to the rapid rise in the sales of varietal wines.

- Wine is increasingly drunk for pleasure and with meals rather than to become inebriated. This has hit fortified wines such as Thunderbird.

- People are moving away from white/sweet/German towards dry/red/French.

Dan thought that within the wine industry, Indiana wines had become identified with Ohio Valley. In order to succeed in the future, Indiana wine producers would have to move away from this image and concentrate on the sales of dry wines to the 25 to 40 year old age bracket. These will be the bulk buyers of the next 15 to 20 years. The final goal should be a line of varietal wines with a price range of $8–12.

Exhibit 7.5 *continued*

Specific Purchasing Issues

When he was asked what made a wine attractive to him as a retailer, Dan gave the following list of attributes.

- Product visibility. Tends to imply consistency of quality, particularly if it is on TV.

- Actual quality. Must be good and consistent.

- Versatility: OK for different situations.

- Attractive presentation. (He pointed out a bottle of Rothschild with a simple but striking label.)

- Price. Preferably retail below $10. This requires a purchase price of around $6.

Dan bought most of his wine from three wholesalers. The most aggressive of these was associated with Gallo. He was under constant pressure to rearrange his shelves, especially when it concerned moving a wine up or down the shelves. He attempted to keep shelf allocation in line with sales.

He was interested in Indiana wines, and would stock Lysander's if he could. However, it was illegal to buy directly from a winery, and the wholesalers were only interested in supplying Ohio Valley's wine. Dan did not have an Ohio Valley stand, and kept its wines on the bottom shelf with the carafe and fortified products. He was aware that Indiana wineries could conduct tasting in shops, and was receptive to any requests, if he was in a position to purchase.

Specific Selling Issues

Most of his Ohio Valley Winery customers were blue-collar workers who also bought beers and other sweet wines. They were extremely loyal to the product and bought it regularly, normally once a month or more. He did not think that this was Lysander's market. 'Yuppies' did come in in numbers on occasion, and he thought that tastings would be a good way to snare these individuals. They tended not to like buying cheaper wines such as Gallo.

His Ohio Valley's drinkers were certainly not typical of his overall customer base. He had never had any enquiries from these customers concerning the provenance of the grapes used by the winery. No customer had ever come in and asked for Lysander wine.

Exhibit 7.6 Trade Opinions (2)

Tim Tompkins (University Mall Cost Cutter Liquor Department Manager)
Ted believed that this store was the town's largest seller of wine by a considerable margin.

Product Quality

Indiana wines were 'not bad', but they were not likely to compare with those from California. He was not sure what they had to do to improve their quality. Their presentation, that is their labelling, had been 'jazzed up' recently. He thought that one of the Indiana wineries had been rated rather highly recently, but he was unsure which one.

Exhibit 7.6   *continued*

Local Market Profile

Tim said that over the previous two years generic wine sales (Chablis, Burgundy and so on) had flattened off. Varietal sales (Merlot, Cabernet and so on) had risen sharply during this period. Many people who had previously drank sweeter and German-style wines had begun to ask for dryer varietals. The consumption of red wines had begun to increase.

The only Indiana wines that the store sold were Ohio Valley's products. All, six of the wines offered were Californian varietals, and they ranged in price from $5.49 to $7.99. They were located in a winery stand at the end of one of the aisles in the centre of the shop.

Tim felt that the sale of Indiana wines was definitely on the upswing. It would be assisted by the production of a better quality product in response to increased customer sophistication.

Specific Selling Issues

The liquor store made its buying decisions on the same criteria as the rest of the shop. By far the most important of these was profit per foot of shelf space. This was a function of price, mark-up and consumer demand. The store had done well out of the general trading up in quality by its wine customers. It liked suppliers that supported awareness through brand advertising. Tim would not take a wine which he could not mark up by 50%.

Vendors did not put much pressure on Tim regarding positioning and shelf space in the shop. As the area's major outlet he was in a dominant position, and made it clear to his suppliers that the decisions would be made by the store. Tim did not think that the larger wine concerns tried to suppress local wineries. They did not perceive them as a significant threat. Most representatives paid close attention to the shelf space and position occupied by their major wholesaling competitors. None had ever commented seriously on Ohio Valley's stand. Several had made jokes about it.

Indiana wines were relatively easy to sell. He would move around 10 to 15 cases per month. Many customers came in and asked for it. The ratio of new to repeat buyers was about 50:50.

The fact that these wines are produced locally was significant in the purchase decision. To increase sales further, he felt that there needed to be an increase in the quality and quantity of advertising in order to increase and sustain awareness in the customer base. A coherent marketing plan and a wider product range would be nice. As with all supermarkets, consistent availability was a real issue.

The majority of his customers for wine were white-collar workers. He did not think that the customers for Indiana wine were significantly different. Most Indiana wine was purchased by regulars who bought one or two bottles four or five times a year. There appeared to be a disproportionate number of women among his regular buyers.

He did not know what his local market share was, but he had heard his manager mention that Cost Cutter now controlled between 50† and 60† of the town's retail grocery market.

Conclusion

Ted pushed the last page of notes back across his desk and took stock of the situation. His initial ambition when he opened the winery had been to make a living for himself and his family by producing and selling wine from one site.

Layout of Typical Town Liquor Store

Points of Interest

░░	Counter
▦	Chilled beer & soft drinks
⠿	Beer and soft drinks
▤	Moderately priced wines
▨	More expensive wines, champagne and spirits
▦	Snacks, kegs, party supplies
①	Local wines

Arrangement of Wine Shelving in Liquor Store

Shelf			
1		QUALITY	European, Californian, etc.
2		BIG SELLERS	Gallo, etc.
3		VARIETALS	Lesser varietals
4	①	ALSO RANS	Branded and unbranded table wines
5	②	SWEET AND CHEAP	Fortified and fruit wines

Points of Interest

① Typical position of a Lysander varietal

② Typical position of a Ohio Valley Winery wine

Exhibit 7.7 *Terence Liquor Stores.*

Lack of money had prevented him from starting off with an integrated winery in a good position. Retailing wine from the site that he had settled for had not been as easy as he had anticipated, despite the fact that he appeared to have the best product in the marketplace.

Ted had spent several years in California, but was not impressed with the direction that the Californian industry was taking. Most of the wineries that he admired were on the Eastern Seaboard, in Michigan, Ohio and Missouri. These wineries tended to be at least 20 times the size of his own company, and many were in the 50,000–100,000 gallon league. This corresponded to virtually the

Exhibit 7.8   Trade Opinions (3)

Randy Fiddler (Manager, Pastel's Restaurant, Armada Inn)

Randy had been bar manager at the Armada Inn for 12 years. He was also bar manager at the Vacation Resort Inn, and was responsible for all wine purchases at both hotels.

Pastel's carried a good selection of premium California wines. It offered no Indiana wines. Sales of California varietals averaged only 12 bottles a month. The bulk of the sales in both restaurant and bar were either high quality or low value carafe wines. Overall wine sales in the restaurants and bar had been flat, and had even shown a slight decline in recent months.

Randy did not see a place in his operation for Indiana wine. This was largely because the consumption of wine was low in most of Terence's restaurants. The type of food and decor encouraged the consumption of beer with food. The main customers of the restaurant were university visitors, meetings and events. Family groups and celebrations tended to use the newer 'ethnic' restaurants downtown for their celebrations. He was not concerned with this as locals never had formed a large part of his consumer base. He had heard that some of these restaurants were doing well, and were beginning to offer more esoteric wines in keeping with their menus.

He did not believe that there was a quality problem with Indiana wines. He admitted that he had never carried any. His only experience of a local product was one instance where a banquet specified an Ohio Valley Fruit Wine as a dessert wine.

---

entire wine production of Southern Indiana. They were set in attractive countryside, surrounded by their own vineyards. As a rule the tasting rooms and shop areas were extensive, and catered for other family activities. Extensive selling occurred through local retailers, restaurants and mail order.

It was Ted's ambition to build his own winery up to this level. If so many other people could do it, why not him? His wines regularly trounced these more successful concerns at wine competitions.

Questions

(1) Read the case that has been given to you. You are a consultant who has been called in by the proprietor of Lysander's Wine Cellars. In the brief the client has said that he has US$5,000 to spend on consulting services for the purposes of improving the marketing of his product. This $5,000 may be used for professional time, secondary and primary research. No further specific instructions have been given.

Write an initial assessment of the situation of Lysander's Wine Cellars for your own purposes in future planning. This should be no longer than 2,500 words. (Six pages single spaced).

(2) You are working for the consulting company that is advising Ted Proctor over the future direction to be taken by Lysander's Wine Cellars. Using information in the case, and any inputs that you have received from your

tutorial, write an internal research proposal. The proposal should have the following major parts:

i) A preliminary problem/opportunity statement. (5%)

ii) A list of possible alternatives. (5%)

iii) A section refining the alternative that you have selected for testing through primary research into a theory, and a statement of your reasons for selecting it in favour of the other alternatives that you presented in Part 2. (10%)

iv) A list of the hypotheses that make up the line of reasoning that will support your theory, and that will need to be individually tested before the theory can be accepted. These hypotheses *must* be listed in a logical manner. (30%)

v) A brief description of the research vehicle that you will use (telephone/focus/mail etc.). Remember to include research targets. (20%)

vi) A list of the questions that you will use to test the hypotheses. Try to avoid questions that result in answers that could be biased or impossible to analyse using statistical techniques should these be appropriate to the research method that you propose to use. (30%)

Parts one to five should not exceed 400 words in total. Part six should consist of not more than ten short questions. (Two sentences maximum.)

CASE 8
The Great Western Brewing Company Limited
Strategic Marketing

Shengliang Deng
University of Saskatchewan, Canada

History and Background

The Great Western Brewing Company was formed on 18 January 1989 with the merger of Molson Breweries of Canada and the North American operations of Elders IXL, an Australian company which owned Carling O'Keefe. The Great Western plant in Saskatoon had previously been owned by Carling O'Keefe. When the company was forced to shut down one of its two Saskatchewan plants, the Saskatoon plant was selected[†].

The announcement of the closure came as a shock to the approximately 40 employees of the Saskatoon Carling O'Keefe brewery who were to be laid off. Their only consolation was that they would receive an early retirement package, enhanced severance benefits and career counselling. The remaining 30 of the 70 employees would be moved to Regina to continue production.

The shut-down of this plant caused the start-up of Great Western. A group of employees considered buying the brewery from Carling and operating it themselves. A package of information had previously been circulated worldwide by one of Carling's former employees to stimulate interest in buying the existing facility. This effort was unsuccessful, however, and led to the employees' decision to buy the plant themselves.

A group of 15 employees put their own money on the line and bought the brewery. The employees then invited Peter McCann to invest and become a shareholder, and also to provide leadership and credibility and assume the position of President and Chief Operating Officer. McCann had spent over 30 years in the brewing industry and gladly accepted the challenge facing the new brewery.

---

† Saskatchewan is one of the 10 provinces in Canada. It is located in Western Canada and has two major cities, Saskatoon and Regina.

The initial launch of Great Western beer saw Saskatchewan beer drinkers polishing off nearly 420,000 bottles. During the first week of sales, Great Western was pegged as having as much as 20% of the total market share. In fact, in several Saskatchewan liquor stores, it topped the 50% mark.

Along with these outstanding sales figures, the province of Saskatchewan has recognized Great Western's success by presenting the company with many awards during the past three years including the Chamber of Commerce ABEX award for best business.

After the novelty of Great Western beer had worn off, sales dropped and Great Western no longer has such a large market share. However, sales are still almost 200% higher than initial projections, and with the introduction of additional beer brands, Great Western is trying to keep its market share as high as possible (see Appendix 8.11).

Finance

In order to finance the purchase of the Great Western brewery, each of the 15 employees invested between $50,000 and $100,000. This worked out at approximately 25% of the $5 million purchase price. Peter McCann also invested in the new venture. Saskatchewan Economic Development Corporation (SEDCO) came up with the rest, while a chartered bank provided an operating loan.

Each of the 16 shareholders in the company has a large stake in the operation both personally and financially. The distribution of shareholdings ranges from 2.3% to 9.9%, with no one person able to control more than 10% of shares outstanding.

The Finance Department at Great Western consists of the manager of finance and an accounting clerk. A computerized financial control system is in use and performance reports are monitored on a daily basis.

Competitors

In the beer industry's shrinking market the three major brewers compete vigorously for market share, with the competition being heavily brand oriented.

Competitors are made up of three main types: mega-brewers, regional brewers, and micro-brewers. The mega-brewers are dominated by Labatt Breweries of Canada and Molson Breweries of Canada Limited. Great Western considers these two companies to be their main competition.

Regional brewers include Pacific Western, Drummond, Northern Breweries and the Great Western Brewing Company. These companies traditionally focus on a local market or region as their target market. Many regional brewers have become more aggressive in their marketing strategies in the hope of capturing a greater market share.

Micro-brewers are local companies that produce beer for consumption in their immediate markets. Brew-pubs are another form of micro-brewery which have emerged in Canada over the last 10 years. The beer is brewed and consumed on the premises and the capacity for production is very limited. Complete market information and comparative data can be found in the Appendices.

Product and Packaging

Great Western takes pride in using as many local ingedients in its beer as possible. Only the finest quality barley malt from Prairie Malt in Biggar (a Saskatchewan town) is used. Specially prepared corn 'grits' provide a lightness of flavour and, together with Canadian No. 1 red spring wheat from CSP Foods, form a small but important percentage of the brewer's recipe. Five different varieties of premium quality hops are selected for their particular aroma and bittering value, and are blended to produce the pleasant, hoppy character of Great Western beers. The mineral content of the Saskatchewan water is ideal for lager brewing and is readily used in production.

When Great Western began production it made only bottled beer. However, by July 1990 it had unveiled a canning line enabling the company to produce both bottled and canned beer. The brewing of canned beer had been opposed in Saskatchewan in the past because there was concern that the market was too small for the economics of a canning process to work.

When the Great Western Brewing Company first began operations it produced two types of beer, Great Western Lager and Great Western Light. The lager is a high-quality, 5% alcohol/volume lager beer brewed using the highest-quality natural raw materials. Great Western Light contains 4% alcohol/volume and has a clean, crisp flavour as a result of a slow, cool brewing process.

Then came Great Western Gold, a smooth, golden malt liquor with 6.5% alcohol/volume. Its heavy wheat content is used in order to identify strongly with Saskatchewan. Prairie 3.2, a beer to appeal to health and weight-conscious consumers, was the next beer to be introduced. It is brewed light and not diluted, to produce a low calorie beer with the full flavour characteristics of much stronger beers.

Great Western's efforts to find new recipes enabled it to introduce other products such as Gibbs Ale, a traditional English-style brew, and a special brand called Christmas Goose. The Christmas Goose brand was introduced during the 1991 Christmas season and is only offered during that season of the year.

On 11 May 1992, Great Western launched the seventh brand to be produced in the Saskatoon plant. Western Dry is 5.5% alcohol/volume and is only available in Saskatchewan at present.

Price

As with all competitors in the Canadian beer industry, the price charged for a case of Great Western beer is regulated by the Saskatchewan Liquor Board (see Appendix 8.12). The price is set according to the type of beer so competition occurs mainly in production costs rather than price. The following were the regulated beer prices in 1992:

Regular and Light brand (bottles)

6 pack	$7.19 including deposit
12 pack	$13.78 including deposit
24 pack	$27.11 including deposit

Price or Generic brands (bottles)

12 pack	$12.45 including deposit

Canned Beer (all brands)

6 pack	$7.66 including deposit
12 pack	$15.32 including deposit
24 pack	$30.64 including deposit

The Drummond beer company tried to overcome its inability to compete on the basis of price by placing CN$2 bills in its cases of beer. The Saskatchewan Liquor Board did not approve and Drummond was eventually punished by having its products removed from the market for 45 days.

Distribution

The sparsity of the population and the immense size of the province mean that the distribution of beer in Saskatchewan presents special challenges. A total of 1,600 licensed outlets must be serviced on a regular scheduled basis with all listed brands to be available for all licensees to order.

The four types of licensed outlets that may buy beer are as follows:

- Saskatchewan Liquor Board Stores. These are located in all cities and most towns.

- Hotels. These are located in all but the very smallest of hamlets, selling beer for consumption on the premises or through off-sale departments.

- Restaurants and bars.

- Special vendors. These are located in small centres with no liquor stores and sell beer along with other retail products in a 'corner store' operation.

All domestically brewed beer is distributed by the Saskatchewan Brewers Association (SBA), a company jointly owned by the two major brewers. As well as distributing beer, the SBA acts as the industry spokesman in discussions with the provincial government, hotel associations and so on whenever an agreed common position is required from the brewing industry.

SBA warehouses are located in the seven major centres across the province.

They receive bulk loads and draught beer from the breweries, which are broken down into loads for local delivery to licensees and liquor stores on a daily basis. The warehouses have no retail sales outlets but are required to operate bottle return facilities.

Beer orders for each of the seven warehouses are received by the brewery daily, via computer, for shipment the following day. The orders are in full pallet quantities of each brand and each order comprises a full truckload of 18, 20 or 24 pallets. Each warehouse's stock level is accessible by brand pack via a computer link to the brewery, as well as brand shipment figures in cases. If one or more brands are seen to be in short supply, the shipper asks the warehouse manager to transfer product in.

Great Western entered the Alberta and Manitoba markets early in 1991, and also works through agents to access US markets. Great Western Lager and Great Western Light are currently available in nine western and mid-western states.

Target Markets

Within Saskatchewan the prime target market area is Saskatoon and district, with the Regina area a very close second. The Saskatoon area has a slightly higher population than Regina, and the highly visible plant location, together with greater existing public awareness of, and loyalty to the brewery, make Saskatoon the number one sales target.

The target market for individual consumers differs for each of Great Western's brands. For example, the new Western Dry brand is targeted strictly towards a market made up of 50% men and 50% women aged between 24 and 35.

Marketing and Promotions

Going into competition with national companies which spend millions on brands and brand identities is a very risky business, but Great Western wisely relied on customer loyalty.

Great Western's main marketing strategy is to put all its efforts into selling beer at the grassroots level. It does not have millions of dollars to put into television commercials so it spends its advertising budget in other ways. The distinctive blue, red and gold Great Western label decorates team shirts throughout the province. Community ball teams, curling leagues, rodeos, King Trapper events, dog sleigh races and Riel Days in Saskatoon have all been supported by Great Western. The company has also funded local sports teams such as the Saskatoon Titans (a junior hockey team), Saskatchewan Storm (a professional basketball team) and several local baseball teams.

The first part of Great Western's marketing strategy is to create awareness and reciprocal support. The second is to offer consumers a unique, quality product they can't resist. With this in mind, the sales staff of seven takes the $800,000 marketing budget and invests it mainly in point-of-sale promotion, radio spots and newspaper ads. The total marketing cost for a brand of beer at Great Western is about CN$1 per dozen beers with less than 10% of that cost being spent on media advertising. Great Western also relies on its marketing representatives to promote its products and persuade people to drink its beer.

While its priority is still focused on the Saskatchewan market, Great Western is also constantly searching for new markets. The newly installed canning facility enables Great Western to ship canned beers to the neighbouring provinces of Manitoba and Alberta since transportation costs for canned beer are less than bottled beer. If Great Western can get 1% of these markets, it would be equivalent to increasing its Saskatchewan market share by 4%.

With the introduction of its newest beer, Western Dry, Great Western shifted its marketing focus to this brand. For the first six weeks after its launch, Western Dry was the only beer to be promoted. It was not promoted for the following six weeks but pushed again for another six weeks after that.

At the same time Great Western introduced its new sales manager. Jack Whyte was hired as vice-president of marketing and sales. He had spent the previous ten months with the Drummond Brewing Company in Edmonton and was with the Pepsi Cola company for seven years before that. Whyte's attitude is that Great Western should become a 'brand' rather than 'brewery' marketer and therefore focus on each brand individually. The new dry beer promotional campaign included two posters featuring local models and all the promotions are produced locally, which is another way Great Western supports its own community.

The Future

With several different beer brands now in production, Great Western is ready to look at the future. Peter McCann says there will be several major promotions during the season, but the company has no plans to launch any additional brands.

The Canadian beer industry is about to undergo a period of change with the removal of interprovincial trade barriers and the drafting of a new pricing structure. So far the industry has been slow to change and it now seems as if everything is changing at once. Imported beers are expected to achieve further penetration of the Saskatchewan market since the interprovincial barriers came down in July 1992.

While its priority is still in the Saskatchewan market, Great Western is always searching for new market developments. As already mentioned, it has entered other markets such as Manitoba and Alberta. The United States market has been another natural target for expansion. Great Western has also made efforts to obtain the licensing rights to produce a Chinese brand beer for sale in the United States.

The Saskatchewan men and women of Great Western Brewing have faith in the future of their province, and look forward to the opportunities and challenges which the future will bring to Western Canada's only employee-owned brewery.

Acknowledgement

This case was prepared as a basis for class discussion rather than to illustrate either effective or ineffective handling of an administrative situation. Appreciation is extended to Mr Peter B. McCann and Mr Jack Whyte who provided valuable information for the case. Acknowledgement is made to Mr Darryl Kotyk for his assistance in preparing this case.

Questions

After a period of three years the company has successfully built a reputation and solid market. With the removal of interprovincial trade barriers, the company faces an increasing number of competitors coming from other provinces and countries. The question is what to do next?

1) How much of the success of the company is due to its total market loyalty – can the company have a continuous success with the disappearance of interprovincial trade barriers?

2) Is the current promotion program used by the company strong enough to maintain the market competitiveness?

3) Do the company's current product lines have enough appeal to a wider market?

4) Is it wise to look into the international market now since the company is quite new and still small in size?

5) How vulnerable is the company since the interprovincial trade barriers have come down and what strategies could the company prepare to deal with a potential failure?

Appendix 8.1 *Estimated Total Sales of Canadian Produced and Packaged Beer in Canada (1990) (hectolitres)*

Month	Draught (A)	Bottles (B)	Cans (C)	Subtotal (A + B)	TOTAL (A + B + C)
January	139,361	870,424	191,287	1,061,711	1,201,072
February	140,965	921,656	192,587	1,114,243	1,255,208
March	165,586	1,092,413	238,110	1,330,523	1,496,109
April	160,469	1,170,657	264,668	1,435,325	1,595,794
May	174,456	1,346,857	334,568	1,681,425	1,855,881
June	175,492	1,468,672	421,148	1,889,820	2,065,312
July	175,527	1,436,462	475,920	1,912,382	2,087,909
August	191,791	1,455,967	480,771	1,936,738	2,128,529
September	144,365	1,055,790	303,282	1,359,072	1,503,437
October	168,091	1,126,054	278,759	1,404,813	1,572,904
November	162,052	1,115,860	247,938	1,636,798	1,525,850
December	150,316	1,369,507	284,321	1,653,828	1,804,144
Total	1,948,471	14,430,319	3,713,359	18,143,678	20,092,149

Source: Brewers Association of Canada, Annual Report, 1990.

Appendix 8.2 *Brands Available in Saskatchewan, August 1991*

Labatt	Carling	Molson
Blue	Fosters Lager	Canadian
50 Ale	*Colt 45	Coors
Budweiser	Miller High Life	Coors Lite
Bud Lite	Miller Lite	*Bohemian
Schooner	Old Vienna	Molson Golden
Labatt's Lite	Old Vienna Lite	Molson light
Guiness	Trilight	Pilsner
Labatt Dry	Extra Old Stock	
† Beer	Calgary Lager	

† Low Price Brand

Appendix 8.3 *World's Major Beer Producers Production (000's hectolitres)*

Country	1989	1988	1987
United States	233,619	232,265	229,297
Fed. Rep. Germany	93,017	92,493	92,602
U.S.S.R.	66,000	55,800	50,700
Japan	60,500	57,894	54,922
United Kingdom	60,015	60,155	59,897
China	60,000	55,000	50,000
Brazil	55,000	47,800	47,500
Mexico	39,131	34,534	29,157
Spain	27,337	26,579	25,842
Dem. Rep. Germany	24,800	24,400	25,000
Czechoslovakia	22,770	22,670	22,228
Canada	22,710	23,149	23,114
France	20,927	20,113	19,894
South Africa	18,680	18,340	18,000
Australia	18,700	19,500	18,765

Source: The Brewers Association of Canada, Annual Report, 1990.

Appendix 8.4 *Total 1988 United States Import Beer Market (Volume † Share)*

	Volume share (%)	Changes
Corona	16.1	+0.3
Heineken	13.9	−1.0
Molson	11.6	−0.8
Labatt's	7.1	+2.7
Becks	4.8	−0.3
Moosehead	4.4	−0.5
St. Pauli Girl	3.3	−0.5
Foster's Lager	3.2	+0.3
Molson Light	2.5	0.0
Dos Equis	2.4	−0.5
All Others	30.5	+0.1

† Volume expressed in 288-oz equivalent units.
Source: InfoScan.

Appendix 8.5   *Total 1988 United States Beer Market (Dollar Share)*

	Volume† share (%)	Dollar share (%)
Low Calorie/Light	34.2	34.2
Premium	31.5	33.4
Popular Price	24.3	18.2
Imports	4.8	8.0
Super Premium	3.2	4.1
Malt Liquor	1.1	1.1
Low/Non-Alcoholic	0.9	0.9

† Volume expressed in 288-oz equivalent units.
Source: InfoScan.

Appendix 8.6   *Comparative Income Statements: 1990 ($000's)*

	Labatt	Molson	Great Western
Gross Sales	5,274,000	2,549,957	8,306
Operating Costs and Expenses			
Cost of Sales, Selling and Administration	4,283,000	1,871,980	7,605
Depreciation and Amortization	134,000	56,847	295
Net Interest Expense	33,000	25,784	283
Operating Income before Income Taxes	231,000	167,296	274
Income Taxes	72,000	59,809	43
Net Income	169,000	117,911	231

NOTE:
1. Labatt's fiscal year end is April 30; Molson's is March 31; and Great Western is December 31.
2. Only 32.15% of Labatt's gross revenue but 75.32% operating income before income taxes were from brewing activities.
3. 53.83% of Molson's gross revenue and 77.31% of operating income before income taxes were from brewing activities.
4. Information regarding Labatt and Molson is from the 1990 Annual Reports of the respective companies.

Appendix 8.7   *Comparative Balance Sheets 1990 ($000's)*

	Labatt	Molson	Great Western
ASSETS			
Current Asset			
Cash and Accounts Receivable	718,000	691,996	910
Inventories	397,000	255,025	1,064
Other Current Assets	69,000	65,131	61
Total Current Asset	1,184,000	707,711	2,036
Non-Current Asset			
Property, Plant and Equipment	1,181,000	538,749	4,787
Other Non-Current Assets	581,000	595,453	0
Total Non-Current Assets	1,762,000	1,134,202	4,787
Total Assets	2,946,000	1,841,913	6,823

Appendix 8.7 *continued*

LIABILITIES
Current Liabilities

Account Payable and accrued liab.	557,000	305,267	1,194
Current Portion of Long Term Debt	26,000	37,996	394
Other Current Liabilities	45,000	49,202	0
Total Current Liabilities	628,000	592,465	1,588
Long Term Liabilities			
Long Term Debt	544,000	252,960	3,741
Other Long Term Liabilities	130,000	270,749	0
Total Long Term Liabilities	674,000	523,709	3,741
Total Liabilities	1,302,000	1,116,174	5,329

SHAREHOLDERS' EQUITY

Convertible Debentures	277,000	0	0
Share Capital	595,000	145,907	1,263
Retained Earnings	801,000	601,641	231
Cumulative Translation Adjustment	(29,000)	(21,809)	0
Total Shareholders' Equity	1,644,000	725,739	1,494
Total Liabilities and S/E	2,946,000	1,841,913	6,823

Appendix 8.8 *Comparative Statistics (1990)*

	Molson	Labatt	Great Western
Net Sales ($'000)	$2,549,957	5,274,000	8,306
Net Income ($'000)	117,911	169,000	231
Number of Employees	13,900	16,000	45
Net Sales per Employee	183,450	339,000	184,578
Profit per Employee	12,036	14,438	6,089
Total Assets per Employee	132,512	184,125	151,622

• Profit per Employee Calculated using Income Before Taxes.
• Great Western's net sales and net income are estimates.
Source: From the 1990 Annual Reports of the respective companies.

Appendix 8.9 *Canadian Market Shares (1972–88)*

	72	73	74	75	76	77	78
Labatt	33.9	36.9	35.9	36.6	37.6	38.4	38.6
MBC	29.2	30.5	31.6	33.5	33.6	33.9	34.1
Carling	30.6	28.3	26.1	25.3	24.9	24.1	23.2
Other	5.3	4.0	6.1	4.2	3.3	2.9	3.2
Imports	0.3	0.3	0.3	0.4	0.6	0.7	0.9
Total	100.0	100.0	100.0	100.0	100.0	100.0	100.0

Source: TMCL, Brewers Association of Canada, and Statistics Canada.

Appendix 8.9 *continued*

79	80	81	82	83	84	85	86	87	88
36.6	36.5	34.9	36.7	36.3	34.6	38.0	39.1	40.3	41.9
36.2	35.9	35.1	35.8	34.7	31.5	30.6	29.8	31.5	31.6
22.7	23.2	22.8	23.1	24.3	28.2	25.0	22.8	22.0	19.6
3.5	3.5	3.8	2.9	3.6	4.2	4.8	4.5	4.7	4.7
1.0	0.9	3.4	1.5	1.1	1.5	1.6	3.8	1.5	2.2
100.0	100.0	100.0	100.0	100.0	100.0	100.0	100.0	100.0	100.0

Appendix 8.10 *Provincial Market Share Data at November 30, 1989*

	Percentage Share			Percentage of
	MOLSON	CARLING	LABATT	Canada Sales
Newfoundland	19	28	53	2.3%
Nova Scotia	–	–	82	3.0
Prince Edward Island	2	–	53	0.4
New Brunswick	–	–	43	2.3
Quebec	33	31	36	26.1
Ontario	40	15	41	39.6
Manitoba	14	29	57	3.9
Saskatchewan	40	23	37	2.9
Alberta	42	20	29	8.2
British Columbia	26	22	44	10.9
NWT/Yukon	–	–	–	0.3
				100.0%

Source: Molson, Labatt Breweries.

Appendix 8.11 *Great Western Brewing Company Limited Proforma Income Statements* ($'000s)

	1991	1992	1993	1994
SALES	8,306	10,902	11,447	12,019
Cost of Goods Sold	4,074	5,339	5,543	5,753
Distribution and Freight	934	1,375	1,589	1,825
Total Cost of Goods Sold	5,008	6,714	7,132	7,577
GROSS PROFIT	3,298	4,188	4,314	4,442
OVERHEAD EXPENSES				
Engineering	415	561	572	584
Brewing	80	108	116	122
Marketing	651	880	943	990
Quality Control	28	38	41	43
Administration	430	564	576	587
Salaries and Benefits	1,288	1,327	1,353	1,380
Interest	283	243	209	180
Out of Province Marketing	0	250	268	281
Total Overhead Expenses	3,175	3,971	4,077	4,166

Appendix 8.11 *continued*

NET OPERATING INCOME	123	216	237	275
Other Income	151	70	72	75
NET INCOME BEFORE TAXES	274	286	309	350
Income Taxes	79	84	93	109
NET INCOME	195	203	217	242

ASSUMPTIONS:
1. 5% growth in sales every year.
2. 1991 sales figures have been adjusted by 27.5% over 1990 figures to reflect 12 months' operations and inflation.
3. 3% inflation in 1991 and 2% thereafter.
4. 1.5% decrease in COGS each year because of increasing utilization of plant.
5. 1% increase in distribution and freight each year because of increasing out of province distribution.
6. Interest payment decreases because of amortization of loan.
7. 25% tax rate for the first $200,000 profit, and 39% on the additional profits.

Appendix 8.12 *Beer Prices for Various Beer Brands (Price in Canadian Dollars and Effective Date 27 July 1992)*

BOTTLED BEER

Beer Brand	Quantity	Price
	(including taxes and deposit)	
GW Gold	6	$7.20
Old Stock	6	7.10
GW Gold	12	13.90
Old Stock	12	13.65
Blue	6	7.25
Bohemian	6	7.10
Budweiser	6	7.25
Canadian	6	7.10
Guinness	6	7.00
GW Lager	6	7.20
Kokanee	6	7.40
Labatt Extra Dry	6	7.40
Labatt Dry	6	7.25
Molson Dry	6	7.40
Old Vienna	6	7.10
Pisner	6	7.10
Western Dry	6	7.20
50 Ale	12	13.95
Blue	12	13.95
Bohemian	12	12.95
Budweiser	12	13.95
Calgary	12	13.65
Canadian	12	13.65
Colt 45	12	13.65
Coors	12	13.65
Gibbs Ale	12	13.90
GW Lager	12	13.90
Kokanee	12	14.25
Bud Light	6	7.25
Coors Light	6	7.10
GW Light	6	7.20
Labatt Lite	6	7.25
Bud Light	12	13.95
Canadian Light	12	13.65
GW Light	12	13.90
Labatt Lite	12	13.95
Molson Special 3.3	12	13.65
OV Light	12	13.65
GW Light	24	27.20
Labatt Lite	24	27.35
Prairie 3.2	6	6.80
Prairie 3.2	12	13.30

CANNED BEER

Beer Brand	Quantity	Price
	(including taxes and deposit)	
GW Gold	6	$7.60
Blue	6	7.70
Budweiser	6	7.70
Canadian	6	7.60
GW Lager	6	7.60
Kokanee	6	7.70
Labatt Extra Dry	6	7.90
Labatt Genuine Draft	6	7.70
Molson Dry	6	7.90
Old Vienna	6	7.60

Appendix 8.12   *continued*

Labatt			Pilsner	6	7.60
Classic	12	15.00	Western Dry	6	7.60
Labatt Extra			Bud Light	6	7.70
Dry	12	14.25	Coors Light	6	7.60
Labatt Genuine			**GW Light**	6	7.60
Draft	12	13.95	Labatt Lite	6	7.70
Labatt Dry	12	13.95	Molson Special		
Lucky Lager	12	11.95	3.3	6	7.60
Molson Dry	12	14.25	**Prairie 3.2**	6	7.45
Old Vienna	12	13.65	Labatt Lite	15	18.25
Pilsner	12	13.65			
Western Dry	12	13.90			
Blue	24	27.35			
Canadian	24	26.95			
GW Lager	24	27.20			
Old Vienna	24	26.95			

CASE 9
PPP
Strategic Marketing

Victor Gray and Rob Lawson
University of Otago, New Zealand

Company History

PPP has one of the longest histories of any recruitment consultancy in New Zealand, commencing business 22 years ago. Three separate companies formed the group and traded separately and profitably through the 1970s and early 1980s. The major shareholders used profits to pursue other business interests during this period. The company was not in a strong position to withstand the substantial downturn in the economy and rationalization within the industry following the 1987/88 stock market crash.

PPP has a forecast revenue for the current year of $2.5m[†], 1.6% of the national market and 3.7% of its geographically feasible market. Its feasible market is greater Auckland which contains quarter of the population of New Zealand. There are 240 recruitment agencies and 110 within the Auckland area. Although research is not available to substantiate it, PPP management are confident that their geographic area has a greater than one-third share of the recruitment business.

The Market

The estimated total market revenues for the next year are divided into five categories:

	$m
Temporary office staff	78
Permanent office staff	34
Professional contracting	28
Executive recruitment	18
Executive search (headhunting)	2
Total	160

[†]All figures in the case refer to NZ dollars. $1 NZ currently exchanges at 40 p.

This is based on an analysis of major daily newspaper advertisements. PPP can rightfully claim at least one-third of that market revenue is within the geographic area it can adequately service. The Auckland area has a higher revenue per head of population than the rest of the country.

Auckland is New Zealand's largest urban area. Greater Auckland incorporates a number of cities and can for almost all purposes other than local authority elections be considered one large urban area. The conurbation is 30 km long from north to south and accommodates more that 850,000 people, a quarter of the country's population. Auckland is also the country's leading port, airport and commercial and industrial centre. The area is New Zealand's fastest growing region, and is considered to be its most cosmopolitan, while the Auckland population reflects the generally high standard of living in New Zealand.

The company operates in the four target areas of recruitment consultancy: executive recruitment, professional contracting, permanent office staff and temporary office staff. To date it has segmented the market as follows

(1) Executive Recruitment
   • Accounting and finance
   • Sales and marketing
   • Legal services
   • Data processing
   • General management
   • Technical engineering

(2) Professional Contracting
Provides executives to any or all of the above segments on a temporary or contract basis.

(3) Office Support Staff
   • Executive secretarial
   • General secretary
   • Computing word processing
   • Account clerks
   • General clerical
   • Payroll
   • Office management
   • Bank personnel
   • Legal secretaries
   • Medical secretaries
   • Sales and marketing
   • Stocktaking staff
   • Warehouse staff
   • Promotional staff
All of the above on a permanent or temporary basis.

The industry is dominated by a few major players (see Appendix 9.1). The top five constitute 48% of the total industry revenue. The remainder of the market is split between a large number of reasonably successful smaller companies and a host of boutique type operations that are dealing in specific market segments.

The management team of PPP are confidently poised to join the big time.

In an attempt to revitalize the company a joint venture (JV) partner from within the industry was attracted. The JV moved to a new location with a resulting change in rent from $12,000 to $200,000. The effect of this increase in overhead was evidenced more in the 1989 than in the 1988 results. The JV failed and litigation between the two partners commenced. The lack of market focus and uncertainty during the last 12 months of litigation has had a negative effect on staff and profit.

To date the company has operated under various trading names, the last being ABC Recruitment. A new company has now been formed called People People People Ltd. It will use PPP as its logo.

The new company will acquire the net tangible assets of the old company and will have a capital of $300,000 shared among the existing shareholders and a major new non-industry partner, Mr R Fraser. The net tangible assets of the company are $600,000 in the form of office furniture and equipment.

A bank loan will be raised to provide working capital for restructuring and development of the business. Two new branch offices will be opened in the suburbs of Auckland. The main office is operating in a high profile building in the heart of the city.

To substantiate the mainly anecdotal information the company had regarding the market, Mr Fraser commissioned a qualitative market research exercise. The highlights of this are as follows.

Market Research

One hundred companies were approached from a range of industries, 75% of which had a turnover of over $10 million annually.

The people interviewed were usually personnel officers or equivalent. Sometimes the appropriate contact was the financial controller, company secretary or general manager.

Question: which companies use personnel consultants?

- Almost 100% had used agencies for seniors through to temps.

- On an annual basis, most small to medium-sized companies used agencies up to 10 times, and larger companies used them more often for temps, short-term and longer-term appointments.

- No companies utilized executive leasing.

- A wide variety of companies were mentioned. Lampen and Drake were always mentioned for temps and clerical, and many others at that level.

Question: *Why do they use consultancies?*

- Access to range of candidates and effective use of management time.
- Candidate screening.

Question: *How do they advertise for recruiting?*

- Almost all sometimes advertise themselves, but usually not simultaneously.
- Many advertise for a few days, then if unsuccessful they use an agency.
- In the past, the economy and employment were stable and good candidates hard to find. Today there are so many good people looking for work that neither the people nor the company need to go through agencies.

Question: *What attracted them to the consultants they use?*

- Personal contact and reputation rated highest, with the other reasons hardly rating at all.
- Comments were that they were attracted by previous association, reliability, professional approach and confidence.
- Personal visits and ability to meet the company's needs.

Question: *Importance of personnel services in order of preference:*

(1) Understanding company's needs.
(2) Personal contact and industry knowledge.
(3) Confidentiality.
(4) Resumé and speed of appointment.
(5) Follow-up work and cost.
(6) Guarantee usually last because, in general, they say agents can only guarantee for a certain time and no one can foresee the future.

Question: *Which companies were they aware of and used?*

- ABC's name – majority had heard of, but a minority had actually used.
- Drake and Lampen – all companies knew and most had used.

- Opal – well known.
- Arthur Young, WD Scott, Ernst & Whinney, Peat Marwick: usually known because they are large accounting firms.
- Used for accounting appointments occasionally, but often used as consultants/auditors, instead of recruitment agents.
- Sheffield and Morgan and Banks used a lot for senior and intermediate staff.
- High tech companies use a lot of specialized agencies.

Comments

Positive comments usually referred to a particular experience where the appointment was successful:

- Good industry knowledge.
- Client kept up to date.
- Experience of agency/consultant.
- Professionalism.
- Specialization.

Negative:

- High fees – pricing themselves out of business, especially in today's economic climate where companies are cutting costs.
- Not screening properly was a widespread comment.
- Sending unsuitable and too many candidates.
- Lack of professional ethics.
- Soliciting from ads.
- Poor resumés and research.
- Concern only with making an appointment and getting fees.
- High turnover of consultants (no continuity).

Recommendations

The following recommendations are based on the information acquired from the research interviews.

Existing Clients

Consultants should make personal visits to companies to keep in touch with their clients' particular requirements, and adopt a professional approach. Let them know you are there to find out about their needs, changes, developments and to see how the agency placements are working out and to receive any complaints and suggestions.

Client servicing

Keep up to date with the client's position, because familiarity with the consultant is important. Ensure the consultant understands the clients' needs and the particular industry they are dealing with.

Personal visits should be made periodically, not just when the client has a vacancy. When there is a vacancy, the consultant should visit the particular manager who is interviewing.

Newsletters/bulletins

- Keep them up to date with any changes within PPP.
- Let them be aware of candidates on file.
- Give your professional view of current employment including trends, salaries and so on.

Fee structure

In today's economic climate it might be advisable to be negotiable on fees if clients feel strongly about paying too much. It should be worth cutting the fee rather than losing a client. Many commented on this and had stopped using agents because of it.

Consultants and candidates

When working on a particular placement, make sure the right consultant is handling the appointment.

Conclusion

Judging from the comments overall, the screening of candidates needs to be more thorough. Perhaps more reference checking is required. Narrow the shortlist to three or four, and start again if these fail.

Make sure you have the right professional, experienced personnel people (with PPP). Too often the consultants are from other backgrounds and have not had the experience in personnel work, interviewing, character judgement, and so on. If they are on commission they must not let this be the driving force for an appointment – they must be able to match the candidate and the company. So much depends on reputation and a professional approach.

Staff Training In-House

Make them aware of the results of this survey, especially the negative responses. Consultants should share experiences, comments, suggestions and complaints. They should be aware at all times of changes and developments/trends within the industries they are dealing with.

Follow-up

Show you care about both candidate and the client. Don't forget about them after the appointment or even the guarantee period.

Thank them for their business. Make them feel appreciated. They will spread the word and recommend your business if they receive good service.

Business Plan

Following the market research the executive team met and decided to reposition PPP so as to actively compete against the market leaders. To do this the management team knows that the company will have to be discernibly different from its competitors.

Listed below are the key aspects of their strategic thinking to achieve the required differentiation.

(1) Full training for all staff as a major priority. Individual training and development programmes will form the backbone of staff training. Regular company sessions will be utilized to develop a team approach to meeting organizational goals.

(2) Replacement or upgrading of consulting staff by attracting industry qualified professionals from competing firms. Consultants will be measured by their individual budgets, using revenue and placement targets that are consistent or better than the industry average. If consultants do not meet their targets over a predetermined time where full support for achieving them has been given by the company, then they will be replaced.

(3) Development of an aggressive marketing programme, including client visits, advertising and prospect development, to reinforce the quality of service provided by a medium-sized company. This will include new brochures, point-of-sale devices, corporate logos, letterheads, direct mail pieces, corporate breakfasts and appropriate image advertising.

(4) Increase the number of consultants by attracting performers from within the industry. Packages will be developed that will include active participation in the organization.

(5) Improve the company's image by emphasis on client paid advertising on a regular basis in the Auckland daily newspaper and other appropriate trade publications.

(6) Implement a detailed financial control package including:
   (a) full budget format
   (b) monthly P & L down to individual consultant
   (c) in-house processing of debtors
   (d) computerized wages for 'temps'
   (e) cashflow reporting

(7) Develop, utilizing 'off the shelf' software, a user-friendly related database that will enable consultants and management to operate more efficiently.

Positioning of PPP (an extract from the Corporate Plan)

The management team of People People People (PPP) believe the company is uniquely positioned in New Zealand as the only New Zealand owned full service recruitment agency.

PPP will focus on two broad market segments: (executive) permanent recruitment, and office support and contracting.

The company must deal with senior executives who are the decision-makers, rather than merely influencers. As a result, long-term client relationships are developed at senior level, and PPP develops its network through the career paths of particular executives as they move through their organization, or from company to company.

The focus must be on strong client bonding to provide understanding of client needs, a personal service, keeping clients fully informed of assignment progress, and developing a high sense of urgency.

The quality of service between both broad segments of the business must be paralleled to ensure overall service standards. The brand awareness programme will lift PPP's profile in the marketplace as the only viable option to the market leaders. Detailed programming of new client prospects and enhancement of the present client base, programmed over the ensuing 12 months, will further develop the company profile.

Resources (extract from Budget)

Turnover projection shows a considerable increase to $3,545,000 (11 months). In principle this is derived by adding new consultants to the existing base.

New suburb

Office Support	1
Office Executive Recruitment	1
Temporary/Office Support	1

City

Office Support	2
Temporary Office Support	1
Executive Recruitment	4
Executive Leasing	1

The start dates of these consultants have been phased, recognizing the lead time required before a consultant becomes productive.

A number of the new staff have already been selected and are programmed to commence within the budget timetable.

Additional overheads have been added:

New Computer System (start-up costs)	$65,000
(to meet marketing targets and improve consultant productivity)	
Financial Consultant	$30,000
(to advise and assist in the computerization of financial data)	
Marketing Consultant	$40,000
(to create and implement a full marketing plan)	

The pre-tax profit projection of $800,000 reflects the increased turnover and improvements in consultant productivity.

Bank funding support of $325,000 is available to service growth and the one-off increases in overhead. The company will, by year end, produce positive cashflow with the overdraft facility projected to decrease by the budget end.

Conclusion

The management of PPP are ready to attack and make their mark. The injection of Mr Fraser's new thinking and enthusiasm have refocused the whole company with a renewed commitment to success. They recognize that people make the difference in a service business. They see themselves as different and hence the expected impact on the market will be significant.

The positioning and overall strategy are set. The funding support of $325,000 is available.

Questions

(1) What are the significant features of buying behaviour for recruitment services?

(2) How may the market for recruitment services be segmented?

(3) What is the competitive situation faced by PPP?

(4) How well does the PPP strategy incorporate the competitive variables?

(5) What do you think of PPP's overall strategy?

Appendix 9.1   *Major Players in the New Zealand Recruitment Industry (as at 1989)*

Name	Owned by	Estimated revenue/ pre-tax profit	Geographic spread in New Zealand	Comments
Opal Consulting	ADT Ltd, a very large UK service firm	$18 m/$1.5 m	Auckland Wellington	Aggressive company, out to grow and increase market share. Considerable expenditure on development.
Morgan and Banks	Select, a UK company	$24 m/$6 m	Auckland Wellington London, USA Australia	Not as focused as it has been in recent years. Sizeable lease programme.
Sheffield Consulting	Private company, restricted shareholdership	$22 m/$5 m	Auckland Wellington Christchurch London, Sydney	Senior executive market. Well respected, high quality of service. Heavy user of newspaper advertising.
Drake Personnel	Drake International, a US-based company	$11 m/ unknown, thought to be negative	Auckland	Very strong in office support market.
Lampen Group	Roger Lampen, a New Zealander	$2 m/ unknown	Auckland Wellington (London)	Strong in office support market. Recently launched into middle management recruitment.

Note Market share figures are unreliable because the industry does not compare like with like service and no two figures comprise the same mix of services. Both Morgan and Banks and Sheffield claim market leadership.
All pay staff on commission except Sheffield Consulting.

CASE 10
Grand Prix Motor Racing Innovation
Innovation Strategies

Brian R. Johnston
University of Westminster

Gordon R. Foxall
University of Birmingham

(1) TEAM LOTUS INTERNATIONAL LTD

Company History

Colin Chapman, a graduate in mechanical engineering, set up the Lotus organization by converting an Austin Seven into a 'special' by adding new plywood body panels and strengthening the chassis. He registered the car as the 'Lotus Mk 1' and successfully competed in trials competitions. Following his national service in the RAF Mr Chapman constructed a Mk 2 Lotus in 1951 for use in circuit racing as well as performing as a road-going car. With the success of the Lotus special in the 750 Formula, Mr Chapman was asked to build other cars for members of the 750 Motor Club. He set up a workshop behind his father's public house in Hornsey where, in 1952, he formed Lotus Engineering. The company at first manufactured and supplied parts for the 750 Formula cars but soon Mr Chapman began designing his own trials competition cars. The Mk 6 Lotus was the first car not based on the Austin Seven but designed and built entirely by Lotus Engineering.

In 1954 Mr Chapman formed Team Lotus to design and build sports racing cars, the first being the Mk 8, the forerunner of several Lotus sports cars that would provide the team with the facilities and experience to produce their own Grand Prix cars. Chapman's ability in chassis design was proven as early as 1955 when he was approached by the Vanwall Grand Prix team to design a new chassis which became the famous 'teardrop' Vanwall. Another Grand Prix team, BRM, enlisted Mr Chapman as a consultant on suspension systems, in which role he increased his knowledge of the current state of Grand Prix racing. In 1955, Colin Chapman left his full-time job with the British Aluminium Company to concentrate on his Lotus involvement. In 1958 Lotus produced its first Grand Prix car, the Mk 12, its inaugural race being the Monaco Grand Prix of that year.

Lotus Elite

Mr Chapman was initially not keen to become a manufacturer of road-going cars, but sales of competition cars were highly seasonal and in order to build up the business the company offered variations on pure racing cars to a wider market. As the company grew, it sought manufacturing methods that were compatible with the short runs of a small firm. Pressed steel chassis and body panels and the tooling they necessitated were expensive and the racing chassis technology (a steel tube space frame on to which alloy panels were riveted) was impracticable.

The alternative was a method well known to boatbuilders but not employed frequently by commercial automobile producers – glass fibre-reinforced plastic. By encasing some of the chassis steel in the glass fibre body material, Lotus produced its first road-going vehicle, the Type 14 Lotus Elite. Although the car was always noisy, it was well received, perhaps largely on account of the racing technology values it incorporated: its 'race bred suspension originally developed for the Type 12 single seater racing car', for instance, as well as 'the splendid rigidity of the body shell, coupled with the almost perfect weight distribution'. Moreover, 'the car handled beautifully and driving it was the nearest thing to driving a racing car' (Crombac 1986; 83). Lotus had become a specialist automobile manufacturer.

The replacement for the Lotus Elite was to have an open top (aimed at the US West Coast market) but it was difficult to attain the required rigidity using glass-reinforced plastic. Chapman conceived a steel wishbone-shaped box chassis that encased the engine and transmission and, more significantly, gave the body shell the rigidity it needed. This design became the Type 26 Lotus Elan.

Lotus Cortina

While sales of the Lotus Elite were strong in volume terms, the company lost money on each car sold. When the new model Elan was being designed, therefore, manufacturing costs were held to a minimum. One of the major capital costs was the engine: the Ford Consul engine was attractive but impracticable. The Ford Motor Company, however, had begun to produce a smaller unit, a 1000 cc engine which, despite its positive qualities, was underpowered for the sports car. At Mr Chapman's instigation Lotus designed a twin-cam cylinder head based around the Ford engine that would increase power sufficiently for the requirements of the Elan.

At this time, Ford was about to introduce a new 1500 cc engine. The company's Director of Public Affairs, Walter Hayes, conceived the idea of combining Lotus and Ford in a project aimed at strengthening the image of Ford's range, with the particular object of attracting the younger market. Using the 'Lotus Ford' twin-cam engine fitted into a standard two-door Ford Cortina saloon car, Mr Hayes 'offered Chapman the heaven sent opportunity to redesign the Cortina's rear suspension, dress the car up a bit and market it as the Lotus Cortina (Type 28) and assemble it at the Lotus factory' (Crombac 1986: 137).

The car, introduced in 1963, became an immediate success both as a road car and as a racing car, although production problems at the Lotus factory delayed Ford's racing programmes that season. Ford later increased the capacity of the Cortina to 1600 cc for racing purposes and Lotus also began to use it in the modified Elan road car. The Lotus Cortina competed in numerous racing categories, through both private entrants and as a 'works' Lotus team, and served its purpose as an 'image builder' for Ford's marketing and promotional programmes.

Ford had been seeking to acquire a small, prestige European car manufacturer to consolidate its racing operations, particularly with a view to winning the 24-hour endurance race at Le Mans. Ford had tried and failed to buy Ferrari in 1962 and other viable firms had subsequently been investigated as potential production facilities for the Ford GT 40 Le Mans project. It was inevitable that the company would see Lotus as a contender for this project given the successful Lotus Cortina project. However, after informal discussions with Mr Chapman, who did not take the threat to his company too seriously, and Lotus executives, Ford did not pursue the takeover on grounds of incompatibility.

The Ford/Lotus Cortina association ended after three successful years during which more than 1,250 cars had been built and the new manufacturer had learned a lot about car production from the established manufacturer:

'they [Ford] gave us support with buying and taught us such things as quality control, and they virtually forced us into developing the management structure so obviously necessary to cope with the increase in output by encouraging us to hire the right type of senior managers and experienced quality controllers' (Crombac 1986: 187).

Production of the twin-cam engine, which eventually came to be fully manufactured and assembled at the Lotus factory, continued until 1975. It was later revived by the Caterham Car Company which took over the manufacturing rights to the Lotus Seven sports car and which continues to produce the car (and spare parts) in small numbers for the Lotus specialist.

The success of the Elan led to the extension of the original range. Having suffered difficulties with the Elan body suppliers, who had difficulty producing the volume required and maintaining quality, Lotus took over the mould and tooling and began producing the bodies itself. The replacement that Lotus Cars Ltd had designed, the Europa (Type 46), used a Renault power unit to avoid overdependence on Ford. Production of the Elan ended in 1973 and that of the Europa in 1976. They were replaced by a new model, the Type 75 again called the Elite, the glass fibre-reinforced plastic bodyshell being moulded by a new vacuum process that Chapman had originally conceived for the manufacture of better quality boat hulls.

The VARI System

The development of glass-reinforced plastic (GRP) as a material for motor vehicles began as early as the 1930s when the German Auto Union company began to manufacture plastic body panels. The material proved to have excellent moulding properties, a good strength-to-weight ratio, and relatively inexpensive production costs. By the 1950s, there were several small British manufacturers producing cars with glass-reinforced plastic body panels, notably TVR, Reliant, Bond and Lotus.

For a number of years, Lotus used 'hand lay-up' methods of manufacture but sought to increase the volume and control of its production by developing a more sophisticated method. With the introduction of the Elite (and later the Eclat and Esprit), aimed primarily at the US market, there was also a need to find a method that could produce bodies that met certain US safety criteria. For example, 'to maintain the car's performance, it was necessary to find a way of controlling the glass/resin ratio and wall thickness of the mouldings. The resin injection system helped meet this need' (Wood 1980: 124).

The moulding is accomplished by vacuum assisted resin injection in which atmospheric pressure is used for mould clampings and the resin is injected into a closed mould previously loaded with reinforced materials after which a vacuum is applied.

By designing the bodies as two-piece mouldings with the joint horizontal along the waistline, Lotus found it could not only simplify each moulding but also, by using only three moulds (one lower and two uppers) produce two body styles. The system, later patented as the VARI (Vacuum Assisted Resin Injection) system, reduced the number of tools required for manufacture, drastically cut manufacturing time and maintained constant quality of the finished bodyshells. Lotus management believed that 'with this revolutionary process, the company was the world leader in fibreglass technology and bettered the quality and cost of the back street manufacturers which constituted most of the industry' (Ellis 1982: 589).

The Ford Cosworth DFV V8 Engine

The governing body of Grand Prix motor racing is constantly reviewing the regulations regarding the design and construction of the cars. Constructors, working towards the goal of producing machines that are both faster and more reliable than those used by other contestants, design cars which are capable of greater cornering and straightline speeds with the result that the dangers of high-speed accidents are increased. In 1961, in an effort to reduce such speeds, the engine capacity had been reduced from 2.5 litres to 1.5 litres. This change was in part a response to the public outcry that had resulted from the deaths of a number of Grand Prix drivers as well as from a general regard for the overall image of the sport which was still clouded by the 1955 Le Mans disaster.

The Commission Sportive Internationale (CSI) announced in 1964 that from January 1966 the World Championship Grands Prix would be contested under a new set of regulations. The most important change was the introduction of engines of up to 3 litres displacement (3000 cc) with normal air induction of 1.5 litres (1500 cc) if supercharged (using forced air induction); also permitted were rotary engines of the Wankel type and gas turbine engines. The change was important for British teams which for some years had been enjoying an upturn in their fortunes. Improvements in chassis design, engine power and reliability had given considerable advantages to teams such as Lotus, Brabham, Cooper and BRM and the new formula's guarantee of greater power output was expected to assist their continued domination of the sport. British Grand Prix teams waited, therefore, to see what the 'home' engine manufacturers would produce under the new rules.

Of the two British engine manufacturers, BRM and Coventry Climax, only BRM announced an intention to produce a new racing unit in the wake of the regulation changes. Early in 1965, Coventry Climax decided on financial grounds to withdraw from further involvement in motor racing. Its decision came as a blow to the Lotus, Brabham and Cooper marques since they were now effectively without an engine supplier. During the succeeding months these teams sought alternative power units with which to start the 1966 season. BRM began the development of its 16 cylinder H configuration 3 litre engine; Brabham opted for a General Motors V8 production unit; Cooper concluded a deal to use the V12 engine produced by the Italian Maserati company (though it later switched to a simplified V12 BRM engine). Team Lotus also initially chose the BRM engine but Mr Chapman subsequently opted for a longer-term view which had far-reaching consequences for the development of Grand Prix motor sport.

Colin Chapman was convinced that there was a need for a light, compact engine around which he could develop a lightweight, aerodynamically superior chassis. He argued that British motor sport had played a significant part in the success of its commercial car industry abroad and that consequently there should be some form of return from the industry. Mr Chapman approached the Society of Motor Manufacturers and Traders with a proposal for an engine that would be financed, designed and developed by one or more of its members. Although this plan received a sympathetic hearing and was the subject of government lobbying, no firm offer was forthcoming. Chapman had talks with the British Ford Motor Company and Aston Martin, but was unable to conclude a deal.

In his campaign to promote the idea, Mr Chapman had met Walter Hayes. Ford had embarked on a worldwide marketing and promotional project, the Total Performance Image, and Mr Hayes was keen to extend the company's involvement in motor sport as part of the major role Ford of Britain was to play in this campaign. Ford's early influence in the sport was extensive, and its position in motor racing had already brought it into contact with Lotus. With the introduction of the Ford Cortina GT (the engine of which had been developed by Lotus, which was also responsible for suspension modifications and the final assembly of the vehicle), Walter Hayes saw the potential in Chapman's idea and in his capacity as Head of Competitions he conceived a proposal for a Ford Grand Prix engine that would spearhead the Total Performance concept.

Together with Harley Copp, Vice President in charge of Engineering for Ford of Britain, Mr Hayes convinced the Ford Policy Committee that the proposal would be beneficial to the company's image. The committee approved a budget of £100,000 for the design and development of two engines, one suitable for Grand Prix racing, the other for Formula Two. The choice of designer was, for Mr Hayes, already settled. Through Chapman and Lotus, he had already formed an association with a company that specialized in competition derivatives of Ford engines. The engine would be designed by its chief executive, Keith Duckworth, an innovative design engineer with practical experience of racing engines. The company was called Cosworth Engineering.

(2) COSWORTH ENGINEERING

Company History

Cosworth Engineering Ltd was formed in 1958 by Keith Duckworth, a graduate engineer, and Mike Costin, a former employee of the De Havilland Aircraft Company. Both men had worked for Lotus Cars Ltd and had discussed the formation of an engineering business to develop and tune racing engines. Initially Mr Duckworth became the major force within the business as Mr Costin had accepted a three-year contract as Technical Director of Lotus Cars and was precluded from pursuing external work during this period. In 1962, he became a full-time director of Cosworth Engineering Ltd.

The company's reputation for high standards of race preparation and the development of Coventry Climax engines ensured a steady workload and a fortuitous involvement with one customer found Mr Duckworth designing and building a Formula Junior racing car. This customer, who worked for Ford of Britain, disclosed that the company was introducing a new engine to power the forthcoming Ford Anglia 105E production saloon car. Thinking that this might make a suitable racing engine for Formula Junior, Mr Duckworth acquired a stock unit, modified it to produce a substantial increase in power output and began to dominate the formula.

In 1963, the CSI announced that Formula Junior was to be replaced by two new classes, Formula Two and Formula Three, the former allowing engines that could be extensively redesigned. Walter Hayes, Ford's Director of Public Affairs, was eager to associate Ford of Britain with Formula Two and, knowing of Mr Duckworth's ability and experience with Ford engines, financed his company to design and develop an engine that was based on the Ford Cortina 116E 1600 cc cylinder block. The resulting unit was fast, efficient and reliable and won the Formula Two championship in 1964 and 1965.

One of the main elements in Hayes's proposed Ford Grand Prix engine was the involvement of Cosworth Engineering as principal design and development engineers and he was able to use Cosworth's success as a major factor in the presentation of his scheme to the Ford Policy Committee. The agreement between Ford and Cosworth was as follows:

'(1) In consideration of the payment by Ford to Cosworth of the sum of £100,000 ... Cosworth and Duckworth agree to design and develop for Ford Formula Two and Formula One engines to be known as 'Ford' engines ... suitable for racing in international competitive events.

(2) That the engines to which the agreement refers are:
(a) a 1600 cc 4 cylinder in line engine designed for the 1967 International Formula Two category designated the FVA using the Ford 120E cylinder block and a light alloy 4 valve per cylinder head, and
(b) a 90 degree V8 3000 cc engine using cylinder heads basically the same as/or developed from the above FVA suitable to race in International Formula One under the regulations which start in 1966.

(3) Cosworth and Duckworth will develop the FVA engine during 1966 and produce at least five engines for racing during 1967.

(4) Cosworth and Duckworth will design, build and develop the Formula One engine and have engines ready for use by May 1967. They will build at least five engines by 1 January 1968 and maintain such engines until 31 December 1968. Cosworth will supply to Ford a total of five engines suitable for Formula One by 1 January 1968 for the purpose of equipping one Formula One team. The choice of team will be at Ford's discretion, Cosworth being available in an advisory capacity if required' (Blunsden 1983: 14).

Mr Duckworth began the design work in March 1986. As the configuration of the engine was to be a 90 degree V8, Mr Duckworth liaised closely with Team Lotus which was to build a chassis to accept the engine. In order to overcome the fact that a V8 layout did not lend itself to efficient chassis design, Mr Duckworth designed the engine to be a 'stressed' part of the car, that is it was to be bolted to the rear of the driver's cockpit and the gearbox, transaxle, suspension and wheels were to be attached via pick-up points.

This innovative approach meant that Duckworth had to incorporate suitable plates for attachment as well as a 'clean' (flat) engine front that mated with the chassis. The overall length of the engine was kept to a minimum with a low centre of gravity, the ancillary equipment, water pump and oil pump, being neatly fitted at sump level below the primary exhaust pipes. The fuel injection and metering units, distributor and alternator were fitted between the Vs of the engine. Once the overall design had been completed, a prototype was built and tested which gave an encouraging power output of 408 bhp, exceeding the target figure of 400 bhp for which Mr Duckworth had aimed. A testing programme in the Team Lotus chassis, carried out in April 1967, showed up some minor weaknesses, notably timing gear problems and clutch failure, but these were subsequently overcome.

Ford had stipulated that the engine should be available for use in May 1967. Mr Hayes wanted its debut to be the prestigous Monaco Grand Prix but Team Lotus was heavily committed to the American Indianapolis 500 race during that month. Consequently, resources were stretched and it was prudently arranged that the Ford Cosworth DFV (Double Four Valve) Grand Prix engine would make its debut in June at the Dutch Grand Prix. It appeared there in a Lotus Type 49 chassis, one driver (Graham Hill) setting the fastest lap time and a second (Jim Clark) taking first place in the race. To underline that this first victory was not just a lucky beginning, the Ford Cosworth powered Lotus 49 claimed three more wins in its first season, though the engine had continual trouble with valve gear and cam drive that took some years to overcome.

The apparent ease with which the car outclassed the opposition in late 1967 prompted Mr Hayes to consider the impact the engine had had on Grand Prix racing. Its primary impact appeared to be a serious reduction in competitiveness since it represented the paradigm technology. As long as the engine was available exclusively to Team Lotus, competitive progress was likely to be seriously diminished and new teams would be prevented from entering the Grand Prix arena. As a result, Mr Hayes was keen to make the engine commercially available to other teams. In 1968, following the South African Grand Prix, the engine was offered for sale by Cosworth Engineering at a price of £7,500 per unit. The first customers were Matra International and McLaren. The following year Brabham began to use the engine and such was its success that as the 1974 season opened, 'there were no fewer than 14 chassis ... ready and waiting to race with Ford engines. The availability of a unit that could guarantee equality with the next man had revitalised the sport' (Nye 1972: 119).

Nor did the loss of its monopoly on the Ford Cosworth DFV appear to inhibit the success of Team Lotus. Indeed, Chapman's innovative DFV based designs, which progressed through ever more aerodynamically efficient shapes, brought the team numerous Grand Prix wins.

Cosworth Derivatives

The Cosworth DFY

From the production of the first DFV engine, Cosworth Engineering have continued to develop the unit to increase its power output and reliability. Throughout the 1970s, it was a consistent winner for a number of teams.

In 1977 the introduction of a turbocharged Grand Prix engine by the Renault team (a legal but long ignored alternative to the conventionally aspirated engine), with an initial power output greater than that of the highly developed DFV brought about the demise, albeit slowly, of this unit. Cosworth continued to develop more power from the engine and it continued in the early 1980s to win races. But widespread adoption of turbocharger technology, with its rapidly increasing reliability and power output, forced Cosworth engineers to produce the DFY engine, a lighter, more powerful unit offering some 520 bhp. This engine's single winning performance in 1983 brought Cosworth's total to date to 155 in 16 seasons. Nevertheless, the domination of the turbocharged engine in Grand Prix racing showed that, in its present form, the Ford Cosworth DFY had reached its limit and development was halted.

A follow-up project was initiated between Cosworth Engineering and Ford, which wanted to enter the turbo arena for research and marketing purposes, to develop a 1.5 litre turbocharged engine. Cosworth had little option but to design this but was known to be opposed to such a venture. Cosworth Engineering designed a new engine (designated GBA) based on its turbocharger experience in the American Indycar racing series and tested it extensively in the new Beatrice/Haas Grand Prix team's Lola chassis. Initial performances were poor due to the electronic management system, but generally the unit was never able to match the power output of other competing engines and the project was eventually abandoned when the rules reverted to normally aspirated units only.

The Cosworth DFX

The Cosworth Engineering DFV engine was developed for use in the American CART/USAC (Indycar) series of races, the most famous of which is the Indianapolis 500. This category of racing is a combination of endurance and sheer speed. Consequently, the engine must be tuned to provide reliability with power. In the search for power, the 'Indycar' regulations allowed turbocharging, though in the early seasons this caused the already highly stressed and fragile engines to 'break' frequently.

At first the engine was a derivative of the DFV with a reduced displacement of 2645 cc. The main problem to overcome was the increase in heat build-up caused by the addition of a turbocharger. New pistons were designed and revised water cooling in the cylinder heads kept the exhaust valves and seats cool. At this early stage, Cosworth was not directly involved in the project, but once the engine had begun to prove itself under race conditions Cosworth saw a market for new and rebuilt DFV units. Accordingly, the company established a production line at the Northampton factory, although at the earliest stages parts were shipped from the United States. During the first full season, 1976, the engine won three races; the following year it won eight; and in 1979 it had won 14 races including the prestigious Indianapolis 500.

Changes have been undertaken by Cosworth Engineering to the extent that the DFX, like the DFV, has become a cost effective, readily available and easily maintained mass produced unit which has allowed more teams to participate competitively. By 1984, the engine had scored more than 80 wins for eight different marques (subsequently increased to over 150 wins) and, more importantly, provided a successful new product to strengthen the company's economic and marketing base.

Ford Cosworth DFL

A change in the regulations for endurance (long-distance) racing in 1972 was the impetus for the Ford Cosworth DFV to be used for the first time in this formula, though the 'official' DFL did not appear until the 1980s. In an attempt to reduce speeds in such racing, a limit of 3 litres was imposed, making the DFV, albeit with detail changes, a natural choice.

Although Duckworth was unhappy with this situation, arguing that the engine was not designed for the stresses of long-distance racing, the company set about modifying the engine by reducing the compression ratios and lowering the rev limit to give more reliability. The unit won the Le Mans 24 hour race of 1975, was second and third the following year, and won again in 1980. That year, following further regulation changes, including the permissibility of turbocharging, the Ford Motor Company decided to develop a long-distance racing car, designated the C100 for 1981 using Cosworth engines. There were to be three different 'sizes' of engine displacement, 3.3 litres, 3.6 litres and 3.9 litres. But when the regulations were finalized they also allowed turbocharging. Consequently, the Cosworth engine became the subject of further development, although the 3.3 litre version did compete in some endurance racing. However, as the turbocharged engine reached an advanced stage of development, Ford withdrew from this category of racing. Cosworth Engineering found that other potential users were not fully committed due to sponsorship difficulties and, in view of escalating development costs, terminated the DFL engine programme.

Cosworth Castings Ltd

Many of Cosworth Engineering's racing engines were based around intricate castings designed by the company but manufactured by external commercial foundries. Cosworth Engineering found that many of the problems encountered with its engines stemmed from the poor quality of these castings. On such items as cylinder heads and engine blocks there was often distortion and cracking (and hence a high scrap rate) that caused not only machining and assembly difficulties but also inherent structural weaknesses so that the engines often 'broke', sometimes terminally. Cosworth Engineering was unable to influence the quality of castings with which it was supplied on account of the small quantities per batch, and the company undertook an analysis of the practices and problems associated with standard sand casting technology.

The establishment of a new foundry and casting process, under the direction of Cosworth Research and Development Ltd, came about as a direct intention to derive an improved process to produce castings for the parent company in Northampton. The technique that was eventually developed (and became known as the Cosworth Process) enabled more precise and accurate castings to be manufactured with greater definition, flatness and structural integrity. The process uses only high purity metals that are cast in zircon sand moulds, a material that has better consistency than conventional casting sand. The molten metal is controlled by a computerized electro-mechanical pump which, it is claimed, minimizes turbulence during the casting process. Complex castings can be made both accurately and consistently, thereby reducing the need for economies of scale usually associated with casting techniques.

Subsequent interest in the procedure has led to Cosworth Engineering establishing Cosworth Castings Ltd to produce commercial castings for customers not only within the automotive industry but also in the aircraft, marine and aerospace industries. The Cosworth Process has been patented and is marketed to establish licensed factory plants.

Mercedes Benz Production Engine

When sales of racing engines, particularly the DFV, declined, Cosworth Engineering sought to fill its production capacity and use its expertise in other areas, the most obvious being performance conversions for road-going engines. A response from the German automobile manufacturer Mercedes Benz provided Cosworth Engineering with the brief to design and manufacture a batch of 200 light alloy, twin overhead camshaft competition cylinder heads for the Mercedes Group B salon car racing initiative. However, the project was suddenly terminated and Mercedes Benz commissioned Cosworth to produce cylinder heads for use in road-going vehicles (basically a de-tuned version of the competition unit) and in far greater quantities than previously. This involved the setting up of a new production facility for manufacture and assembly of the cylinder heads to the rigorous quality control standards laid down by Mercedes Benz. This initiative, instigated to broaden Cosworth Engineering's product base, used the design knowledge and precision engineering capabilities derived from the company's racing engine tradition.

Ford Cosworth Sierra RS

This road-going production vehicle began, like the Mercedes Benz as a competition car commissioned by the Ford Motor Company to compete in Group A saloon racing. To qualify, Ford had to sell a minimum of 5,000 similar road-going cars in 12 months and looked to Cosworth Engineering to design and manufacture the power unit. However, unlike the Mercedes Benz project, Cosworth was not only to manufacture parts but also to assemble the complete units for dispatch to the Ford assembly plant.

A significant aspect of the project was an emphasis on the Cosworth name and its racing and engineering pedigree, an aspect of marketing that some of the major motor manufacturers have used to sell 'niche' cars (cars marketed to specific market segments and having a different visual and performance identity from those of a general production model and which use high performance engines). Cosworth Engineering believed itself to be well-placed to continue to serve this growing sector of the automotive industry. The Ford Sierra Cosworth partnership, from which other derivatives have since emerged, is an association that actively seeks to promote the technological excellence of both companies with overt marketing and advertising.

(3)   WILLIAMS GRAND PRIX ENGINEERING

Company History

One of the racing teams to emerge in the late 1960s was founded by Frank Williams, a keen motor enthusiast who had once been a management trainee with a Nottingham-based automobile distributor. After working as a mechanic on a Formula Junior car in the early 1960s, Mr Williams began trading in spare parts for racing cars and in June 1967 established Frank Williams Racing Cars, a business specializing in the preparation, maintenance and running of racing cars. The company worked from premises in Slough and started with the race preparation of a Formula Three car for the driver Piers Courage in a race at Brands Hatch. The following year this partnership moved into Formula Two with a Brabham BT23C, as well as undertaking preparation for customers of other formulae. In 1969 Mr Williams moved into Grand Prix racing, preparing a Ford/Cosworth powered Brabham for Courage. The following year Williams switched to an Italian de Tomaso which Courage drove throughout the season until his death in the Dutch Grand Prix of that year.

The 1971/72 season saw Williams contest Grands Prix with Ford/Cosworth powered March cars but:

> 'there were many disadvantages in running proprietary cars, so when FOCA (Formula One Constructors Association) began organizing charter travel and race promoters introduced sensible start and prize money, the time was clearly ripe for Williams to build his own Formula One cars' (Nye 1986a: 241).

One of Williams's sponsors, the Italian toy company Politoys, put up £40,000 and the resulting car was known as the Politoys Cosworth FX3. By using off-the-shelf proprietary parts in his own chassis, Williams became one of the first Grand Prix 'kit car manufacturers', a derisive term for those competitors whose cars ostensibly comprised purchased items which they had merely bolted together.

The following season, backed by sponsors Iso Rivolta and Marlboro, Williams's cars, effectively modified FX3s, became known as Iso Marlboros. Success was elusive for the underfinanced team between 1973 and 1976. Mr Williams employed a succession of drivers who competed in cars that were often cobbled together from other teams' discarded parts. During 1975 the Iso Marlboro cars were redesigned and designated FWs, the first chassis to bear the Williams name, the FW04 being run under sponsorship from the Swiss Ambrozium concern. Still underfinanced, the team struggled to improve and develop its cars and in 1976 was offered financial help by the Canadian oil equipment millionaire, Walter Wolfe, who was seeking to build up a Grand Prix team. Wolfe bought a controlling stake in Frank Williams (Racing Cars) Ltd and by late 1976, after disagreements and a disastrous season, Frank Williams was shouldered out of Wolfe's racing plans.

That year Mr Williams formed Williams Grand Prix Engineering Ltd (WGPE) and was joined by Patrick Head, an ex-Lola designer who had been with him prior to the Wolfe takeover. They worked from premises in Didcot, Berkshire, and initially the team contested the 1977 Grand Prix season with a March 761 while designing their own chassis, known as the FW06, for future competitions. It was at this time that Williams obtained sponsorship from the little known but expanding Saudi Arabian airline, Saudia. This was a significant event for two reasons: first, it gave WGPE some measure of financial security at a time when the team's track record showed promise rather than achievement; and, second, Saudia was setting a courageous precedent by lending its reputation to a racing team when other airlines had kept clear of motor sport. The Cosworth-powered Saudia Williams contested all the Grands Prix in 1978 and although the team lacked experience in aerodynamics and wind tunnel testing they produced a reliable though conventional car. The first major success came in 1979 when the FW07 won the British Grand Prix, the first of five victories during the season. The car was further developed during the next season and in 1980 WGPE won the Constructors' Championship as well as the World Drivers' Championship.

The FW07, now in its 'C' specification, had by the end of 1981 reached the end of its development life and was replaced for the following season by the FW08. Developing a new car is a long and expensive process, for

> 'much of the expense of Formula One disappears into parts never used and some idea of this "wastage" can be gained from experimental engineer Frank Dernie's wind tunnel programme. Of all the underwing profiles designed, developed and tested, only marks 1, 4, 6, 7, 13, 18, and 24 were actually raced, the rest just weren't good enough' (Nye 1986a: 241).

With the advent of the turbocharged Grand Prix engine the conventionally aspirated cars, mostly Ford Cosworth powered, were being outclassed. Williams Grand Prix Engineering, a staunch supporter of the DFV engine, struggled to gain an advantage by aerodynamic use of the negative lift or ground effect principle. Nevertheless, the company produced the best chassis/engine combination of 1982 which was sufficiently successful to secure the Drivers' Championship of that year.

A change in regulations for 1983, banning ground effects underwing sections and allowing only flat bottomed cars, led to the wind tunnel testing of the FW08 in preparation for the 1983 season. However, even with a more powerful

Judd-developed Cosworth engine, the car struggled against its turbocharged rivals. The introduction of turbochargers into Grand Prix racing signalled the end of the Williams/Cosworth association. Even though the Cosworth was a reliable and powerful unit, it was no match for the new generation of forced induction engines that could be tuned to develop power outputs far in excess of anything the normally aspirated engines could deliver. During the winter of 1982, Frank Williams had negotiated a deal to use the Japanese automobile manufacturer Honda's new turbocharged engine.

The WGPE/Honda Partnership

Honda's first attempt at Grand Prix racing had been in the early 1960s and had come about as a result of the motorcycle company's diversification into automobile production. To gain knowledge of four-wheel vehicles, Honda built up a Grand Prix team to develop its own cars. Early engines and chassis were based on motorcycle technology and were vastly overweight. A partnership with the racing driver and former motorcycle racing champion, John Surtees, gave Honda access to current Grand Prix technology (as well as a British base) and it began to achieve some success. Yet in 1968, with a single Formula One win to Honda's credit, its management directed that all resources be put into refining production cars for the US market where safety and pollution control were becoming significant marketing parameters.

By contrast with this early incursion, Honda's reappearance in Grand Prix racing in the 1980s was a low key operation. Honda had learned that poor showings and bad publicity (the result of the death on the track of one of the team's drivers) as well as limited technical capability had only hindered the company image. Its reasons for a second attempt at Grand Prix racing were twofold. First, by the late 1970s the domestic Japanese automobile market had reached saturation level and manufacturers were looking for export-led growth. Second, such a programme would give Honda engineers access to new and current technologies.

At that time, the emerging turbocharged engines were beginning to dominate but meeting a variety of electronic, structural and fuel problems related to the addition of the turbocharger units. Consequently, Honda concentrated on developing its expertise in engine technology rather than seeking to become a fully fledged constructor. A partnership with the newly formed Spirit Grand Prix team (more experienced teams had not been interested) made little technical progress and the team was uncompetitive. The partnership was terminated in 1983 having contested only six Grands Prix. Among other reasons, 'Spirit were too new and too small an outfit to cope with Honda and its high ambitions' (A. Staniforth in Bamsey 1988: 110). Honda announced in 1984 that it would be supplying only Williams Grand Prix Engineering with its output of engines.

A new chassis, the FW09, was designed to accept the engine and a development programme began. The Honda engine was a heavy unit and set the Williams team two major tasks. It was necessary, first, to produce a car that was sufficiently lightweight to compensate for the engine; and, second, to design a turbocharger layout – Honda supplied no intercooler or exhaust parts – that was thermodynamically efficient, a crucial element in engine reliability. Honda's technical limitations soon became apparent to Williams Grand Prix Engineering. The 1983 season was to be a time of testing and development for both Honda and Williams Grand Prix Engineering with a view to making a competitive entry in 1984.

Technically, the Honda engine suffered from poor fuel consumption and piston failures and Williams engineers were faced with the task of designing a chassis that the overweight and awkwardly designed engine would fit. Developing the 'engine package' involved Honda working with Japanese firms for development work since, until 1984, it worked from its Tokyo headquarters.

While Honda R&D engaged in a massive engine development programme, Williams Grand Prix Engineering designed a new chassis based on lightweight carbon fibre composite materials as well as undertaking a study of aerodynamic forces. The results of testing in late 1983 were encouraging and the team entered the car in the last race of the season in South Africa where it took a respectable fifth place. Honda continued to develop the engine, incorporating many technical lessons learned on the track, producing more reliable and powerful engines and, it was rumoured, using ceramics and heat resistant coatings on parts susceptible to overheating. During the winter months, Williams Grand Prix Engineering moved into larger, purpose-built premises which also housed the Honda engine workshop to which only Honda personnel were admitted.

The following season was a period of development and adjustment for the Williams/Honda partnership and, in its first full turbo year, with an estimated budget of £4 million, the team finished sixth in the Constructors' Championship. Further engine development took place and a new chassis, the FW10, was designed for the 1985 season. The combination, one of the fastest of the turbocharged generation of cars, achieved four wins during the season. In the light of a change in the regulations reducing fuel allowance by 25 litres, the partnership continued to develop both engine and chassis to such good effect that in 1986 the Williams Honda FW11 won nine out of the 16 races and only narrowly missed winning the Drivers' Championship for the third time. Nevertheless, Williams won the World Constructors' Championship.

Late in the season, Williams Grand Prix Engineering and Honda signed a new two-year agreement extending the partnership until 1988. In this same season, Frank Williams was seriously injured in a road accident and was thereafter confined to a wheelchair.

Throughout its Grand Prix involvement Honda has been secretive about technical data and specifications, even keeping its engine operations separate within the Williams organization. With its engine arguably the most powerful and reliable of its kind, Honda decided that, as from 1987, it would supply Team Lotus, who were struggling with the comparatively underpowered Renault unit, as well as the Williams team. In supplying both teams, Honda deemed it appropriate to move its engine facility into separate premises. Despite the personal tragedy, 1987 proved to be another successful year for the Williams Honda partnership: as well as winning the World Drivers' Championship, the team were also Constructors Champions with nine wins out of 16 races.

The announcement later in the season that the partnership had been terminated after only one year understandably provoked surprise, if not shock. In a press release, Honda said:

> 'We have won six races out of 10 with Williams this year. If we want to win more races next year, there is no doubt that the short cut would be to continue our relationship with Williams. We know each other well, and worked together most excellently. But on the other hand it means that we will no longer be able to find new aspects to stimulate each other. Since we resumed our Formula One activities in 1983, winning has always been on our minds' (quoted in *Autosport*, 10 September 1987).

For the 1988 season, Honda would supply the McLaren International team with its own engine rather than Williams Grand Prix Engineering, as well as continuing its association with Team Lotus.

With a change in the regulations banning the use of turbocharged engines after 1988, the Williams team opted to use a normally aspirated engine in order to begin a development programme for 1989, although the sudden withdrawal of Honda left them with little choice of supplier. Like many teams adjusting to a transitional period due to a change in regulations, Williams Grand Prix Engineering struggled in 1988 to remain a competitive force, though it undertook the necessary development programme aimed at producing a winning engine/chassis combination.

Acknowledgement

This case study was compiled as part of a research project funded by the Economic and Social Research Council under its History of Innovation Initiative, grant number WB07250004 to the second author. It is intended to provide a history of events as the basis of class discussion of the issues involved, and implies no criticism of the managerial and technical issues described. The authors are grateful to Team Lotus International Ltd, Cosworth Engineering and Williams Grand Prix Engineering for their helpful cooperation.

Questions

(1) Describe the main differences between the Team Lotus and Williams Grand Prix Engineering commercial and technical strategies.

(2) Analyse the relationship between Cosworth Engineering, Team Lotus and the Ford Motor Company with respect to the design and development of the DFV V8 Grand Prix engine project.

What were the most significant factors from each organization's point of view?

(3) Outline the significance of **sponsorship** to Grand Prix racing, in general, and Williams Grand Prix Engineering in particular.

References

Bamsey I. (ed.) (1988). *The 1000 BHP Grand Prix Cars*. Yeovil: Haynes

Blunsden, J. (1983). *The Power to Win*. London: Motor Racing Publications

Crombac, G. (1986). *Colin Chapman: The Man and His Cars*. Wellingborough: Patrick Stephens

Constanduros, R. (1984). *Williams*. London: William Kimberley

Court, W. (1990). *Power and Glory: The History of Grand Prix Motor Racing. Volume II: 1952–1973*. Wellingborough: Patrick Stephens

Ellis, R. J. (1982). Group Lotus Car Components Ltd. *Cases of Golbal Competitive Business Environment*. London

Foxall, G. R. and Johnston, B. R. (1991). Innovation in Grand Prix motor racing: the evolution of technology, organization and strategy. *Technovation: The International Journal of Technological Innovation anc Entrepreneurship*, **11**, 387–402

Frostick, M. and Gill, B. (1984). *Ford's Competition Cars*. Yeovil: Haynes

Grant-Brabham, B. (1990). *Williams: The Story of a Racing Team*. Swindon, Wiltshire: The Crowood Press

Henry, A. (1991). *Williams: The Business of Grand Prix Racing*. Yeovil, Somerset: Patrick Stephens

Nye, D. (1978). *Motor Racing*. Blandford Press, London

Nye, D. (1972). *The Story of Lotus 1961 to 1971*. London: Motor Racing Publications

Nye, D. (1986). *Theme Lotus 1956 to 1986. From Chapman to Ducarouge*. London: Motor Racing Publications

Nye, D. (1986). *The History of the Grand Prix Car 1966–1985*. London: Hazleton

Robson, G. (1991). *Cosworth: The Search for Power*. Yeovil, Somerset: Patrick Stephens

Sakiya, T. (1987). *Honda Motor. The Men, the Management, the Machines*. London: Kodansha International

Setright, L. J. K. (1973). *The Grand Prix 1906 to 1972*. London: Nelson

Wells, K. (1987). *Cosworth*. London: William Kimberley

Wood, R. (1980). *Car Bodywork in Glass Reinforced Plastic*. Wellingborough: Patrick Stephens

CASE 11
Cifra
Strategic Marketing

Fiona Davies and Luiz Moutinho
Cardiff Business School, University of Wales College of Cardiff

Company History

Cifra is a corporate group operating in Mexico. Its core business is supermarket retailing, which generates about 80% of its sales. Cifra was the first retailer in Mexico to offer food, clothing and hardware under the same roof, the first to introduce own-label brands, and the first to undertake a multiple chain strategy. Cifra currently has the industry's most technologically advanced operating systems, and is pioneering new retail formats to the Mexican market, such as the warehouse club and the supercentre concept. In 1993, in a survey by the journal *Euromoney*, experts on the Latin American market voted Cifra the best-managed company in Latin America.

This case study concentrates on Cifra's core business, its supermarket operations. The firm incorporates five supermarket chains: Aurrera, Bodega Aurrera, Superama, Club Aurrera and Wal-Mart Supercenter (the last two are partnerships with Wal-Mart Stores Inc., the largest US retailer). This partnership is likely to ensure that Cifra continues to dominate the Mexican retail sector, and, indeed, it could be said that Cifra aims to become a Mexican Wal-Mart.

Exhibit 11.1 gives a summary of Cifra's operations, including the fashion chain Suburbia and the restaurant chain Vips, which are not considered in this study.

The Supermarket Chains

Aurrera

Aurrera has 35 stores with about 400 employees each, and is Cifra's largest chain in terms of sales volume. Aurrera stores offer an extensive selection of food,

Exhibit 11.1 *Cifra's operations*

Chain	Sales breakdown 1992 (%)	Units [†] Cifra	Joint venture	Total	Average store size [†] (m^2)
Cifra	100.0	211	24	235	—
Total for supermarkets	79.4	104	11	115	—
Aurrera	37.0	34	1	35	6,900
Bodega Aurrera	23.6	35	4	39	4,300
Superama	12.8	35	2	37	1,300
Club Aurrera	6.0	—	4	4	9,000
Wal-Mart Supercenter	0.0	—	—	—	—
Suburbia	15.6	28	—	28	5,000
Vips	5.0	79	13 [‡]	92	205 [§]

† Up to June 1993.
‡ 13 units are franchised.
§ Average number of seats.
Source: Company Data.

clothing and general merchandise. Stores are typically located in open air shopping malls featuring a wide selection of complementary services to provide one-stop shopping for customers from all income groups. The chain also includes three hypermarkets called Gran Bazar, which are larger and stock a greater selection of products. A refurbishment programme for Aurrera stores was completed in 1993, improving their attractiveness and layout and incorporating fast food bars and other services into several stores.

Aurrera stores target a wide range of social and income groups, emphasizing product variety and competitive pricing. Their strategy of 'everyday low prices' was introduced in 1992. However, recent market research by Aurrera on prices and image has shown that they are perceived as having higher prices than their competitors, even though on average their prices are lower. This may be linked with the quality image with which Aurrera was associated – polished marble-type floors, some carpeted departments, well-distributed articles, better customer service, and so on.

Another consumer study recently led Aurrera to introduce the concept of 'Buyer Worlds'. Shops are partitioned into Clothing World, Home World, World of Health, Beauty and Hygiene, Childhood World, Teenager World, Do It Yourself World and Sport World.

Bodega Aurrera

Bodega Aurrera, the fastest growing segment of Cifra, is a group of 39 discount warehouse stores targeting medium and medium-to-low income groups. These consumer segments register thin penetration by organized supermarket chains, thus offering attractive growth potential. The chain has gained gradual acceptance among lower income customers due to its no-frills warehouse-style appearance and emphasis on discount pricing. This policy necessitates minimal product mark-ups and therefore a narrow gross margin, so it is essential that sales volume is high and operating costs low. The product assortment is composed primarily of branded, frequently purchased merchandise, and generally excludes perishables and frozen foods. Most stores are located in the urban perimeter of Mexico City, where targeted consumer segments live and land costs are low.

Superama

The Superama chain comprises 37 smaller, more expensive supermarkets, employing about 250 staff each, located in prosperous residential neighbourhoods. They sell mainly grocery items with a high percentage of imported products, and cater for people who can afford to pay a little more for the convenience of shopping near home. Sales per square metre of Superama store space are almost twice those of Aurrera and Bodega Aurrera stores. The 'Buyer World' concept is also being incorporated in Superama stores as in the Aurrera chain.

Club Aurrera

Club Aurrera is a warehouse club, based on the US format, and half-owned by the US retailing giant Wal-Mart. It offers a narrow selection of products, specially packaged in bulk, at very low prices. Seasonal and availability factors result in variations in the product mix. Over half the merchandise is imported. Customers must be 'club members'. Membership is open to business owners and other selected people, all of whom pay an annual membership fee. This is a low margin operation, relying on high sales volumes and low operating expenses (for example, basic warehouse facility, little surplus stock held). The warehouse club format has quickly become popular, with a typical clientele including business people buying office supplies, shopkeepers buying in bulk for resale, and housewives buying imported food and clothes.

Wal-Mart Supercenter

The two Wal-Mart Supercenters are another partnership with the US retailing giant Wal-Mart, and combine a Wal-Mart general merchandise discount store with a supermarket under one roof. Stores feature everyday low prices on a large variety of items across all product categories: shoes, clothing, toys, cosmetics, electronics, household goods and a full selection of grocery items. One store is in Mexico City, the other in Monterrey, 900 kilometres further north.

Cifra's Marketing Strategy

Cifra's strategy is to target different income groups with the variety of store types described above, offering varying product ranges and prices. Surveys show that almost half the population of Mexico use supermarkets or self-service stores, and the middle and higher social classes prefer to shop in this way (rather than in smaller local stores or open markets). Cifra gave priority in the 1980s to consolidating the market position of its three food formats, Aurrera, Bodega Aurrera and Superama, within the Mexico City metropolitan area and surrounding region.

Own-label Brands

Aurrera was the first Mexican supermarket to introduce own-label brands, with the *marca libra* (free brand) product line. The intention was to offer value for money through cheaper products with the same quality as brand name products. However, a study by Nielsen de Mexico showed that the products were in fact perceived as lower quality. Aurrera carried out a repositioning exercise, renaming the line *marca propia* Aurrera (Aurrera own brand) and offering products of as good or better quality than brand name products, at a reasonable price.

Promotion

The Aurrera division of Cifra places great importance on promoting itself to customers and potential customers. It is a central element in its strategy for market penetration and growth, and is used as a competitive advantage. The main promotional instruments are:

- *Guia del Ahorro (Saving Guide)* – a free booklet containing information about Aurrera's 'everyday low prices' policy. This is distributed door to door in the supermarkets' catchment areas, and is also available at the supermarket entrance. Most issues have a central theme, such as Christmas, Back to School, Mothers Day, and so on.

- *Siempre en Familia (Always in Family)* – a free magazine containing advice on cooking, healthy eating, beauty, fashion, household hints, and so on. This is also distributed door to door. The magazine is used by Aurrera to influence its customers' shopping habits; for instance, a recent edition included an article on the advantages of frozen over canned food. Frozen food is not such a frequent purchase in Mexico as in the United States and United Kingdom, and by its promotion Aurrera hopes to change customers' buying habits.

- *Radio* – advertisements, plus a one-hour weekday programme called *En Su Tienda Aurrera* (Inside Your Aurrera Supermarket). This is a phone-in programme, with specialist guests speaking on various topics and members of the public ringing in with questions about what to buy, and when and where to shop.

- *Television* – used selectively and only for special promotions, as TV advertising is extremely expensive.

- *Newspapers* – used to advertise special offers and some 'everyday low prices' products, but not a preferred method of advertising as non-working Mexican women (the majority of regular supermarket customers) do not often read newspapers.

Geographical Coverage

Cifra has concentrated its activities in the urban area of Mexico City and adjacent areas in central Mexico, where 75% of its stores are currently located. This area has the highest population density in the country, and above average GDP per capita compared with the rest of Mexico, resulting in a highly lucrative but also highly competitive retail market. Cifra's stores' central location also enables direct store delivery of over 95% of its merchandise, as most suppliers are also located in or near Mexico City. Cifra chains thus benefit from strong name recognition within Central Mexico but are virtually unknown outside this region. The Monterrey Wal-Mart Supercenter is well outside Cifra's traditional trading region, and capitalizes on the Wal-Mart name, likely to be better known than that of Cifra. However, continued expansion into other areas will be necessary for Cifra to maintain its leading position in Mexico.

Exhibits 11.2 and 11.3 show the locations of the different types of Cifra stores.

Competition

Mexico's supermarket industry is highly fragmented and Cifra's competitors include regional supermarket chains, independent retailers, government-operated supermarkets and street markets. The main competitors, however, are the two large supermarket chains Comercial Mexicana and Gigante. These two formed joint ventures with US retailing groups at about the same time as Cifra started its joint venture with Wal-Mart, and have also copied the Bodega Aurrera concept, opening Bodega Comercial Mexicana and Bodega Gigante. Gigante in particular has pursued a policy of geographical diversification, with numerous outlets in the major cities of Mexico City, Monterrey and Guadalajara as well as many smaller towns. Its focus is now on middle-sized cities, where there is less competition and profit margins are higher. It has opened, jointly with the largest US wholesaler Fleming, a non-membership 'price-impact' supermarket in the small town of San Juan del Rio, and intends to open about 10 similar stores a year. Although Comercial Mexicana has pursued a national growth strategy, the majority of its outlets are still located in Mexico City.

Exhibit 11.2 *Cifra's supermarkets (June 1992)*

Town	Aurrera	Bodega Aurrera	Superama	Club Aurrera
Acapulco, Gro	—	1	—	—
Aguascalientes, Ags	1	—	—	—
Celaya, Gto.	1	—	—	—
Cuernavaca, Mor	1	1	3	—
Guadalajara, Jal.	4	2	—	—
Leon, Gto	1	—	—	—
Mexico City	22	32	32	3
Monterrey, N.L.	—	—	—	1
Morelia, Mich.	1	—	—	—
Pachuca, Hgo.	—	1	—	—
Puebla, Pue.	2	2	2	—
Queretaro, Qro.	1	—	—	—
Toluca, Mex.	1	—	—	—
Total	**35**	**39**	**37**	**4**

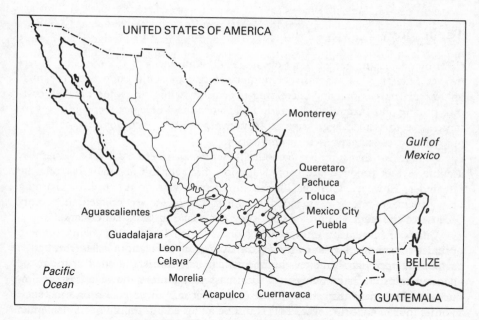

Exhibit 11.3 *Location of Cifra stores.*

The Benefits of Cooperation with US Retailers

Mexican companies like Cifra, Gigante and Comercial Mexicana, which have formed joint ventures with US retailers, have immediate access to US technology, marketing expertise, distribution and buying power. US partners can also provide finance to enable faster expansion. Cifra believes that Wal-Mart's technology will help in stock control and also in improving distribution channels to enable further expansion outside central Mexico. Wal-Mart has extensive experience in distribution, and as Cifra expands geographically, keeping distribution costs down will be a major factor in maintaining its current high profit margins. Fleming is helping its partner Gigante with scanning goods to improve stock control, and also advising on store lighting and layout. Liverpool, Mexico's most upmarket retail chain, has formed an alliance with K-Mart, which it is hoped will allow it to expand into different markets.

The Mexican companies realize, however, that increased consumer spending in Mexico must be matched by increased export revenues. Exports in 1990 accounted for only 16% of GNP. Thus both Cifra and Liverpool are making use of their US partnerships to promote Mexican goods in the United States via jointly-owned import–export companies. Cifra also works with the Mexican Development Bank in helping its smaller suppliers, by providing low interest rate loans and advising them on how to become more competitive.

Technology

Cifra pioneered the use of point-of-sale (POS) equipment in the Mexican supermarket industry. Only a fully computerised system could cope with the high volume of transactions and increasing expansion, while providing detailed costing, pricing and turnover information. Advanced technological capabilities were imperative to realize aggressive store network growth incorporating both geographic and consumer-based diversification.

Cifra insists that suppliers barcode all merchandise before delivery. Generally, around 95% of products are barcoded, and other retailers manually barcode the remainder. However, Cifra has forced suppliers to take on this task by charging very expensive rates for uncoded products. Suppliers are obliged to comply because of the high volume of sales they can make in Cifra supermarkets.

Cifra's management information system (MIS) is currently being used to optimize inventory levels while maximizing individual store sales through a customized merchandising programme which determines the shelf space to be allocated to products by analysis of local customer preferences. The system produces product maps that show the exact product mix to be placed on each shelf in order to maximize turnover. This is still being tested but should be implemented in the very near future.

The MIS also allows quick repricing of products, which can be done during opening hours thus reducing overtime working.

The next major development expected is the introduction of Electronic Data Interchange (EDI) systems, which connect retailers directly with suppliers.

Cifra's partnership with Wal-Mart should enable it to use Wal-Mart's technological experience and expertise in the analysis of customer data to extend even further its use of technology.

Distribution

Mexican retailers have generally relied on manufacturers and wholesalers to deliver directly to stores in central Mexico. Aurrera accepts delivery of over 95% of merchandise at its stores. In contrast, Grupo Gigante, with much wider geographical coverage, has built up a distribution system which handles 20% of merchandise.

Superama is implementing a new electronically based delivery system, details of which are confidential, which dispenses with complex administrative procedures and thus eliminates waiting in the reception area in over 95% of cases. In fact, the most time-consuming part of deliveries is now the physical unloading of merchandise.

Cifra will benefit, as it expands geographically, from Wal-Mart's extensive knowledge of distribution and distribution technology.

Finance

Cifra's share prices have risen fast over the past few years. Over the period 1988 to 1992, they showed an annual yield of 109%.

Both operating margins (5.5% in 1992) and sales per square foot are the best in Mexico. Operating profits rose by 32% in 1992. From 1988 to 1992, Cifra reduced its expenses to sales ratio every year. Cifra is strong financially, with no long-term debt, financing itself by large cash balances from its operations. Its stock turnover period averages about 30 days, while suppliers typically give 45 to 60 days' credit, leading to profits from interest income. However, Mexican interest rates are falling, and Cifra is now concentrating on increasing operating profits rather than relying on interest income. Management are confident that growth in sales and profitability in the next two years will be four or five times overall Mexican economic growth.

SWOT Analysis

Cifra's strengths and weaknesses are summarized in Exhibit 11.4.

Some further comments could be made on this exhibit. The strengths of a company should be visible to customers, and Cifra now dominates the Mexican retail market in terms of marketing, finance, own-label products and management. Although Gigante owns the largest number of sales outlets, many are non-productive or badly run, and are a drain on the group's resources.

Cifra has pioneered innovations in the Mexican retail industry. It was the first company to introduce multiple supermarket chains targeting different social groups, to introduce point-of-sale systems, to undertake a joint venture with a US company, to introduce own-label products, and to offer shares in the Wall Street market.

Exhibit 11.4   SWOT Analysis

	Major strength	Minor strength	Neutral	Minor weakness	Major weakness
Marketing					
Company reputation	x				
Market share	x				
Quality reputation	x				
Service reputation	x				
Manufacturing costs	x				
Distribution costs	x				
Promotion effectiveness	x				
Sales force effectiveness	x				
R&D and innovation	x				
Geographical coverage				x	
Finance					
Cost/availability of capital	x				
Profitability	x				
Financial stability	x				
Manufacturing *(marca propia)*					
Facilities		x			
Economies of scale		x			
Capacity		x			
Able dedicated workforce	x				
Ability to deliver on time	x				
Technical manufacturing skill		x			
Organization					
Visionary capable leadership	x				
Dedicated employees	x				
Entrepreneurial orientation	x				
Flexible/responsive	x				

Another major strength is Cifra's low cost structure. This may not be so obvious to customers, especially considering the recent refurbishment of the Aurrera chain, but compared with its competitors, Cifra's supermarkets are run more effectively and with fewer staff. For example, a store manager will take merchandise orders with an infrared gun, use his personal computer to prepare sales reports, and solve problems with both customers and staff. Every supervisor in the organization is responsible for on average 7 to 15 staff, and in every area of work productivity studies are done to make comparisons with international organizations and determine areas for improvement.

Although geographical coverage has been cited as a weakness, it is one which the company is addressing. With Cifra's current advantages over its competitors, geographical expansion should not be a problem.

The *marca libre* products used to be a weakness of Aurrera due to their image as low price and low quality products. Their repositioning as *marca propia* products succeeded in converting a weakness to a strength.

Opportunities and Threats

The main opportunities and threats are as follows:

Opportunities

- Unsaturated market outside central Mexico.
- Joint venture with Wal-Mart providing access to its resources and expertise.
- Growing population.
- Further use of technology.
- Influence over suppliers.

Threats

- Changes in consumer behaviour – open markets becoming more popular.
- Possible market fluctuations causing changes in consumer purchasing power.
- Market becoming more dynamic due to advances in technology and communications.
- Entry of US companies to Mexican market as permitted by NAFTA.

The Mexican Economy

The Mexican economy was in recession in the 1980s, with the average per capita income being reduced by 46% between 1982 and 1987. Recent years have shown recovery, but incomes are still nowhere near their 1982 levels. This may have some connection with observed changes in consumer shopping behaviour which show increased use of open markets.

In 1993 the Mexican market showed only a small increase in value of around 4%. Mexico's stock market was valued by the analysts Bear Stearns of New York at 11.9 times 1993 earnings, making it relatively cheap compared with Argentina and Chile, which had multiples of 16.5 and 14 respectively.

Mexico has a population of 85 million which is growing fast. 73% live in urban areas. The major cities are Mexico City (population over 20 million) and Guadalajara and Monterrey, both with a population of over 3 million. In the Guadalajara area, in the north close to the US border, and around the major oil producing region of the Gulf of Campeche in the south, are several smaller cities with populations of between 250,000 and 1 million. Half the population is aged under 20. As more young people enter the workforce and have money to spend, demand for consumer goods is likely to increase, so the forecast is for consumer spending to grow much faster than the overall economy.

Major industries in Mexico include oil production (it is the world's fourth largest oil producer), agriculture and tourism, which is a major earner of foreign currency.

Market Conditions

Despite the aggressive store opening programmes of Cifra and its competitors (see Exhibit 11.5 for details of Cifra's supermarket sales floor growth), the total supermarket selling area per head of population in Mexico is small compared with many other countries. Although the urban area in and around Mexico City itself is perhaps close to saturation as regards supermarkets, there is ample room for growth in the rest of the country. Retail profit margins average 6% on sales – approximately double the US figure. As more large supermarkets open, small shops lose business to supermarkets, and the smaller supermarkets lose business to the large chains, most of whom have formed alliances with US retailers. This is enabling Mexican consumers to have a wider choice of products, many of which are imported. However, small Mexican suppliers are likely to suffer if they cannot produce goods in the volume required and to the specifications insisted on by bulk buying retailers.

A big change in the market is likely to occur with the implementation of the North American Free Trade Agreement (NAFTA) which will allow US companies to trade in Mexico. The biggest American retailers have created joint ventures with Mexican companies to learn about the market and get their names known in Mexico, but once they are allowed to enter the market freely, aggressive competition can be expected.

Exhibit 11.5   *Cifra supermarket sales floor growth*

Chain	Sales floor 1987 (m^2)	Sales floor 1992 (m^2)	Annual growth (%)
Aurrera	215,600	243,000	2.4
Bodega Aurrera	34,900	169,200	37.1
Superama	34,200	46,900	6.5
Club Aurrera	—	27,100	—
Total	**284,700**	**486,200**	**11.3**

Acknowledgement

The authors would like to thank Luis Alvarez for providing the necessary information and allowing it to be used as a case study.

Questions

(1) What benefits does Cifra gain from its alliance with Wal-Mart? Are there any disadvantages in this alliance?

(2) How has Cifra segmented its markets? How has it positioned its different types of store in order to target these segments?

(3) How does Cifra differentiate itself from its competitors?

(4) Cifra wishes and needs to expand geographically. Summarize what you believe should be the company's expansion strategy.

(5) Appraise Cifra's current promotional strategy for Aurrera. Does Cifra need to extend or supplement these promotional activities as it expands? If so, how?

(6) What benefits does Cifra gain from its use of new technology?

CASE 12
Asea-Brown Boveri
Strategic International Marketing

Erdener Kaynak
Pennsylvania State University, Harrisburg, USA

Company History

Representing the merger of Asea of Sweden and Brown Boveri of Switzerland, Asea-Brown Boveri (ABB) was created in 1988 as a pan-European firm. This merger serves as a case study on how businesses positioned themselves for the advent of the European single market in 1992.

ABB is an electrical engineering firm employing 180,000 people with annual sales of about $18 billion. Asea and Brown Boveri have equal shares in the firm but each retains a separate stock market identity, and each has excluded a few assets from the merger. The breakdown of revenue by country is shown in Exhibit 12.1 and by sector in Exhibit 12.2.

ABB located its corporate headquarters in Switzerland for several reasons. It is near Zurich airport and has easy access to other European centres. Having a Swiss partner has helped the firm to recruit and retain the most talented Swiss engineers. Switzerland's lenient tax structure contribute to the company's profitability.

The location, however, does have one disadvantage. Although ABB, with 70% of sales and nearly its all manufacturing in Europe, vigorously maintains that it is the most pan-European of all electrical engineering firms, national preference is so ingrained that local firms have a definite and usually a decisive advantage. As a firm outside the European Union after 1992, ABB may continue to suffer from discrimination in public procurement in those EU countries where it lacks subsidiaries to compete with the domestic businesses. Examples of national preference include GEC and Northern Engineering in the United Kingdom, Siemens and AEG in Germany, General Electric and Westinghouse in the United States and Hitachi in Japan. In practice, the only truly open markets in the European power-related business are those, like Denmark and Austria, that lack a national producer.

Exhibit 12.1 *ABB revenues by market (1988)*

	Turnover ($m)	Share (%)
Eastern Europe	180	1
Japan and Australia	540	3
North America	1,620	9
Developing countries	3,240	18
Nordic countries	5,580	31
European Community	6,840	38
Total	18,000	100

Source: Company Reports.

Exhibit 12.2 *ABB sales revenue by sector (1988)*

Sectors	Sales revenue ($m)	Share (%)
Power transmission	3,492	19.4
Power distribution	2,304	12.8
Power plants	2,106	11.7
Environment	1,998	11.1
Industry	1,602	8.9
Financial services	1,206	6.7
Line building	990	5.5
Wholesaling	702	3.9
Transport	702	3.9
Telecommunications	594	3.3
Other	2,304	12.8
Total	18,000	100.0

Source: Company Reports.

Apart from discrimination in the procurement policies of some European governments, ABB's greatest handicap is the apparent overcapacity in the European power industry. In an effort to overcome this problem, ABB has attempted to diversify geographically by signing an agreement with Westinghouse of Pittsburgh giving Westinghouse a 55% share and ABB a 45% share in two joint ventures; one in the manufacture of power generation and the other in power distribution and transmission equipment. In effect, the deal gives ABB access to Westinghouse's trademark and its American utility customers for $500 million in exchange for the 55% share. There is one problem, however: the American market is even more depressed than Europe's.

Power remains the core of ABB's business, and both partners are strong contributors to the cutting edge of power technology. For instance, ABB leads the world in the manufacture of high-voltage direct current systems. Asea contributes pressurized fluidized bed combustion (PFBC), an efficient, cheap and environmentally sound way of burning coal. For its part, Brown Boveri provides a high-temperature nuclear reactor that stabilizes at a safe temperature, diminishing the risk of a core melt-down.

Industry experts maintain that the demand for power is still growing by approximately 2% a year in industrialized countries and 6 to 8% in developing countries. The prospect of brownouts and blackouts will eventually persuade utility commissions around the world to upgrade. The upturn is expected to occur first in the United Staes where, by the end of 1990, facilities capable of generating about 100 gigawatts of power were 30 or more years old.

Power, however, is only one of ABB's areas of expertise. Niche opportunities are opening in its other businesses, thanks to the superiority and effectiveness of its R&D effort which challenges Japanese manufacturers of industrial robotics. In locomotives, ABB is already the main supplier to the national railways of Switzerland, Scandinavia and Germany. Its expertise in mass transport systems is also producing impressive results. For example, ABB has produced a high-speed train that, unlike Japan's Bullet and France's TGV, operates on existing track, thus reducing costs considerably.

In view of the overall slackening demand for power equipment, ABB's main competitors have diversified into consumer electronics, defence equipment and medical products to reduce their dependence on the electrical engineering industry in general and the power industry in particular. For instance, for Siemens of Germany, electrical engineering equipment now represents only about 40% of total sales, for General Electric of the United States 30%, for GEC of the United Kingdom 45%, and for Hitachi-Mitsubishi Electric-Toshiba of Japan 25–30%. For ABB, however, electrical engineering equipment represents 100% of the total sales.

Percy Barnevik, the Swedish chief executive of ABB, emphasizes profits over volume and market share. Specifically, he avoids signing new contracts at inadequate profit margins that result in unprofitable manufacturing capacity. He fears that if ABB does not turn away marginally profitable business, it will find itself left with overcapacity that would be much better scrapped.

The firm has recently restructured its organization. Originally it did not possess an effective matrix organizational structure. Each of its subsidiaries located in various countries had its own management structure, and undertook its own marketing, research and production, thus duplicating costs and dissipating strategy. The conversion of the firm from a geographical structure to a product divisional structure, and the establishment of about 3,000 profit centres has been advocated by the corporate management. The proposed profit centres would have greater autonomy in purchasing and be closer to their markets and customers, which would mean shorter decision lines.

As a manufacturer of capital goods whose main customers are governments, ABB suffers a disadvantage compared with consumer-products companies. For instance, when Electrolux, a Swedish white-goods multinational, acquired Zanussi of Italy, it was able to transfer the production of washing machines from Italy to France, and refrigerators from Sweden to Germany. Nestlé, a Swiss chocolate-maker, had a similar opportunity to shut down inefficient operations and concentrate production in efficient factories. However, ABB is largely unable to engage in this type of manoeuvre. The firm realizes that it has little chance of winning a contract from either a statal and/or a parastatal government body in an industrial country, when in competition with domestic rivals, unless it has a significant manufacturing base in that country.

ABB, however, does possess the strategy to break into developing country markets. The firm wants to be part of the infrastructure, which has heavy electrical engineering as its core, when newly industrialized countries come onstream. ABB's aim is to operate in developing country markets as 'an insider, not an invader'. The company cites joint ventures in South Korea and Taiwan as indications of things to come. The potential for growth is great, and the demand for power in the newly industrialized countries is growing at least three times more quickly than in the old industrialized countries. Only a shortage of foreign exchange and credit prevents these countries from giving ABB more business.

Where will ABB direct its attention? Perhaps the joint venture with Westinghouse will give it the opening into the world's largest utility market for which Asea and Brown Boveri individually have longed. In the electrical equipment field, Westinghouse has run a distant second to General Electric. It is possible that ABB will pass every other test only to fail the one that really matters – the test of the marketplace.

Source: Adapted from Asea-Brown Boveri Power Play, *The Economist*, May 28, 1988, pp. 19–22.

Questions

(1) How is ABB going to keep itself busy and profitable while waiting for world demand for its core business to pick up?

(2) Can ABB be used as a successful strategic model for other European industries?

(3) Why might ABB experience problems after 1992, with the emergence of the European Union on 31 December 1992?

(4) Should ABB invest money on R&D? What kind of product developments has such investment procured in the past?

(5) What benefits has ABB seen as a result of the merger of Asea and Brown Boveri? What needs to be done to maintain this merger in a satisfactory manner?

CASE 13
Medical Research Incorporated
Patents and Legal Implications

Kip Becker
Boston University, USA

PART A

The Company's Background

Medical Research Incorporated (MRI) is a diversified biomedical firm specializing in the development, manufacture and sale of disposable products for open heart surgery and speciality pharmaceutical devices. The firm has enjoyed a high growth rate and generated record revenues of $12.2 millon in 1991. Health-care product revenues increased by 36% in 1991 compared with 1990. The increase included growth of 71% in the sales of specialized hospital supplies (a 37% rise in volume and a 34% rise in prices), an 8% increase (4% decrease in volume and 12% rise in prices) in the sales of proprietary pharmaceutical products and a 30% decrease (29% decrease in volume and 1% increase in prices) in the sales of private label solutions.

The company has carved out a strong niche in the cardiovascular disposable business through innovative, high quality products. Its cardioplegia (heart muscle preservation) products are leading the way to continued growth in earnings. Medical Research Inc. became a public company in 1974 and is listed on the NASDAQ.

Initial Development

Medical Research Inc. did not start out in the medical field. The business of the company until 1982 was land development. It was then that the company made their first move into the medical area with an over-the-counter processing solution called RNCO. In its initial form RNCO was not considered to be a drug. It was, however, Medical Research's intention to introduce an improved product, RNCO-2, and to apply for a product licence for drawing, separating, storing, thawing and reinfusing blood platelets. RNCO, in its over-the-counter form, was used for the long-term storage of blood platelets. If RNCO-2 received approval it would allow the 210,000 cancer patients who undergo chemotherapy each year to use their own blood after therapy. Patients with aplastic anaemia, leukaemia and solid tumours suffer from a decrease in the number of blood platelets after chemotherapy. This can cause haemorrhaging which was a leading cause of death among patients receiving treatment. The available product provided for a shelf life of about 72 hours when stored at non-freezing temperatures. Using RNCO-2 a patient's own blood could be extracted prior to chemotherapy and used during the treatment phase. Blood platelets stored with RNCO-2 would have a shelf life of three years. The broader market use of the product was that platelets could be 'banked' in large quantities of pre-typed, single donor platelets for emergencies.

Initial Structure

The organizational structure of the company at this time (1982) was fairly simple (see Exhibit 13.1).

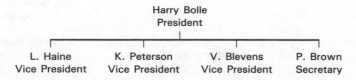

Exhibit 13.1 *Organizational structure (1982).*

Of the six members of the board of directors, two were not officers of the company, and V. Blevens was an officer and not on the board.

The company's financial position was excellent as its major assets were its large land holdings, which continued to increase in value.

In 1983, Gary Davis was hired as president to reorganize the firm. Mr Davis was selected as a result of his strong background in medical products which was felt to be the new direction for the company. His experience in the medical industry included working with Baxter-Travenol and Abbott-Sorenson. Under Mr Davis's leadership the company developed the growing and profitable product base from which it now derives most of its revenues.

An early business strategy of Mr Davis was to focus on the development and distribution of an open heart surgery catheter. The open heart catheter is a device used to take blood from the heart to a heart–lung machine during the open heart operation. Medical Research Inc.'s product would allow blood to be taken from two heart chambers by one catheter. While other methods were being used to accomplish the transfer of blood, Medical Research Inc. believed that its design was far superior to existing products. This is why Gary Davis left his position with a *Fortune* 500 pharmaceuticals company to head Medical Research Inc. He firmly believed that the MRI product could be the focus of the company's strategy to move from being primarily a real estate company to become a major force in health-care devices. He brought with him two seasoned veterans in the health-care device industry. Nancy Holtz would head corporate communications and Mark Givins would head operations.

The organizational structure as the company entered 1985 is shown in Exhibit 13.2.

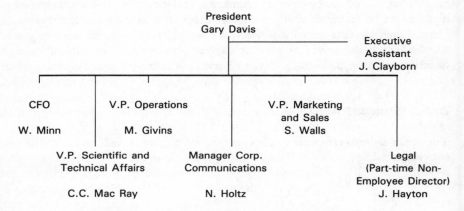

Exhibit 13.2   *Medical Research Incorporated organizational chart, board of directors (1985).*

Initially proceeds from the sales of MRI real estate holdings were used to fund research and development. By 1987 this was no longer necessary as health-care operations were generating a positive cash flow. The firm continued to derive some revenues from property sales and carried over $4 million (book value) in real estate on the 1991 balance sheet (Appendix 13.1).

The Success of the New Product

The Strategy of MRI

Under Mr Davis's direction MRI researched, produced and marketed its first new product, a dual drainage venous disposable return catheter. The business strategy of Medical Research Inc., as developed by Mr Davis, was to identify markets ranging from $10 million to $25 million which were too small to attract major medical device producers but could be highly profitable to a smaller firm. It was the policy of the company to develop unique products for such niche markets and then protect its position by entering each new niche with a product that was based upon patented innovations. The development of patent protected products was essential if a small firm was to exist in a marketplace dominated by multinationals with deep pockets.

The market niche of dual drainage catheters was considered important. There are approximately 350,000 bypass operations conducted in the United States and 625,000 worldwide each year. It was felt that the growth potential for the product was enormous. As more nations developed the internal sophistication to perform the bypass surgery operations the market would expand dramatically. India, for example, was estimated to have a market potential of 50,000 operations a year, South Korea 20,000 and South Africa 18,000.

Part of MRI's strategy was to develop loyal customers who were decision-makers. Mr Davis had no desire to become involved with the entanglements which surrounded the sales of medical devices through hospital purchasing channels. Such channels were slow to adopt new ideas, and normally over-burdened with paperwork and bureaucratic layers of approvals. Finding the actual decision-maker for even small purchases could become an overwhelming source of frustration. Mr Davis had developed a strategy which focused on low cost products that, due to their disposable nature, needed to be continually reordered. A key was that their purchase was authorized by the surgeon who would use them.

By focusing on the physician two important outcomes were realized. The first was that the sales force knew exactly who to contact concerning the product. This type of sale had the secondary benefit that it tended to make the users of the product a part of the 'research and development team'. Ideas from physicians at the operational level were to play an important role in both the improvement of existing products and the development of new ones. MRI, early on, established a record of providing financial rewards to physicians who contributed usable ideas. This practice encouraged those who were closest to problems to become involved in solutions. In addition to providing valuable feedback to MRI, this approach tended to develop a satisfied customer base.

MRI's Patent

MRI applied for a patent for its catheter in 1984 and simultaneously entered the marketplace with this dual drainage venous return product. For marketing purposes Mr Walls, Vice President of marketing, suggested that the product be called the ARIS. The product followed Mr Davis's corporate strategy of focusing on a small market niche, new patented product with superior technology and few competitors. Unfortunately, the significant competitor in the market was the multinational corporation Tri D which owned a patent for a similar product. MRI firmly believed that its technology was advanced and the design sufficiently different so as not to infringe upon the Tri D product. It knew that product protection was an essential element in any business strategy. It was soon to find out how important.

Product Protection

There are several means by which a firm can attempt to protect its product in the marketplace. One method is to establish an early entry and thus 'train' the consumer to relate the product to the company name. This has been the case with firms such as Kleenex, Xerox and Clorox.

To legally protect intellectual property a firm may seek to obtain a patent on newly developed products and in some cases services. Patent protection, however, tends to be a short-term strategy good only over the life of the patent itself. Such protection can range from 5 to 17 years depending on the type of product or service and the type of protection sought. Patents, of course, will not protect against a new and different superior product. For this reason a patent can rarely be the only product defence strategy. Positioning consumer issues such as quality, reliability and after-sales service is essential for continued sales after patents expire. For example, the German multinational corporation Bayer continues to market its aspirin at above-average prices long after its patent protection expired by focusing on perceived quality. Although the ingredients in Bayer's aspirin and generics are similar, if not identical, Bayer has a strongly held world market share. One multinational which marketed a very successful ulcer drug discovered that the day after the firm's patent protection expired its high priced drug lost significant market share. The company had failed to establish its product as different from a generic which was now priced at half the price.

MRI's strategy was to develop products for small market niches, provide a patent protected superior product and generate a loyal customer base. Mr Davis had worked hard to ensure that research, production and the sales force all 'pulled' together to accomplish this objective.

Luck Like the Seasons Changes

First the Good News

The MRI catheter was just such a product. Developed to meet a specific niche market the product was believed to be technologically different and superior to Tri D's product. The MRI product was well accepted by the medical community and a patent had been applied for. It was an important day for the company when, in early 1984, the patent was awarded. Mr Davis and his team were delighted. The move he and several others had made from Abbott-Sorenson to MRI seemed to have paid off. They had invested a great deal in the move and the energy they had put into the ARIS product seemed to present everyone with an exciting future. It had not really been that long since Mr Davis had joined MRI. He recalled how the firm was, at that time, struggling for an identity. Once a real estate company, it had decided to use its land profits to enter the medical industry. Often investors viewed the little public company more as a venture capital start-up than an honest competitor in medical devices. The fact that the company's catheter was a new design, worked and was well received by the medical community certainly gave everyone at MRI a reason to celebrate – at least for a few months.

Then the Bad News

2 October 1984 was an upsetting day for Mr Davis and MRI. The company lawyer Mr Hayton informed him that the multinational corporation Tri D was suing MRI for patent infringement. The lawsuit stated that MRI's catheter product was based on Tri D's Armine two-stage venous return catheter which had been patented in 1977. Both devices were used during heart surgery to take blood from the heart to a heart–lung machine. They both employed openings at the end of the catheter and openings further down the tube to allow blood to be taken from two heart chambers by one catheter.

The Tri D product had been patented in 1977 by Bruce Armine who was at that time a design engineer for Sarns Inc. Sarns Inc. was purchased by Tri D after the catheter had been developed.

Davis Meets Goliath

Mr Davis knew that MRI was in trouble. He and Mr Hayton had spent long hours reviewing the ARIS patent to assure themselves that the product was sufficiently different from others on the market. They had proceeded only after all avenues of investigation had demonstrated to them that their patent was defendable.

No matter how defendable the patent was, the idea of having to fight a multinational was a bit overwhelming for a small company. The first thought that came to Mr Davis's mind was that Tri D probably had more lawyers in its patent division than he had total employees. In most cases a small firm would not have sufficient funds for a legal defence, which could cost $1 million to $2 million. A large multinational could easily destroy a small company. Mr Hayton knew that Tri D could prolong a case long enough to deplete the resources of most small firms. The medical devices side of the business was not reassuring. MRI had a market capitalization of about $10 million to $20 million with $500,000 in revenues from its catheter product. If it were to rely only on product sales it would be impossible to defend the case without bankrupting the firm. Mr Hayton felt certain that Tri D was keenly aware of this and would use the larger firm's financial superiority to force MRI into bankruptcy and thus secure Tri D's market position. He wondered, 'How could the legal system be so constructed so as to allow a major multinational this advantage?' 'It's not fair,' he thought, 'they can take our most important product because we cannot afford the defence of our patent.'

Mr Davis called his staff together to discuss the predicament. His words echoed what the others had said to each other prior to the meeting. 'ARIS is the product we have built our total strategy upon. It is our *raison d'être*! There is really no company without it'.

Everyone sitting around the table was well aware that Tri D had taken action against another major medical player, the company Ztec. Ztec was much larger than MRI and better able to fight. Even Ztec, however, had not wanted to take on Tri D and had yielded to the mammoth. Ztec had accepted a licensing agreement to market and sell its product in return for handing it over to Tri D. It choose not to enter a patent fight. By accepting the licensing arrangement Ztec received less profit but would still be in a position to benefit from its prior efforts. Mr Davis silently wondered, 'Would Tri D make such a licensing deal with us?' He turned to those in the room and asked, 'What do we do?'

Questions

(1) What are Mr Davis's options?

(2) Can Medical Research return to being a land development company?

(3) What are the strengths of a MNC which can be brought to bear against a small company?

(4) What would be the advantages and disadvantages of the different options?

(5) Can MRI afford a fight?

PART B

The Phone Call

'Let's try to deal,' replied Mr Hayton. 'If we can strike the right deal we may be able at least to sell our product. In this way we may be able to continue with our strategies.' There was general agreement. No one liked the idea of giving Tri D the product. Each felt he or she had something to do with ARIS. There was the development, marketing, legal work and then actual sales. Everyone had worked long and hard. No one felt good about a deal but what else could a small firm do? 'Mr Hayton is right,' Mr Davis thought, 'They sure do have a lot of lawyers to keep busy.'

Mr Davis knew that dealing was not a great alternative but certainly trying to take on Tri D looked much less appealing! The call was made to Tri D and the question asked, 'Would Tri D consider a licensing arrangement with Medical Research similar to the Ztec agreement?' The next days were tense and everyone at MRI was a bit short tempered. Mr Davis asked Mr Hayton. 'Have we done the right thing by asking for a settlement?' If we give in on this product will we be fair game for every product we develop? Is the request for a settlement in everyone's best interest?'

Mr Hayton reiterated his previous position 'Tri D is certainly large enough

to stop us dead in our tracks. It has done so to Ztec which is larger than us.'
Mr Hayton also knew that if Tri D defeated MRI it would be in a position to
set prices for consumers and dictate terms to distributors. Oligopolies liked this
luxurious position and did not like small firms trying to muddy the waters. In
addition, with Ztec out of the way and only MRI to knock off, Tri D would
be in an excellent position to scare off any new small firm that dared to enter
'their' devices market. Large firms liked that too! Mr Davis knew that with the
introduction of the ARIS product Medical Research Inc. had, almost overnight,
become a medical device contender. While the new found success was enjoyable,
none of the company's managers felt overly confident with having only the one
major product. Half to convince Mr Davis and half to convince himself Mr Hayton
said, 'This was the best decision.'

The Phone Call Is Returned

It had been two weeks since the initial contact with Tri D when Mr Davis's phone
rang. 'It is the legal representative from Tri D for you', the secretary announced.
Mr Davis slowly picked up the phone. He had not looked forward to this moment.
Suspense turned to surprise when he heard, 'Tri D is not interested in a deal
with Medical Research. We are asking you to voluntarily get out of the market.'
He put the phone down and asked his secretary to notify the board that they would
meet the following day. 'Now what?' he thought. Tri D had clearly considered
MRI to be a weak player and one which would be threatened out of the market.
Perhaps it was.

Mr Davis explained the previous day's call from Tri D to the board and again
stated that the legal staff firmly believed that the patent, which protected the ARIS
product, was defendable. They, however, did not really know how much it would
take to defend it. Whatever it was, it was going to be very expensive.

Mr Davis then turned to the board and again asked the question, 'What do
we do?' It was now a much more determined and angered group which responded,
'We fight!' Each board member knew that the ace in the hole for MRI was
the company's large reserve of cash from the land assets. Their's was a unique
situation. No small firm in a start-up phase would have this level of cash reserves.
Drawing on them would certainly use capital which could be allocated to research.
Mr Davis knew, however, that if MRI lost the fight there would be no company
left to do research. There was no option for the company. It now had to fight
for its life.

Mr Davis had carefully considered the numerous issues involved. What the
suit meant to the firm, its development of the product, the Tri D position and
the consequences of the suit to MRI. Could the company really afford to take
on a multinational in a major suit? Perhaps it could not afford not to. Mr Davis
knew that Tri D was banking on its powerful reserves to defeat his small company.
Could Tri D break the company with its size, reserves and legal teams? Hours
had been spent going over the documents, designs and R&D records. Mr Martin

Givins, VP operations, strongly believed that the product was not only substantially different from Tri D's product but it was also substantially better. It was their product and they would not let it go without a battle! Mr Davis started to put together a team that would lead the fight.

The Sun Comes Out for Medical Research

The Case Drags On

Mr Davis found it interesting that Tri D filed its suit in Salt Lake City, Utah. While this was the corporate home of Medical Research Incorporated, it would have been normal to try to locate the trial in a more neutral area. Everyone at MRI felt that this was indicative of the MNC's belief that it would steamroll the process with size and resources and did not have to worry about side issues. The legal representative from Tri D informed MRI that the reason it was following through with the patent suit was that Tri D 'Is a good corporate citizen. If the Tri D patent was not valid then they wanted to know about it.' 'What a marketing line!' thought Mr Walls. He did, however, worry that MRI would not be able to financially maintain its defence.

The case was now moving towards its third year and it was getting hard to keep the daily enthusiasm going in his department. Everyone felt that if this continued much longer the overall operations of the firm would be in danger.

Inequitable Conduct

The twenty-fourth of October 1987, was a happy Friday afternoon for Mr Davis and MRI. David Smithe, the District Judge, had just ruled that Tri D did not have a case. The man who claimed to have invented the Armine two-stage venous return catheter 'did not invent' the device. While Mr Armine had claimed that the ideas which led to the development of the product were his, several prominent heart surgeons with whom he had met and corresponded at the time clearly showed that the invention was a combination of ideas that were already available in the medical community. The judge ruled that, 'No subsequent actions by Tri D or its competitors, can overcome the clear and convincing evidence that Armine did not invent the [catheter] and that the apparatus described in the patent would have been obvious in March 1977, to one of ordinary skill in the art of venous return.'

It was particularly uplifting to Mr Davis that the court ruled the Tri D patent as invalid and procured through inequitable conduct. The court had recognized that Tri D was attempting to muscle MRI out of business and did not like it, he thought. It also appeared that no one had bought the 'good neighbour' line. Gary once again considered how lucky they were to have had the resources to see the case through. He knew, however, that MRI was not yet out of the woods. An appeal was expected, and would cost additional time and much needed cash.

The Door Slams on Tri D

Mr Davis reached for his ringing phone. The calendar on the desk read 17 October 1991. He was expecting word from the court house today as a final decision on the Tri D appeal was due. It was Mr Hayton with the news that the Federal Circuit Court entered its judgement in favour of Medical Research Inc. and had upheld all aspects of the District Court's decision. Not only was Tri D forced to acknowledge the legitimacy of Medical Research's patent but it was also to pay costs and attorneys' fees. These were in the range of $613,000. Mr Davis knew that the awarding of legal costs was most unusual and represented a clear understanding that Tri D had been wilfully attempting to use its strength to destroy a competitor through predatory action. The strategy had failed.

Nancy Holtz, manager of corporate communications, released the company press statement, notifying the business community of the decision. In it Mr Davis stated, 'We are pleased that this legal matter is resolved. However, it is of even more significance to our shareholders that we have emerged from this situation as the worldwide market leader in the legally contested product arena of dual-stage venous return cardiovascular catheters. We now are the only company participating in this market with a patented dual-stage venous return catheter product, and sales of this product continue to grow rapidly.'

A Strange Turn of Events

On 4 June 1991 Medical Research Inc. was issued a patent for the firms muscle preservation balloon catheters. The patent involved both design features as well as the method and use of self-inflating balloon retrograde cardioplegia devices. The patent applied to the company's Retroplegia (R) balloon catheters, its pediatric retrograde balloon catheters and the recently introduced Normoplegia (Tm) balloon catheters.

Mr Davis stated in a June fifth press release that the patented self-inflating balloon technology addressed a market potential of approximately $100 million in the 625,000 open heart surgeries performed annually worldwide. In the same release Mr Davis stated that, 'This long awaited patent is extremely important to the corporation, as our line of balloon cardioplegia devices is the company's most rapidly growing line and strategically import product.'

It was assumed that the patent would better enable the company to defend not only its commercial interests in the expanding heart muscle preservation market, but also the intellectual property of its development partner.

After the patent award one of MRI's first acts was to file a patent infringement lawsuit against the firm CRC Inc. MRI claimed that CRC had infringed on their patented technology involving retrograde venous cardioplegia catheters and their methods of use and manufacture for heart muscle preservation. Mr Davis stated in a press release, 'Medical Research Inc. intends to pursue all legal remedies available to it which arise out of the infringement activities of CRC Inc., and to aggressively defend our leadership position in this growing market.' Mr Davis could not but wonder with their cash reserves high due to both their continued revenue from land holdings and the recent settlement from Tri D if they now were not the 'Big Bad Wolf'. It was certainly clear to him that patents had become an important element in a firm's business strategy.

Acknowledgement

The author would like to express his appreciation to the President of the firm represented as Medical Research Inc. for his interest and dedicated assistance in the preparation of this case. While the names, companies and products have been changed, the case is based on actual events.

Questions

(1) In what ways can a firm protect a new product? What is the best method? What are the underlying costs and returns?

(2) Discuss Gary Davis's leadership and decision-making role in the patent case.

(3) What means are available to protect a firm in the service industry from competition?

(4) Why do you think Tri D did not fight to have the case heard outside MRI's home town?

Appendix 13.1

Five Year Consolidated Summary of
Operations and Selected Financial Data

(In thousands except per share data)

	1991	1990	1989	1988	1987
Revenues	$12,175	$10,880	$ 7,640	$ 5,834	$ 6,037
Cost of sales	4,756	4,972	3,267	2,316	2,211
Interest expense		205	539	552	556
Income tax expense	1,365	970	410	305	290
Net income	2,471	1,414	791	492	368
Earnings per share	0.41	0.25	0.16	0.10	0.08
Total assets	18,503	14,622	14,704	14,381	13,766
Long-term debt	–	–	1,706	1,943	2,040

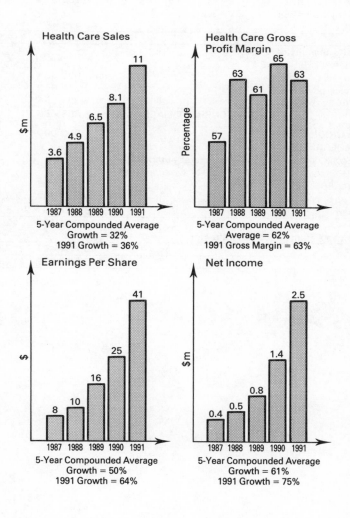

Health Care Sales

$m

3.6 / 4.9 / 6.5 / 8.1 / 11

1987 1988 1989 1990 1991

5-Year Compounded Average
Growth = 32%
1991 Growth = 36%

Health Care Gross Profit Margin

Percentage

57 / 63 / 61 / 65 / 63

1987 1988 1989 1990 1991

5-Year Compounded Average
Average = 62%
1991 Gross Margin = 63%

Earnings Per Share

$

8 / 10 / 16 / 25 / 41

1987 1988 1989 1990 1991

5-Year Compounded Average
Growth = 50%
1991 Growth = 64%

Net Income

$m

0.4 / 0.5 / 0.8 / 1.4 / 2.5

1987 1988 1989 1990 1991

5-Year Compounded Average
Growth = 61%
1991 Growth = 75%

Appendix 13.2

Consolidated Balance Sheet

	June 30	
	1991	1990
Assets		
CURRENT ASSETS		
Cach and cash equivalents	$ 875,216	$ 2,041,949
Short-term investment	4,140,000	
Accounts receivable	2,321,256	1,603,800
Current portion of notes and contracts receivable	126,055	243,256
Inventories	1,544,202	1,568,100
TOTAL CURRENT ASSETS	9,006,729	5,457,105
LAND HELD FOR RESALE	4,309,219	4,424,472
OPERATING PROPERTY	4,109,874	3,793,033
NOTES AND CONTRACTS RECEIVABLE	597,698	331,163
OTHER ASSETS	479,457	616,402
	$18,502,977	$14,622,175
Liabilities and Shareholders' Equity		
CURRENT LIABILITIES		
Account payable	$ 522,058	$ 421,121
Accrued taxes payable	241,863	358,626
Other accrued expenses	334,565	231,399
TOTAL CURRENT LIABILITIES	1,098,486	1,011,146
DEFERRED INCOME TAXES	800,000	805,000
SHAREHOLDERS' EQUITY		
Common Stock, par value $0.50 per share; authorized 20,000,000 shares, issued 5,928,394 shares in 1991 and 5,509,966 shares in 1990	2,964,197	2,754,983
Additional paid-in capital	5,277,737	4,196,370
Retained earnings	8,362,557	5,891,354
	16,604,491	12,842,707
Notes receivable from officer and director		(36,678)
	16,604,491	12,806,029
	$18,502,977	$14,622,175

Appendix 13.3

Consolidated Statements of Sharehold

	Year Ended June 30		
	1991	1990	1989
Revenues			
Health care product sales	$11,067,604	$ 8,159,564	$6,472,109
Real estate transactions	809,526	2,399,136	857,494
Interest and other	298,332	321,048	310,650
	12,175,462	10,879,748	7,640,253
Costs and Expenses			
Cost of health care product sales	4,071,407	2,851,246	2,507,887
Real estate transaction costs	684,233	2,120,916	758,866
Research and development	661,162	516,908	500,399
Interest		205,015	538,978
Selling, general and administrative	3,160,330	2,501,439	2,133,586
Settlement of litigation		300,000	
Divestiture of implantable assets	(237,873)		
	8,339,259	8,495,524	6,439,716
INCOME BEFORE INCOME TAXES	**3,836,203**	**2,384,224**	**1,200,537**
Income taxes	1,365,000	970,000	410,000
NET INCOME	**$ 2,471,203**	**$ 1,414,224**	**$ 790,537**
EARNINGS PER COMMON AND COMMON EQUIVALENT SHARE	$0.41	$0.25	$0.16
AVERAGE COMMON AND COMMON EQUIVALENT SHARES OUTSTANDING	6,013,000	5,666,000	4,960,000

CASE 14
The Scottish National Orchestra
Strategic Non-Profit Marketing

Matthew J. T. Caminer
Allied Distillers Ltd

Introduction

The Scottish National Orchestra is Scotland's most distinguished professional orchestra, giving concerts and making recordings throughout Scotland and the rest of the United Kingdom, as well as making overseas tours. Like all British professional orchestras, the management of its affairs is dominated by financial matters, the problem being more one of survival than of growth.

The SNO has a considerable pedigree, is acknowledged to give performances of the highest artistic calibre, and has an enthusiastic following throughout Scotland. The management team is small and new, and upon it lies the burden of responding to the challenge of a changed operational environment in the face of severe financial constraints.

Overview of the Situation

It is early in 1990, and the Chief Executive of the SNO is in conference for the first time with the newly appointed marketing manager. They are discussing the major and difficult challenge currently facing the orchestra and must make immediate plans to deal with the short-term situation.

Glasgow is already enjoying a high profile as European City of Culture, and the Scottish National Orchestra is preparing for its move from the City Hall to the larger Royal Concert Hall upon its opening in October. Newly appointed pivotal senior managers have had little time to lay their plans. The Scottish National Orchestra had been innovative in being one of the first British arts organizations to introduce subscription tickets, but for many years the orchestra's marketing environment had not been progressive and disciplined strategic planning had not been considered a prerequisite for its continued success. The focus had instead been concentrated on the more urgent, short-term need to attract public funds and industrial sponsorship to guarantee survival and to permit growth. This emphasis had placed a considerable burden on the management team, leaving less time for longer-term strategic issues. Now, with the opening of the Royal Concert Hall only six months away, they have no choice but to address themselves to the immediate task of exploiting the opportunities presented by the new concert hall to the full.

General Background

History

The SNO was founded in 1891, although it has only existed in its current, full-time form since 1950. Until that time, known as the Scottish Orchestra, it had operated on a part-time basis except for a short break during the First World War. Since the 1950s it has been known as the Scottish National Orchestra.

It is therefore an organization with a considerable history and, in Scotland, its reputation in its field is second to none. It is very much part of the national establishment, and its professional excellence in public concerts and in the recording studio is recognized both at home and abroad.

Activities

The organization's activities are described in the annual report as 'to administer the Scottish National Orchestra which gives performances of symphonic, operatic and choral music. The subsidiary company, Scottish National Orchestra Society (Properties) Limited, is responsible for the operation of the SNO Centre.'

The activities thus described combine public performances, studio recordings (for broadcasting companies and the record industry), tours of the United Kingdom and overseas, participation in major festivals, and the promotion of and participation in educational activities.

Although the orchestra's base is in Glasgow, it is in the nature of the Scottish population that, even when 'at home', a considerable amount of time is spent touring within Scotland, the winter subscription season from September to April involving intensive travelling between its four regular venues, Glasgow, Edinburgh, Dundee and Aberdeen.

The subsidiary company, SNO (Properties) Limited, owns and operates the SNO Centre, a refurbished church building in the West End of Glasgow, comprising a hall known as the Henry Wood Hall, and a recently constructed office suite housing the orchestra's management. Although primarily used by the SNO itself as a rehearsal hall and recording studio, the Henry Wood Hall is also hired out to outside musical bodies when available. Since the early 1980s it has been a popular venue for small and medium-size concerts.

The Organization

The organization comprises 89 players, all of them specialists on their chosen musical instruments. The board of directors includes two members of the orchestra, representatives of outside bodies such as the Scottish Arts Council and local authorities, several non-executive directors, and the Chief Executive (see organization chart: Exhibit 14.1).

The representative strength of the local authorities and the Scottish Arts Council on the board reflects the major sources of the orchestra's funds. Their concerns, frequently politically motivated, tend to dominate internal discussion, which is hardly surprising given the marginal financial basis upon which the orchestra operates. The board includes individuals with standing in Scottish public life and industry who provide the necessary balance. Given the nature of an orchestra, the playing members are indispensable: without altering its nature in a radical manner, the numbers and specialities involved could not be changed.

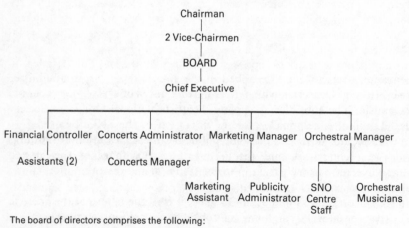

The board of directors comprises the following:

Chairman	2 Orchestral Players	Financial Controller
2 Vice Chairmen	7 non-executive directors	(ex officio)
Honorary Treasurer	Chief Executive (ex officio)	

Representatives from 13 Scottish Regions
Assessor from the Scottish Arts Council
Four assessors for the convention of Scottish local authorities

The full board meets 6 times a year, operational authority being delegated to the Chief Executive and his team.

Exhibit 14.1   *Organizational structure of the SNO.*

Similarly the supporting management team is so small and specialized that changes could not easily be made.

The musical profession is not well paid, at either the performing or the management level. Within the SNO, the prevailing atmosphere reflects vocation and commitment. A great deal of dedicated effort is the reason for the excellent artistic results, and in this respect, the players, management and staff are all of a high calibre.

In the management team, there have been new appointments in all the senior positions in recent years, bringing to bear a combination of experience, new values and a vibrant, innovative approach. As several staff members reached well-earned retirement, the Chief Executive has had the opportunity to rationalize the establishment, at the same time selecting with care the replacements where required, in some cases by internal promotion.

The work of the Scottish National Orchestra takes place in an environment that is constrained by exceptional financial hardship. For example, the fact that the most lucrative work for orchestras and their players is often to be found in London or overseas has the potential to tempt the best players to move away.

The Product

It is easy to itemize the activities of the SNO. At the heart is the winter season of concerts, comprising performances in four major cities, as well as a short summer series of Proms in the same cities. (The details are given in Exhibit 14.2.) In addition, and important either as revenue sources or for future audience building, are broadcasts, recordings and schools concerts.

It is less easy to explain these activities as a product, however, or to establish whether in marketing terms they represent a product or service. For instance, it is unclear whether the SNO belongs to the serious music or entertainment industry; whether it is a commercial organization or one performing a social service; and so on.

A clue may be found in an analysis of the work it chooses to undertake. It is open to the SNO to perform *only* popular classics, or *only* 'highbrow', esoteric compositions; it could reflect its Scottish heritage with a heavy bias towards native compositions; it could ensure a hearing for more difficult, modern music. Each type has its advocates and its opponents; and each appeals to its own audience. There is a middle road, combining a little of each type, leaning slightly towards the safer, more conservative programmes, and this policy is followed by most orchestras as a means of appealing to the broadest possible cross-section of the audience, thus filling seats and at the same time presenting an attractive proposition to potential industrial sponsors.

In the same way as an industrial company, therefore, the SNO has to make strategic marketing choices of a very businesslike nature. This choice is dictated by the SNO's own strategy, described below. Its execution results in a mix of the elements described above, thus meeting all the commercial and organizational criteria for a well-balanced symphony orchestra.

Exhibit 14.2   Performances and audience capacities (1989/90 & 1990/91)

Location			1989/90 Capacity	Concerts	Potential	1990/91 Capacity	Concerts	Potential
Aberdeen	Winter		1,200	8	9,600	1,200	8	9,600
	Proms		1,200	3	3,600	1,200	4	4,800
Dundee	Winter		2,525	8	20,200	2,525	10	25,250
	Winter†					2,205	2	4,410
	Proms		2,525	3	7,575	2,525	3	7,575
	Proms†					2,205	1	2,205
Edinburgh	Winter		2,414	22	53,108	2,414	21	50,694
	Winter†		2,215	4	8,860	2,215	5	11,075
	Proms		2,414	4	9,656	2,414	4	9,656
	Proms†		2,215	2	4,430	2,215	2	4,430
Glasgow	Winter	Sat	1,216	26	31,616	2,417	22	53,174
	Winter	Sat†				2,065	4	8,260
	Winter	Thurs	1,216	9	10,944	2,417	7	16,919
	Winter	Thurs†				2,065	1	2,065
	Proms		2,000	12	24,000	2,000	12	24,000
Winter				77	134,328		80	181,447
Proms				24	49,261		26	52,666
All				101	183,589		106	234,113

† Concerts with choir resulting in smaller audience capacity.

Just as it was difficult to analyse the product of the SNO, so it is unrealistic to suggest that there is such a thing as an average consumer (concert-goer, record purchaser, radio listener, and so on). People's motives for going to an SNO concert vary widely. These include a genuine love of music, a wish to enjoy music at a superficial level, the need to go out and be with other people, a need to support and identify with national institutions, whatever their nature, and the psychological need to be seen in the 'right' place on a particular night.

The SNO is musically capable of meeting all the needs at the narrow, musical end of the spectrum, and certainly covers all the other needs more than adequately. By the choice of repertoire within the context of the organizational strategy, the SNO could potentially confine itself to specific elements, but in fact takes the broader stance described above.

Organizational Strategy and Market Mission

These were described in the following terms by the Chief Executive:

'The Scottish National Orchestra aims to be a leading contributor to the cultural life of Scotland. Within the harsh financial constraints of the classical music industry, we attempt to offer a well-balanced programme to the public, a realistic form of sponsorship for our supporters and a stable source of employment to our players. The orchestra's association with a number of distinguished conductors has provided focus both musically and commercially, leading to improved audiences, increased sponsorship and extensive recording commitments. It is the intention that the SNO should continue to look outwards to the needs of the community which it serves, with particular emphasis on the young, the audiences of the future. While it might be pleasant to indulge in programming of an esoteric nature, this would be impractical, and our strategy is to appeal to as broad a range of the people as possible. Only thus can the orchestra expect to survive the financial hardships which will always be present as long as the current system of funding continues.'

Organizational Culture

The influence of finance on the orchestra is obviously of the greatest importance. The financial position is dealt with elsewhere, but everything is geared to doing as much as possible with as little money as possible. Thrift plays a major part; so does a concentration on excellence, without which the orchestra cannot survive. The orchestra continued with the active participation of the same Musical Director, Sir Alexander Gibson, for 25 years until 1984. His influence affected the culture of the orchestra as much as the artistic policy and musical standards. Whether artistic excellence has always in the past been matched at a managerial and operational level is open to debate.

For many years, the long-service administrative staff have been supported by numerous very active part-time, volunteer workers throughout Scotland, helping in many small ways, such as manning stalls and hosting Friends' events. Their approach has tended often to be non-innovative and conservative both musically ('We know what we like and we like what we know') and organizationally ('We've always done it this way'). It could be suggested that this approach typifies the hard-core SNO audience, who do not take kindly to change.

The central professional managers, however, are quite the opposite, striving towards excellence although frequently deprived of the resources with which to pay more than lip-service to such an approach. It is observed that their enthusiastic, hard-working attitude has begun to rub off on the organizational culture generally.

The SNO is only able to operate as an independent organization up to a point: the funding of its activities is derived to a greater extent from public funds than from the paying public. Thus market needs and competition alone could never wholly dictate the nature of the product, the policies and strategies: this lack of freedom inevitably colours the culture of the SNO.

Three senior management figures, the Musical Director, the Chief Executive and the Chairman, have quite distinct roles in shaping the destiny and public image of the SNO.

The Musical Director is responsible for the artistic policy of the orchestra. As well as choosing when and what he will conduct, he liaises with the Chief Guest Conductor to discuss his concerts. Up to a point he is involved in the remaining concerts, recordings, and so on, and has a role in developing a musical plan several years into the future. He has drawn attention to the frustration of having to be governed by commercial and box-office considerations rather than by artistic ones when planning the season's concerts.

The Chief Executive is ultimately accountable to the board for the effective and efficient management of the orchestra. He is responsible for ensuring that the musical content of the orchestra's life is well constructed, although this aspect is handled on a day-to-day basis by the Concerts Administrator, who negotiates with artists, and arranges programmes where these have not been selected by the Musical Director. The Marketing Manager reports to him on all aspects of marketing and publicity, including sponsorship seeking. Most human resource questions, including new appointments, are also his responsibility, although the Orchestral Manager deals with day-to-day aspects of such matters.

The function of the Chairman is less easy to define. His role involves providing an objective overview, at the same time undertaking a selective public relations function. This is particularly important with regard to the SNO's relationships with the Scottish Arts Council, local authorities and the sponsors.

Environment

Cultural Environment

Reference has already been made to the broad nature of the product/service offered by the SNO. The changing social environment is a strong influence, one in which values have altered, tastes evolved, and people's entertainment needs have become increasingly influenced by high unemployment.

Thus when the SNO undertakes concerts in schools throughout Strathclyde Region, it is not simply fulfilling a cultural and educational need for today; it is also staking its claim to the interest and involvement of tomorrow's potential concert-goers, and thereby investing in the future.

It is not simply a question of musical tastes. People who do not think twice about spending £10 on a round of drinks in the pub complain about spending the same amount on a concert ticket providing an entire evening's entertainment. Television has contributed to the decline of all kinds of live entertainment, as have hi-fi systems and all the other leisure opportunities that have developed over the last 20 years.

As discussed in greater depth below, Glasgow's nomination as the European City of Culture in 1990, and the anticipated opening of the new concert hall, have had a particularly strong influence on the cultural environment.

It is in this environment that the orchestra seeks not only to sell tickets and records, to engage world-famous artists and to employ the best available players; but also to convince those who fund it, the Scottish Arts Council, the local authorities and its sponsors, that by supporting the SNO they are engaged in a worthwhile undertaking.

Competitive Environment

In addition to the environmental factors described above, there exists a large amount of artistic competition in Scotland. Glasgow, a city of nearly 1 million inhabitants, is home not only of the SNO but also the BBC Scottish Symphony Orchestra, Scottish Opera, Scottish Ballet and the Citizens' Theatre, all professional bodies of a high calibre and of equal ambition. As well as these, many small professional and amateur organizations exist, all competing for the same finite audience.

Competition is not restricted to arts organizations. From a financial point of view, the ability of organizations like the SNO to obtain funds from public sources, principally the Scottish Arts Council and commercial sponsors, can make the difference between survival and collapse. Political factors influence both the total amount and the criteria for distribution of public funds, while the competition for industrial sponsorship is huge, not only from arts organizations but also from the sports world and charitable bodies. Furthermore, companies undertaking sponsorship are themselves subject to market forces which may effectively force them to discontinue some or all sponsorship.

Financial Environment

In recent years, it has become increasingly necessary for orchestras to build their entire existence upon the difficulty of surviving within the financial environment. Public money is a major factor in keeping arts organizations afloat, either through the Scottish Arts Council or through local authority funding. It is not possible to expect these sources to increase automatically, and very often the sums available remain static or even shrink in real terms.

The growth of sponsorship has led to a growth in professional sponsorship management and consultancies, chief among which is the Association for Business Sponsorship of the Arts, encouraged and supported by the government's award scheme for arts sponsorship. Whether sponsors really hope to gain commercial benefit from their sponsorship or are simply being altruistic is very difficult to determine. In the United States sponsorship can be written off against tax, but this is not so in the United Kingdom, making it hard to obtain support for what many people think of as a minority interest. It is not only a problem of the competitive environment, therefore, but it is also a financial one because the industrial sponsor who was the mainstay of the organization's industrial sponsorship last year may not be in a position to provide any support at all this year. Thus even though it has always been relatively easy to predict trends on the expenditure side of the equation, from the income point of view the Finance Director's task in creating realistic financial budgets is an extremely difficult and high-risk exercise.

European City of Culture

The nomination of Glasgow as European City of Culture for 1990 introduced a number of new factors. From a positive point of view, it provided the stimulus for constructing a purpose-built concert hall (see below). It also aroused intense interest in the city, attracting major international orchestras and stars who previously would never have considered visiting Glasgow. This has inevitably heightened local awareness, and created great anticipation for such visitors as the Bolshoi Opera, the Berlin Philharmonic, Luciano Pavarotti and Jessye Norman. The SNO has certainly benefited from this heightened awareness and from the increased media attention for the arts.

From a tourism point of view, Glasgow has experienced a major influx of visitors enjoying the rich cultural choice available to them and at the same time providing an important additional source of income for the SNO and other arts organizations.

These same benefits create their own difficulties, however. In a city where the competitive arts environment has in the past been largely controllable and predictable, and where there is a largely finite amount of disposable money for entertainment, people have suddenly been exposed to new and exciting artistic opportunities. The potential casualties could have included the arguably less glamorous, ubiquitous organizations like the SNO.

Concert Hall

For many years, the orchestra's Glasgow home was the much loved St Andrew's Hall. A quarter of a century ago, following a boxing match, the hall burnt down. In the intervening period, the orchestra's 'temporary' home has been the City Hall. In a city of nearly 1 million inhabitants, there has been little marketing challenge for a major institution like the SNO in filling a municipal assembly hall holding an audience of only 1,216 people. The heavy advance sale of subscription tickets rendered conventional marketing more or less redundant.

Despite much public hand-wringing by the authorities, there was never enough stimulus to build a new concert hall until the nomination of Glasgow as European City of Culture. Once the decision was taken, it was too late to make full use of the opportunity, because the new hall would not be completed and opened until nine months after the Year of Culture was finished.

The significance of the new hall from the SNO's point of view was that it would nearly double the available seating capacity for its Glasgow concerts, and would increase its total capacity for the winter season by 35%. Given that many subscription holders renewed year after year with little fluctuation in numbers, the sale of these additional seats would become a major challenge, especially as other organizations using the hall would face exactly the same challenge.

This difficulty in appealing to a finite audience would be compounded by the fact that, whereas international orchestras had avoided Glasgow as a venue because of the absence of an acceptable performing venue, they would now be including the city in their tours, not only in 1990, but after the Year of Culture was over. This would have the potential both to dilute audiences and to create pressure at an artistic level because instant comparisons, which had previously been denied to most regular Scottish concert-goers, would now be possible.

Finance

Introduction

Exhibit 14.3 summarizes the profit and loss, and sources of income and expenditure for the SNO for the last seven financial years. Not surprisingly, it is by no means uncommon for the orchestra to be in deficit, and the situation would be worse were it not for occasional subventions from the Charitable Trust, which exists to provide fundamental capital support for the SNO.

Sources of Funds

The orchestra obtains its funds from four major sources: the Scottish Arts Council (40%), box office receipts (40%), sponsors (10%) and local authority grants (10%).

The SNO was one of the earliest British organizations to import the subscription ticket concept from the United States. By selling a very high proportion of tickets for all the concerts in the season before it starts, the system provides a guaranteed audience and certain income, minimizing the need for heavy marketing expenditure, as well as creating a positive cash flow. Sales in this way have ranged from 80% of capacity for the Edinburgh series to 95% for the Glasgow Thursday series.

As discussed above, the SNO is subject to political decisions which can quite radically affect the orchestra's welfare, often due to factors which are totally unrelated to the arts in Scotland. Thus, while the SNO is able to keep its head above water, overnight changes in government policy and short-term crises in local government finance could cause immediate problems for the orchestra. An example of this in recent years has been the non-payment of council tax, which has severely damaged the ability of local authorities to maintain their budgets. The victims, inevitably, have been 'non-essential' activities including, of course, the arts.

Sponsorship represents a small proportion of the income, the amounts and proportions of total income fluctuating over the years, demonstrating the instability of sponsorship as a guaranteed source of income. Some of the reasons for not obtaining sponsorship have already been explained. Over the last five years, the SNO has experimented both with using a sponsorship consultancy and with employing a full-time sponsorship manager. Since it persevered with neither appointment, it has been difficult to judge the efficacy of each approach. It is interesting to note, however, that Scottish Ballet has for some years employed a

Exhibit 14.3   Profit and Loss Statement 1984–1990†

(£'000)	1984	1985	1986	1987	1988	1989	1990
Turnover							
Concert receipts	459	465	522	577	523	678	725
Hire of orchestra	139	147	260	114	185	199	117
Broadcast/TV fees	75	130	65	48	49	43	40
Concert sponsorship	49	83	116	73	184	145	131
Recording sponsorship	28	19	48	80	91	136	142
Net gain on record sales	1	—	1	2	1	—	—
Corp. members/advertising	28	37	57	45	48	47	44
Hall rental income	—	—	—	—	—	—	21
Total turnover	779	881	1,069	940	1,081	1,249	1,220
Other Operating Income							
Miscellaneous	2	—	—	—	—	—	
Donations	42	38	43	43	17	33	90
Friends of the SNO	9	5	2	3	3	2	7
Total other operating income	53	43	45	46	20	35	103
Operating Costs							
Salaries/subsistence	1,323	1,471	1,487	1,553	1,751	1,910	1,949
Artists' fees	103	130	177	127	151	126	197
Hall rental	80	97	95	103	116	106	55
Hire of music, instruments	21	25	27	18	27	18	18
Misc. concert charges	70	101	82	105	92	99	102
Recording costs	23	38	59	98	128	139	92
Programme printing	41	42	56	56	58	59	69
Depreciation	14	18	18	16	16	24	38
Printing & advertising	130	145	132	135	140	167	156
Transport & travel	69	71	73	68	122	36	56
Gala concert net proceeds	—	—	29	—	—	—	—
SNO Centre direct costs	—	—	—	—	—	—	8
Total operating costs	1,874	2,138	2,237	2,278	2,602	2,683	2,741
Gross Deficit	1,042	1,214	1,123	1,292	1,501	1,399	1,418
Administration Expenses							
Office administration	201	203	272	294	322	345	555
Sponsorship consultants	4	4	2	11	—	—	—
Total administration expenses	205	207	273	305	322	345	555
Loss Before Exceptional Items	1,247	1,421	1,396	1,596	1,822	1,745	1,973
Exceptional Items	0	0	0	0	0	(41)	421
Net Operating Deficit	1,247	1,421	1,396	1,596	1,822	1,786	1,552
Other Income							
Scottish Arts Council	926	996	1,251	1,332	1,389	1,444	1,481
Regional/district authorities	273	281	172	191	211	221	260
Interest received	5	5	7	8	2	14	—
Carnegie UK Trust	3	3	2	2	—	2	—
SNO Endowment Fund	50	—	48	—	—	—	—
Others	—	—	—	2	2	1	22
Total other income	1,257	1,285	1,480	1,535	1,603	1,682	1,763
SNO Properties Surplus/(Deficit)	(2)	(5)	59	(11)	(16)	(8)	(22)
Surplus/(Deficit) for the Year	8	(141)	143	(72)	(235)	(111)	188

† Totals may not add due to rounding.

full-time sponsorship manager whose exclusive task has been to obtain sponsorship, both new and repeated, the stability of the appointment being reflected in a more predictable pattern of sponsorship income. It reflects nothing but credit on the SNO that it succeeds as well as it does in the absence of such a concentrated view of seeking sponsorship.

Expenditure

Salaries represent by far the largest drain on the orchestra's resources. Some international artists are beyond the scope of the SNO. This presents a dilemma: without attracting international stars, there is a limit to the lucrative external engagements (such as one-off concerts, broadcasts, recording contracts) that can become available as revenue sources. On the other hand, the engagement of expensive artists would result in an unacceptable financial drain. The SNO attempts to strike a balance in this regard, tempting concert-goers with a satisfactory blend of programmes and artists.

The situation is complicated further by the differing costs of a single programme. In some weeks, one programme of music is prepared for performance in only two concerts, but in other weeks there can be as many as five performances of that single programme. The rehearsal and other costs tend to be largely the same; as a result two apparently similar concerts can have very different expenditure potential against a fixed income.

The small organization, in terms of staff and property, means that the overheads are low in real terms, although they represent a drain that must constantly be kept in check.

From 1990 onwards, however, there has been an additional constraint. In some cities, the 'resident' orchestra is charged a greatly reduced fee for using the concert hall. In Glasgow, however, the managers of the new concert hall have made it clear that no such benefits would accrue to the SNO or other Scottish orchestras. Thus, in the face of increased competition from visiting orchestras, the SNO has had no competitive edge at all, and in the meantime, the orchestra's costs are increasing at a faster rate than its income.

Marketing

Marketing Orientation

The SNO is dedicated to the excellence of its product. Financial considerations influence how it uses that product. It is that excellence that ensures that all the financial sources described above can be maintained and put to the best possible use.

Until now the SNO has not had a marketing department. There was, however, a press and publicity department, whose activities overlapped with a number of marketing roles. Despite their lack of specialist, professional marketing skills, the individuals concerned maintained exemplary control over short-term activities. The SNO's most recent person in a marketing-related management position was the full-time sponsorship manager. Upon her departure, however, the board recognized the need for dedicated marketing skills with the very recent appointment of an experienced marketing manager, demonstrating a shift in the SNO's marketing orientation.

Product policy, however, remained the combined province of the Artistic Director and the Chief Executive. The marketing manager's function was to market a pre-defined product without the ability to influence the future of the product in the light of marketing forces.

Marketing Budget and Management

The marketing budget is set as part of the overall SNO budget package, and is then broken down on a top-down basis. Exhibit 14.4 shows a typical breakdown of the marketing budget expenditure.

Exhibit 14.4   A typical breakdown of the marketing budget expenditure

Activity	%
Subscription series brochures, summer proms series brochures, posters and street banners	60
Media advertising	30
Small advertising items, point-of-sale items, gift items, etc.	10
	100

The activities were very much geared to selling subscription tickets, which was not so much a marketing activity as a financial necessity. There was a finite number of seats actually available for casual sale on a concert-by-concert basis given the high rate of subscription pre-sale described above, and it could therefore be argued that there was little need for a formal marketing function.

The SNO face a new situation with the opening of the new concert hall, with a doubling of the capacity for its Glasgow concerts and an overall 35% increase in capacity for its winter series. While it might have been imagined that Glasgow's position as European City of Culture for 1990 and the opening of the new concert hall would have been seen as a sufficiently strong catalyst for an earlier appointment, the fact remains that only in early 1990 itself did dedicated professional skills become available within the SNO.

For the opening season in the new concert hall, the marketing manager had the option to use the normal mailing approach, upon which was superimposed an additional activity for which commitments had already been made by the board. This comprised a Glasgow-centred poster campaign, based upon a two-month burst of 48-sheet advertising alternating over 60 sites. As a medium this was preferred to television advertising, which was also seriously considered. The campaign was funded partially by an increased marketing budget and partially by donations from five corporate sponsors, and by the concert hall itself.

Planning Process

No formal marketing plan has been produced by the SNO, nor has there been a longer-term company marketing strategy within which such a plan could operate. What marketing planning there was at the SNO had been directed wholly at the subscription ticket scheme and had been undertaken each summer, at the end of the previous season. It amounted basically to a project-planning exercise for the production and distribution of brochures by mail and in strategic distribution points (for example, ticket office, public libraries, and so on). Given that these were normally produced to specification and were distributed on time, this approach worked very well. The same could be said for the parallel, but smaller, project of marketing the Proms series held in Glasgow, Edinburgh, Aberdeen and Dundee each summer.

Innovation

Within the United Kingdom, the SNO was a pioneer in the introduction of subscription tickets, and in the artistic sphere its Musica Nova festival of contemporary music every three years has represented the breaking of new ground. It has nevertheless been felt that within the very narrow confines of the SNO's activities, as described in the annual report, there has appeared to be little scope for further innovation. Marketing opportunities do, nevertheless, exist, even without 1990s twin challenges, and these have previously been exploited without maximum effect.

For instance, programmes bought by concert-goers have traditionally been a marketing province within the music business; they are frequently made into self-financing and even profit-generating publications, the production costs being met entirely by advertising revenue, the cover price remaining a revenue source. For many years, the SNO has ignored this approach, and has considered the programmes to be a province of the Concerts Manager. Expenditure and receipts from printing and advertising/cover price respectively have been treated as part of the income and expenditure outcome of a concert. As a result of this approach, SNO concert programmes have either carried no advertising at all, or only that of some of the sponsors, for whom free advertising was part of the deal. The result is that programmes were probably a drain on funds rather than a revenue source.

At its Glasgow concerts, the orchestra has permitted an outside organization to erect a stand selling albums and cassettes in direct competition with its own stall (see below). No fee has been obtained for this activity which the SNO sees as offering a service to the public.

The SNO erects a stall on concert nights. In Glasgow, it is manned by members of the office staff who are traditionally paid a retainer for doing the task, and elsewhere by students in exchange for free tickets. The stall carries a full range of the orchestra's recordings, as well as an attractive range of advertising items (coffee mugs, aprons, pens, and so on). This is obviously an important source of income. The drain on potential sales of SNO recordings, due to the competitive circumstances mentioned above, is a further example of a poorly exploited marketing opportunity. Similarly, possibilities exist for substantial improvements in the somewhat unimaginative sales layout and presentation.

None of these three items in themselves would prove to be substantial sources of revenue, but given that the orchestra operates within a very tight financial framework, such activities could prove valuable.

Marketing Information

It has not been considered necessary to develop a marketing information system at the SNO. No research of any kind has been undertaken, whether *ad hoc* or omnibus, qualitative or quantitative, and no audit data has been bought. Provided that subscription holders renewed each year, it was implicitly accepted that concert-goers were satisfied with the nature of the product, the type of music performed, the timing and whereabouts of concerts, the artists engaged, and so forth. The current pattern of SNO activities had continued unchanged for many years, and little merit had been seen in investing the time and money needed to build up an audience profile and other details that would have been included in a marketing information system, given the perceived limitations on the effectiveness of doing so.

Conclusion

The SNO is a vibrant organization, whose performances are of the highest international standard, and whose management succeeds in maintaining a good balance of housekeeping and progress, against pressures of a turbulent and changing environment. The SNO provides a quality product, one with which its customers and funders are generally satisfied. Given the traditional nature of a symphony orchestra, few opportunities have in the past been recognized for change or innovation, and within this scenario the SNO has operated efficiently and has achieved its objectives.

The greatest cause for anxiety remains the question of finance: the SNO's vulnerability to political change creates insecurity but is beyond the management's control. At the same time, the exploitation of industrial sponsorship as a means of raising further finance is at an undeveloped stage and its full potential has still not been realized. There is, therefore, immense pressure on the management team. This pressure is compounded by the strategic opportunities presented by the European City of Culture nomination and the opening of the new concert hall, both factors carrying major marketing implications.

The SNO has previously believed that heavy investment in sophisticated marketing tools was a luxury that it could not afford and did not need. Marketing planning and the development of marketing information systems were not considered to be business priorities, and management believed that the introduction of strategic marketing planning would not result in any significant improvement. That this is a major long-term issue has clearly been recognized and acted upon by the board, given the recent appointment of a marketing manager. What is less certain is the extent of his role and the contribution he will eventually make.

Questions

(1) Write the job description for the newly appointed marketing manager, giving:
   (i) The background within which the position exists
   (ii) A summary of the position
   (iii) Five key tasks
   (iv) Three duties and responsibilities associated with each of the key tasks

(2) Does the SNO sell a product or a service, and what is its nature? Who is the target consumer, and what need does the SNO satisfy?

(3) Do the marketing needs of arts organizations differ from those of profit-making concerns? If so, explain the points of difference.

(4) On not more than two sheets of paper, brief a research agency that you wish to conduct audience research. Your brief should indicate the objectives of the research, the preferred research method and the time scale.

(5) What would be the financial implications of a 100% increase in industrial sponsorship and a 25% decrease in the Scottish Arts Council grant? Would the two balance each other? Explain your answer in financial terms.

(6) In the form of a diagram, produce a comprehensive SWOT analysis based on the case study. Select one item from each of the four sections and explain why you have included them in your analysis.

Question for Group Work (suggested size – five people)

Your group represents a marketing services consultancy, about to make a presentation to the SNO's new marketing manager. Present your strategy for the orchestra, covering product policy, price strategy, promotional activity, target audience and financial objectives. Your presentation should focus on how each of these elements will be affected by the opening of the new concert hall.

PART 2

Managing the Marketing Mix

The Marketing Mix

Marketing management deals with developing a marketing mix to serve designated markets. The development of a marketing mix should be preceded by a definition of the market. Traditionally, however, the market has been loosely defined. In an environment of expansion even marginal operations could exist profitably, so there was no reason to be precise, especially since the task of defining the market is at best difficult. Besides, corporate culture emphasized short-term orientation, which by implication stressed a winning marketing mix rather than an accurate definition of the market.

Product strategies specify the market needs which may be served by offering different products. It is the product strategies, duly related to market strategies, which eventually come to dominate both the overall strategy and the spirit of the company, and opportunities and threats are seen accordingly. Product strategies deal with such matters as number and diversity of products, product innovations, product scope and product design.

Positioning helps in differentiating the product from competitive offerings. Positioning is achieved by using marketing-mix variables, especially through design and communication efforts. While differentiation through positioning is more visible in consumer goods, it is equally true of industrial goods. With some products positioning can be achieved on the basis of tangible differences (such as product features); with many others, intangibles are used to differentiate and position products.

New product development is an essential activity for companies seeking growth. By adopting the new product strategy companies are better able to sustain competitive pressures on their existing products and make headway. The implementation of this strategy has become easier because of technological innovations and the willingness of customers to accept new ways of doing things.

Top management can affect the implementation of new product strategy. First, by establishing policies and broad strategic directions for kinds of new products the company should seek. Second, by providing the kind of leadership that will create the environmental climate needed to stimulate innovative drive in the organization. Finally, by instituting review and monitoring procedures so that the manager is involved at the right decision points and can know whether or not work schedules are being met in ways that are consistent with the broad policy direction.

Pricing strategy is also of interest to the very highest management levels of a company. Yet there are few management decisions that are more subject to intuition than pricing. There is a reason for this. Pricing decisions are primarily affected by factors which are difficult to articulate and analyse, such as pricing objectives, cost, competition and demand. For example, assumptions must be made about what a competitor will do under certain hypothetical circumstances. There is no way of knowing this for certain; hence the characteristic reliance on intuition.

If a firm operates in an industry where there are opportunities for product differentiation, it can have some control over pricing even if the firm is small and there are many competitors in the industry. This may occur if customers consider one brand to be different from other competing brands; whether the difference is real or imaginary, they will not object to paying a higher price for their preferred brand. To establish product differentiation of their brand in the minds of consumers, companies spend heavily on promotion. Product differentiation, however, offers an opportunity to control prices only within a certain range.

Distribution strategies are concerned with the flow of goods and services from manufacturers to customers. Six major distribution strategies may be distinguished: channel-structure strategy, distribution-scope strategy, multiple-channel strategy, channel-modification strategy, channel-control strategy, and channel-conflict-management strategy.

The channel-structure strategy determines whether the goods should be distributed directly from manufacturer to customer or indirectly, through one or more intermediaries. The distribution-scope strategy specifies whether exclusive, selective, or intensive distribution should be pursued. The question of simultaneously employing more than one channel is called a multiple-channel strategy. The channel-modification strategy involves evaluating current channels and making necessary changes in distribution perspectives to accommodate environmental shifts. The channel-control strategy focuses on vertical marketing systems to institute control. Finally, resolution of conflict among channel members is examined under the channel-conflict-management strategy.

Promotion strategies are concerned with the planning, implementation and control of persuasive communication with customers. These strategies may be designed around advertising, personal selling, sales promotion, or any combination of these. The first strategic issue involved here is how much money may be spent on the promotion of a specific product/market. The distribution of the total promotional budget among advertising, personal selling and sales promotion is another strategic matter. The formulation of strategies dealing with these two issues determines the role that each type of promotion may play in a particular situation.

Clear-cut objectives and a sharp focus on target customers are necessary for an effective promotional programme. An integrated communication plan consisting of various promotion methods should be designed to ensure that customers in a product/market cluster get the right message and maintain a long-term cordial relationship with the company. Promotional perspectives must also be properly matched with the product, price and distribution perspectives.

Development of an optimum promotion mix is by no means easy. The promotion decision should be made in the context of other aspects of the marketing mix. Managers should examine the relevance of other marketing decisions to the promotion mix. The price and quality of a product relative to the competition have an impact on the nature of its promotional perspectives. Higher prices must be justified to the consumer by actual or presumed product superiority. Thus, in the case of a product which is priced substantially higher, advertising achieves significance in communicating and establishing the product's superior quality in the minds of the customers.

The promotional mix is influenced by the distribution structure employed for the product. If the product is distributed directly, the salesforce will largely be counted on to promote the product. Indirect distribution, on the other hand, requires greater emphasis on advertising since the salesforce push is limited. The further the manufacturer is removed from the ultimate user, the greater is the need for the advertising effort to stimulate and maintain demand.

Strategic matters explored in the area of personal selling are those concerned with designing a selling programme, supervising sales people and the use of information technology as a strategic weapon in salesforce management. Today's business and marketing managers are faced with a continuous stream of decisions, each with its own degree of risk, uncertainty and payoff. With reference to marketing, operating decisions are the domain of marketing management. The typical objective of these decisions in a firm is profit maximization. During times of business stagnation or recession, as experienced in the past few years, efforts to increase efficiency have typically encompassed a cost minimization perspective. Under these conditions managers are pressured into shorter and shorter time horizons. All too frequently decisions are made regarding pricing, discounts, promotional expenditures, collection of marketing research information, inventory levels, delivery schedules and a host of other things with far too little regard for the long-term impact of the decision. As would be expected, the decision that may be optimal for one time period is not so in the long run. The degree of control that management can achieve over the components of the marketing mix varies by industry, product/service type and market conditions. Particularly important is the performance of the entire marketing mix in the marketplace, not just the effectiveness of any one component.

Marketing Mix Cases

Some cases in this section focus on specific parts of the marketing mix, while others consider the overall development of a marketing mix strategy. The *Flying Waiters Ltd* case examines key aspects in the establishment of a new business with an innovative service offering. Issues raised by the case include the definition of a service policy, the pursuit of future corporate and marketing strategies, segmentation, targeting and positioning issues, design of a marketing plan, promotion considerations and the measurement of marketing effectiveness.

The *Home From Home* case again looks at a new business venture, a residential home. The case introduces the company's managerial economic, financial and investment plans, its marketing plan and implementation plan, and marketing, service, pricing and promotion strategies. The new company has to consider ethical and consumer behaviour issues, market analysis and planning, segmentation, positioning, pricing, communication and promotion strategies, and investment analysis.

The *MIT Tractors* case is designed to familiarize students with possible pricing objectives and strategies, as well as to dispel the myth that pricing decisions are tactical in nature and to assert their strategic implications. It also demonstrates the possible application of the buy-response approach to pricing research.

Pricing is also the focus of the *POK Electronic Systems* case, which allows for a comparison of 'skimming' versus 'penetration' pricing in new product introductions. The case shows the relevance of demand, competition and cost factors in pricing decisions.

The *WEDR-FM Radio Station* case analyses the success of a black-run radio station in Miami, Florida, which implemented a series of strategic moves to lift it out of ratings obscurity to become one of the top five stations serving the area. The case focuses particularly on segmentation and on advertising to particular target audiences.

The *Aroma* case concerns a commercial distribution firm in a sector where there is great competition from both large area stores and small specialist establishments. Students have the opportunity to analyse the firm and its capabilities, its decision to reposition itself, and its subsequent advertising strategies.

The *Langport Building Society* case looks at the possible marketing objectives of a medium-sized building society, the main features of a new financial product it is about to launch, and the marketing plan required for this new issue. The case concentrates on the anticipated advertising campaign, and which are the 'best' advertising channels for the newly envisaged product.

The development of a new financial planning service is the focus of the *Windsor Building Society* case. The case situation revolves around the analysis of the marketing approach used by the company, which was based on a strategic synergy between personal selling and direct marketing techniques.

The *Southwest Bank* case deals with the choices facing a bank in defining its approach to corporate customers with specific emphasis on small businesses. It highlights the impact of some environmental factors on banks and how increasing customer responsiveness can aid banks in differentiating their offerings, and also considers approaches to product and customer policy. Key issues raised are customer service, service quality, customer care programmes and customer base management, as well as the development of new market opportunities, product mix management, pricing and profit performance.

The *Avis Rent-a-Car Limited* case is designed to familiarize the student with franchising as a vertical-marketing system, as well as some of the advantages and disadvantages of franchising for both the franchisor and the franchisee.

The *Ulaanbaatar Carpet Factory* case tells the story of a Mongolian company struggling to adapt to rapid social and economic change, and examines to what extent traditional marketing concepts such as marketing information systems, segmentation, targeting and positioning can be applied in an unusual market environment. Students are challenged to develop specific marketing mix and international marketing strategies within the Mongolian socio-economic context.

In the *Strathspey Centre* case the student is introduced to the different stages of the new product development process in the leisure industry. The case presents and discusses many factors involved in the design of marketing mix strategies, and shows the importance of analysing demand patterns and market trends. It also allows students to prepare an advertising budget and a promotional strategy.

The *London Underground Ltd* case analyses the application of marketing strategies and techniques in a public sector organization which is highly visible, has a complex technological environment and is strongly influenced politically in its operations. The key issues are related to performance indicators, market segmentation and targeting, marketing communication strategies and the analysis of future strategic implications.

Finally, the *Scottish Football League* case illustrates the difficulties of properly marketing a sport, especially at the League/Association level. It provides students with the opportunity to develop marketing policies, strategies and marketing mix programmes in a non-traditional situation. Important concepts considered are budgeting, sponsorship, segmentation, targeting and promotional strategy.

Reference

Jain Subhash C. (1985). *Marketing Planning and Strategy*. Cincinatti, OH: South Western Publishing Co.

CASE 15
Flying Waiters Ltd
New Service Development

Luiz Moutinho
Cardiff Business School, University of Wales College of Cardiff

Company History

Early in 1993, an international group of students, hard pressed with their studies and constantly eating out, sat around the large house they shared wondering what sort of project they should consider submitting as part of their MBA course.

As usual, thoughts turned to food and they decided they would have to go out, regardless of the bad weather. The usual row broke out as to where they would go. Donald Smith wanted plain English cooking, Christos was homesick and wanted to eat in a Greek restaurant, while the four remaining members of the group wanted to go to a Chinese restaurant. Mary said, 'If only there was a local service we could call which would send waiters flying round with our food.' All six obtained an MBA and now they are the managing partners of a firm called Flying Waiters Ltd.

The Marketing Environment

The Players and the Company

Flying Waiters (FW) is a people-based service trying to create, meet and satisfy the personal needs of discerning customers. The company delivers quality food from a wide product mix for in-house consumption.

The Flying Waiters service philosophy is expressed in the sign-off line 'professional service with the personal touch'. This philosophy is embodied in a number of 'augmented service' facets: a complimentary rose, home delivery, polite, conscientious, smart and courteous staff, convenience of service and an excellent and varied choice.

The staff are trained to leave a favourable impression and decrease the consumer uncertainty over a new experience.

The Suppliers: Establishments of Distinction

Top restaurants provide the food that FW resells. The chosen establishments are of excellent quality, formal and relatively exclusive, and will supply a high-quality menu under a negotiated contract with the company. FW cannot survive without the quality food supply and support provided by these selected restaurants.

The Flying Waiters Products

Flying Waiters not only sells food, it also sells quality. It offers a professional home delivery service with a personal touch. Seven international cuisines are available: French, Italian, Greek, Indian, Chinese, Spanish, Mexican, as well as Carvery and a Fish Menu.

Menu variety results in great consumer choice and an impressive depth of product mix.

Establishing the Flying Waiters Service Difference

The following factors will help establish and sustain FW as the best choice for the discerning customer: quality food, beautiful presentation, service with a smile, punctuality, reliability, consistency, flexibility, attention to detail and focus on customer satisfaction.

A combination of the above will increase customer confidence, decreasing the uncertainty surrounding service exchanges.

Customers – The Focal Point of the Flying Waiters Philosophy

Clichéd it may be, but for a service-oriented organization such as this, the customer is, and must always remain, the focal point of all company operations. Losing sight of this factor will threaten the very existence of the organization. Research conducted by the company has identified a potential target market lying within social categories A, B, C_1. These socio-economic groups living within inner London spend more per head on quality food than any other area in the United Kingdom. Flying Waiters must achieve the highest level of competence in order to satisfy their requirements and retain their custom.

The Competition – No Margin for Complacency

The company is moving into a currently unoccupied market niche. Within the market spectrum, at a lower level, are the pizza delivery services. Above Flying Waiters one could find in-house food preparation being located in the perceptual map. The company managers feel that, for the moment, the niche potential is entirely theirs. The objective is to establish sufficient standing and competitive advantage in the market so as to restrict the effective entry of competitors. FW's managers sense that exclusive restaurant contracts, targeted growth, experience effects and economies of scale will help, but there can be no room for complacency.

How does Flying Waiters identify possible competitors?

Assume a member of FW's targeted social classes returns home, tired from a hard day's work.

- What desire does he/she want to satisfy? (Desire competitors) socializing, exercising, eating?
  If the answer is eating, then:

- What does he/she want to eat? (Generic competitors) home-cooking, eat in ready-made or going out to eat?
  If the answer is eat-in ready-made, then

- What type of eat-in ready-made food does he/she want? Take-away, home-delivery, ready-made frozen or chilled food?

If the last choice is home-delivery, then FW represents an exciting new alternative to the pizza/pasta options. The exclusive characteristics of FW differentiate the company from existing alternatives and satisfy many predicted scenarios, for example, no food in the house, boredom with existing home delivery, reluctance to eat out, desire for quality food and home comfort, unexpected guests, pre-planned dinner parties and unwillingness to cook.

What Do Customers Want From Flying Waiters?

The company knows it has the ability to satisfy the key targeted customer needs in terms of providing a novel eating experience. The directors had perceptions of the main requirements they could satisfy, but in defining their total service they had to gauge the opinions of potential customers.

The customer survey

As a result, FW conducted cross-sectional open interviews over a weekend with 150 households located in the year one target area.

Respondents were initially briefed on the idea in a neutral manner. This was not a hard-sell exercise. Questions were not disguised and were open-ended to encourage greater information, versatility and flexibility. Because of the friendly manner in which the interviews were conducted, few refusals were obtained. The interviews lasted about 30 minutes. This was a non-probability sample and, therefore, a statistical level of confidence cannot be assigned to responses. The company also accepted the limitations related to interviewers' bias. Some of the questions posed to respondents included the following:

- What are your initial impressions of the FW service?
- How could we improve the service?
- What cuisines would you like included?
- How often do you think you might use the service?
- What factors would contribute most to your enjoyment of the service?
- How do you feel about the proposed delivery charge?

Despite the limitations of the marketing research approach, the managers were encouraged by the positive responses. Respondents identified the following factors as important to their potential enjoyment:

- Quality (including presentation and temperature)
- Variety
- Value for money
- Ability to order in advance
- Emphasis on quality rather than speed (within reason)
- Manner and appearance of staff
- Capacity limitations, that is ordering for big parties
- Credit card payment facilities
- Willingness to try something new
- Ordering by fax
- Customer complaints procedure.

The managers used the findings to reinforce and refine the final FW service content. Exhibit 15.1 shows a perceptual map indicating FW's product positions strategy.

Corporate Strategy

The home delivery food market has been successfully exploited in the United States. Only now are British food retailers awakening to its huge growth potential. At one end of the spectrum is the affordable, but limited, pizza delivery option; at the other, a full butler service, to prepare, cook, serve and clear up your meal.

FW managers believe that a golden opportunity lies between these two extremes. In creating FW, they aim to fill that niche.

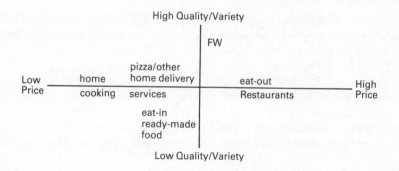

Exhibit 15.1 *Flying Waiters market position (as defined by price and quality/variety).*

Why Use Flying Waiters – A Possible Scenario

Have you ever returned from a hard day at work only to find an empty fridge? You do not feel like cooking and your favourite restaurants are fully booked. Yet you really feel you have earned a good meal. You could get a take-away, but the choice is limited and the food often indifferent. You don't have many options.

Now there is an alternative. Flying Waiters offers home delivery of a superb variety of top quality international cuisine, freshly prepared by your favourite London restaurants. Delicious food, immaculately delivered to your door by professional and dedicated staff.

Looking Towards the Future

- What are the long-term objectives?
- How is FW going to achieve them?

Collectively, FW management has defined its ultimate goal: 'Flying Waiters aims to become *the* generic term for the home delivery of quality cuisine.'

Company Objectives – Strategic Hyperbole or Operational Necessity?

The following objectives are the backbone principles of a company determined to succeed:

- To establish and maintain a service difference unseen and unsurpassed in the home delivery food market.

- To continually identify, highlight and respond to the varying and challenging needs of the FW customer base and potential market.

- To never forget that without its customers FW will be nothing. Total customer satisfaction and fulfilment should be, is, and always will be the company's primary focus.

Building on Success – Investing in FW's Future

Assuming financial viability at the end of year three, implementation of phase two of the company's growth will commence. Possibilities under consideration include:

- Increased expansion of the London target market area covered.

- Setting up in geographical areas outside London.

- Extension of the range of available FW services, business office lunches and 'the Flying Butlers'.

- Franchising is the long-term objective that really excites FW managers. The possible advantages include: transference of investment costs to franchisees, initial franchise fees and royalties on gross franchise sales.

- Adherence to franchise guidelines and practices, thus maintaining the quality image.

- The chance to become the 'Interflora' of its marketplace, held in esteem by customers and restaurateurs alike.

The Implementation Plan

Realizing the goals of Flying Waiters.

'Flying Waiters Is Only As Good As Its People'

The company depends on the appearance, behaviour and inter-personal skills of its staff, as well as the quality of its food. Delivery drivers must act in accordance with the selective image of the FW service, inspiring customer confidence and decreasing uncertainty.

Training – A Fast Track to Service Excellence

The company must effectively recruit, select, train, evaluate, compensate and motivate people. This will help facilitate internalization of the FW service philosophy and of its specific role expectations.

Why Join Flying Waiters? – Attracting the Right People

- Excellent remuneration – well above London courier service averages.
- Personal use of a company vehicle.
- 'Driver of the month competition'.
- Association with a progressive, innovative and ambitious company.

Recruitment Schedule

Demand projections necessitate the employment of 49 people by the end of year three: six managers, 40 drivers and three telephonists/secretaries.

Location

Premises are located in Acton (costing £120,000) and only five miles from the initial target area.

The Restaurants

Ten establishments in close proximity to each other in the Kensington/Chelsea vicinity. Meals will be purchased at a pre-agreed discount on retail menu prices. Second and third year expansion will necessitate the addition of extra restaurants closer to the new target areas. This will reduce delivery times and will prevent over-extension of restaurant capacity.

Opening Hours

- Monday to Saturday 10 am to 12 pm. Orders accepted by fax anytime and by telephone after 3 pm.
- Sunday 3 pm to 12 pm.
- Last orders accepted at 11 pm.

Customer Ordering Process

- Orders encouraged one day in advance, whenever possible.
- Personal and order details are logged into the computer to assist the following: direct mail shots, monitoring buying behaviour, that is, preferred restaurants, average order size, purchase frequency, peak demand periods and best geographic areas.
- Credit card payments are encouraged.

The Delivery Process

- Order received and price quoted.

- Order telephoned to restaurant(s) and time estimate received.

- Customer notified of abnormal time delays.

- Driver sent to collect order (supervisors will expect drivers to coordinate more than one order at a time whenever possible).

- Order delivered with a red rose, receipt and customer satisfaction questionnaire.

Drivers' hours are 6 pm to 12 pm with one day off a week on a rotational basis. A greater number of drivers than vehicles will ensure optimum delivery potential seven days a week.

Coping with Crisis and Dealing with Demand

The labour intensive nature of the business permits rapid response to deviations from anticipated demand levels.

Responding to a downturn

- Reduce staff levels

- Reduce the number of vehicles

- Decrease advertising and promotions (reluctant measures due to necessity of consumer awareness)

- Dispense with the roses

- Look for new services innovations

- Vary the advertising and the marketing mix

- Change restaurants

Satisfying increasing demand

- Widen the target area
- Increase the number of drivers
- Increase the number of vehicles
- Increase the number of restaurants
- Bring forward expansion of services
- Renegotiate restaurant contracts for higher volume

  Cost considerations and the marketing background of two of the FW directors will dictate corporate strategy. The company is, in essence, an intermediary. Previous employment contacts have resulted in favourably priced support services being readily available to the company when needed. The marketing director will coordinate the implementation of the corporate strategy.

Marketing Objectives

What Is FW Trying To Achieve?

- To establish itself as market leader in a new niche within the home food delivery market.

- To create and sustain awareness and differentiation among its customer base.

- To achieve recognition among 50% of the initial 30,000 mailshot campaign.

- To encourage 40% of the above to try its service at least once.

- To convert approximately 24% of them into regular customers, using the service three times a month.

- To facilitate a successful year two expansion into the second target area and likewise during year three.

- To create a perception of outstanding customer service and value for money, both for customers and associated restaurants.

- To facilitate justification of higher profit margins in order to sustain a competitive advantage over aspiring competitors.

How Is FW Planning To Achieve the Marketing Objectives?

The marketing department has a sizeable allocation of £51,300 available in the first year. This is in recognition of the extensive advertising and promotion necessary for building consumer awareness within the target market. This has been apportioned among the following items and activities.

Creating market awareness

Flying Waiters' managers are conscious of the need to create rapid market awareness if demand forecasts are to be fulfilled. The company is embarking on a new operation in a new market niche and must achieve rapid penetration of its target market. It is therefore embarking on a proactive advertising and promotion campaign.

Menu packs

High quality promotional menu packs will be delivered to 30,000 households located in the company's initial postal target areas of London. These menu packs are of an innovative design, thus encouraging people to retain them, rather than throw them away. Each pack incorporates the FW livery and contains individual menu sheets from the 10 restaurants in use. An additional 10,000 packs will be held in surplus to satisfy demand from the freephone information line.

Print and production requirements:

- 40,000 A4 sized sheets folded to A5 with an insert pouch, printed in two colours both sides.
- 400,000 A5 sized sheets printed in two colours, both sides.

The packs will be delivered on a single day by the Post Office, as cost considerations prohibit the purchase of mailing lists.

Newspaper advertising

First year newspaper advertising will be in the *Evening Standard* newspaper one Friday per month, and *Time-out* magazine likewise. Advertisements have been costed for half-page size and will mention target area restrictions. The company recognizes the large 'target miss' factor in such advertising, but it is aiming for general awareness, assisting expansion during years two and three.

Printing requirements:

- mono half-page bromide
- two colours half-page bromide

Years two and three

A broad continuation is proposed subject to first experiences. Requirements have been upscale to incorporate remailing of existing target areas, as well as penetration of the new target areas during the following months. Costings have been adjusted in line with company forecasts, and inflation rates of 10% in 1994 and 9% in 1995 (see Exhibit 15.2).

Getting the message across

FW service philosophy will be communicated throughout all advertising and promotion media with the following corporate sign-off line:

'Professional service with the personal touch'

Newspaper and magazine advertising will be designed around the following message:

Exhibit 15.2 Projected Financial Performance

Profit/Loss

	1994	*1995*	*1996*
Sales	1,105,950	3,412,800	5,378,400
Cost of sales	(901,425)	(2,757,888)	(4,302,729)
Gross profit	204,525	654,912	1,075,680
Expenses	(289,329)	(672,565)	(1,066,863)
Profit/loss	(84,804)	(17,653)	8,817

Cash flows
The cash flows are £5,536, £13,974, and £40,840 for 1994, 1995 and 1996, respectively.

Investment Appraisal
(a) NPV = £48,478 (over a five-year period)
(b) IRR = 23.9% (cost of capital = 14%)

Breakeven Analysis

Years	*Contribution/unit*	*Fixed cost/unit*
1	5.81	8.60
2	6.44	6.63
3	6.93	6.85

Other Information
(1) A 20-year term mortgage of £80,000 was obtained at the launch of the company. The capital repayment is £8,000 a year with an initial holiday of nine months and the annual interest is static at 13%.

(2) Taxation is only due on profit surplus after losses have been deducted and therefore does not apply to 1994 and 1995; taxation of 1996's profit is due in September 1997.

(3) As annual turnover exceeds £35,000, the company has to register for VAT.

(4) PAYE is calculated as 25% of both the employers' and the employees' salaries.

(5) Inflation is estimated at the rate of 10% in year one, 9% in year two and 8% in year three.

(6) Profit margins are calculated at 15% in year one, 16% in year two and 17% in year three.

(7) A further loan of £80,000 to assist with the initial set-up costs of Flying Waiters was provided by the bank.

(8) All six managers/partners contributed £30,000 each of initial capital.

'We have Mexican, Greek, Chinese and French,
Indian and so much more,
For great food in the home,
Just pick up the phone,
And FLYING WAITERS will deliver to your door!'

Future straplines include the following:

- 'Home has never seemed so good'
- 'When only the best will do'
- 'Chez vous, mangez toutes'

Measuring the Response

Considerable attention will be given to ensuring that all customers are questioned as to how they became aware of the service. A contingency plan has been developed for years two and three, highlighting the following alternatives if response to a particular medium is unsatisfactory:

- Alternative magazines – *The Tatler*
  – *The Economist*
- Newspapers – closely targeted freesheets
- Radio advertising
- Billboard posters
- Filofax inserts
- Joint promotion with Telephone Information Services Ltd
- Bus and Underground poster campaign

Measuring the Performance, Quality and New Needs

Having launched the new FW service, continuous feedback needs to be gathered from customers. This will allow for identification of possible weaknesses in performance, quality levels, complaints and new needs.

A large survey of FW customers will take place at the end of each year. This can be combined with the promotional tool of posting seasonal greetings cards to the regular customers of Flying Waiters.

Acknowledgement

The author would like to thank Dimitrios Koufopoulos, Mattheos Dimopoulos, Kwok Wai Leung, Adrian James O'Reilly, Mark Alan Squire and Charalambos Xylouris for providing the necessary information and allowing it to be used as a case study.

Questions

(1) (a) How could the company define a strategy designed to 'manage the evidence' of the Flying Waiters Service?

    (b) What concerns should the company have with synchronizing supply and demand?

(2) Based on the financial information provided in the case, make a summary assessment of the projections for the financial performance of Flying Waiters Ltd.

(3) What are the main considerations that the company should use when formulating a future service/market strategy?

(4) Comment on some key criteria and procedures that could be utilized by Flying Waiters Ltd in order to develop a segmentation, targeting and positioning strategy.

(5) Comment on the strategic planning process and key strategic marketing decisions that are likely to have an impact on the company.

(6) Devise a realistic and pragmatic marketing plan for Flying Waiters Ltd.

(7) Define the key criteria that could be used by the company in determining the promotion mix.

(8) What techniques and mechanisms could Flying Waiters Ltd apply in evaluating and controlling marketing performance?

CASE 16
Home From Home (HFH) Limited
New Service/Business Development

Luiz Moutinho
Cardiff Business School, University of Wales College of Cardiff

Introduction

Home from Home (HFH) Limited is a residential home whose future, despite the recession, appears to be promising. In the United Kingdom, the future market for residential homes is dependent upon the level and age structure of the elderly population. Pensioners are steadily increasing in numbers and by the year 2025 there will be an estimated 12.3 million of them.

In the United Kingdom there are still a considerable number of elderly people whose needs for care have not been met. Because HFH is entering a new market the company is faced with many threats. There is a great deal of competition in Aberdeen, so the company's competitive advantage lies in its offering a variety of services. HFH believes that it will obtain a competitive position and good reputation by implementing the proper strategies.

Managerial Economic and Financial Plan

Analysis shows that the investment plan is a feasible and profitable one. Much attention needs to be paid to achieving an occupancy level above the breakeven sales volume of 15 beds.

The company's activities are based on a total of 20 beds, with 13 paid staff and one unsalaried manager selected from among the directors, and assumption that the company can achieve 70% occupancy level for the first six months after opening and 90% for the rest of the period until the end of the third year.

It is estimated that HFH Ltd will make a profit before tax of £13,460, £56,199 and £68,586 in the first three years, respectively.

The return on capital employed ratio for the first year is less than 10% due to the substantial initial outlays, but the ratio improves significantly to achieve over 30% for the second and third years.

Assuming that the life cycle of HFH Ltd is five years, it is calculated that the internal rate of return of the company will be 18.28%, exceeding the base rate (cost of capital) of 13.5%. The finding suggests that the investment is worthwhile for acceptance.

Through cost–volume–profit analysis, it is estimated that the breakeven sales volume is 15 residents for the first year and 13 residents for both the second and the third year.

The use of sensitivity analysis suggests that the breakeven sales volume is the most critical factor to the success in achieving the company's objectives.

Additional Investment Plan

Taking into account the feedback, suggestions and findings derived from a survey carried out with potential residents and their relatives, the company is planning to invest some additional financial resources in order to improve the features of the 'total service offer' (that is, furnishings, safety standards, administrative functions, and so on).

HFH management is in the process of choosing between two additional invest-ment programmes (A and B) as shown in Exhibit 16.1.

HFH managers are currently calculating the payback periods of both invest-ment programmes.

Exhibit 16.1   Investment alternatives (cash inflows of £10,000 investment)

Year	Investment Programme A	Investment Programme B
1	5,000	1,500
2	5,000	2,000
3	2,000	2,500
4		5,000
5		5,000

Summary of Marketing Plan

HFH managers have identified the key marketing objectives so as to maintain a high occupancy level and to sustain quality residential care. Research has shown that the two major considerations governing residential home choice, by potential residents and/or their relatives, are service quality, location and staff care cover. Market analysis reveals that there are 52 residential homes in the Aberdeen area which are potential competitors. The company is to adopt a high passive pricing strategy and focus attention on non-price factors, especially quality service. The company is to advertise in local newspapers and *Yellow Pages*. Personal selling channels will also be cultivated to achieve 'word of mouth influence'. In the short term, the company has no intention of setting up a marketing department so the directors and the secretary will take up the marketing responsibility.

Implementation Plan

Whenever a new venture is begun, the individuals involved normally construct a systematic plan on paper. Although in many instances this is a relatively easy task, the actual implementation of the plan is very difficult indeed, and is thus not underestimated in the case of HFH Ltd. The execution of the business plan consists of many steps including: competitor analysis, examination of all forms of associated legislation, purchasing properties and securing bank loans. The latter seems to be the most important aspect of implementation, because without finances the business cannot begin. Although implementation is an extremely important process it should be used in conjunction with all the elements necessary in establishing a new venture, including strategy, marketing and financial affairs.

Marketing Plan

Marketing Objectives

- Maintain a resident occupancy level of equal to or greater than 18 out of the 20 possible beds. Available information and research indicate that occupancy levels of 85% to 90% are currently being maintained in residential homes for most areas. To sustain a profit-making company, and keep to the company's expansion programme, it must therefore aim to fill at least 18 of the beds. Should it fall below this level at any stage, then HFH will have to advertise in one of the local newspapers, which is the best advertising technique for immediate response.

- Follow a business expansion programme to ensure a level of employment of over 30 staff in three years.

- Sustain high-quality residential care for the elderly population.

Market Analysis

Industry Background

The accommodation needs of the elderly vary greatly and can be divided into three distinct types:

(1) Sheltered accommodation,
(2) Nursing homes
(3) Residential homes

Residential homes

These are registered with the local authority and offer residents rented accommodation, board and the degree of attention which they might expect from a caring relative at home. Residents are, in general, still mobile and do not require nursing care. Most homes do not cater for anything other than minor illness.

Typical Structure of the Market

The market has been dominated by small operators, usually a husband and wife team with a single unit. Once an initial home has been established, it is common for the small operator to either sell on and purchase or build a larger unit, or add an extension to the existing home. In some cases operators move on to a second home and a small number have built up a cluster of homes.

Expansion usually takes place around 18–36 months after first entry into the market. First homes tend to be in the 10–20 bed range with second homes/extended homes ranging from 20 to 60 beds.

There are currently 52 residential homes in the Aberdeen area. The average size of residential homes opened in 1991/92 was 13 and nursing homes was 25. It is difficult to establish the life cycle of the market due to its lack of maturity but there are indications of operators withdrawing after 3–5 years.

In the last two to three years a number of corporate players have entered the market and tend to operate larger units of 40 or more beds. These include:

Hotels and leisure groups	Stakis
Private health care groups	BUPA
Start-ups that have grown to corporate size property companies	McCarthy & Stone

Market Trends

The majority of residents in nursing/rest homes are in the 60 + age bracket, which is the major segment of the market in which the company is interested.

There is evidence of resistance to large institution type homes from both the market and from registration authorities.

Market implication of influences from socio-economic environment

Market size and government support are related. 50% of residents in private sector homes are supported by the government. Despite this, many residents receive additional help from relatives. It is therefore expected that running a residential home with a mix of private and government sponsored (that is DSS) residents should produce higher profitability.

Consumer Needs

The total population in the 65+ age bracket in the United Kingdom is 8.2 million. There are 262,313 elderly people in the Aberdeen area. HFH target clients are retired women aged 60–75 and retired men aged 65–75, 47,478 in total. They are in general:

- People who tend to be frail, relatively immobile or recovering from surgery. They might expect personal services and help with daily living.

- Residents who are still mobile but need 24-hour close attention.

- People who stay away from home for reasons other than those mentioned above, for short- and long-term, with or without a caring relative at home.

They can be classified into five categories:

(1) Mental problems, that is dementia or senility
(2) Alcohol dependence
(3) Drug dependence
(4) Physical disability
(5) Old age

In considering their needs, it is understood that the following attributes carry much weight in their decision to stay in a particular home:

- Staff care cover and staff–residents ratio
- Service variety and quality
- Facilities
- Accessibility
- Space per person
- Diet
- Environment

Future Marketing Strategy

The future market for residential homes is dependent upon the level and age structure of the elderly population. The retired population of the United Kingdom is becoming progressively older.

The retired population as a percentage of the working population will remain fairly stable until after about 2001 when it is expected to increase.

The most 'profitable' section of the population for residential homes is the under 75 year olds, an age grouping which is more active and needs fewer services. The development of sheltered housing is increasing, and will attract those people with capital mobility, and independence, who will generally be the 'younger' section of the retired population. It is therefore likely that the average age of residents in residential homes will increase. This may in turn reduce their profitability as generally the dependence of the older residents will increase.

The increase expected in the number of residents over the age of 75 is likely to result in an increased demand for nursing rather than residential care in the future.

To meet this anticipated demand it is the company's intention to obtain dual registration (under the Registered Homes Act 1984) from the Grampian Regional Council, as a residential and nursing home within three years.

Service Strategy

The attributes, features and services that HFH intends to provide at the residential home include:

- A fully registered residential home.
- A private home of the highest standard with well experienced, caring and dedicated staff providing 24-hour care.
- An ideal location, close to the shopping centre, public transport facilities and public parks.
- Delicious home cooking with a well balanced and varied menu to cater for the personal and medical needs of the residents.
- Single and double/shared rooms.
- Long- and short-term stays.
- Full central heating.
- An attractive, spacious and secluded garden.
- A large dining room and two TV lounges.
- An intercom system in all rooms with a comprehensive fire detection and alarm system.
- Resident guest room for family or friends.
- Government-sponsored residents are welcomed.

In addition to the above features, the company also intends to provide the following services:

- A small in-house library.
- A regular hairdressing service.
- Free chiropody and dental service when required.

Residents will also be encouraged to pursue their own personal hobbies and interests. If residents so wish, they are also welcome to furnish their own rooms with their own furniture. Surrounding the resident with his/her belongings would help create a more homely atmosphere.

Day trips will occasionally be offered to the residents. A minibus will be arranged to take the residents to the seaside or to a night at the theatre, for example.

Additional services to be provided by the home are birthday and Christmas parties. Residents will have the opportunity of inviting a limited number of family or friends along to celebrate together.

Pricing Strategy

A high passive strategy is to be adopted in order to keep fees competitive with other residential homes. The company does not aim to compete with other players in the market through price cutting. According to the result of a study, the potential consumers in the market are not very price conscious. It is the quality of the services which count most in their decision of choosing where to go. So HFH does not aim to emphasize price strongly in advertising, personal selling or other promotional activities. Instead the emphasis will be on non-price factors (such as 'caring and professional' services) and trying to relate its service characteristics to clients' needs. Thus the company is positioned in the 'High Passive Strategy' band (see Exhibit 16.2).

The fees currently charged by residential and nursing homes in Scotland are about £180–240 (see Exhibit 16.3).

There is no complete official regional information on fees currently charged by residential homes in the Aberdeen area. It is understood, however, that the prices are closely related to the running cost, most importantly cost values per bed.

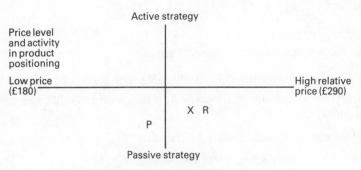

X   HFH price position relative to competition
P   The Heather House's price position (£200)
R   The Blue House's price position (£265)

Exhibit 16.2   *Pricing positioning map.*

Exhibit 16.3   Residential and nursing home fees charged in the United Kingdom

Area	Residential home (£ per week)	Nursing home (£ per week)
Wales	170–210	220–290
North	170–220	220–280
Midlands	180–240	220–290
London	210–350	250–400
Scotland	180–240	220–290

The going concern values vary greatly from region to region and depend on many factors including location, quality of care, breakdown of patients, and so on. This is illustrated by the following:

(1) Heather House, a fully occupied 13-bedded and 16-staffed residential house in Aberdeen, is charging £200 per person per week, whereas the value per bed is £25,000.

(2) The Blue House is a well-established home on the outskirts of Aberdeen with 33 staff and 34 residents. It previously charged £95 per person. However, last April, the home obtained dual registration as a residential and a nursing home. The charge for nursing home status per resident is £265 a week. This charge in registration was accompanied by an increase in capacity of the home from 34 to 44 beds.

Thus there are major local variations in pricing, ranging from approximately £170 to £400 per week. It is believed that such a wide price range in the market is attributable to the consumers' low price sensitivity. Most of the residential homes succeed in differentiating themselves from their competitors through featuring their services rather than adopting a pricing strategy.

Reaction to Competitive Actions

Despite the current economic recession in the United Kingdom, the residential home sector is a booming industry. Available information and research indicate that occupancy levels of 85% to 90% are being maintained in most areas. Therefore HFH believes that competition in the market will remain relatively stable.

Nevertheless, precaution is still exercised in case there is any unexpected change in the market situation. HFH reactions to competitive actions will focus on service improvement, which includes provision of personalized services such as hairdressing and special diets. Since the demand of elderly people for residential home services is rather inelastic, fee cutting will not be an effective means of meeting competitive actions.

Communication and Promotion Strategy

The main promotional techniques will be advertising and personal selling.

Local newspapers will be used as one method of advertising the home. Market growth in residential homes is shifting away from the traditional coastal resorts towards the growing centres of population. The trend is now also towards retirement close to family support. It is highly likely, therefore, that most if not all the potential residents will have lived in the Aberdeen area for many years. Local newspapers are thus a very important local medium because they are delivered weekly to over 110,000 homes throughout the Aberdeen area.

The company proposes to publish a 10 cm × 10 cm advertisement for three weeks prior to official opening, two weeks during the first month after opening, and one week monthly until the end of the second year, at a cost of £200 per insert. It will then be published for one week every other month for the whole of the third year at a cost of £100 per 10 cm × 5 cm advertisement. The advertisement will detail the overall attributes and services that will be provided by the residential home.

The company also intends to list the home in the *Yellow Pages* at a cost of £200 a year.

HFH also intends to use direct mailing as an advertising medium because it has a high degree of audience selectivity. This direct mailing will be done by both post and direct house delivery to certain areas. The leaflets will again endeavour to be tastefully worded, emphasizing HFH's strengths as a residential home. This direct mailing will also be done before the home opens and during the first weeks/months of operation.

Another major marketing tool that the company intends to cultivate is the personal selling method. It will concentrate on developing the personal communication channels both before and after the residential home has opened. HFH will promote the home via 'expert channels' including:

- The Department of Social Services.
- Local nursing homes, hospitals and the Area Health Authority.
- Social workers.
- General Practitioners in the Aberdeen area.
- Local nursing home associations.
- Help the Aged and voluntary organizations.

In addition to these 'expert channels', 'social channels' of communication will be developed. This will involve forming a good relationship with the family and friends of residents to promote the reputation of the home. Residents and potential residents will be asked how they came to hear of the home and this will help in evaluating the successful aspects of the advertising programme.

These personal communication channels will develop a 'word of mouth influence' which is likely to become a most effective and persuasive method in the marketing campaign.

Marketing Implementation Plan

In terms of organization, responsibility for marketing is taken by the directors and implemented by the secretary. No marketing department is intended to be set up during the early years of operation for the following reasons:

- Running a residential home is a management oriented business rather than a marketing oriented business. Promotion through advertising in newspapers and *Yellow Pages* will suffice since there is an excess demand for residential home services.

- Staffing costs make up the largest percentage of the cost of running a residential home. The directors believe that setting up a marketing department will be as much of a hindrance to the company's expansion as a help, in terms of the heavy costs to be incurred.

- The management still holds a contingency view of marketing. The directors believe that in due course a marketing department will be necessary when the company's development and environmental changes call for it.

Questions

(1) Should the ethics of routine 'business' marketing be the only major consideration driving the corporate strategy of HFH?

(2) HFH is planning to carry out marketing research in order to find out the importance of various elements contributing to residential home choice. List these 'product' attributes which will make up the 'universe of content' for subsequent questionnaire design.

(3) What considerations should be taken by the company when implementing the process of market analysis and planning?

(4) What innovative approaches could be used by HFH to segment its market, and develop a positioning and differentiation strategy?

(5) Comment on the pricing strategy and price positioning chosen by the company.

(6) How could HFH use a hierarchy-of-effects communication model to assess the effectiveness of its promotion strategy?

(7) Calculate the payback periods for both additional investment programmes. Criticize the application of the payback method by pointing out its shortcomings and disadvantages.

CASE 17
MIT Tractors
Pricing Policy

Douglas T. Brownlie
University of Stirling

In 1987, the MIT tractor company entered its fourth year of manufacturing and marketing a basic four-wheel-drive overland jeep called the *Little Shifter*. Since its introduction, the company had been selling the vehicle in the United Kingdom through a network of 8 distributing agents and 12 franchised dealers. The latter also acted as sole distributors of the firm's core product, its line of agricultural tractors.

In line with the company's aim to target the jeep at what it thought to be a very price sensitive UK market, its very competitive retail price of £4,799 in the introductory year had only ever risen in line with retail inflation, at an annual rate of 5%. The product was marketed as a no-frills, but reliable and tough working vehicle that would appeal to farmers, estate managers and land owners.

As a result of mounting feedback from its dealership network, MIT has recently become sensitive to the growing market potential for an up-market version of its jeep. Seeking to react quickly to this business opportunity the company has designed the *King Shifter*. Based on the chassis and engine of the Little Shifter, the new vehicle incorporates modifications of the suspension assembly, transmission, interior decoration, fittings and body finish thought to be consistent with customer perceptions of quality. The underlying marketing theme was being geared to encourage and exploit the evolving cult status of such vehicles and their associations with a young, successful, leisure-oriented and trend-setting, but well-heeled and independent lifestyle.

The Director of Marketing is about to advise the board of the price he believes MIT should set to dealers and end customers for the King Shifter. He and his team normally have the authority to take strategic marketing decisions where their budgetary implications are at least manageable, if not known. On this occasion, however, the MIT board looks likely to set what it will consider to be a conservative target return-on-assets (ROA) of 10%, as an average to be achieved over the first three years of the project. This is consistent with the hurdle rate used by the board on all MIT capital investments. Furthermore, it would not be unreasonable to expect the board's target ROA to increase dramatically in later years.

The Director of Marketing, Tony Edwards, has before him an executive summary of the factors he must consider in coming to his decision on price. This summary is reproduced in Exhibit 17.1. What price policy and strategy would you recommend that Mr Edwards set for the launch of the King Shifter? Compare

Exhibit 17.1   Executive Summary of Price Considerations

(1)   At current levels of productivity, the company has enough manufacturing capacity to produce up to 5,000 units per year of the new model.

(2)   To exceed this quota by more than 20%, is expected to require investing in new plant capacity.

(3)   The Director of Manufacturing is known to favour a production planning volume of 5,000 units in year one, building to full capacity in year two.

(4)   The Director of Finance accepts the logic of economies of scale in production, but he will express some caution on the grounds that economies of scale in marketing may not be forthcoming if the selling-in process proves difficult. He will also stress the working capital implications of large stocks of finished goods and work-in-progress.

(5)   The Total Fixed Costs (TFC) of producing and marketing the King Shifter are estimated at £5 million. This includes selling and promotional expenses, which are budgeted to account for about 10% and 15% of TFC respectively.

(6)   The Total Variable Costs (TVC) are estimated at £5,000 per unit, 90% of which is accounted for by direct labour (50%) and direct materials (40%) (direct costs plus manufacturing overheads plus trade discounts and commissions).

(7)   It is expected that assets of about £40 million would be employed during the first year of the launch of the King Shifter.

(8)   The leading competitor of the three already in the market is producing a high-quality overland jeep which is currently retailing at £7,000. The competitor charges its dealers £5,600 per vehicle and is expecting to sell about 6,000 vehicles this year. It is estimated that the competitor's net profit margin is about £450 per vehicle. An estimated return on assets (ROA) of 5% is being achieved.

(9)   At a recent trade show, the King Shifter model on display received very favourable reviews, 70% of the enquirers interviewed noting that the King Shifter seemed better designed and fitted than competing models. *Ad hoc* pricing research was conducted at the trade show on the firm's behalf. The buy-response technique was applied to a sample of non-owners/users of jeeps. The data collected was used to plot the buy-response curve of Exhibit 17.2, which shows the price above which the propensity to purchase might fall off.

(10) A group of industry analysts often used by the MIT board has projected 1988 sales of leisure-oriented jeeps at 12,000 units. This represents an expected growth rate of 40% on 1987 sales. A 50% average rate of growth is thought likely to persist into the early 1990s as younger car owners switch to status-giving vehicles and new market segments continue to evolve.

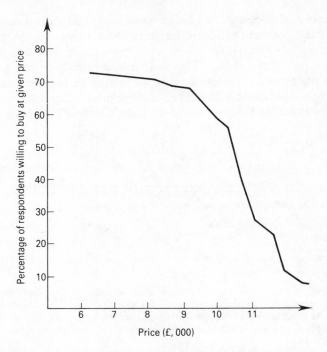

Price (£, 000)

Exhibit 17.2 *Customer response to various price points.*

and contrast possible cost and market-based pricing approaches that Mr Edwards might use.

Questions

(1) What are the total costs that will be incurred in producing and marketing 5,000 vehicles?

(2) What net profit margin is consistent with the ROA target?

(3) What dealer price should be set?

(4) What effect does the dealer's margin have on the retail price?

(5) How many vehicles must be sold to break even?

(6) What is the safety factor?

(7) What impact should inflation of 10% on direct variable costs have on the safety factor?

(8) What effect will a price increase (and decrease) of 10% have on the break-even point?

(9) How many vehicles does MIT have to sell at a retail price of £9,000 (and £8,000) to make the same net profit?

(10) What turnover is required to achieve a 15% NPM target?

(11) Negotiations with a nationwide chain of vehicle outlets have identified five prime sites that could be franchised at a cost of £150,000 and could generate a 5% increase in sales. Should MIT go ahead?

(12) Is there a case for doubling the promotional budget?

(13) What level of sales is needed to maintain the NPM if the following changes are introduced simultaneously?
   (a) Promotional budget increased by £500,000
   (b) Variable labour costs are cut by 10%
   (c) Variable material costs are cut by 20%
   (d) The franchising agreement proceeds

CASE 18
POK Electronic Systems
Pricing Policy

Luiz Moutinho and Fiona Davies
Cardiff Business School, University of Wales College of Cardiff

Introduction

In July 1982, POK Electronic Systems faced a major pricing decision with respect to its new teleconferencing system. 'We're really excited here at POK Electronic Systems,' exclaimed Mr Paul Kruger, the founder and president of POK Electronic Systems. 'We've made a most significant technological break-through in telecommunication systems.' He went on to explain that the marketing plan for 1983 for this product was now his major area of concern, and that what price to charge was the marketing question that was giving him the most difficulty.

Company History

POK Electronic Systems was founded in Glasgow, Scotland, in 1977 by Mr Kruger. Prior to that Mr Kruger had been a senior lecturer in electrical engineering at one of the local universities. Mr Kruger founded POKES to manufacture and market products making use of some of the electronic inventions he had developed while at the university. Sales were made mostly to the car industry and the military. Sales grew from £200,000 in 1978 to £4 million in 1981. Profits in 1981 were £2.6 million.

The Teleconferencing System Project

During the last four years, Mr Kruger had been trying to reduce the company's dependency on government and auto-manufacturers' sales. One of the diversification projects to which he had committed research and development investment was the so-called TCS – teleconferencing system project. The objective of this project was to develop a system whereby a television picture, which could be displayed on a screen as big as 8 to 10 feet diagonally, could be used for small to medium-sized meetings and conferences within corporations and different types of institutions. By installing this system in different locations, executives are enabled to conduct their business meetings without having to move out of their offices. In the area of information technology, there is a growing trend towards the utilization of value added networks, such as the teleconferencing system. In late 1981, one of POKES's engineers made the necessary breakthrough. The rest of 1981 and the first few months of 1982 were spent producing working prototypes. Up until June 1982, POKES had invested £400,000 in the project.

Teleconferencing

Teleconferencing – a new concept in which meetings are conducted before a camera and relayed via satellite to video screens in several locations simultaneously – is changing the way a number of corporations and associations do business.

Teleconferencing will not replace the business meeting nor will it take the place of the rapport and personal interaction of businessmen and women meeting together. It's not a replacement, it's a complement, a supplement.

Clearly, something is afoot. In view of all the current activity, and the strong opinions about teleconferencing – pro and con – it seems necessary to attempt an informed assessment of the new medium.

Is teleconferencing here to stay, or merely the latest technological hula-hoop? Teleconferencing is not entirely new. The technology which permits satellite communications has been with us for almost 20 years. Only recently has it become economically feasible to use the technology on a mass scale.

The history of most new technologies follows a similar pattern. Initially, the new technology is too expensive and too bulky in size to be practical for anything other than large business, government and institutional use.

Pocket calculators, for instance, originally sold for many times their present cost. Computers were once huge in size and economically practical only for multi-million pound operations. Now they are priced within the reach of small businesses and households, and can fit on table tops.

Such is the consistent history of technological innovations. Being the first buyer of new technology is not necessarily the best position to be in.

The superlatives and underlying sense of excitement surrounding tele-conferencing today have a familiar ring. In the 1950s and early 1960s, similar words were used to tout Closed Circuit Television (CCTV) as the next great advance in business meetings.

'Users in every part of the country report savings in travel and other expenses,' said an RCA executive at that time, 'when television has been utilized to bring together their staffs in regular conventions or for special occasions such as the kick-off of a new product. They also have lauded the effectiveness and impact that results when meetings are televised to remote locations, thus enabling field men to receive the "word" direct and simultaneously from top management rather than secondhand from travelling teams. . . .'

Even the term 'teleconference' was first used in reference to CCTV. As early as 1952, CCTV was being used for a variety of events: heavyweight prize fights, the Metropolitan Opera, Broadway shows, medical and educational seminars, fund raising, government and trade association meetings, stockholders' meetings, new product introductions, press conferences, dealer and salesmen meetings.

CCTV did not gain wide acceptance for broadcasts beyond special events primarily because it was not cost-effective. The cost of telephone land line transmission was expensive, and satellite transmission was limited and financially prohibitive at that time as well.

AT&T's Picturephone – telephones that transmit both voices and the faces of callers – is another example of communications technology that did not gain the mass acceptance first predicted for it.

Originally introduced and demonstrated at the 1964 World's Fair, Picturephone was launched with great fanfare. In 1970, the company predicted that by 1975 the service would have 70,000 sets in use in 30 cities. By the 1980s, AT&T speculated, Picturephones would be widely used by business and the general public, replacing some forms of transportation.

The analysts were wrong. Picturephone as originally conceived was a commercial failure, not because of its technology, but because of its high cost. 'Cost, and cost alone,' was the problem, said former AT&T Chairman John De Butts in an interview. 'Those sets each cost us a bundle to manufacture. Don't forget that a Picturephone has everything in it that the camera in a TV studio has, along with all the works that are in your home TV receiver – all in a compact desk-top unit.'

Initially, AT&T concentrated on selling the service to businesses, institutions and other large customers in a few major cities, including New York, Washington, San Francisco, Chicago and Pittsburgh; but the installation charges proved higher than most firms would pay, and not enough subscribers signed up to establish a practical network.

With new technologies, history has shown that caution is a wise and necessary response.

The new telecommunications technology permits teleconferencing to be offered to large businesses and associations as a cost-effective tool that delivers more for less and in less time. This is the reason why big business and associations are the prime movers behind the early use of teleconferencing.

It appears that every company or association that has had the teleconferencing experience has nothing but praise for it. Most users report time and money saved, ease and effectiveness of presentation, and a dramatic increase in the number of participants reached.

In October 1980, Symposiums International (SI), a Los Angeles based medical educational company, used the HiNet system to reach thousands of nurses in 77 cities. Noel Reede, President of SI, said the teleconference was an outstanding success. 'During one four-hour period we were able to put a distinguished team of doctors and nurses in front of thousands of nursing specialists, giving them the opportunity to learn the latest techniques in emergency nursing from some of the medical profession's top performers.

'The introduction of our promotion was a smashing success,' said Daniel McMaken of North American Van Lines. 'The HiNet Communications concept gave us the opportunity to announce our new programme to our agent family without the expense of either touring the country to visit a number of locations with a small entourage of corporate personnel, or bringing the agents together at a single location for a two-hour presentation.'

'We have to figure out the right formula to make teleconferencing profitable for all parties,' says Gary Badoud, president of VideoNet, and the man who almost single-handedly started the rapid growth of satellite video teleconferencing.

Because of the tremendous savings teleconferencing offers the corporate world, Badoud says, trying to stop teleconferencing at this point would be 'like putting your shoulder to a glacier.'

Teleconferencing System Designed for World Use

A teleconferencing system designed to meet worldwide transmission standards has been developed by Compression Labs Inc., San José, California. Called REMBRANDT, the system offers full-motion video teleconferencing on bandwidths that give users a choice of picture quality and transmission cost.

International teleconferencing is possible because the system offers conversion between National Television Standards Code video used in the United States, Canada and Japan, and Phased Alternative Line video used in Europe, South America, the Middle and Far East.

The system also offers RGB, the worldwide video standard for graphics that are of high quality.

Additional features include higher resolution graphics and video switching for Simulvision, an option that allows the display of two or more video images at the same time, and extended network line communications.

Compression Labs, a publicly held company, designs, manufactures and markets full-motion colour video teleconferencing systems for use by business, government and other organizations.

Among its customers are AT&T Information Systems, ITT Europe, Sony Corp., US Telecom and Vitalink Communications.

Video Screen Television

Extra large screen television systems were not new. There were a number of companies who sold such systems both to the consumer and commercial (pubs, restaurants, discos, and so on) markets. Most current systems made use of a special magnifying lens that projected a regular small television picture on to a special screen. The result of this process is that the final picture lacked much of the brightness of the original small screen. As a result, the picture had to be viewed in a darkened room. There were some other video systems that did not use the magnifying process. These systems used special tubes, but also suffered from a lack of brightness.

POKES developed a system that was bright enough to be viewed in regular daylight on a screen up to 10 feet diagonal and this was complemented with an innovative multi-person audio system for teleconferencing. This process was protected by patent, and Mr Kruger thought it would take at least two to three years for any competitor to duplicate the results of the system.

A number of large and small corporations were active in this area. Admiral, GEC, RCA, Zenith Electronics, Sony and Philips were all thought to be working on developing large screen systems directed at the consumer market. Sony was rumoured to be ready to introduce a 60-inch diagonal screen system that would retail for about £2,000. A number of small companies were already producing similar systems although without the multi-person audio unit which was tailored for teleconferencing purposes. PRIMETECH, a small East Anglian company, claimed to have sold 3,500, 84-inch diagonal units in two years at a £3,000 price. SOLO Electronics claimed one-year sales of 4,000 50-inch diagonal units at prices from £1,000 to £2,000. Mr Kruger was adamant that none of these systems gave as bright a picture as POKES's and that no other company came up with the idea of applying the core system to the potential market area of the teleconferencing business. He estimated that about 10,000 large-screen systems were sold in 1981.

Cost Structure

Mr Kruger was analysing the possibility of using a well-known industrial distributor to market the new system. This move would permit POKES to minimize some marketing costs as well as to provide a wider market coverage since this particular distributor had a strong customer base, salesforce, and also provided after-sales service. Mr Kruger expected about 50% of the suggested final selling price to go for the distributor's margin. He expected that POKES's direct manufacturing costs would vary depending on the volume produced. Exhibit 18.1 presents these estimates. He expected direct labour costs to fall at higher production volumes due to the increased automation of the process and improved worker skills.

Exhibit 18.1 *Estimated production costs of POKES's teleconferencing system.*

	Volume		
	0–5,000	*5,001–10,000*	*10,001–20,000*
Raw materials	£400	£380	£350
Direct labour	£450	£400	£200
Total direct costs	£850	£780	£550

Material costs were expected to fall owing to less waste due to automation. The equipment costs necessary to automate the product process were £50,000 to produce in the 0–5,000 unit range, an additional £30,000 to produce in the 5,001–10,000 unit range, and an additional £20,000 to produce in the 10,001–20,000 unit range. The useful life of this equipment was put at five years. Mr Kruger was sure that production costs were substantially below those of current competitors including Sony; such was the magnitude of POKES's technological breakthrough. Mr Kruger was unwilling to produce over 20,000 units a year in the first few years owing to the limited cash resources of the company to support inventories, and so on.

Market Studies

Mr Kruger wanted to establish a position in the business market for his product. He felt that the long-run potential for this company was greater there than in the consumer market. With this end in mind he hired a small marketing research consulting firm based in London to undertake a business market study to determine the likely reaction to alternative final selling prices for the system. These consultants undertook extensive interviews with corporate executives of potential purchasing organizations, and examined the sales and pricing histories of similar competitive products. They concluded that: 'POKES's teleconferencing system would be highly price elastic across a range of prices from £2,000 to £5,000.' They went on to estimate the price elasticity of demand in this range to be between 2.5 and 4.0.

The Pricing Decision

Mr Kruger was considering a number of alternative final selling prices. 'I can see arguments for pricing in order to skim the market or to penetrate the market and gain a foothold in the future,' he said.

Questions

(1) What factors should be considered in setting a price for POKES's teleconferencing system?

(2) What price should Mr Kruger set for POKES's teleconferencing system? Why?

POK Electronic Systems – Case Study Update

Introduction

Since the 1980s, the teleconferencing market has expanded and has seen a proliferation of different products. The new digital telephone technology (ISDN) during the 1980s permitted video teleconferencing via telephone lines, but it was still restricted to '*point to point*' expensive full time circuits, generally leased over a one- or three-year period. The development of the CODEC, again by CLI, enabled video teleconferencing to make effective use of the emerging digital telephone transmission medium.

The Gulf war in 1991 and the Lockerbie air disaster gave the medium a real boost as large organizations, particularly in the United States, turned to video teleconferencing systems, rather than risk the danger of terrorism.

Newly agreed international standards like the H.320 as well as advances in semiconductor technology made possible in the early 1990s the launch of a new way of video teleconferencing, the small groups or '*rollabout*' or '*rollaround*' systems. These systems allow mobile video teleconferencing without the need for the establishment of dedicated conference rooms.

In recent years, we have also seen the introduction of desktop video teleconferencing or multimedia teleconferencing, where users of PCs at different sites can view each other on their screens, as well as share data (documents, photographs, drawings, videos, and so on) and work collaboratively on them, with the use of appropriate '*groupware*'.

AT&T's Videophone 2500 as well as BT–Amstrad–GEC–Marconi's videophone launched in 1992, have been characterized as stellar accomplishments, but it remains to be seen if they will succeed, or if they will become the PicturePhones of the 1990s. Finally in 1993, AT&T's Picasso, a still image phone, which is still video-audio based, tapped a new segment of the teleconference market and provided further evidence of the fragmentation of the visual communications market.

Teleconferencing Markets and Products

One way to model the teleconference markets and their products is according to the combination of audio, video, groupware and telecommunication medium they utilize. Exhibit 18.2 shows such a model.

On the top are the high end systems while at the bottom are the lower end, less functional, but not always cheaper systems. A definition and description of these markets and their products follows.

Exhibit 18.2 *Teleconferencing products*

Price		Functionality
	• Dedicated Broadband Video Teleconferencing	
	• Dedicated ISDN Video Teleconferencing	
	• Small Group Systems Video Teleconferencing	
	• Desktop Video Teleconferencing	
	• Videophone	
	• Business Television	
	• Still Video – Audio-based systems	
	• Group Audio/Paper-based systems	
	• High Quality Audio Teleconferencing	

Dedicated Broadband Video Teleconferencing

This market requires products that can handle video teleconferencing between groups usually of 6 to 10 people and can ensure broadcast-quality video picture, that is they require the use of a broadband telecommunication medium, with a bandwidth of at least 2 Mbps up to 140 Mbps (for the very high end systems), to deliver at least 30 fps video picture quality. Thus they employ dedicated special telephone lines, or cable lines, or satellites, or any combinations of these broadband media.

They use also dedicated, specially designed, studio-type conference rooms with big public screens and/or PCs, equipped with the appropriate software for groupware and group decision support. Multipoint Control Units (MCU) can connect more than two of those rooms to enable multipoint teleconferencing.

Owing to the high cost of this infrastructure, only big multinationals can afford these systems.

Dedicated ISDN Video Teleconferencing

This market was a direct derivative of the one for the system described above. Owing to its high bandwidth costs, not many companies could afford it and they had to either pay heavy charges to interconnect private equipment, or use public facilities. The introduction of switched digital services – particularly switched ISDN – and the CODEC meant that more users could justify the cost of installing their own videoconferencing systems.

Such ISDN-based systems provide more or less all the services the previous system does, but at less cost.

Small Group System Video Teleconferencing

The need for portability and flexibility, which the Dedicated Video Tele-conferencing systems could not offer, was fulfilled by Small Group Systems Video Teleconferencing.

These systems are designed for departments and small to medium-sized companies. They are the *'plug and play'* type and include a monitor, camera, audio system, video CODEC, document camera, hand-held remote control or desktop touchscreen and network interface in a compact, rollabout cabinet. This is why they are also known as *'rollabout'* or *'rollaround'* systems. The system also provides connections for optional peripherals, such as VCR.

They are ISDN compatible and include powerful self-diagnostic and remote diagnostic capabilities, upgradeable software and MCU support. They can operate outside a dedicated studio environment, in any office which provides adequate lighting and low noise volumes, thus proving their flexibility and portability.

Desktop Video Teleconferencing

Desktop VC systems can provide audio/video communications on the PC together with shared groupware. They are a combination of powerful processors, using new global communication standards like the H.320 that ensure inter-operability between different vendors' equipment, and digital telephone services that provide the communication link.

They include microphone, camera, video compression and communications adapter, collaboration software and a PC. All these components can usually be added to a 486 or a Pentium PC, but new generations of PCs with all these components already integrated on them are coming out.

They permit free sharing and manipulation of user data, providing at the same time subtle, yet critical non-verbal communication cues (in the video equipped versions) associated with in-person meetings. Groupware supports these activities with various tools and interfaces and its purpose is to improve productivity by making communication easier between members of the team.

In Olivetti's PC, AudioTalk stores dialling information and controls con-ventional telephone calls made with a handset linked to the PC. FormTalk provides cooperative form filling on screen. TextTalk enables two-way real-time text conversation, used as an alternative to voice contact to ensure privacy or in situations where two-way audio conversations are difficult to conduct. Whiteboard enables each user to annotate simultaneously on-screen information, in much the same way as traditional whiteboard, and then save the new file. FileTransfer allows fast file exchange between users. PhotoFax permits transmission of true colour, high definition images. VideoTalk provides full point-to-point real-time videoconferencing.

Other collaboration software like Lotus Notes 3.0, SunSolutions and ShowMe 2.0 can be used for the same purpose. Another relevant term is *'Meetingware'*, a type of Group Decision Support System (GDSS), which is a set of software and hardware tools that can enable 'electronic' meetings and decision conferencing.

The degree of collaboration required during any given session will vary throughout the course of the meeting. There may be short bursts of very high data transmission when sending a file; low transmission, when for instance, a keystroke is transmitted; or no data transmission when the collaboration software is not required. Thus in order to maintain a natural interaction between participants, the system supports rapid dynamic bandwidth allocation and mode changes.

MCUs are also now available for this market, enabling *multipoint bridging* and thus *multisite conferencing*. With the introduction also of new Vision Processor (VP) and Vision Controller (VC) chips from companies like ITT, new PC-based products are now available which are able to compress and decompress video signals at rates up to 30 fps – the standard for full motion video.

Videophone

This is a telephone equipped with appropriate CODEC, which compresses video and audio signals to below 20 Kbps for use on normal analogue telephone lines, and a small, usually 3.5 inch by 3.5 inch, LCD screen. It also includes a charge coupled camera with a fixed focus, which works quite well up to a range of 9 feet.

Picture quality is currently unacceptable for a business system, but makes it acceptable for the consumer electronics market. It is also dubbed a 'granny phone' since it is primarily aimed at social workers to provide social and practical support to elderly and handicapped people who live in their own homes, and wealthy grandparents who want to see their children and grandchildren and can afford its high (for the moment) price.

Products include BT's Videophone priced at £400 (1993) and AT&T's Videophone 2500 priced at £1,000 (1992). Analysts believe that prices will need to drop and picture quality improve before substantial markets are found for these products.

Business Television

Business Television is a type of broadcast television, the earliest type of private television. Most Business Television applications require presentations to be 'broadcast' simultaneously to many locations and to receive questions or answers via the telephone – in other words, one way video and two way audio. It can be used in conjunction with desktop presentation, which allows the complex process of slide production to be performed in-house, with the option of integrating company data directly into the presentation. Prices are at the £20,000 level and main applications are found in company training and information provision.

Still Video Audio-based systems

The Still-Image Phone allows high-resolution, full colour, still images to be transmitted over standard analogue phone lines. They are captured through an attached device and displayed on a standard TV monitor at the receiving end. The base unit and user interface is a telephone through which ancillary devices are connected. The resolution it provides is very good and it can offer simultaneous two-way audio and the ability to display real-time interactive annotation of images using a mouse.

The market for this kind of product is businesses that are highly image-intensive and collaborative such as advertising, engineering, manufacturing, retail and remote health care. The only product in this category (May 1993) is AT&T's Picasso priced at £2,197. This price is high for horizontal market penetration, but it will not be a barrier in those vertical markets which it is aiming at.

Group Audio/Paper-based systems

These systems provide two-way audio communication via a telephone, supported by facsimile for the exchange of text and graphics. They are a cheaper way of conducting a teleconference supported by some kind of 'visual' elements.

High Quality Audio Teleconferencing

Audio teleconferencing allows people in remote locations to use standard telephone equipment to take part in meetings. The participants need a standard telephone, and either ISDN or analogue telephone lines, so the capital required is very low. It is, however, possible to use audio-conferencing terminals, which are hands-free, desktop units containing several microphones so that anyone sitting around the table can take part.

To organize a conference, the host simply rings the dedicated operator with the phone numbers of those who are to participate and the time at which they are required. The operator will then make the connection, welcome the participants and introduce them to the meeting. Alternatively, and for a slightly lower cost, those taking part can phone in at a pre-determined time and be connected.

BT and Mercury have also introduced several other optional services such as simultaneous translation, transcription and recording of the discussion. Recordings can be either delivered on tape, or reviewed immediately after the conference, by phoning the operator and using a pin code to gain access to the material. Other functions that are growing in popularity are voting and questionnaire facilities.

A recent surprising new area of application is in justice. The *Daily Telegraph* reported in 1994 that: 'Teleconferencing between lawyers and judges has become so popular that in the 5th Appellate District Court, which covers a wide area of rural central California, more than 90% of the cases are now dealt by telephone.'

Finally, another potential application is in market research, where a selection of respondents could be asked a series of questions in a much shorter time and at less cost, than using traditional methods.

Teleconferencing Suppliers & Business Alliances Issues

With the convergence of the technologies used in audio, video, television, computer and telecommunications industries, barriers between these markets are breaking down. This has led to the teleconferencing market being characterized by continual alliances between suppliers of different technologies.

Some characteristic strategic alliances are the following:

- Compaq–PictureTel for the design and manufacture of standards-based personal conferencing products. The resources of the videoconferencing leader and the PC leader are combined to produce a new generation of products scheduled to appear in the worldwide market by 1995.

- PictureTel–Lotus, for operating the PCS 100 desktop videoconferencing system from within the Lotus Notes environment, and PictureTel-IBM, for directly selling PictureTel PCS 100 products and fully integrating them within the Person to Person collaborative computing software. Such alliances will help with the future integration of videoconferencing into existing desktop software.

- Videologic–BT–Motorola to design and produce a PC-based Videophone and multi-media based chipset.

- P&P–Northern Telecom–PictureTel to bring new videoconferencing and desktop communications to the corporate market place.

- ICL held talks in 1993 with four CODEC designers in the United Kingdom (BT), Finland (Bitfield), Japan and the United States to choose two of them and to develop a PC-based videoconferencing system.

- ICL–Novell alliance, which for ICL will act as a springboard towards becoming a system integrator, while for Novell it means access to proven groupware technology and a major endorsement for its UnixWare system.

- Motorola produces a chipset that works on a videoconferencing workstation being developed by BT–IBM.

- AT&T–NCR produce the Personal Video System, a PC-based desktop video system, that allows live video on Windows.

- BT–IBM unveiled a PC-based videophone while similar systems are provided by CLI–Apple (Cameo) and by PictureTel–IBM–Siemens.

- AT&T–McCaw Cellurar, two telecommunications giants joining forces. This was followed by Microsoft–McCaw Cellular–Teledisc (a small US company) and their ambitious project to launch 840 low-flying satellites for offering wireless data, digital voice, video and text, and a global wireless communications network by the next century.

- Microsoft–Apple–AT&T–IBM–Erricsson–Siemens, to support the National Semiconductor Isoenet Multimedia Application Standard, which brings together data and voice technology into a single data stream, across local and wide area networks.

- Intel–CLI–AT&T and 10 others to write PC conferencing standards.

The above examples show that traditional suppliers of small group systems type of videoconferencing equipment, like PictureTel and CLI, since they are not able to compete on price and on collaboration provision with the new desktop videoconferencing products, ally with computer systems suppliers like Compaq, Apple and IBM to develop their own video PCs.

Other multi-industry partnerships will continue to emerge to establish new standards and develop the information super-highway.

Market Analysis and Trends

Teleconferencing and more particularly videoconferencing has matured as a strategic business tool, on desktops as well as in boardrooms, with industry analysts seeing the service mirroring the rapid growth pattern fax machines. It will not be long before business cards carry video numbers as well as fax and voice telephone numbers. Just as networks have miraculously sprung up between hardware boxes over the last few years so the dial-up telephone network could be the next and ultimate local network. The industry has moved from $100,000 semi-functional systems to high quality desktop units priced at less than $10,000 in the span of three years.

Equipment prices are falling by 30% to 40% a year. International standards for the production of equipment and digital transmission have been agreed, technological advances have been made, and digital dial-up lines are now on offer, all aiding the rise of videoconferencing. Also, because equipment is getting cheaper, the purchasing decision is moving down the management ladder.

The disappointing financial performance of the US market leaders PictureTel and CLI, which together hold 75% of the videoconference systems sold in 1992 in the United States, was interpreted by analysts as a downturn in the video-conferencing market. Forrester Research Inc. of Cambridge, Mass., predicted in 1991 that videoconferencing suppliers would not have the runaway growth that many expected. However, these indicate not a downturn in the market but that increased competition is making price a more critical issue.

Videoconferencing initially tended to be used only by senior executives. But increasingly lower-level managers in marketing, production and administration are using it, according to London consultancy Ovum Ltd. A market scenario by Ovum concerning the multimedia market is described below:

- Phase 1: 1992–95
  Videoconferencing revenues will continue to come from sales of conventional equipment (dedicated and small group systems). Most multimedia applications for business users will be stand-alone, though a few value added resellers and large organizations will start to build networked applications.

- Phase 2: 1996–98
  Revenues from video PCs will exceed those from conventional videoconferencing equipment (Exhibit 18.3). Sales of desktop software will take off as users start to take advantage of the facilities available on networks. Strong growth will take place in the consumer market.

- Phase 3: 1999 onwards
  Sales of video PCs will climb, hitting revenues from video traffic on wide area communications services. The business market will expand more rapidly than the consumer market, fuelled by matured tools for information retrieval and groupware.

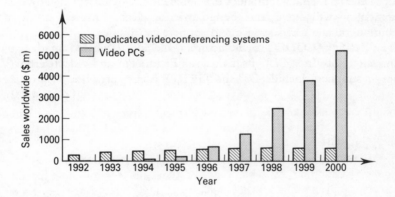

Exhibit 18.3 *Desktop versus dedicated videoconferencing sales by 2000.*
Source: Ovum Ltd.

Ovum adds that suppliers of conventional videoconferencing equipment will not be able to compete on price with these products, though they can form partnerships with computer systems suppliers to develop their own video PCs. They should offer increased quality, rather than lower prices. This could be done by:

- adding new options and features to existing equipment, to support applications such as distance learning and remote consultations;

- encouraging third party software vendors to develop software tools that integrate communications with other facilities, such as decision support and information retrieval;

- ensuring that all their products are compatible with the higher levels of the emerging H.320 standards for audiovisual telephony.

These products will be used as quality equipment for applications in vertical markets. Within an organization they will have a role to play at departmental level, where the market is likely to develop in a manner similar to that for other office equipment such as photocopiers or fax machines.

Finally, telecommunications revenues from video teleconferencing based traffic will be generated by four types of equipment (Exhibit 18.4): dedicated videoconferencing systems, small group systems, very small group and individuals systems, and video PCs.

Revenues from dedicated equipment, including large group systems (studios), will continue to make a major contribution throughout the period to the year 2000, because the systems are used for much longer periods over expensive leased lines. The effect of the massive growth forecast for video PCs will not become apparent until the end of the decade.

New competitive advantages and differentiation criteria will keep emerging. As the group videoconferencing market moves through its product life cycle, the uniqueness of vendors' product development strategies will rapidly diminish. Differentiation will move from design towards classic business issues such as distribution channels and service and support capabilities.

The leading CODEC manufacturers include US-based market pioneer Compression Labs Inc. (CLI), its main rival, PictureTel, and Videotelecom (VTel). European suppliers include BT and GPT. BT currently has 80% of the UK

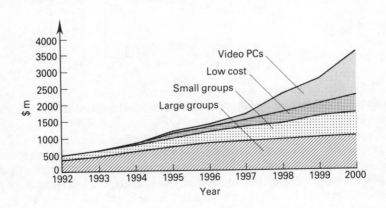

Exhibit 18.4 *Growth in total service revenues from videoconferencing.*
Source: Ovum Ltd.

market, 50% of the European market and 15% of the world market for video-conferencing. It plans to take 30% of the French market in the next three years.

Personal Technology Research Group forecasts the market profile of the videoconferencing market by 1997 as shown in Exhibit 18.5.

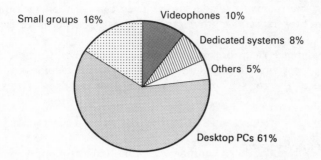

Exhibit 18.5 *Video teleconferencing market breakouts (1997).*
Source: Personal Technology Research Group.

Estimates of 1997 revenues vary between $850 million and $12 billion. The considerable divergence among all the forecasts shows the volatility of the teleconference market, which makes any estimation or prediction both difficult and inaccurate.

Installed videoconferencing units are predicted to be quickly adopted by the US market, while the European market follows at a slower pace, considerably outperformed by the former.

Within Europe the most developed markets are the United Kingdom, Germany and France.

A more specific analysis of the major segments of the teleconferencing market follows.

Dedicated Systems

Today's average price for a room videoconferencing system, about $45,000, has dropped by an order of magnitude from $500,000 in the mid-1980s. This included designing and renovating conference rooms, in order to convert them to studio-like rooms, as well as create an optimal videoconference atmosphere.

They are the oldest segment of the market and have typically been used by senior executives in large organizations. Although they will remain an important part of the overall market, growth will probably not be as spectacular as that of smaller systems.

Small companies that could not afford these expensive systems had a second option, to use public rooms provided by national PTTs. The introduction of ISDN and later the Globand as telecommunication media, replaced the high speed and expensive dedicated networks, and made these rooms an even more competitive offer.

The availability of the switched digital services gave rise to this new kind of public room as well as a new kind of public room service. Large users with their own videoconferencing facilities can recoup some of their investment by renting out their private rooms to smaller users. They can list their facilities with conference room brokers, service providers that act as go-betweens for facility owners and users.

The conference room broker service is quite common in the United States, but, because most videoconferencing users are bringing facilities in-house due to the decrease in the costs involved, it may be that the days of this service are numbered.

Small Group Systems

The introduction of products like Eclipse by CLI brought sub-$20,000 prices, standards compliance and PC front-end architecture in this market. A report by ENS indicates that the technology and price/performance points of the leading suppliers are now clear. Clients that have delayed investments due to the volatility of the market can buy now with confidence (ENS, 2 August 1993). The report states also that all three videoconferencing leaders – PictureTel, CLI and VTel – have placed their low-end group systems strategies on PC platforms, indicating the move towards this segment of the market.

The report does not find any clear sustainable advantage in any videoconferencing company. Since the margins are not high (they are about at the level needed to fund the enormous service, support and R&D that videoconferencing, demands), and because the cost structures are roughly equal, it would be silly for any vendor to proactively start a price war in this business for quite some time.

Desktop Systems

For years the videoconferencing market was dominated by a handful of speciality vendors like CLI, PictureTel and VTel. The introduction of the video PC made several mainline computer companies enter the new, promising, desktop videoconferencing market.

But critical mass will be slow to come due to the technology's high cost – currently £3,000 to £5,000 excluding the cost of the PC. When more integrated products come out, prices will fall and sales will rocket. Exhibit 18.6 shows a forecast by Personal Technology Research.

An ENS report also states that the desktop videoconferencing industry will be characterized by hundreds of new vendors and products, with a dizzying array of different implementations on all fronts. Some of them which were bitter enemies will collaborate on the desktop, while other partners will split up and directly

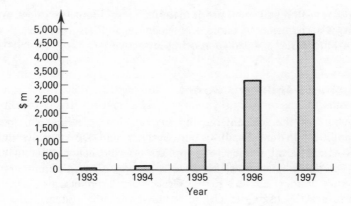

Exhibit 18.6 *Desktop videoconferencing systems sales.*
Source: Personal Technology Research Group.

compete against each other for this lucrative market. Vendor survival over the planning horizon is also quite unpredictable (ENS, 6 December 1993).

Meanwhile Ovum Ltd predicts that early video PCs with a 14-inch screen and a telephone handset are not likely to prove acceptable for sustained use. Users will require:

- larger screens, capable of displaying several video windows simultaneously;

- higher resolution;

- improved audio, with echo cancellation and background noise reduction;

- hands-free telephony to enable them to use the keyboard and mouse at the same time.

Even with these improvements, leading computer systems suppliers will find it difficult to compete on price in the longer term. These products are likely to follow other PCs, becoming a commodity market.

The growth of video PCs in the multimedia world will be followed by a parallel growth of a new generation of software communications tools, to support applications such as audio and video mail, groupware, conferencing and all forms of cooperative work.

The groupware market is likely to grow at a significantly higher rate due to new networks, powerful new video PCs, the steady acceptance of common technical standards, the likely incorporation of elements of artificial intelligence and the change in ways of doing business (business teams, industry deregulation, flattening of corporate structures, trend towards contract work, mergers and acquisitions).

The interest in video PCs can be explained by the fact that big-name vendors, in a time of recession and small profit margins on traditional products, are seeking new ideas. The addition of audio and video capabilities could boost sales and profits, making desktop videoconferencing attractive.

Products and Industry Supply

The segments of the teleconferencing market that it seems will face a kind of 'commoditization' are Small Group Systems and Desktop Systems. There is already a significant number of suppliers offering many different choices of products, platforms standards, bandwidth of operation, different applications, video picture frame rate and price. Groupware suppliers also offer software solutions to desktop users, which are bundled with the system.

Conclusion

It is apparent that technological advances will bring the necessary improvements which these systems need to meet the needs of this new and promising market. Growth opportunities will keep emerging during the next five years, especially in the desktop segment. For the first time all the critical pieces are coming together to drive market demand for, and acceptance of, desktop visual communications.

Chip-makers have announced and are selling silicon solutions to enable this new class of product to be. Equipment manufacturers have already introduced new systems. Developers are delivering collaboration software tools. Digital communications services are widely available and transmission costs are declining. The deployment of the ISDN capability is accelerating and the ratification of the new standards lifts proprietary platform barriers by ensuring inter-operability between standards-compliant offerings.

These developments have made possible the emergence of a new class of desktop products that are available at price/performance ratios unthinkable just a few years ago. These advances are fuelling user interest also. Organizations are starting to explore how best to leverage the benefits of desktop visual communications for their maximum competitive advantage, and videoconferencing facilities and collaborative software are also coming to be perceived by managers as status symbols.

Acknowledgement

The authors would like to thank Konstantinos Kormazos for the research he did on the teleconferencing industry, which has formed the basis for this update.

Questions

POK Electronic Systems successfully penetrated the market in the 1980s with its teleconferencing system. After two years, it achieved its sales target of selling 20,000 units a year, until 1991 when sales began to decrease slightly. Mr Kruger believes it is necessary for POK to get into the desktop videoconferencing market.

(1) (a) What factors should Mr Kruger consider in formulating a marketing strategy for POK's entry into the desktop videoconferencing market?
   (b) What should be his strategic aims?

(2) (a) What should be the major directions of POK's strategic orientation?
   (b) What would be the advantages and disadvantages to POK of embarking on a strategic alliance with a computer manufacturer, as many developers have done?

(3) What marketing strategies could POK use on its entry to the desktop videoconferencing market?

References

ENS, Research Note (2/8/93) *Group Videoconferencing Technology Directives Are Set*, Gartner Group Continuous Services
EENS, Research Note (6/12/93) *Desktop Videoconferencing Key Issues for 1994*, Gartner Group Continuous Services
Computer World (17/5/93) *Deskwardbound*
Daily Telegraph (22/2/94) *Special Report on Telecommunications*
Economist (26/3/94) *Infrastructure in the Sky*
Ovum Ltd (January 1994) *Networked multimedia*

CASE 19

WEDR-FM Radio Station
Advertising – Segmentation

Jonathan Goodrich
Florida International University, USA

Introduction

WEDR-FM is a black-run radio station in Miami, Florida. In 1962, it was purchased for approximately $25,000. Its logo once was 'STAR FORCE 99'. Its present logo is '99 JAMZ'. In 1991, WEDR-FM became one of the leading radio stations serving the Miami–Fort Lauderdale area of Florida, through excellent programming, recruitment of top-notch personnel (such as DJs, programme director), and by replacing a 165-foot antenna in Liberty City (part of Miami) with a 926-foot antenna much further north in North Dade, off Highway 441. This taller antenna allowed WEDR to broadcast much more powerfully, with better transmission/reception, and to a larger geographic area than before. The station could now be picked up within a 90-mile radius of the station on Highway 826 North (Palmetto Expressway) in Miami, which was not the case before.

The success of WEDR (99.1 FM) illustrated that a black-run radio station playing music by blacks for blacks could be among South Florida's top radio stations, AM or FM. It also underlined the growing importance of the black market, as the station's success came amid intense competition for black listeners.

Service

According to Jerry Rushin, Vice President and General Manager, WEDR's main service consisted of selling air time, that is, commercials. Advertisers included large and small white businesses and black businesses. Some of the largest advertisers were Frito-Lay, Sun Bank, J. Byrons clothing stores, and Calder race track.

Exhibit 19.1 is a sample of the rate card for 60-second advertising spots on WEDR. Note that these spots are more expensive between 5.30 am and 10.00 am

Exhibit 19.1 Sample Rate for 60-Second Air Time on WEDR

GRID		I	II	III	IV	V	VI
MON–FRI	5.30 am–10.00 am	300	275	250	225	200	185
MON–FRI	10.00 am– 3.00 pm	240	220	200	180	160	150
MON–FRI	3.00 pm– 8.00 pm	275	250	230	200	185	175
MON–FRI	8.00 pm– 1.00 am	125	125	125	125	125	125
MON–FRI	1.00 am– 5.30 am	40	40	40	40	40	40
SAT	6.00 am–10.00 am	100	100	100	100	100	100
SAT	10.00 am– 3.00 pm	275	250	230	200	185	175
SAT	3.00 pm– 8.00 pm	240	220	200	180	160	150
SAT	8.00 pm– 1.00 am	125	125	125	125	125	125
SUN	8.00 am–11.00 am	150	140	130	120	110	100
SUN	11.00 am– 3.00 pm	170	160	150	140	130	120
SUN	3.00 pm– 8.00 pm	95	95	95	95	95	95
SUN	8.00 pm– 1.00 am	75	75	75	75	75	75

Notes News/Sports/Gospel Sponsorships additional 10%.
⅓, ¼ TAP Plans 85% of applicable Grid average.
TAP = Total Audience Participation. Advertisers who buy this plan have their ads spread over the entire day.
ROS = Rotation of Schedule or Run of Schedule. An advertiser with a ROS plan will have his ads played at different times during a pre-specified time period, between 5.30 am and 5.30 pm.
ROS Plans Mon–Sun, 5.30 am–5.30 pm, 65% of applicable Grid.
30-second rate, 85% of applicable 60-second rate.
All rates are based on availability at time of purchase and may be subject to change without notice.
Consult your 99 JAMZ Representative for current specials and promotions.

and 3.00 pm and 8.00 pm that at other times of the day. The least expensive spots are during the early morning hours, 1.00 am to 5.30 am. The rates for 30 seconds are 85% of those applicable to 60 seconds. The grids refer to the frequency of advertising spots during a given time period. For example, between 5.30 am and 10.00 am, each of the six 60-second advertising spots in Grid VI will cost $185, whereas each of the three 60-second spots in Grid III will cost $250. WEDR sold about 12 minutes of commercial time during each hour, equivalent to roughly $12 \times 24 = 288$ minutes (4.8 hours) of commercials for every 24 hours of operation.

WEDR also performed other services in addition to selling air time to advertisers. For example, it devoted approximately 1 minute of every hour to public service announcements (PSA) It also had regular news programming, and music for blacks. The 'black music' included blues, rhythm and blues (R&B) , jazz and some rock n' roll, for example. Some of the black artists featured were well-known, such as B.B. King, Stevie Wonder, Ray Charles, the late Z.Z. Hill, Chuck Berry, Aretha Franklin, Dionne Warwick, Whitney Houston, James Brown ('Godfather of Soul') , Little Richard, Smokey Robinson and Luther Vandross. Only about 1% of air time was devoted to music by white artists. There were also informational programmes for blacks, for example relative to education, jobs, religion, politics and community activities.

While WEDR was owned principally by a white family from Stuart, Florida, the station was run by a black staff headed by Jerry Rushin. WEDR was the only top-rated black music station in South Florida with an audience that was almost entirely black – 85% to 90%.

Competition

WEDR competed for listeners with some 41 AM and FM radio stations that served the Miami–Fort Lauderdale area. Jerry Rushin said that WEDR's three main competitors were Y-100 FM, Power 96 FM, and Hot 105 FM. Of these, Hot 105 was the closest in terms of programming almost all black music, although it had very few black employees. Other competitors included Magic 102.7 FM, WVCG 1080 AM and WAVS 1170 AM. (In an indirect way, it could be said that WEDR also competed with local and national television stations for listeners.)

In 1988 WEDR was the number 2 station overall in South Florida. Then around September 1988, Hot 105 began to play music mostly by black artists. At the same time, other urban contemporary and dance music stations added more black artists to their play lists. By the spring of 1990, WEDR had dropped to number 16 in the Arbitron quarterly ratings in the South Florida market.

Advertising and Promotion

WEDR's advertising and promotion can be divided broadly into two categories:

(1) promoting itself; and
(2) promoting clients' products and services.

In terms of promoting itself, Mr Rushin believed that the best vehicle for promoting a radio station, and WEDR in particular, was the station itself. Hence WEDR had many of its own commercials promoting itself, and its disc jockeys did a good job of regularly reminding the listening audience to keep tuned to 'WEDR-FM, 99 JAMZ'. WEDR also had a large billboard immediately outside the station with the station's name and logo. It used television advertisements about twice a year, and had an ad in Southern Bell's *Yellow Pages*. Of course, other inadvertent methods of promotion for WEDR were the sales people in the field who sold air time, and word-of-mouth from listeners.

In terms of promoting clients' products and services, in 1991 WEDR had nearly 700 different advertisers a month, up from 400 in 1988. In a month, the station can run about 4,200 spots, which represented $500,000 in revenue. A year before, that same number of spots brought in less than $200,000. Some products advertised regularly on WEDR were automobiles, foods, clothing, real estate, magazines, music videos, office supplies and electronic equipment. Services advertised included education, medical, legal, entertainment and banking.

Pricing

Pricing, relative to a radio station, is concerned with the price advertisers pay for air time (commercials). Exhibit 19.1 shows the prices of 60-second air time for different times of the day, and was explained earlier. Companies that advertised heavily on WEDR received slightly better rates than those shown in Exhibit 19.1.

Distribution

The distribution point for a radio station is the station itself. From the station flows its entertainment, news, sports, gospel, community affairs and other programmes, and the radio commercials. The sales people who sell air time, as well as the management and staff who are engaged in community activities on behalf of the station, can also be viewed as part of the radio station's distribution system.

Company Structure

Personnel

WEDR had 20 full-time and 4 part-time employees. Full-time employees included the Vice President and General Manager Jerry Rushin, a sales manager and six account executives (sales persons), a music director, a programme director, a production manager and six disc jockeys.

Market Segmentation

WEDR segmented the market on two broad levels: geographic and demographic. On the geographic level, the station served the Miami–Fort Lauderdale area. On the demographic level, the station targeted mainly 25–54 year-old blacks. This age group segment was known in the trade as the 'money demo', that is, the demo(graphic) segment with the income and willingness to spend. This large market segment could be broken down further into young adults (21–30 years old) and middle-aged adults (45–55 years old). Music could then be geared to these age groups; for example, rap music for the younger audience, and jazz and R&B music for the older segment. Educational and other entertainment programmes were similarly arranged and aired at different times of the day.

Programming

Programming was a major ingredient of a successful radio station. Good programming – music, type and arrangement, news, gospel, community programmes,

PSAs, talk shows, and so on – helped to maintain and/or increase audience size. Larger audiences meant higher Arbitron ratings, and higher ratings meant the station could charge more money for its air time. All this translated into more revenues and profits.

How WEDR Rose to the Top

Jerry Rushin orchestrated many things in his effort to increase WEDR's market share, ratings and visibility in the Miami–Fort Lauderdale marketplace. First, he increased the station's broadcasting wattage, penetrating north Broward and Palm Beach counties, by removing the 165-foot antenna in Liberty City and replacing it with a 926-foot antenna in North Dade County just off Highway 441. (The highest radio station antenna height permitted by Dade County ordinance was 1,000 feet.)

Second, Mr Rushin improved the programming. The format was made tighter, slicker and hipper. Play lists were shortened and meticulously planned. Programmes were aired that appealed to a broader audience of black listeners. 'Our disc jockeys used to play songs by feeling. Now the lists of songs are prepared by our programme director and computerized,' Rushin said.

WEDR ended production gaffes, such as sequencing directly from words to commercials without the disc jockey's voice smoothing the transition. The moves paid off. In the first quarter of 1991, the station was ranked equal third in audience size in the Arbitron ratings of some 41 radio stations in South Florida. According to interim Arbitron ratings, the station was ranked number 2 overall during the first half of 1991.

With the higher rankings came higher revenues, since the station charged more now for its air time than when the ratings were lower. WEDR's 1991 revenue reached $5 million, double that for 1990.

Third, as well as the much taller antenna and improved programming, Mr Rushin lured top DJs and other experienced personnel away from rival stations. All this helped to enhance the station's performance. Finally, the station's logo was changed from 'Star Force 99' to '99 JAMZ'. '99 JAMZ' was an action term. To blacks (and whites) the terms 'to jam' or 'jamming' meant to have fun, to be in the groove, to dance, and so on. So when a black person said, for example, that 'the party was jamming', he or she meant that the party was good, hot, hip, full of life.

Because of its higher ratings, WEDR was able to attract a more diverse group of advertisers – not just black advertisers, but white companies too – who paid more for a radio 'spot.' A few years ago, many of WEDR's advertisers sold products and services to blacks almost exclusively, or had a disproportionately high number of black customers. These included hair-care products, beer and flea markets. Now WEDR was securing general-market advertisers like Frito-Lay and Sun Bank.

Questions

(1) What strategies did WEDR-FM radio station follow to become one of the top-rated radio stations in the Miami–Fort Lauderdale area?

(2) What is a black radio station?

(3) Discuss the segmentation strategies followed by WEDR.

(4) Comment on the pricing of advertising at WEDR.

CASE 20

Aroma
Advertising – Positioning

Enrique Bigné and Marcelo Royo
University of Valencia, Spain

Background

Grupos Gala is a firm with a long tradition and experience as a wholesaler of *droguería*[†] products and perfumes, supplying mainly traditional shops, supermarkets and small retail chains. The firm is a shareholder in a buying group made up of nine *droguería* and perfume wholesalers which in 1991 made group purchases of Pta25,000 million, and had sales of Pta48,940 million (of which Pta2,500 million were made by Grupos Gala). It is 23rd in the ranking for total sales of Spanish *droguería* and perfume firms and 15th at provincial level in the ranking of distribution businesses.

The evolution of the distribution sector in Spain is characterized by both a trend towards the association of business and vertical channel integration, which implies a loss of power for the traditional wholesaler; and the tendency for small traditional businesses to disappear in favour of large businesses with more competitive prices and higher standards of service (see Exhibit 20.1). In 1986 the executive director of Grupos Gala took the strategic decision to integrate its function as a wholesaler with that of retailer, creating a chain of shops specializing in *droguería* and perfume products under the business name of Aroma. He was motivated by the company's loss of power as a wholesaler and the consequent loss of business profitability in the near future.

The first Aroma shop opened in 1987 in a medium-sized town of 20,000 inhabitants. New shops subsequently opened in other places, until reaching in 1991 a total of nine establishments, all located in the province of Alicante.

[†] The Spanish term *droguería* refers to household and personal cleaning materials, paper products, and the shops that sell them. The product lines are described in more detail in the text.

Making use of its specialization as a wholesaler, the range of products offered to the consumer consists mainly of *droguería* and perfume products, but this is broadened with lines of top-quality perfumes and cosmetics of a number of brands for which it holds exclusive distribution rights.

The Aroma Chain of Shops

The Aroma shops are rented, with a surface area of between 200 and 250 square metres, and a location which is as central as possible in the town. The *droguería* products make up the greater part of the goods on display, which include: detergents, paperware, personal care products, household cleaning materials, and insecticides and air fresheners. Customers serve themselves.

The high-quality perfume products for which Aroma has exclusive distribution rights (Barbara Ward, Gisele Denis, Lancaster, Rochas and so on) are divided into two sections, high-quality perfumes and cosmetics, which are sold by specialist staff at counters. Next to these there is also a small accessories and custom jewellery section.

Between the counters and the self-service sections there is no real change in atmosphere even though both sections are distinguishable within the shop. In the most recently opened shop, however, there is a clear distinction in the atmosphere between the two sections.

The staff usually consists of a manageress and a cashier. The manageress's main duties are to act as a coordinator between the shop and the chain, to check on the cashier and to be responsible for sales at the counter, giving advice on high-quality perfumes and cosmetics. The cashier, besides operating the till, is responsible for restocking the shelves.

The prices of the *droguería* products are usually lower than those of the competition, and many offers and promotions are carried out. The sales prices of perfumes and cosmetics usually include a discount, although lately this practice has been varied, with a personalized discount being made at the time of sale in the presence of the customer.

Communication is carried out by direct advertising – delivered to domestic letter boxes in areas close to the shops – on sheets of paper of one colour showing the name of the shop, products, prices, promotions and offers. On occasions the shops act as sponsors of local events.

The evolution of sales is positive in both of the sections, however as can be seen from Exhibit 20.2, the share of *droguería* products in total annual sales has decreased from 60% to 48%, while that of the perfume section has increased correspondingly from 40% to 52%.

The Competition

The particular characteristics of the range of products which Aroma supplies to the market means that the competition comes from two different areas:

Exhibit 20.1   Evolution of Establishments

TYPE OF ESTABLISHMENT	JANUARY 1987 Number	% of total	JANUARY 1988 Number	% of total	% change	JANUARY 1989 Number	% of total	% change
SELF-SERVICE SHOPS	16,893	33.6	17,893	34.7	5.9	18,410	35.4	8.9
SMALL SUPERMARKETS	4,146	8.2	4,689	9.1	13	5,217	10.9	25.8
LARGE SUPERMARKETS	552	1.1	603	1.2	9.2	691	1.3	25.1
HYPERMARKETS	89	0.18	99	0.2	11.2	108	0.2	21.3
SMALL DROGUERÍAS	15,719	31.2	15,466	30.0	−1.6	15,017	28.4	−4.4
LARGE DROGUERÍAS	6,734	13.4	6,680	12.9	−0.8	6,498	12.5	−3.5
PERFUMERIES	6,179	12.3	6,104	11.8	−1.2	6,012	11.6	−2.7
TOTAL	50,312	100	515,344	100	2.4	51,953	100	3.2

Source: Nielsen Yearbook 1991.

Exhibit 20.2   *Evolution of retail sales volume.*

Year	No. of outlets	Total Pesetas	Droguería Pesetas	%	Perfumes Pesetas	%
1988	4	74,711,379	44,623,684	59.73	30,087,695	40.27
1989	5	109,278,554	62,394,774	57.09	46,883,780	42.91
1990	6	153,148,429	79,620,342	51.99	73,528,087	48.01
1991	9	254,694,124	122,177,106	47.97	132,517,018	52.03

- *droguería* products; and
- perfumes (high-quality perfumes and cosmetics)

In the case of *droguería* product lines, the competitive position of Aroma looks vulnerable in the future given the strong competition of the large stores such as supermarkets and, especially in these lines, hypermarkets. The 'Mercadona' chain of branch supermarket stores which had, in 1991, 154 establishments in Spain and a sales turnover of Pta146,000 million, and 'Consum', a chain of branch and franchised supermarkets in the Spanish Levante area (Murcia, Alicante, Valencia, Castellón and Barcelona), with a total of 135 shops and a turnover of some Pta48,000 million, are two large chains well established in Alicante city and province. They occupy the first and second place among distribution firms at provincial level, and fifth and thirteenth positions respectively on a national level. All the establishments stock the same brands, and the prices are very competitive, with little differentiation between branded and mass consumption products. In addition there are the shopping habits of an important segment of consumers who prefer to make one large weekly purchase in establishments which stock all types of goods.

In the case of high-quality perfume and cosmetic product lines the competitive postition of Aroma could be more favourable and sustainable in the future. Its competitors do not have the same depth of product lines as Aroma given the characteristics of such products: high price, greater differentiation between brands and more selective consumption. Equally important is the special atmosphere required in the shop and the need for a more personalized sales technique where what counts particularly is advice, specialized information and personal attention

Exhibit 20.1 *Continued*

	JANUARY 1990			JANUARY 1991	
Number	*% of total*	*% change*	*Number*	*% of total*	*% change*
18,377	35.7	8.7	18,072	36.2	6.9
5,647	11.9	36.2	5,941	11.9	43.2
725	1.4	31.3	746	1.5	36.1
128	0.25	43.8	151	0.3	69.6
14,608	28.4	−7	13,581	27.2	−13.6
5,858	11.4	−13	5,686	11.4	−15.5
6,011	11.7	−2.7	5,747	11.5	−6.9
51,348	100	2	49,924	100	−0.7

from staff. The main competitors in these types of products are the traditional perfume shops – a counter with personal attention – and the large stores, that possess a small range of these products and only a few of the quality brands.

Market Research

Objectives

Taking into account the need for information which would enable us to decide the future positioning of Aroma as a perfume shop instead of a *droguería*, market research was carried out in two areas in which Aroma shops were located[†].

The objective was to determine the positioning of Aroma and of its competitors, as well as the attributes of the establishment and other marketing stimuli on which perceived differences could be based.

Preliminary Research

To get to know the business and Aroma's immediate competitors, various interviews were carried out with the executive director of Aroma and the staff of the shop to find out their opinions and obtain information in this respect.

The most immediate competitors identified in this case fall into two groups: chains of supermarkets stocking all types of products such as Mercadona and Consum, and small traditional shops specializing in perfumes such as Caricia, Soler and Gloria and which compete strongly with each other.

Formal Research

The techniques of commercial research which were used were focus group interviews and the personal interview.

[†] In the present case reference will only be made to one of them, though there were no great differences between their results.

Qualitative analysis

The focus group exercises on the one hand confirmed the information given by the employees in relation to the competitors, and on the other, and this was the main point, revealed which characteristics of the establishments were most significant for the consumer and would help in designing the interviews. The group was made up of women aged between 20 and 50, all of whom had been approached on coming out of the Aroma shop and invited to take part in a focus group interview.

The focus group interviews brought out the most valued attributes of Aroma and details about the competition. These were the personalized treatment of the customer; the proximity of the establishment to the customer's home; having staff specialized in perfumes; the variety, depth and modernity of the different product lines; the ease of buying and the price depending on the type of product, the latter being important in the cases of *droguería* products but not so in the case of high-quality perfume and cosmetic products. With respect to Aroma, no real formed image was observed, and it stood out only for its prices in *droguería* products. Other attributes which did not indicate any advantage or real difference with respect to the competitors were that the establishment was functional – the self-service system meant that customers did not have to wait to pay for their purchases – and that the shop offered *droguería* products or brands of a similar level of prestige to those of the supermarkets and traditional *droguerías*.

It was also found that in the case of the weekly purchase or the big shopping session there was a preference for supermarkets since the customer only had to queue once to pay, all types of products were available and it was easy and convenient to serve oneself, whereas in the case of a sporadic purchase or urgent need for one type of product, the preference was for the nearby and traditional shops, particularly in the case of heavy items.

With respect to high-quality perfumes and cosmetics, the preference was for the specialized perfume shops among women of middle to high socio-economic levels and women between the ages of 20 and 35. However, for women of lower middle to lower socio-economic levels, the range of perfumes and cosmetics present in the supermarkets was sufficient, their demands with respect to advice and service being less.

Quantitative analysis

The questionnaire included a number of questions with diverse objectives; however, we will only make reference to the part related to the technical multivariable analysis which was used (see Exhibit 20.3).

The population was made up of housewives, that is women who habitually bought *droguería* products, perfumes and cosmetics, aged between 20 and 55 and living in the town. 369 interviews were carried out, which made it possible to work with a sample error of ±5% with a 95.5% significance level. The sample units were chosen using the sampling method called Random Route among housewives

Exhibit 20.3 Items Used in the Correspondence Factor Analysis

F.01	Going shopping is fun
F.02	It has everything I need
F.03	The products are of good quality
F.04	It has prestige brands
F.05	It has the most modern products
F.06	The establishment is clean and tidy
F.07	It is a big establishment
F.08	It is a small establishment
F.09	It is well lit
F.10	It is a modern establishment
F.11	It has good shop windows and displays
F.12	It is easy to find the products
F.13	You serve yourself
F.14	The products are well arranged
F.15	The prices are high
F.16	It is good for buying goods on special offer
F.17	It gives good value for money
F.18	The prices are lower than in other places
F.19	You get personalized discounts
F.20	They give presents and run raffles
F.21	They make special offers
F.22	Their opening hours are good
F.23	Uninterrupted opening hours
F.24	They send leaflets with information about products and prices
F.25	You can pay quickly
F.26	You can pay by credit card
F.27	You can order by phone
F.28	They deliver your shopping to your home
F.29	The staff are pleasant and friendly
F.30	They let you try the product
F.31	They have staff specially trained in perfumes
F.32	The staff advise me
F.33	The staff inform me about the products in a personalized way
F.34	The staff are slow, they keep me waiting
F.35	You only have to queue once to pay
F.36	It specializes in *droguería* products
F.37	It specializes in perfumery products
F.38	It specializes in both
F.39	It specializes in all types of products
F.40	It is well placed
F.41	It is near home
F.42	It has a name suitable for the establishment

living within 10 minutes walking distance of Aroma during the period between 20th March and 2nd April 1991.

After applying the Correspondence Factor Analysis we obtained the positioning map shown in Exhibit 20.4, which provides a simplified illustration of the similarities or differences between establishments, as well as the variables and factors causing them. Thus two establishments which are situated close together on the positioning map must be understood to be perceived as being similar. For this reason, if a variable or attribute is situated very close to or very far from an establishment, this indicates respectively a close or distant association with the establishment. With respect to the analysis of the information shown on the map it is worthwhile bearing in mind that points situated close to the origin of the coordinates should not be considered, as they represent characteristics perceived as ones which all the establishments analysed possess and as a result do not show any important differences between them.

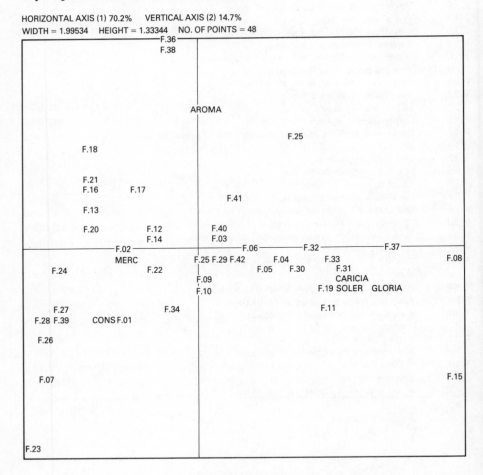

Exhibit 20.4 *Positioning map.*

The first two axes or factors account for 85% of the variance, that is, they contain 85% of the information obtained from the responses to the questionnaires. They therefore possess a high explicative power of the phenomenon under study. The interpretation of the axes or factors was carried out using the absolute and relative contributions of the variables in the formation of the factors.

The following interpretation of the factors was established:

* Factor-1, horizontal, represents the greater explanatory power with 70.2% of the variance and it was interpreted in its negative dimension as large supermarkets with all types of products, and in its positive dimension as small specialized perfume shops with high prices.

* Factor-2, vertical, which has a lesser explanatory power than Factor-1, accounts for 14.7% of the variance, and was interpreted in its positive dimension as establishments specializing in *droguería* products and in *droguería* and perfume products, while in its negative dimension no interpretation was made due to the absence of identifying attributes.

Analysis of the Positioning

With respect to Factor-1, Aroma has no clearly defined positioning due to its central position. It represents an establishment somewhere between the supermarkets and the traditional specialized perfume shops. However, it positions itself quite clearly with respect to the positive dimension of Factor-2.

Aroma is perceived as an establishment specializing in *droguería* products (F.36) and in both *droguería* and perfume products (F.38), but not one specializing in perfumes (F.37).

The price level is good and even cheaper than in other places (F.17, F.18 and far from F.15). It is also perceived as a good place to buy products on special offer (F.16) and it makes good offers (F.21); however, it is not perceived as an establishment in which people are given a personalized discount (F.19).

It is perceived much more as a self-service (F.13) than as an establishment which uses the traditional concept of selling (F.33, F.30, F.32). Nor is it associated with prestigious brands (F.4) nor modern products (F.5) nor with having specialized staff in the perfume section (F.31) who inform in a personalized way about the products (F.33) and who allow the products to be tried out (F.30). On the other hand it is not perceived as being a large establishment (F.7) though not a small shop either (F.8) and furthermore it is not perceived as having good window displays (F.11).

With respect to the competition, two groups of competitors (both with each other and with Aroma) can be observed:

A) Mercadona and Consum
B) Caricia, Soler and Gloria

A) Mercadona and Consum

These establishments are perceived as being large (F.7), they have all sorts of goods (F.2), and they offer other complementary services such as orders by telephone (F.27), home delivery of the shopping (F.28) and payment by credit card (F.26). It can thus be seen that they are not considered as specialists in *droguería* (F.36) or perfume products (F.37), but they are considered as being specialized in all types of products (F.39). Shopping in this type of establishment is considered to be fun (F.1), although a bit slow in the case of Consum.

With respect to price, they are not perceived as having either high or low prices although Consum is perceived to be slightly more expensive than Mercadona. Also, Mercadona (compared with Consum) is closer to the following attributes:

- giving gifts and holding raffles (F.20);
- sending information leaflets (F.24);
- good for buying products on special offer (F.21); and
- giving good value for money (F.17).

B) Caricia, Soler and Gloria

These establishments are found very close to each other on the map, which implies a perceived similarity among them and as a result a high degree of competition.

They are clearly perceived as being specialists in perfume products and as having staff specialized in them (F.31). They are considered to be small (F.8), with high prices (F.15) and with good window displays (F.11). The staff give information in a personalized manner (F.33), they advise (F.32), they allow the customer to try the product (F.30) and give personalized discounts (F.19).

Questions

(1) Indicate the strengths and weaknesses of AROMA and its competitors in the lines of *droguería* and perfumes.

(2) Determine the aspects to be improved by the AROMA chain on the basis of the market research.

(3) Analyse the decision to reposition AROMA as a chain specializing in perfumes, and define the basis of the marketing strategy as regards pricing, product and associated services policy.

(4) Discuss the basis of the advertising strategy: objectives, budget, message, media selection and evaluation. Consider various types of campaigns and media: mailing, mass media, and so on.

(5) Suggest other promotional activities.

CASE 21
The Langport Building Society
Advertising Management

Arthur Meidan and Tom Lloyd
Sheffield University Management School

Introduction

Mike Clark, the marketing manager for the Langport Building Society, was engaged in planning an advertising campaign to attract depositors' funds to the Society. The Langport was an old-established society which, in spite of a soberly conservative image, had reached and held, with £2,500 million assets, a position just outside the top 10 in order of size of building societies. The problem that faced it was the recurring one of shortage of funds to meet the demands for mortgages, at the current borrowers' interest rate of 7.99%. It was calculated that a further £50 million in deposits was necessary to clear the waiting list of acceptable mortgage applications before the expected fall in interest rates, which the government was being urged from all sides to initiate, brought about an increase in demand for mortgages.

The Board had decided, and Mike had concurred, that a new high interest share be instituted, paying a guaranteed 1.5% above the standard interest which was currently at 5.375%. The new share was provisionally named the Topshare for purposes of internal communications but the final decision on the name under which it was to be marketed had yet to be made.

There had been dissenting voices raised at the Board meeting. Most of the objections arose out of perennial deeply-felt concerns over the fundamental objectives of the Society but Mike was rather nettled by some contributions to preliminary discussions over the projected advertising campaign to launch the new share. One director had quoted a recent article to the effect that the Cranston Building Society, Langport's nearest rival, had a higher market share in terms of deposits but had a lower market share of advertising expenditure than did Langport. This led to comments on the tone of Langport's recent TV advertisements which seemed to portray both Langport's depositors and borrowers as seedy comic characters. There was clearly some indignation felt: 'Makes us look as if we are laundering the proceeds of petty crime!'; 'Should we be subsidizing self-indulgent out-of-work film directors?'; 'An insult to our members!', and so on. Mike defended the TV advertisements. A respected consultant had advised that there was a trend among aspiring under-30s to regard 'bounded disreputableness' as rather chic. It was to reach this segment, under-represented among Langport members, that an experimental approach had been tried. Mike continued: 'I concede we may have been ahead of the times; innovators usually are! However, that same article pointed out that our branches are bringing in an average of over £9 million each in savings yearly compared with Cranston's average of £7.5 million. That seems to validate our overall strategy!' (See Langport and Cranston balance sheets in Exhibit 21.1 and demographic distribution of Langport depositors in Exhibit 21.2.)

Exhibit 21.1   Current Balance Sheets for Langport and Cranston Building Societies

Langport Building Society

Liabilities and reserves	*£'000*
Shares	2,211,354
Deposits and loans	257,150
Taxation and other liabilities	70,205
Deferred tax	2,834
General reserve	99,892
	2,641,435

Assets	
Mortgages	2,109,946
Investments and cash	494,465
Fixed assets	35,208
Other assets	1,816
	2,641,435

Cranston Building Society

Investors' balances, liabilities and reserves	*£'000*
Shares	2,624,194
Deposits and loans	599,587
Taxation and other liabilities	56,186
Deferred taxation	7,541
General reserve	128,007
Reserve for future taxation	37,135
	3,452,650

Assets	
Mortgages	2,709,902
Investments and cash	677,476
Fixed assets	63,102
Other assets	2,170
	3,452,659

Exhibit 21.2 *Results of an in-house sample survey of characteristics of Langport depositors compared with the population of the United Kingdom.*

	Langport depositors (%)	Population of United Kingdom (%)
Male	58	49
Female	42	51
Age groups		
15–24	16	19
25–34	10	18
35–44	11	15
45–54	18	16
55–64	21	14
65 +	24	18
Socio-economic groups		
AB	15	16
C1	38	22
C2	37	32
DE	10	30

Mike had been instructed to produce a Topshare advertising plan, designed to bring in £50 million extra deposits, and he had started by considering the product as envisaged by the Board.

A pilot survey indicated that questions related to marital status might be too sensitive to allow for a satisfactory response rate and investigation of those variables was not undertaken. Geographical distribution of depositors was outside the scope of the survey; adequate information on that score was already in the Society's records. Broadly speaking Langport was strong in the North, fairly strong in the industrial conurbations of the Midlands but significantly less strong in the South.

Commenting later on the probable validity of the survey, a newly appointed director with a strong statistical background said the survey was 'methodologically unsophisticated' but probably didn't seriously distort the overall picture.

The Product

Topshare presented considerable attractions to depositors:

(1) The current interest rate of 6.875% with compounding half-yearly interest giving 6.99% provided a return virtually unbeatable in the building society field. Even if interest rates fell these shares would give a high yield relative to investments of comparable security.

(2) Topshare combined high returns with high liquidity at a modest cost. Ninety days' notice was required for withdrawal but deposits could be withdrawn immediately at a penalty of 90 days' interest on the sum withdrawn. Indeed, for accounts with more than £10,000 left after the withdrawal, no penalty was imposed.

(3) The generally sober image and practices of Langport still convey an impression of security to depositors.

(4) The rather low minimum deposit of £1,000 made it attractive to depositors with modest sums of long-term savings to invest. If anything, Topshare was too attractive to institutional investors, and to reduce the burden of interest payments it was decided to limit the maximum investment in these shares to £50,000. Further, the shares' term was limited to two years.

The Marketing Plan

Mike started drafting out the marketing plan for presentation to the Board. So far he had written:

Marketing Objectives

(1) To improve the volume of deposits into Langport.
(2) To position Langport clearly and competitively within the savings market.
(3) To encourage increased holdings among existing users.
(4) To decrease the rate of withdrawal.

Advertising Objectives

(1) To present Langport Topshare as an attractive investment for private individuals, and for organizations, with up to £50,000 to save by drawing attention to the highly competitive interest rate and assured liquidity.
    At this point he stopped. What did they want the advertising not to do? Certainly they didn't want to alienate existing customers as the previous campaign had apparently done, but what other traps did they want to avoid?
    His mind drifted to what was, for him, the more congenial task of thinking over concrete, specific details – £50 million, about equivalent to a fortnight's deposits. It could be done but it wouldn't be cheap. He reached for the current issue of *BRAD* and started jotting down notes.

	Circulation (in millions)	Cost per insertion
Daily Mail	(1.08)	SCC[†] £82 Full page £20,664
		Colour £30,000 (35 cm × 7 columns per page)
Daily Mirror	(2.7)	Full page ROW[‡] £25,900 Fixed day £29,800
Guardian	(0.4)	Full page ROW £15,500
The Times	(0.4)	Full page ROW £15,000
Daily Telegraph	(1.1)	Full page ROW £33,500
Observer	(0.5)	Full page ROW £23,750
Sunday Times	(1.2)	Full page Sec A (News) £47,000
		Full page Sec E (Business) £45,000
Sunday Telegraph	(0.6)	Full page £24,000
Yorkshire Post	(0.3)	Full page £5,871

† SCC = Standard Column Centimetre.
‡ ROW = Run of Week.

He thought for a moment. Past experience suggested that they would have to be good, or lucky, to raise £100 deposits per £1 advertising expenditure. He continued thinking: 'Assume 33.3% decay per insertion.'

He turned the pages of *BRAD*, making notes:

Total ITV households about 20 million
LWT Saturday night 30 second spot £25,000 in March/April
£21,000 July/August (Pre-emptible?) ITV households
(incl. overlaps) 4390 K.

Peak viewing 30 second spots

Yorkshire ITV £14,000 C4 £7,000 ITV/C4 £20,000
Tyne Tees ITV £7,000 C4 £3,500 ITV/C4 £10,000

Yorkshire 2150 K households 'Tyne T' 970 K
Guaranteed Target Audience Packages? 100, 50 or 10
TVRs for Men, Women, ABC1 Adults ...

He continued musing: What was it that consultant said? Something about blinkers as far as advertising was concerned? What about an airship trailing a banner?... Be serious! He turned the pages: 'National Solusites 16-sheet display at 775 sites at major shopping areas or on main roads leading to them £27–34,000 depending on time of year.'

He then turned to NRS material and to other handbooks (see Exhibits 21.3 and 21.4).

Exhibit 21.3 *Socio-economic aspects of newspaper readership.*

Newspaper	Percentage of readers who are ABC1	Percentage of ABC1 population who are readers
The Times	85	5
Daily Mail	56	18
Guardian	79	7
Daily Telegraph	81	16
Daily Mirror	24	18

He continued for some hours, making occasional phone calls. Deciding the final marketing name of the share was a problem, but he had set in motion a brainstorming session to come up with a shortlist of possible names for consideration. Now it was a matter of getting down to the number crunching. But not just yet: there were things that might have to be rethought. And there might be something that had been missed. For example, he kept thinking about an interjection overheard from a noisy good-humoured political argument in a corner of the staff restaurant that day: 'You are way behind the times! The proles are already bourgeoisified: 14% of privatization shares bought by individuals, not companies, were bought by DE people!'

Perhaps it was necessary to go back to basics, asking simple questions.

Exhibit 21.4   Extracts from Mike's Jottings

Percentages for households reached by ITV is socio-economically identical with the percentage for total UK households.

(*Source*: BARB)

Personal income Percentage of taxpayers with income >15,000, by region

North	28.6	South-East	38.1
Yorkshire and Humberside	30.0	North-East	30.1
East Midlands	29.9	West Midlands	30.2
East Anglia	32.5	North-West	29.4
Wales	28.7	United Kingdom	32.0
Scotland	31.5	Northern Ireland	28.5

South West Region. % of average gross income coming from investments = 5.8 (Regional Trends).

For the United Kingdom as a whole it is 3.5%.

Average personal income taking into account housing subsidies, etc.

Bottom quintile	£4,130 pa
Middle quintile	£7,020 pa
Top quintile	£17,260 pa

Top 1% has 6% of income; bottom 50% has 22.7% of income   (Social Trends)

Percentage of adult population with building society accounts 64%

1978   43%   1968   15%

Percentage of adult population with National Savings Bank accounts 7%

1978   18%   1968   37%

Percentage of adults with TSB accounts 12%

1978   17%   1968   18%

Percentage of adults reading national daily newspapers by region

Paper	North Y & H,	E & W Midlands	E. Anglia & SE	Greater London	SW & Wales	NW
Sun	23	30	27	30	28	18
Daily Mirror	25	30	21	24	22	26
Daily Mail	7	9	14	14	11	9
Daily Telegraph	3	5	9	7	7	5
Guardian	2	2	5	8	2	4
The Times	1	2	5	6	3	1

Questions

(1) What should be the target market, assuming the Topshare launch goes forward? What are its characteristics?

(2) Comment on the advertising campaign suggested. How should the budget be allocated, what method(s) could be employed and what calculations will be required?

(3) Which media are feasible given the product, the nature of the message and the segment of the population selected? What would be the CPT (cost per thousand) in the target market?

(4) Is Langport's marketing objective – as presented in this case – a realistic one?

(5) (i) Is Cranston necessarily getting better value for money out of its advertising?
    (ii) Does Langport really need to launch Topshare?

CASE 22
Windsor Building Society
Personal Selling and Customer Management

Luiz Moutinho

Cardiff Business School, University of Wales College of Cardiff

Introduction

Theoretically, investment management is more important than distribution; however, in reality, sales and marketing skills are crucial to success, no matter how good the investment management. For example, Citibank has concentrated its mutual fund efforts on developing a sales culture rather than focusing on investment management. Chase Manhattan Bank has hired mutual fund industry personnel and is developing its own salesforce in retail and private banking. Banking organizations that are most likely to succeed are regional financial institutions – consumer banks and building societies with a strong regional franchise in areas outside the major media markets where customers are not exposed to high levels of mutual fund advertising and broker solicitation. While there is no single recipe for success, the necessary ingredients include top management involvement, a commitment to a marketing budget, a servicing plan, marketing research and reasonable investment results.

In the United Kingdom, banks and insurance companies have been brought under a single corporate roof during the acquisition and joint venture boom of recent years. The key to making the combination work lies in the creation of a common culture among banking and insurance people. Stronger mass marketing skills should be introduced to the financial services industry. The industry also needs to commit itself to defining, producing and then delivering the ideal range of services. Reaffirming that the customer is the top priority would send out a crucial message to the market: that the industry recognizes that it owes all its customers a duty of care. In the financial services arena, where trust is paramount, the importance of this pledge cannot be overstated. To achieve this, banking groups will need to spread this culture across the range of their operations.

The developing unification of European economies into a single market of some 340 million relatively affluent consumers has implications for the financial services sector, where the shrinking of economic barriers between nations is also eroding the barriers between industries. Banks and insurance companies are considering the possibilities of cross-selling and other affiliations. For the most part, European banking and insurance practitioners are sharply divided regarding the appropriate channel through which insurance should be marketed to a bank's client base. Some favour a dedicated insurance saleforce, while others believe that branch personnel can be trained to sell insurance products on the premises. While all observers agree that commercial bankers are not well-endowed with the marketing instincts of a direct insurance salesforce, they can effectively market insurance products to their retail clients. The banks have carefully chosen products that require a minimum of individual selling effort and are similar to core banking products.

Putting financial institutions, such as banks and building societies, into the business of marketing property and casualty, life, and annuity products is good for the consumer, the agent, the financial institution and the carrier.

Marketing Financial Services Through Technology

Virtually all banks have a customer information file (CIF), but many have failed to capitalize on the information collected there. Some are now beginning to utilize the CIF in customer service, sales and marketing. Relational database technology is the most effective method of utilizing the CIF, but many new software products, often personal computer-based, are available to help banks tap the data contained in CIFs. Outside service firms are available to perform analysis and market segmentation of CIF data. Bankers can engage in relationship banking with a CIF, but its most effective use is in marketing and sales. The CIF database can be used to identify existing customers for appropriate new product solicitations. The quality and the depth of information contained in the CIF will also determine how effective it can be. The information must be accurate and continually checked to ensure quality.

Bank marketing managers increasingly are becoming aware of the competitive advantage that can be gained by harnessing the full productive power of the CIF as a source of marketing data. In order to maximize the capabilities of their CIFs, bank marketing managers will have to achieve two important goals. First, they will have to take a more active role in integrating the CIF into the overall market planning process. Second, they will have to expand their expertise in information technology to assume a greater leadership in the development of appropriate computer hardware and software to support the CIF. The CIF can assist in resolving a wide range of marketing problems, the most noteworthy being the development of better marketing strategies. In addition, the CIF can be used to build demographic and geographic profiles of each segment and to identify important customers therein. These individuals can then be used in further research on consumer behaviour. As banks are moving to database management systems to handle transaction processing, it should become more cost-effective to build CIFS.

In the meantime, at one of the major British clearing banks, customer service representatives (CSRs) are using a new branch automation system to sell additional products. CSRs use the colour monitor on their personal computer to present the features and benefits of the bank's products in ways that hold the customers' interest. This capability is helping the bank's branches make the transition from basic order-taking environments to comprehensive financial information centres. With just a few simple keystrokes, employees can:

(1) request detailed information on the customer's total relationship;
(2) call up uniform, scripted presentations that describe products;
(3) provide detailed information on speciality products;
(4) handle deposit transactions; and
(5) tie into the bank's branch mail system for alerts and product changes.

Branch automation has meant more personalized selling for CSRs. Automation also makes it easier for the bank to monitor its sales strategies.

A large building society, with potential for a £1.5 million payoff, has created a sophisticated IBM OS/2-based front end to its host-based applications that is expected to provide a significant competitive advantage and improve customer service. This particular financial institution determined that its rates were competitive but reasoned that, if it could promise the participants in a real estate transaction a virtually on-the-spot mortgage commitment backed up by more accurate data, it could gain a lead of a point or more over its competitors. The idea was to use laptop computers to create an online conference of sorts, bringing together all parties and all vital information. Now about 70 loan officers in the field use Compaq Computer Corp.'s 286/LTE laptops, which tie into a mainframe via an IBM PS/2 Model 60. The financial product, Mortgagevision, is expected to create a chain reaction of satisfaction among customers. Estate agents can more easily qualify buyers, and the banking institution can reduce the amount of paperwork and employees needed while its business increases.

Selling Financial Services Direct

New research from Mintel shows that the financial services sector is turning its back on independent advisers and is establishing its own salesforces in-house.

There have been tremendous changes in the way financial services are sold, although they have largely gone unnoticed by the consumer. Behind the scenes, however, there has been a dramatic change of attitude by life insurance companies, banks and building societies.

Financial sales people have never gone quite as far as the double glazing salesman who is said to have offered to sleep the night on the sofa while a couple made up their minds, but they do have a reputation for the hard sell. Naturally, this makes potential investors wary. So when Windsor, the only top 10 building society that has retained its independent status, decided to set up a financial-planning operation in 1992, it reckoned a telephone-based system would help potential customers to feel they were in charge.

Windsor has been monitoring the competition very closely in terms of the strategic use of telemarketing in the financial services sector. In particular, Windsor managers have been focusing their attention on the moves of the largest building society and market leader which opened an inbound telemarketing unit in 1990 to:

(1) reduce call volume to branches;
(2) pre-sell and prepare prospects going to branches; and
(3) provide existing customers with the opportunity to open additional accounts by telephone.

The results are considered an unqualified success and management is exploring additional ways to use this effective new resource. Since the competitor already has a telephone system that supported many locations in England and Wales, it was easy to add a new multistation inbound sales unit, complete with automatic call distributor. Since this was the competitor's first attempt at telemarketing, no benchmark for productivity had been established. Measuring second-year results against those of 1990, the volume of calls increased by approximately 1,000 a month, while sales volume almost doubled. Growth is expected to continue along these lines, with promotional support to boost totals during slow periods.

Mintel has recently researched the move by financial services companies towards using more directly employed salesforces, as opposed to taking the self-employed or independent financial adviser (IFA) route. This enables us to examine why the employed salesforce is now a cost-effective option, how providers are setting up their new salesforces and what they hope to achieve.

The Financial Services Act 1986 has not had quite the effect that was intended. The anticipated increase in IFAs has failed to materialize because they found the costs too high – both the cost of compliance and the need to keep up-to-date on thousands of products in order to provide the best advice. The number of IFA firms has fallen from 10,600 in 1988 to fewer than 6,500 in 1993. In addition, the realization that the in-house life office can provide additional income, as opposed to the independent which represents a cost, has led suppliers to come directly to the market. The result has been the establishing of employed salesforces. This has been most dramatic among banks and building societies.

The latest research by Mintel has concentrated on the nature of the sales teams that are being put together. The average (median) age of sales personnel is the mid-30s, which is beneficial because much of the selling effort is currently targeted at the family formers (their peer group). In almost all cases, the financial services sector maintains its sex bias with predominantly male salesforces. The building societies are proving the exception, with a fairer split. The sector has also acknowledged its lack of experience in this type of selling and is tending to recruit from outside the financial services sector.

Of particular interest is the low attrition rate now being experienced which is providing added stability to the industry and will go a long way to help it overcome the image of fly-by-night sales people. Also helping to rid financial services of their poor image is the fact that the salesforce is doing no cold calling, with all leads being supplied by databases from the marketing group. This is a restructure for many companies, allowing them to share customer information without falling foul of the Data Protection Act. The result of all these changes should be an increasingly committed salesforce which is less likely to sell and run.

However, the research concludes that the demise of the IFA is unfortunate, since independent advice should provide the customer with the best service. By June 1993, 15 major financial services companies had set up their own salesforces.

Windsor Building Society: The New Pronto Financial Planning Service

In November 1990, the Windsor Building Society was awarded its second National Training Award for a programme with the aim of training all branch staff in the skills of marketing the society's lending services. Research had revealed that the perfect training programme would need to cover an enormous range of knowledge and skills related to lending, including induction, referrals, interviewing, arrears counselling and business development. The programme was designed for both new starters and others up to senior staff level. For the new starters, emphasis was placed for the first time on lending rather than investments and it was supported by a follow-up pack for the trainees' managers. For staff that have been with the society for more than five months, the learning began with a self-teach package on unsecured lending, followed by audio cassettes and a paper-based package covering all the elements of lending. The financial results were spectacular, with mortgage applications 28% above target for the first quarter of the following year.

Michael Harrison, assistant general manager in charge of Pronto Financial Planning (PFP), said mailshots had gone out to selected bands of customers, such as all Tessa holders who were with the Lexington Building Society before it was taken over by Windsor. It is up to the clients if they want to make a phone call. A financial consultant based in a Manchester office takes down brief details about the customers and their objectives and talks about the range of options. This is all put down on paper, and within a couple of days a summary of the details plus the recommended course of action is sent off with a large reply-paid envelope.

Windsor is now planning to decentralize the Pronto Financial Planning service into 10 selected branches covering the most important target market areas. 'When our clients ring us up, we know they want to buy. It's a soft sell approach. They can put down the phone on us at any time,' said Mr Harrison.

Around a quarter of those who receive a report act on the advice. Most inquiries are related to pensions, investment and insurance. Any queries about mortgages can also be handled by the new Pronto Financial Planning service, although some of these information requests are referred to local Windsor branches which are not currently offering the full PFP system. 'Our customers are traditional building society investors. We err on the side of caution; they don't like to take risks.'

Windsor Pronto Financial Planning supplies fact sheets on topics such as personal pensions and critical illness insurance. But it will also make specific recommendations.

For instance, John Carter, one of the advisers, dealt with a client who wanted to buy a personal pension. The report sent to him said three companies would be suitable: First Equitable, Clerical Health and United Amicable. But it went on to single out United Amicable as the most suitable, and included a brochure and application form. 'We think people want guidance. They don't want to be left to make the decision themselves,' said Mr Harrison.

The Pronto Financial Planning team aims to return to clients three or four times a year to review their needs. A summary of the major leading indications in the economy which includes a clear analytical interpretation of these trends will be sent out to clients on a periodic basis to give a view of the changes. Windsor has considered charging a fee for the service, but at the moment it is free to customers, with the profits drawn from commission.

Windsor advisers will be taking part in Capital Radio's Finance Advice Week. Between 6 pm and 9 pm a team will be on hand to give confidential advice over the telephone. Michael Harrison was confident about the success of this new financial product but he was wondering about how to assess the overall effectiveness of his strategy.

Questions

(1) Comment on the concept and key attributes of the new Pronto Financial Planning service.

(2) How would you assess the role of a personal selling strategy in the financial services industry?

(3) Is telemarketing a suitable strategy for selling a financial product?

(4) How could Michael Harrison find the right promotional synergy when combining personal selling with direct marketing efforts?

(5) Comment on the so-called 'soft-sell' approach mentioned by Michael Harrison.

(6) How would you segment and target the current and potential customer base of the company?

(7) Comment on the decision made by Windsor to decentralize the new service into some selected branches.

(8) Do you agree with the currently prescribed policy for the new product?

(9) How would you help Michael Harrison define ways to evaluate the overall effectiveness of his strategy for the new Pronto Financial Planning service?

CASE 23
The Southwest Bank
Customer Management

Luiz Moutinho
Cardiff Business School, University of Wales College of Cardiff

Introduction

There is a cold wind of change blowing down the United Kingdom's High Streets. Established businesses are disappearing overnight, and the multitude of 'For Sale' signs sit like wooden vultures above not-so-busy streets. The old order is disappearing, not least the British bank manager. Some would argue this is a result of the recession. But throughout history there have been those who have been ready and waiting to find advantage in human tragedies.

While business people everywhere have cut profit margins to the bone to survive and remain competitive, the banks have been piling on the pressure and the charges: from £12.50 for a telephone call, to applying the wrong rates of interest, and overcharging in some cases by thousands of pounds. The bewildered, hard pressed, small business community waited anxiously for the Chancellor's announcement that he was going to curb these excesses: from the hotelier in Devon paying 15.72% interest on his business overdraft, to the property developer in Cheshire overcharged by £78,000 in an 11-month period. The announcement came, and was shocking in its lack of understanding. There was to be no enquiry, no questions, the banks could carry on as before. As a sop to the masses, the Banking Ombudsman Scheme was to be widened to include small businesses with a turnover of under £1 million.

It takes at least 12 months to get a case investigated by the Ombudsman. How can a business survive while waiting for the outcome and still being hard pressed by the bank? The Ombudsman is funded by the banks. How can we be confident of his impartiality? He spent £2 million in 1992 investigating 722 cases out of 10,109 complaints. How much is he going to need for all our cases? None of these questions were answered, nor indeed asked, but they are being asked now in Parliament, on our behalf. It is said the British come out fighting when their backs are against the wall and injustice is running riot. The banks and the Chancellor would do well to remember this.

These comments are the opinion of Patricia Griffiths, national coordinator of the Bank Action Group, who calls for banks to give business a fairer deal (see *Marketing Business*, 19 April 1993, p. 3). The thrust of the Bank Action Group's argument is that errors, overcharging and an unreasonable attitude to some customers are bankrupting small businesses in their thousands.

The Consumers Association found in a survey in November 1992 that one in 10 customers are unhappy with their bank or building society account (*The Observer*, Sunday 29 November 1992).

Bank Services and the Small Business Sector

It has been a fraught half hour for the four directors of Kendall Technical Services. They have been trying to persuade the Southwest Bank's manager to agree to a £70,000 overdraft to help their machinery maintenance business get off the ground. Among their difficulties are the limited funds – just £20,000 – that they can put up as share capital and uncertainty surrounding the contracts they hope to win from two large local manufacturing companies.

The manager seems to be questioning whether Kendall Technical Services has thought through the nature of the payment terms on those contracts and whether the two manufacturing companies are financially sound. He seems very pessimistic – everyone's going to go bust on the bank's money!

It has not been an easy session. The bank manager has questioned the directors closely on their backgrounds and was reluctant to lend without security in the form of personal guarantees. He doesn't seem to understand Kendall's business operations. Although he has asked a lot about the directors' individual backgrounds, this has mostly been about their previous money management. He hasn't asked about competitors or the type of service Kendall is going to offer. The bank manager hasn't explored any ideas to raise further capital or any helpful areas at all. At this point, John Smith, one of the four directors of the company, felt that it was unlikely that they would be able to raise the money. The Southwest Bank branch manager seemed to be annoyed by the argumentative approach of one member of the Kendall Technical Services team.

Lending to Small Companies

With the banks taking an increasingly tough line on lending to small companies in the present recession, knowing how to get on with your bank manager and how to put a convincing case for funds are crucial. 'They put you on the spot,' said Helen Morecombe, director of Silcox Engineering of Birmingham. 'They ask you why you haven't brought in certain information when you didn't know they wanted it.' 'The rules have changed,' commented Peter Jackson of the Cardiff-based First Design Company. 'You find yourself second guessing them.'

Many small business managers do not fully understand some of the specifics of financial management. Take the question of gearing. Many managers are surprised at how, apparently, small changes in interest rates can radically alter an investor's return from a particular investment. Another crucial area is the development of cash flow forecasts. These are not difficult to prepare but are one of the key documents a bank manager will expect to see.

Companies that fall frequently do so after a very good year's trading, warned James Spalding, a former chief accountant with McCarthy Transport Services. 'Fast growing companies often run out of cash. They do not realize that cash and profits are not the same thing.'

Businesses often run into problems because they do not collect on time the money that is owing to them. Their turnover may shoot up but the business is still short of cash to pay wages. There are also transactions that will affect a business's cash flow without showing up on its profit and loss (P&L) account. Buying an expensive item of equipment will have an immediate impact on the cash available in the business but the P&L will only record the amount by which that equipment is depreciated in any year. Similarly, the P&L will not take into account spending on stock but only the amount used up, which may be smaller.

Small business managers should draw up a 12-month cash flow forecast so as to calculate the size of the loan they will need to ask for. This brings home the implications of a large customer making them wait two months for payment.

Campari Style Analysis

A cash flow forecast is a crucial part of any approach to a bank manager, but forms only one of the criteria by which you will be judged, Spalding explained. Bank managers will normally base their discussion with the customer on the Campari style analysis or a similar system. Campari stands for:

- *Character* – bank managers are expected to take into account the stability of your personal life and the length of time you have been a customer.

- *Ability* – do you have a successful track record in business and is it relevant to the business you now want to set up? The banks are not renowned for taking a positive view of previous failures.

- *Margin* – the rate of interest will reflect the manager's view of the risk.

- *Purpose* – the bank will obviously want to know what the loan is for. The manager may have burned his or her fingers in a particular sector, such as property, or the regional office may have set down exclusions.

- *Amount* – the bank will probably not want to lend more than the sum you are putting into the business, but it is also not in its interest for you to start up with too little finance.

- *Repayment* – will the small business company meet sales forecasts and achieve a large enough margin to repay the loans?

- *Insurance* – the bank will usually want security even if its other criteria have been met. This may be fixed against a specific asset or floating against all the assets of the business.

The small business manager will probably have to explain these issues to the bank manager but include them in more detail in a written business plan. This should include projections for sales – broken down by customer and market – as well as cash flow and profit forecasts.

Financial Criteria and Ratios

Increasingly, bank managers are looking at financial criteria at the expense of the possibly more subjective elements in Campari-style analysis, Spalding explained. At the heart of their analysis are certain key financial ratios. Spalding suggests three key figures:

- *The acid test*. This measures the small business company's ability to pay its creditors. Divide debtors and cash by your current liabilities. A result of 1 or more indicates the business has enough cash to pay its outstanding bills.

- *Interest cover*. This indicates whether the small business company can repay the interest on loans. Divide profits before tax and interest by the interest due. Bankers do not usually like this number to fall below 2.

- *Return on capital employed*. Divide profits before tax and interest by shareholders' funds and loans and multiply the answer by 100%. The figure arrived at should not, over the long term, fall below what could be earned if the small business company left the money on deposit or what the company pays in interest.

Small business managers should try to expand a simple cash flow forecast so that it could become a more extensive business plan with details of pricing and promotion policies and forecasts for cash flow, profits and balance sheets. Following this approach, the four directors of Kendall Technical Services have now put a convincing case to the Southwest Bank branch manager who offers to provide what has now become an £80,000 overdraft at 5% above the base rate. However, this appears rather expensive to the directors of Kendall Technical Services, who have a potential corporate backer in the wings, so they retire to think about the bank manager's offer.

Performance Ratios and Codes of Practices

Life may have become tough for the small company seeking business but it has not got any easier for the bank manager either. Exhibit 23.1 shows how the major British banks say they will treat their customers by comparing the performance ratings of UK business banking codes of practice.

The Southwest Bank managers were carefully analysing the findings included in Exhibit 23.1 in terms of their major competitors' standings and pondering on how they would have rated the Southwest Bank on the basis of the listed criteria. Their own Code of Practice was old fashioned and set out a series of principles for carrying out banking business, but few of the staff or even the customers knew much about it, although it featured in very small print on the back of the bank's loan forms and other literature.

The bank's managers had, however, decided to offer a more specific charter to small businesses and had commissioned a firm to undertake some research to identify what expectations small businesses had of a bank and its staff and services. An extract of the results which represents the top 16 most important expectations is given in Exhibit 23.2.

The Southwest Bank's customers were not convinced that its branch managers really understood their business, and complained of both high overdraft and interest charges as well as other bank staff forgetting to action instructions such as cancelling standing order payments or transfers between current and deposit accounts. Two other main complaints were highlighted: personnel at some branches were slow to respond to individual enquiries, and staff changes and training rotations meant most counter staff did not know the regular customers and while they acted professionally they were mostly unwelcoming.

The Southwest Bank management were most concerned about these results and believed the best response would be to design an effective and well balanced marketing strategy aimed at improving bank customer care.

Exhibit 23.1 *How the banks say they will treat their customers (%)[†]*

	Midland	Lloyds	NatWest	Barclays	Bank of Scotland	TSB	Royal Bank of Scotland
Legality & principle	57	14	86	43	50	43	100
Contracts & complaints	50	0	100	50	25	50	100
Charges	86	86	86	86	86	86	86
Borrowing	70	27	53	53	77	44	83
Security	33	33	33	33	50	33	83
Performance monitoring	38	13	26	26	26	25	50
Overall	63	33	63	53	63	48	82

[†] A rating of the bank's recent business codes by the Forum of Private Business.
Source: Financial Times, 17 March 1994.

Exhibit 23.2 Small Business's Expectations of Southwest Bank

(1) Account information is accurate.
(2) Banking information is confidential.
(3) Accuracy of written communication (i.e. bank statements).
(4) Promises made by bank staff are upheld by head office.
(5) Low bank charges.
(6) Low interest rates.
(7) A bank manager who is trustworthy.
(8) A bank manager who makes decisions quickly.
(9) Other bank personnel who do not make errors.
(10) Staff who can be relied on to do what they say they will do when they say they will do it.
(11) A bank manager who understands your business.
(12) Information concerning accounts is readily available to you.
(13) Easy access to decision-makers when telephoning.
(14) A bank manager who has the authority to make decisions which affect your business.
(15) Transactions are dealt with quickly.
(16) Bank charges are clearly defined and explained.

Source: Taken from Anne M. Smith, Service Quality: Relationship between Banks and their Small Business Clients, *International Journal of Bank Marketing*, 7(5), 28–35.

The Customer – Bank Relationship

In the summer of 1991, the chairmen of the Big Four UK clearing banks were summoned before the Chancellor of the Exchequer. This move followed a spate of bad publicity surrounding the treatment of the banks' business customers.

Following these discussions the Chancellor recommended that codes of conduct between banks and their business customers should be initiated. To varying degrees the business charters produced by the major clearing banks complied with the minimum standards outlined by the Chancellor.

In 1992, the Royal Bank of Scotland was voted Small Business Bank of the Year for the second consecutive time by the readers of *What to Buy for Business*. According to the independent Forum of Private Business (FPB), the Royal Bank of Scotland's Charter is the most effective response to the Chancellor's call for codes of conduct to be introduced.

The FPB, which has over 19,000 members, gave it top rating with a score of 82%. As can be seen in Exhibit 23.1, overall the Royal Bank of Scotland has a clear 19 percentage point lead over its nearest competitors – Midland, NatWest and Bank of Scotland.

The FPB's Chief Executive, Stan Mendham, has said: 'The Royal Bank of Scotland has set a new standard by promising to tailor each individual relationship to suit the business concerned. It also gives a commitment that overdraft facilities will only be removed in exceptional circumstances and, wherever possible, with notification.' The result will be less anxiety for small businesses, especially those who are borrowing.

Questions

(1) How would you assess the handling of the Kendall Technical Services case by the bank manager?

(2) How would a 'tough line' policy on lending to small companies in the present recession affect the generation of new business by a financial institution in the future?

(3) How would you rate the degree of usefulness associated with the utilization of a Campari-style analysis? What other or further criteria could be used?

(4) How would the Southwest Bank go about persuading its customers that it had a real commitment to helping its customers' businesses to prosper?

(5) What actions can a bank branch manager take in order to more effectively monitor the profit performance of his or her financial product mix?

(6) What are the benefits of improving customer service and what are the key features of a customer care programme?

(7) What are the key strategic implications arising from the given survey results?

CASE 24
Avis Rent-a-Car Limited
Distribution Management

Anthony W. Dnes
Nottingham Trent University

Introduction

Avis is a worldwide operation, initially established in 1946, in the USA, by Warren E. Avis who opened in Detroit with just three cars. Today it operates 4,200 locations in over 142 countries with an estimated fleet of 330,000 vehicles. Around 21,000 employees work in the international Avis system. Franchising was adopted early in the history of the US parent company.

Avis Rent-a-Car Limited was formed in 1965 to develop car rental in the United Kingdom. It did not adopt franchising until 1984. However, expansion through franchised outlets has been rapid and there are now 44 of these as well as 54 agency arrangements and 71 company-owned rental stations (1992). Company outlets are located at airports and wherever business clients tend to demand a high proportion of one-way rentals; their number has remained virtually static since 1986. Agencies are used at present to expand into the corporate market; agents are paid 20% commission for renting out vehicles belonging to Avis, sharing overhead costs with other businesses such as petrol retailing. Franchises are created wherever Avis hopes to increase its penetration of local, and typically private rather than business, markets, where there is a need for detailed local knowledge and entrepreneurship. Avis hopes to have one or other type of station in all towns and cities with populations of 50,000 or more as soon as possible. Avis belongs to the British Franchise Association. There is also a franchisee association which was set up by Avis.

Strategic Issues

The company's current strategy is one of expansion into previously neglected local markets for car hire. According to data supplied by Avis for this case study, in 1991, out of a total UK rental market worth £404 million, it had a 19% share. However, the share was more like 38% for airport rentals, and 8.5% for local business and leisure use. Of the total market, about two-thirds is local hire business which is mostly covered by small, local firms. Avis has increased its penetration of local markets from a 2.5% share in 1988 and attributes this to franchising. Current business strategy is to continue moving the Avis brand name into local markets while consolidating the corporate ones. Rental fleets consist of cars and light vans. About 75% of any outlet's fleet will comprise cars.

Avis's policy is generally to seek experienced motor-trade business people as franchisees. In 1986, the requirement was for single-use sites operated under the Avis logo. However, some motor dealers operated a franchise as part of a larger operation and some franchisees found that they could most easily rent a site as part of a service station. These dual-use sites turned out to be most successful, reflecting a natural economy of scope. Avis now encourages the policy and does not insist on stand-alone operations. Multiple franchisees are not ruled out by Avis but the preference is for 'hands-on' franchisees, as expressed by Mr Alan Rimell, the Network Relations Manager. Avis prefers to have a large number of franchisees rather than have whole areas of the country tied up by one franchisee. The fear is that a large multiple franchisee would operate in a manner detrimental to the interests of Avis and of other franchisees.

Avis has recently begun moving towards certification of its entire system, including franchised stations, under the BS5750/ISO9000 (UK/European Union) quality standards. Much UK business is currently seeking this type of recognition, which definitely helps in dealing with other established companies. The standards check the performance of a company against its targets and industry standard practices. By August 1992, Avis had fast tracked 11 of its departments into early recognition under the scheme and hoped to complete the process by November. Mr Rimell believes this is a good illustration of the manner in which franchising is an important and fully integrated element in current strategy.

Nature of the Franchise

Avis offers a full business-format franchise with manuals covering all operating, sales and administrative procedures. A computerized administrative system (Wizard) which links with centralized Avis reservations and 23 countries, is available for franchisees. No financial assistance is given to franchisees and Avis in fact regards their ability to raise finance independently as an important part of the selection procedure. A finance scheme specially tailored to Avis franchisees has been developed by the National Westminster Bank and preferential leasing arrangements are available from major companies like Ford Motor Credit.

Franchisees are directed to this. Avis can show its owned outlets as working models for franchisees.

Mr Rimell sees franchisees' obligations as honouring the franchise agreement, and maintaining service levels at least equal to those of the company-owned stations. In turn, he sees Avis as providing technical and product innovation, giving marketing and operational support, and using purchasing expertise to obtain good fleet and insurance deals for franchisees.

A franchisee essentially receives the rights to operate under the Avis brand name, to use centralized booking arrangements, and to participate in a system of one-way vehicle hire. The Avis franchise system is illustrated in Exhibit 24.1, where dotted lines are used to show trading links over which franchisees have free choice, and where arrowheads show the direction of sales. No product is sold by Avis. Franchisees may choose to use company supply lines to hire or to purchase vehicles from manufacturers. The lease arrangements are particularly attractive with manufacturers being very keen to place their cars into hire fleets as a promotional device. The cars are leased for 10,000 miles over three to nine months. All the same, it is becoming clear to Avis that franchisees are most profitable when they are able to buy and sell their own cars, which does require particular skills. The boxes illustrating the rental market in Exhibit 24.1 show the segmentation of internationally and nationally generated rentals into business and leisure hirers in the approximate proportions in which these arise. In addition, the franchisees are shown to be more involved in local as opposed to international business. Strictly speaking, the franchisees are not free to choose whether to service any

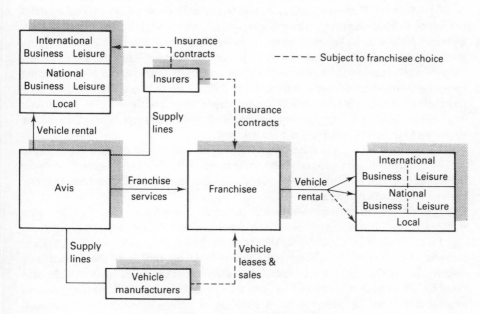

Exhibit 24.1 *Avis franchise system.*

particular customer, as they must accept centrally booked and nationally negotiated hires and must service cars rented on the one-way systems.

The Franchise Relationship

Avis uses a written franchise agreement to clarify its relationship with franchisees. This specifies the marketing and operating support which is provided, the fees that are charged for franchise services, the monitoring of franchisee quality that Avis undertakes, and the network systems in which the franchisees participate. It is a minimal agreement which does not try to legislate for every eventuality.

Essentially, the franchisees agree to work to Avis operating standards, to participate in a system of one-way vehicle rental and to report their rental turnover (time and mileage plus collision-damage-waiver fees) at monthly intervals. They pay a sales royalty and a lump-sum initial franchise fee. In addition, the franchisees agree to spend 2.5% of their time and mileage charges on local advertising; as part of this, standardized *Yellow Pages* and telephone directory entries must be placed.

Avis undertakes to promote the brand name nationally, to help the franchisees with vehicle and insurance procurement, to be available for consultation, and to supply all brand-name-specific displays, stationery and uniforms for the franchisees' use.

The franchisees always agree upon an initial vehicle fleet and a plan for its growth when setting up with Avis. Hire rates are not fixed, however, for this would be illegal under UK competition law. The franchisees do abide by internal transfer prices for vehicles hired on the one-way system, under which they may be left at an outlet from which they did not originate and may then be used by the receiving station, preferably as a means to make a return journey. The renting company (Avis or a franchisee) must pay 60% of time and mileage charges to the owning company. This discourages a station from holding on to a one-way vehicle. The franchisees service vehicles which are in their area if required to do so by Avis or another franchisee, even if they are not their own; the franchisees are paid for such work at rates agreed from time to time.

Franchisees may leave Avis by giving six months' notice of their intention to do so. The franchisor's grounds for termination of the franchise agreement cover breach of any contractual term by the franchisee, the latter's insolvency and any case of substandard operation.

Apart from the written agreement the franchise relationship is subject to a number of understandings which have developed over time.

First, there is an expectation that the franchisor will undertake a significant amount of national advertising, although technically this is at the franchisor's discretion. In the 1991–92 financial year, an expenditure of £10 million was planned. The figure was reached by Avis using a task-and-method approach, where expenditure is set to meet certain advertising objectives (for example, television exposure to be equal to that of rivals). The feeling at Avis is that large expenditures are required as part of a means of keeping good franchisees in the network and attracting new ones.

Second, there is an expectation held by the franchisor that franchisees will operate vehicles meeting Avis quality standards. This 'no-lemons principle' refers to the exclusion of cheap, low-quality cars from the business on this criterion. While the maintenance of standards is emphasized in the agreement, particular details of this kind are not spelt out and rely on an informal understanding.

Third, it is accepted that Avis will take part in the selection of a franchisee's personnel. This is a strong addition to control over management appointments, which relates only to the managing director and operations manager, provided for in Section 11 of the agreement. Normally this involvement in selection arises when Avis offers the assistance of its district managers or franchising personnel to the franchisee.

Finally, it is understood that Avis vehicles may be used by new franchisees at uncontrolled local rates until their business begins to be established. Then they may be used only at national, Avis rates. This represents a little initial support for the franchisee and will be applied in a discretionary manner by Avis's regional managers. Franchisees confirmed the existence of this initial help.

Monitoring of the franchise network is fully integrated with that of company outlets. Daily conduct of the business is observed by district managers, on average about once a month in the case of franchisees. Apart from the requirement in the agreement for monthly performance reporting, copies of each day's rental agreements are sent into a franchisees's district office. For the first three months of operations copies also go to the head office in Hayes.

Mr Rimell feels that the agreement should not be continually quoted at franchisees but, rather, exists as a last resort to clarify issues in a business relationship. He would feel that the company was failing in its work if franchisees ever had to report one another over substandard operation. It was in fact necessary to terminate approximately 10 early franchise contracts, where franchisees' lack of business experience had led them into ill-advised financial schemes. A further five franchisees left voluntarily in the period between 1988 and 1992. It is important to note that Avis makes it easy for franchisees to leave after giving six months' notice of their intention. Many of these franchises proved to be resaleable.

The changes represent the move from an early stage with very high hopes for franchising to one where the arrangement is viewed more realistically. Avis still expands by franchising, where it really needs entrepreneurship in local markets, but uses company stations – and particularly agencies – where a lot of one-way rental is required. Franchising is not suited to transferring services around a system. In this sense, there has been a modest retreat from franchising since 1988, when there were 54 franchisees mostly on stand-alone sites.

The monitoring system is reinforced by the possibility of centralized complaints indirectly alerting Avis to under-reported rentals. Also, Avis claims to have a good idea of what business an outlet should produce. Under-achievement would lead to investigation so that, again, honest reporting is encouraged. Monitoring costs are very low for the franchised network relative to company outlets as so much daily supervision can be left to the franchisee.

Why Franchise?

Avis gains largely from an influx of entrepreneurial talent at the local level. The company's wish to expand into local markets requires that branches make efforts to drum up local sales, for example going out to local business people to establish new accounts. It is felt that this is most likely to happen when a branch is run by a financially committed franchisee. In addition, Mr Rimell can point to service standards among franchisees which are at least as high as those achieved by Avis-owned outlets. Finally, capital-raising advantages are perceived: Avis sees franchising as a low-cost method of adding additional stations to the network.

Mr Rimell believes that Avis offers a huge brand-name advantage to franchisees. In addition, central reservations and a national sales team which is active in the pursuit of company accounts both generate rental business for franchisees. The vehicle and insurance supply lines are also an advantage which Avis has to offer. The operating system used is held to keep costs to a minimum, which helps franchisees to weather better any demand recessions. Finally, Avis employs two business managers, one each for the North and the South, who advise franchisees on business methods and strategy.

Fees and Returns

The franchise agreement allows for a 10% royalty which is levied on turnover excluding value added tax (VAT). In addition, the lump-sum initial franchise fee stood at between £20,000 and £30,000 in 1992, depending on expected business for an area. This figure may be negotiable in exceptional circumstances for a franchisee with an established rental site. The negotiation occurs for two reasons. First, Avis is keen to move its logo on to established sites as a matter of business strategy, as this aids expansion into local markets. Second, Avis's costs in starting up a franchisee are lower for an existing business. The start-up package includes such things as help with shopfitting, provision of uniforms, launch advertising, three-months' stationery requirements, training and promotional materials. Avis does not aim to make a profit from the initial fee. Franchisees confirm that the initial fee is spent by Avis in starting them up in business. VAT is added to all fees paid to the franchisor and is claimed back by the franchisee.

Full set-up costs for a franchisee are in the region of £50,000. An example of an Avis supplied profit and loss projection, as a hypothetical fleet is built up to 30 cars and 10 vans, is given in Exhibit 24.2. The franchisee's income as a manager is not included in costs. Fairly healthy operating profits are shown from the first year of operation. No longer-term projections are available. It should be remembered that fleets are expected to build up to higher levels in subsequent years. Also capital costs do not feature in the projection.

Sales targets are not set as such but fleet projections do form part of the agreement. Mr Rimell believes that franchisees show better returns than would be common in the vehicle rental business. Avis is very happy with its overall UK profits which increased by about 350% between 1984 and 1987, and reached an all time record in 1991.

The Franchisees

Franchisees vary in their backgrounds and in the size of their businesses. Details of three of them are summarized in this section of the case.

All three operate from sites located on service stations in urban areas. They regard this as efficient. In two cases, the service stations belong to the franchisee who divides his time between his interests on the site. In the third case, the franchisee believes that the ready availability of vehicle services and the proximity to the motoring public are of benefit to him. Observation of such sites shows that the Avis brand name is not lost.

The three franchisees all emphasize the value of the brand name to them in explaining their decision to join Avis rather than go it alone. The brand name is thought to reassure customers that they are buying a quality service with a full national back-up in terms of vehicle support and the availability of one-way hire. To the franchisees, this means that they are less dependent on price as a competitive instrument: higher perceived quality for hirers translates into better hire rates for the franchisee.

The central reservations system can generate as much as one-half or as little as one-tenth of a franchisee's business depending on its location. Locations in areas which attract tourists or business people from overseas tend to benefit most. The facility is seen as valuable by franchisees but is not emphasized to the same extent as the benefits of the brand name.

Company supply lines for vehicles and insurance are not as highly valued as Avis managers may think. The three franchisees all take at least one-half of their fleets on this basis but do not emphasize the benefits of the arrangement. The benefits are in terms of vehicle-lease charges and a saving of the franchisee's search and negotiation costs.

The franchisees believe that their personal investment in their businesses acts as a commitment-increasing device. They feel confident that Avis could not obtain the same level of local entrepreneurship by motivating employed managers with profit-sharing schemes. Franchisees typically have a high proportion of their personal wealth along with their reputation as business people sunk irretrievably into their franchised outlets. Not just failure, but lack of real success, would seriously jeopardize their futures. No employee has quite this incentive to be completely vigorous in building up business at the local level. Vigorous local entrepreneurship

Exhibit 24.2   Avis Profit and Loss Projection, 1992 (£)

Month	1	2	3	4	5
Revenues					
Back to back	11,130.00	8,619.00	3,457.00	4,517.00	7,811.00
One way	1,110.00	2,241.00	1,004.00	226.00	2,475.00
Petrol refuelling @ £4.40 per rental	330.00	290.40	334.40	338.80	396.00
Delivery/Collection charges	250.00	250.00	250.00	250.00	250.00
Other charges	7.50	6.60	7.60	7.70	9.00
Total revenues	12,827.50	11,407.00	5,053.00	5,339.50	10,941.00
Expenditures					
ROYALTIES	1,113.00	861.90	345.70	451.70	781.10
Credit club charges	489.60	434.40	178.44	189.72	411.44
One way solit @ 70%	777.00	1,565.70	702.80	158.20	1,732.50
Insurance	1,224.30	948.09	380.27	496.87	859.21
Petrol refuelling costs	198.00	174.24	200.64	203.28	237.60
Fleet charges @ 75% utilization	2,871	2,231	1,360	1,893	3,556
Sub total	6,673.01	6,218.44	3,167.85	3,393.10	7,577.41
Balance	6,154.49	5,188.56	1,885.15	1,946.40	3,363.59

is what the franchisees believe they offer Avis; and this is of course what Avis is seeking.

Because of the emphasis on brand-name effects, the franchisees' main expectation of Avis is that full efforts be made to develop the brand nationally. These efforts are expected to include multimedia advertising, the operation of a national sales team to promote contracts with major companies, and the more general support of an active marketing department.

None of the three franchisees has any serious grievance. Individuals speak of occasional gripes but of nothing more. Some network difficulties arose in the early days of franchising over payments for vehicles in the one-way system. There were complaints that Avis was quick to charge a franchisee for vehicle recovery. However, payments from Avis were relatively slow when a franchisee recovered vehicles. One franchisee felt that he incurred high costs when attending to vehicles which belonged to other stations when these were in his area. This problem essentially disappeared when franchisees were targeted on areas unlikely to generate much one-way business.

Franchisees speak of an easy-going relationship with Avis which is based on common interests. Franchisees appear happy with their situation including their profitability: everyone interviewed expressed an intention to remain in the system.

Summary

The Avis franchise offers a brand name and a national rental network to franchisees. In return, Avis is able to draw on local entrepreneurship to develop local business by franchising. The development of local rental markets is Avis's

Exhibit 24.2 *Continued*

6	7	8	9	10	11	12	Total
10715.00	10,605.00	7,640.00	8,360.00	8,078.00	8,338.00	8,751.00	98,021.00
947.00	2,650.00	1,527.00	2,376.00	2,250.00	2,475.00	1,947.00	21,228.00
431.20	602.80	541.20	532.40	651.20	734.80	664.40	5,847.60
250.00	250.00	250.00	250.00	250.00	250.00	250.00	3,000.00
9.80	13.70	12.30	12.10	14.80	16.70	15.10	132.90
12,353.00	14,121.50	9,970.50	11,530.50	11,244.00	11,814.50	11,627.50	128,229.50
1,071.50	1,060.50	764.00	836.00	807.80	833.80	875.10	9,802.10
466.48	530.20	366.68	429.44	413.12	432.52	427.92	4,769.96
662.90	1,855.00	1,068.90	1,663.20	1,575.00	1,732.50	1,362.90	14,859.60
1,178.65	1,166.55	840.40	919.60	888.58	917.18	962.61	10,782.31
258.72	361.68	324.72	319.44	390.72	440.88	398.64	3,508.56
4,062	3,831	3,111	3,511	3,867	3,849	4,089	3,142
7,700.47	8,805.04	6,475.81	7,678.79	7,941.89	8,205.77	8,116.06	46,864.81
4,652.53	5,316.46	3,494.69	3,851.71	3,302.11	3,608.73	3,511.44	81,364.69

principal current strategic goal. Franchisees are found to have a high level of commitment to developing the business. Avis's returns come mainly from a royalty which is levied on rental turnover. The single-use site does not materialize among franchisees, who commonly set up on service stations, and this appears to have been accepted by Avis as efficient. Brand presence is not lost but may be diluted. Some fairly minor problems existed in the early days over fitting the franchised outlets in with the company stations. Overall, the current phase of Avis's development as a major UK vehicle-rental company is progressing successfully with growth in profitability and in the size of the network. Franchising is an integral part of this strategy but is now seen as applicable in local markets where vehicles tend to stay in a well-defined area.

Questions

(1) Why did Avis introduce franchising into its vehicle-hire network in 1984?

(2) What does Avis sell to its franchisees?

(3) What advantages and disadvantages are attached to franchising for the franchisor?

(4) What advantages and disadvantages are attached to franchising for the franchisee?

(5) Has Avis achieved its marketing objectives over the 1984–92 period?

(6) How does Avis maintain its brand image throughout its franchise network?

(7) What incentives do franchisees have to perform well, within the franchise system?

(8) In what ways is franchising a substitute for close monitoring of the satellite businesses? Give an in-depth analysis of control issues in your answer.

(9) Does franchising solve all of Avis's problems?

(10) Refer to the data in Exhibit 24.2 (Avis's profit and loss projection). Assume an initial investment of £50,000 and a required annual income for the manager of £18,000. Calculate:

(i)   Return on sales.
(ii) Return on investment.
(iii) Internal rate of return.
(iv) Net present value, assuming cost of capital 8%.

CASE 25
Ulaanbaatar Carpet Factory
Marketing Mix Strategies

Luiz Moutinho
Cardiff Business School, University of Wales College of Cardiff

Introduction

From ancient times, generations of Mongolian nomads have been handing down to each other the traditional art of making woollen carpets. Machine production of carpets started in Mongolia comparatively recently. However, these products have already won a good name with both Mongolian and foreign customers. Many of them have merited high awards at international fairs. The rich colours and beauty of ornaments resulting from the combination of classical and traditional patterns, as well as the durability ensured by the high-quality wool of Mongolian sheep and fine workmanship, are the most salient features of carpets manufactured at the Ulaanbaatar Carpet Factory.

The Company

The Ulaanbaatar Carpet Factory is a 100% private, shareholder-based company. The main corporate goal is profit maximization. The organization has a total of 550 employees and was first established in 1971. Most of its machinery was imported from the former East Germany, Poland and Hungary. The company upgraded some of its equipment in 1989 and the main supplier was again the former East Germany. The plant facility is large and the company has quite spacious and clean installations. The machines are modern, well kept and well maintained. The manufacturing process uses very good quality wool as its prime raw material. The painting section (used for the application of different dyes) has less sophisticated technology and less modern machinery, whereas the sewing shop is large, clean and delivers a high-quality end-product. The company has a group of designers for drawing the different patterns used in the carpets and the design section on the shop floor is mainly responsible for the elimination of deficiencies in all the items within the product range. Nearly 150 different patterns can be used in a given carpet.

Constant work is in progress to upgrade production methods. Half the machines are operated and assisted by workers, while the others perform totally automated tasks. Productivity in the factory as measured by output per employee has been steadily improving even when weighted and adjusted by product quality ratings. The company has been able to improve the total quality of the manufacturing process even though it uses a somewhat unsophisticated method for quality control (through visual detection and touching the carpet – procedures carried out by a group of specialized workers). Another traditional method applied in the factory is the use of a *sampin* (a Mongolian hand computer) in the raw material processing section for calculations of waste production.

The total production capacity of the factory is $400,000 \, m^2$ a year. The market demand curve is inelastic since there are a considerable number of unsatisfied customers who cannot purchase the carpets due to non-availability.

The manufacturing schedule revolves around two production shifts with working hours from 7.00 am to 10.00 pm. The level of noise pollution is high in parts of the factory but some workers wear ear muffs and mouth protectors.

The total sales revenue of the company in 1991 amounted to 269 million tugriks, of which 51% represented export sales. Total fixed costs amounted to 41 million tugriks. The average selling price per square metre is 1,115 tugriks while the average variable cost per square metre is 780 tugriks. The average price mark-up used by the carpet factory is 30%. Total company profits amounted to 69 million tugriks in 1991.

Product Mix

The main types of machine-made carpets of the factory are Altanbulag, Ulaanbaatar, Solongo and Altai. The first two product lines are made of 100% pure wool whereas the others are made of 70% pure wool and 30% synthetic fibres (staple). These four carpet lines also differ in pile composition, pile height and weave density. The height of pile of each carpet varies from 5 mm to 10 mm. The size of each carpet varies from 50 cm to 2,200 cm. The weave density ranges from 26 to 50 knots/10 cm by warf and from 28 to 68 knots/10 cm by weft. All product lines are manufactured with dyes belonging to 16 major families of colours. A new high-quality, 100% wool carpet was launched in 1990 under the brand name Otgontenger which was chosen by the director of the factory and is the name of the highest mountain in Mongolia. Since its launch this new product line has only been sold in the domestic market, although there are plans to start exporting this relatively new type of carpet.

The factory's product mix also includes KharHorin carpets which are handmade in line with the traditions of oriental carpet weaving art.

Markets

The carpet factory's products are sold throughout the Mongolian market. The country has a population of 2 million people and its capital, Ulaanbaatar, accounts for around 25% of its inhabitants. The most important product applications are for home and office furnishings. The company does not sell directly to the final consumer. In the past, the products were sold to a central state organization which would then sell them on to department stores and small shops. More recently, with the transition to a market economy, the company places its products on the 'commodity exchange' for sale to merchant wholesalers which in turn sell the carpets to large and small retailers. The mark-ups used by wholesalers vary from 8% to 10% whereas the retailers' mark-ups can vary widely (the most common margins are in the region of 40% to 50%). A limit of 50% margin for retailing outlets has been imposed recently by the government. Mongolia's economy is in difficulty at present; for example, GNP experienced a decrease of between 12% and 20% in 1991.

The carpet factory exports 57% of its output, mainly to former Eastern bloc and other socialist countries as well as to Japan, Austria, Hong Kong and Finland. The company relies on two foreign trade corporations – Mongolexport and Mongolimpex – for its export marketing efforts. The promotional material (mainly brochures) is published by the Mongolian Chamber of Commerce. The carpet factory has almost completely changed the designs of its carpets to suit market demands and every year it renews a considerable part of its product mix. Customization in production is possible in terms of design patterns provided a certain minimum number of each batch are ordered. Therefore, the company is able to accept orders according to the customers' preference as well as specific samples provided by clients.

Competition

The Ulaanbaatar Carpet Factory has two major competitors: Erdenet with a total production capacity of 1,200,000 m^2 a year and Choibalsan with a production capacity of 600,000 m^2 a year. There is no reliable information on each competitor's market share either in units or in value. Exhibit 25.1 shows a product positioning map which plots the three competitors in terms of customer perceptions with regard to two important purchase criteria: price and quality of the product.

As can be seen from the positioning map, the Ulaanbaatar Carpet Factory is perceived as having a high-quality product mix sold at somewhat higher prices than its competitors. Erdenet is perceived as offering a 'middle-of-the-road' product range in terms of quality and price level. Choibalsan is in a more difficult position since it is perceived as providing the lowest carpet quality in the market at higher-than-average prices.

The key dimensional vectors associated with the psychological positioning

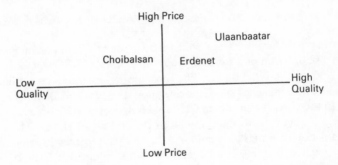

Exhibit 25.1 *Product positioning map of Mongolian carpet manufacturers.*

(in the customers' minds) used to assess the total product of the three companies in the industry are as follows:

- Level of quality of the product.
- Degree of texture (soft versus hard carpets).
- Level of comfort provided by the product.
- Degree of heat preservation.

The Role of Marketing at the Ulaanbaatar Carpet Factory

The company is still strongly production-oriented although it is trying to move towards a marketing orientation. It has just set up a small marketing department headed by a marketing director who has a degree in economics and joined the company in January 1992. He is assisted by two young graduates, one in charge of the sales accounting procedures while the other deals with cost analysis and pricing calculations. The marketing department is also about to hire a new member of staff who will be responsible for carrying out research, sales forecasting and 'industrial espionage'.

Owing to the size of the department and its recent creation, marketing operations are not developed within a line function but are positioned as a staff function in the organizational chart reporting directly to the managing director. In terms of its development stage, the marketing department is seen as a provider of marketing-related services to the company. A recent horizontal and vertical marketing audit of the company, performed by an outside consultant, provided the following information:

Marketing Information System

- No marketing research studies have been undertaken by the company.
- No attempt has been made to analyse consumer behaviour or organizational buyer behaviour.
- There are no marketing research companies in Mongolia.

- No attempt has been made to assess key trends in the marketing environment.

- The company does not apply any systematic market and sales forecasting techniques or procedures.

- There is no marketing information system in place, let alone a computerized one.

- The company pursues an undifferentiated marketing approach. No market segmentation, targeting and positioning techniques have been used.

Marketing Mix

- The company has a good and balanced product mix and manufactures a high-quality product.

- The organization is aware of the important role played by new products in terms of total profit contribution and is willing to invest in internal new product development.

- There is no clear strategy for the development of brand names. Recent brand names were chosen by the managing director.

- The company uses two different pricing methods: cost-plus for the domestic market and export pricing for specific international markets (the organization exports directly to foreign customers). The company has recently increased the price of its products by 30% and this decision did not have a negative impact on the level of demand.

- The carpet factory does not provide any product guarantees or warranties.

- Up to now, the organization has not invested any substantial amount in promotional efforts or advertising, except for the production of promotional brochures published by the Mongolian Chamber of Commerce.

- At the present time, there are only two advertising agencies operating in Mongolia.

- The company has no salesforce. A good illustrative example is that some foreign customers have placed orders with the company after having seen the products being displayed in some retail shops.

- The organization has no clear strategy with regard to its channels of distribution.

- There is no formal physical distribution function being performed at present, except for materials handling and order processing. Furthermore, there is no policy of stock control (not even a safety stock) and the delivery time to customers is quite long. Some retail customers (department stores and small shops) collect the product themselves directly from the factory.

- The 'order taking' philosophy is the prevalent one at the carpet factory.
- There is no marketing planning system in place although the company is now trying to develop a formal marketing plan.
- The organization has never attempted to design effective marketing strategies.
- A new marketing budget is currently in preparation.

Confronted with the findings of the marketing audit report, the new marketing team of the Ulaanbaatar Carpet Factory were wondering which key marketing issues needed to be addressed in the short run. They were also wondering how to implement some critical turnaround marketing strategies that would enable the company to face up to the rapid social and economic changes taking place in Mongolia.

Questions

(1) What organizational factors or actions could make an important contribution for the adoption of a marketing orientation by the carpet factory?

(1) Design a pragmatic marketing information system which could be implemented by the company and comment on its overall and specific benefits as well as the tasks to be performed within the system.

(3) Make some recommendations with regard to the company's product policy, including the new product development process and the issues related to branding.

(4) Analyse the cost–volume relationships presented in the case (including the use of breakeven analysis) and evaluate the most important considerations linked with the design of a pricing policy and strategies.

(5) Develop an effective promotional mix strategy tailored to the realities confronting the carpet factory.

(6) Comment on the most important building blocks that would enable the organization to implement a totally new distribution strategy.

(7) Define and comment on three segmentation, targeting and repositioning strategies that could be used by the carpet factory.

(8) What advice could you give the company on the development of an effective international marketing strategy?

CASE 26
Strathspey Centre
Marketing Mix Strategies

Luiz Moutinho and Fiona Davies
Cardiff Business School, University of Wales College of Cardiff

Company History

After a week's skiing at one of the prestigious resorts in the Highlands, Moira Thomson and Steve Smith had arranged to meet to talk about their newly hatched plans to become partners in developing a new and different skiing haven in Scotland. It all started when Moira's former economics school classmate and other friends of long standing who shared an eight-person apartment during the week became disgusted with standing in lift queues, paying £15 daily for tickets, gulping down tasteless food in a crowded subterranean tavern and picking their way across poorly maintained, and alternately icy and muddy, walkways. Also, their favourite chairlift had broken down twice during the week, forcing them to take to the intermediate slopes for most of each day.

Among the group that had skied together annually for more than a decade were a lawyer, the owner of an electronics firm, a stockbroker, a doctor and two high-level executives, all of whom felt sanguine about the prospects of banding together, investing £50,000 to £100,000 of seed money each, and financing the remainder through loans and venture capital to launch their dream. The clincher of the deal was immediate availability of a friend and fellow skier's non-working property, covering 3,560 acres and contiguous on one side to abandoned timberland and on the other to a Forestry Commission area that happened to be marked, along with six or more other sites in the district, as a potential ski area. There were numerous creeks on the property, a trout stream and a sizeable river that was part of the property's boundary line.

Nature has endowed the region with magnificent mountain ranges offering unparalleled winter recreational potential. Major skiing and winter holiday areas include such destination resorts as Aviemore, Cairngorm, Lecht, Glenshee, Glencoe and a new centre, Aonach Mor, near Fort William. Acreage for the proposed site is relatively isolated in the north-central part of Scotland, about an hour's drive from Inverness and Fort William. An airport about 70 miles distant, served by one major and three regional airlines, is linked to the potential ski resort by a two-lane road that is well maintained. There are good bus and train links.

The project idea was discussed in a heated conversational manner among the potential development partners. Many important issues were raised through comments such as 'snow tractors cost £100,000', 'snow-making systems would cost millions', and 'we'll have to contract for an environmental impact study – I hear they cost around £40,000'. This was a particular issue of concern as the so-called 'green lobby' was perceived as having an increasingly important role concerning legislation for the protection of the environment. 'However,' said the stockbroker, 'the Aonach Mor development did not seem to have too much trouble with environmental regulations. I'm sure we can make just as good a case for our project.'

Thinking of a suitable model on which to pattern their resort project, they first considered Aviemore. This famous ski resort, located 28 miles south of Inverness, was the epitome of popular ski areas in the United Kingdom. The group knew that starting to compare their project with Aviemore would be impossible, with its surface lift, chairlifts, runs, hiking trails, fishing, hunting, camping and caravan sites, multiple excellent hotels and lodging facilities, restaurants and pubs, tennis courts, swimming pools, ice rink, golf courses, equestrian centres, sites for performing arts, child care centre and many tourist shops. Also Aviemore's ski school was renowned, and its ski touring trails abundant. 'Perhaps,' the doctor intervened, 'we should consider another model, say, Lecht?' And so the brainstorming discussion went on.

The Stirling lawyer added a note of caution:

'In 1986 my wife and I, and our two children, could visit Aviemore for a week's ski holiday and spend about £700, including travelling expenses; next trip we'll spend about £1,400 for the same package. Transportation costs, lodging and lift tickets have gone up faster than the consumer price index (CPI). I think we should act with caution and realize that only those with a moderate to high discretionary income will be able to afford it. Leisure time alone won't create the demand we want for the resort.'

What they would settle for provoked a lively discussion based on spirited disagreement: slopes offering good skiing varying from broad, gentle glades, to steep chutes. Steve thought that three double chairlifts would be a good beginning. Others wondered about emulating the Nevis Range's gondola installation – six-seater gondola cabins running on a continuous cable, used by non-skiers as well as skiers. Soon they concluded that a lot more information was needed about breakeven volume and about all the services required to create a well-planned, attractive and pleasant ski complex. And what other resort facilities, they asked themselves, would be required to attract summer visitors and tourists to help cover overhead costs? Then one of the executives, Neil Robertson, said, 'The Aonach Mor development seems to be doing well since it started up in 1989. It's a larger scale operation than we're looking at, but perhaps we can get some ideas from them. I have a friend who owns a hotel in Fort William and was quite involved with the development. He may be able to give us some advice.'

In relation to other aspects of the project, the group knew that daytime temperatures in the area were usually comfortable, the snowfall was light and dry at that 1,150 foot elevation, and they could expect a good average snowfall throughout the season. They were close enough for Aviemore and Lecht customers to start patronizing their ski resort. They estimated there were 300 to 400 rooms available at nearby hotels and guest houses, as well as bed and breakfast accommodation within a 20 mile radius, to help cope with the visitor traffic until development began at Strathspey Ski Centre. This was the tentative name submitted by Steve, and quickly approved by all.

The group realized they could not go much further with their plans without much more information. As a first step, they agreed to meet a week later by which time Neil would have been able to find out as much as he could about the development of Aonach Mor and the Nevis Range.

Nevis Range

When the group met again they certainly had much to consider. Neil had found out a lot about the Nevis Range, and not all of it was good news. The developers had formed a company, Nevis Range Development Company plc, to manage the project, the estimated cost of which had been £6.58 million. This included the gondola, chairlift, ski tows, buildings, infrastructure, design costs and professional fees. £2.8 million of public sector finance was made available through the Scottish Development Agency, Highland Regional Council and Lochaber District Council, and the Highlands and Islands Development Board gave the company a £400,000 grant. The remainder of the finance was raised by the company through a share offer.

The group were a bit concerned by these figures. What they were planning was not that much smaller a development than Nevis Range, which had a gondola, one chairlift and six ski tows. Having already financed one such ski area, would public funding bodies look favourably on their requests for money, especially as their project was in an area already better served with ski facilities than Fort William had been? Would most individuals who had the inclination to put money into a ski resort already have bought shares in Nevis Range?

They studied the facilities available at Nevis Range: ski runs of all standards from easy to very difficult, the gondola, chairlift and six tows, a shop and Alpine-style restaurant at the top of the gondola, snack kiosk on another tow, cafe in the car park, ski school with 20 fully trained instructors also offering snowboarding instruction, 500 sets of skis for hire, creche, and ticket-reading turnstiles which enabled selling of tickets at other locations. In addition, mountain bike hire was available from the car park, forest trails had been designed in the area by the Forestry Commisssion, and several easy walks were possible from the mountain restaurant to stunning viewpoints. The area also offered numerous other outdoor activities such as climbing, hill walking and cycling, many indoor leisure facilities, and a wide range of accommodation facilities – 38 hotels (many providing evening entertainment such as discos, folk nights, ceildihs, and après-ski evenings), over 200 guest houses and bed and breakfast establishments, plus caravan and camping sites and youth hostels.

Would the partners be able to raise money for ski facilities to rival those at Nevis Range? Or should they set their sights on a different type of development?

Neil had also brought records of skiers at Nevis Range. The most useful measure is skier days per annum, and Nevis Range has established a market share of 10% to 15% of all Scottish skier days. In 1989–90, the first year it was open, there had been 58,148 skier days (as against estimates by the developers of 77,000), and skiing had taken place on 99 days out of a possible 132 days in the season. The following year, with skiing on 120 days, skier days were up 60% to 91,750. But the poor conditions experienced by all Scottish ski resorts in 1991–92 had led to the slopes only being open 73 days, and a drop to 60,473 skier days. Nevis Range had attracted several major events, such as the British Speed Skiing Championships, British Telemark Championships, Scottish Mogul Championships, Scottish Snowboarding Championships, and several regional championships, as well as children's races, ski instructors' races, husky races and a 'Fun Week' with events for both skiers and non-skiers. But in the 1991–92 season most of these had been called off due to the poor conditions.

'I think,' said Moira, 'we need to be very careful. A newly set up ski resort in this area could be ruined by one or two years of bad snow conditions, if there are no other attractions for visitors. Maybe we need to cater for a broader spectrum of visitors, with skiing as only one attraction among many.'

One of the keenest skiers objected, 'But if the snow conditions are no good, our visitors can always go to Aviemore. It's less than half an hour's drive.'

The lawyer disagreed, saying, 'I think nowadays people expect to have all their holiday facilities on the doorstep. I agree with Moira – we should be looking at a "Strathspey Centre", with facilities for summer and winter tourists.'

More spirited discussion ensued. Some group members were still highly enthusiastic about a dedicated ski centre, while others were being swayed towards the idea of a broader type of resort, making use of the excellent outdoor facilities in the area for walking, mountaineering, canoeing and mountain biking as well as skiing – or even supplementing these with a 'holiday village' type development containing a wide range of indoor leisure activities which were not dependent on the weather. Moira pointed out the wide range of clientele who could be considered apart from skiers – sports clubs and other interest groups, corporate clients looking for somewhere a bit different for a conference or training course, families looking for activity holidays with different activities for different family members, the growing over 50s market, and so on. They were also eager to discuss alternative design concepts. Should they go 'luxurious' or 'utilitarian and economic'? What target markets should they consider? How could they assess and analyse market potential indices in those segments? How could they develop specific marketing mix programmes tailored to each target segment? The group then agreed that they had to seek advice and guidance from a marketing consultant.

Market Information

As an initial step, the marketing consultant engaged by the group provided them with much background information on the UK leisure market and on the specific sub-markets they had discussed.

The UK Leisure Market

Current influences on the market include:

(1) An increase in holiday entitlement. Average holiday entitlement with pay has been steadily increasing since the 1960s.

(2) There has been a general trend for an increasing number of people to take more than one holiday each year. The proportion of adults taking two or more holidays a year increased from 18% in 1976 to 20% in 1984 and 26% in 1992. Among Scottish adults, however, this figure was only 18% and among those in the North of England 24%.

(3) The income of those in work has risen in real terms. This has given many people, especially those in the ABC1 socio-economic groups, an increase in their disposable income.

(4) There is an increased trend towards flexible and part-time working, so short-break holidays, for those who can afford them, may be taken at various times of year and during the week as well as at weekends.

(5) There is a generally increased interest in fitness and health, although active participation in outdoor activities is still very low. The most popular activity is walking and rambling, in which 20% of the population participated at some time during 1990.

In 1990–91 the average UK household spent 8.6% of its income on leisure activities. The percentage was highest in London and the South-East, while Scotland and Yorkshire/Humberside each spent 8.4%, the North of England 7.0% and the North-West of England 8.9%; 36% of UK adults took a UK holiday in 1990, and 26% of UK adults took UK holidays only. 12% took a winter break in the United Kingdom, while only 2% took a winter break abroad. The number of European visitors to the United Kingdom is steadily increasing: 9,222 in 1991 (4% increase on 1990), 3,737 of whom came for a holiday (10.1% increase on 1990).

The potential market for holidays in the Strathspey area is likely to be mainly Scotland and the northern parts of England, which include the Manchester and Liverpool areas, and Yorkshire and Humberside. There are a total of approximately 15 million adults (aged 15 or more) in these areas.

Holidays can be categorized by length into five different categories, which also vary in other ways:

(1) *The long holiday of two weeks or more, traditionally taken in the summer.* In 1989 40% of European adults took a holiday of this type.

(2) *Shorter holidays lasting 8 to 13 days.* People who are of independent means or retired, or those with flexible leave arrangements, may opt for such holidays. They are also popular with young people and those on medium incomes. Holidays abroad of 10 or 11 days are now frequently offered by tour operators.

(3) *Shorter holidays lasting five to seven days (generally Monday–Friday or Saturday–Saturday).* These are often popular with older single or widowed women, one week being long enough to have a change from the everyday monotony of life, but not too long to totally disrupt their routine. They are also popular with those living in rural areas, and workers who in addition to their two or three weeks' summer holiday have a 'winter week'.

(4) *Short breaks of three to four days.* These are frequently taken over a public holiday. Executives, senior civil servants, and others who work a long, 60–70 hour week, often find this type of break a good opportunity to wind down and relax. City dwellers, and people living in two or three person households, are also frequent takers of short breaks.

(5) *Two-day or weekend breaks.* These are favoured by people in the higher socio-economic groups, and by both single travellers and those in four or more person households (perhaps busy parents taking the chance to enjoy themselves with the family for a couple of days). The main takers of such breaks are the self-employed and professionals.

The Short Break Market

A short break is generally defined as a holiday of between two and four days, usually taken not far from home and at any time of the year. The private car is the most common form of transport used. In the United Kingdom, over the period 1973–87, there was little change in the total number of short break holidays taken, but the demand shifted from non-commercial accommodation (such as staying with friends or relatives) to commercial accommodation, with a growth of 78% in the number of holidays taken at licensed hotels. The number of short breaks in hotels and guest houses increased by nearly two-thirds in the period 1978–88. Exhibit 26.1 shows the proportions of trips, nights and spending for different holiday types.

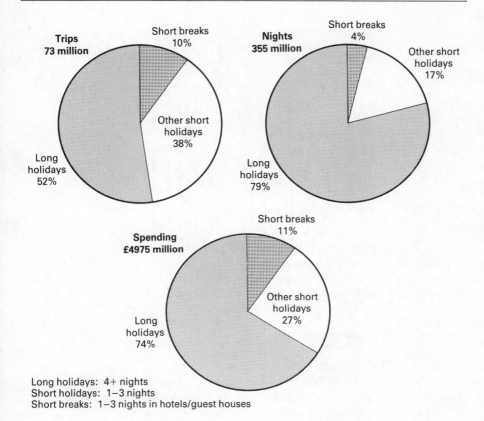

Exhibit 26.1 *UK holidays 1988.*
Source: British Tourism Survey 1988.

Exhibit 26.2 shows the spending per person per night for the different types of trip, indicating that spending is higher on short breaks than any other category of trip and more than twice the average for all trips. This is partly because takers of short breaks are predominantly from the higher income groups.

Short breaks are less subject to seasonality than longer holidays (see Exhibit 26.3). The majority take place at the weekend, and many hotels that cater for business customers during the week target the short-break market at the weekend, often by investment in sport and leisure facilities such as swimming pools, gyms and saunas. Other attractions can include theme weekends, for example based around a fake murder which guests have to 'solve', and breaks based around a sport (such as golf) or around guided visits to local attractions.

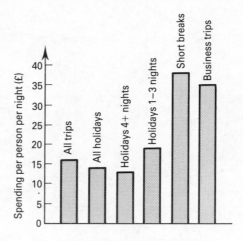

Exhibit 26.2 *Holiday spending.*
Source: ETB (1989).

Booking of Shorter Holidays

The shorter a holiday, the more spontaneous the booking decision tends to be. While many people book their main summer holiday six months or so in advance, for shorter holidays (that is, 2 to 13 days) only 8% book six months ahead, and 16% two to three months in advance. 28% book one month in advance, and the largest proportion, 30%, only book one week in advance. 18–24 year-olds (43%) and single travellers (42%) are most likely to be late bookers.

The UK Skiing Market

Since the 1960s there has been an overall trend of steady growth in participation in skiing in the United Kingdom. It is estimated that there is a core group of around 450,000 to 500,000 adults who ski on snow regularly (that is, at least once every two years).

Membership of ski clubs is also a measure of participation in skiing. There are an estimated 250 ski clubs in the United Kingdom with approximately 51,000 members. The largest is the Ski Club of Great Britain, with, perhaps, 12,000 members resident in the United Kingdom. Another sign of skiing's increased popularity has been the growth in the number of dry ski slopes (now well over 100 in the United Kingdom).

The ski holiday market for UK visits abroad is split into three principal components: packaged holidays, school ski groups and independently arranged holidays. Estimates indicate that in 1985/86 approximately 525,000 skiing holidays

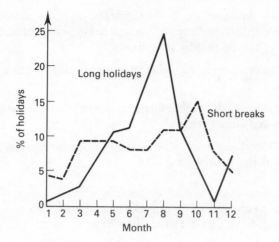

Exhibit 26.3 *Month of UK holidays by UK residents.*
Source: British Tourism Survey, 1988.

were sold – 260,000 packaged holidays, 115,000 independent holidays and 150,000 school ski places. The total is almost double that of 1978/79, with packaged holidays rising at the fastest rate. More up-to-date figures are not available, but it is estimated that the growth is continuing for all holiday types, though at a slower rate, around 5% per annum. As the market becomes larger and more broadly based, market niches are developing, such as group chalet holidays in upmarket Austrian resorts, and school skiing holidays in the popular French ski areas.

Many UK residents generally confine their skiing to overseas winter holidays. Of most interest for this study may be the number of skiers using Scottish ski areas, which is currently estimated at 60,000 to 70,000. A large number of Scottish schoolchildren ski, with 68% of schools having ski clubs and 41% including skiing in the curriculum (figures from a 1985 Highlands and Islands Development Board survey). Studies show that the prime market for Scottish skiing is Scotland itself and the North of England.

Three distinct market segments of the Scottish ski market can be identified:

- Day trips at weekends, by Scots, usually multivisit.
- Weekend stay, mainly Scots, several visits.
- Holiday – weekend/weekday, mainly English, one visit per year.

The five resorts tend to cater for different markets:

(1) Aonach Mor/Nevis Range – weekend, holiday and day trip market, high proportion of long stays in the area, wide Scottish and large English market, also some overseas visitors. There are many other attractions in the Fort William area, so visitors may stay a while in the area but only ski on one or two days.

(2) Cairngorm – a weekend and holiday market, high proportion of long stays, wide Scottish and large English market. A long-established ski area with about 50% of the market in skier days.

(3) Glenshee – local day trip or weekend market, wide Scottish catchment area.

(4) Glencoe – predominantly local Glasgow day trip market, attracting more experienced and rugged skiers.

(5) The Lecht – local day trip market for beginners or families mainly from Aberdeen and the surrounding area.

In all areas, most skiing is done on Saturdays and Sundays; 40–55% of skiers (depending on area) are under 20 years of age, and over 75% under 30, with only around 1–2% over 50. There are around twice as many male as female skiers at most resorts.

The vast majority of skiers visiting Scottish resorts travel by private car, although bus and train links to the Strathspey area are also good. Exhibit 26.4 shows distances in miles by road from the major Scottish cities to the main ski areas.

Exhibit 26.4　*Distance of ski areas from Scottish cities*

	Glasgow	Edinburgh	Dundee	Aberdeen
Nevis Range	111	139	116	172
Cairngorm	150	133	107	104
Glenshee	101	84	45	67
Glencoe	74	106	97	159
Lecht	175	158	87	57
Strathspey	165	148	105	75

Other Outdoor Activities

Increased interest in health and fitness has led to an increase in the number of people undertaking some sort of sporting activity on their holidays. Five million people holidayed in Scotland in 1990, 64% of these for four nights or more, with an average trip duration of six nights; 29% of these cited some activity as the main purpose of their holiday, the most popular being walking (defined as hiking, hill walking, rambling or orienteering) in which 9% participated. Looking at activities pursued during the holiday, whether main purpose or not, the number taking part in some activity rises to 53%. Walking is again most popular (22%). Exhibit 26.5 shows details of the percentages pursuing each activity.

Exhibit 26.5 Percentages of Holidaymakers in Scotland Pursuing Various Activities

	Main purpose	*Main purpose or secondary activity*
Motorboat cruising	–	1
Other sailing/yachting/boating/canoeing/windsurfing	1	4
Water-skiing/power boating	–	–
Swimming	3	12
Fishing – sea angling	–	2
Fishing – coarse or game	2	3
Shooting/stalking/hunting	1	1
Horse riding/pony trekking	–	2
Tennis	–	1
Golfing (not mini-golf)	3	5
Cycling	1	2
Hiking/hill walking/rambling/orienteering	9	22
Mountaineering/rock climbing/abseiling/caving/ potholing	1	1
Gliding/flying/hang gliding/parachuting	–	–
Snow skiing	3	3
Any other particular sport	1	3
Multi-activity package	–	–
Watching any sport/sporting event	1	2
Field study/nature study/bird or wildlife watching	1	4
Watching performing arts – theatre/cinema/concert/ opera/ballet	2	4
Visiting theme park/activity park	2	4
Visiting heritage sites – castles/monuments/ churches etc.	6	19
Visiting artistic or heritage exhibits – museums/ art galleries/heritage centres etc.	3	9
Other particular hobby/special interest holiday	1	1
Other particular activity	–	1

Source: The UK Tourist: Statistics 1990. Based on United Kingdom Tourist Survey, sponsored by the statutory tourist boards of the UK

Holiday Villages

Holiday villages were first built in Europe in the 1950s, and since then have undergone many developments, making them an important holiday option in countries with unpredictable weather. The first holiday villages comprised between 20 and 200 cottages or chalets, designed for summer occupation by families with children. They were located in areas with natural attractions, and sometimes provided additional outdoor facilities such as tennis courts, swimming pool, or children's playground. They usually had a restaurant and grocery shop on site.

Holiday villages built in the 1960s contained more substantial bungalows, with central heating, which were suitable for all year round occupation. Indoor leisure facilities were also introduced. As well as the smaller villages, the 1960s also saw the first of the large-scale developments with 400–700 bungalows. These led the way to projects such as Center Parcs, with massive indoor 'water leisure centres'. These include a large pool with features such as artificial waves, slides, rapids, whirlpools and floating carpets, children's pools, terraces with deckchairs and cafes, saunas and steambaths, palm trees and tropical plants, all in a comfortable temperature much higher than that of a normal swimming pool. Such large-scale villages also have numerous indoor and outdoor leisure facilities, such as tennis, squash, badminton, fitness training, golf, mini-golf, dry slope skiing, surfing, sailing, canoeing, bowling and children's games.

In 1987 Center Parcs introduced the new concept of having a whole village centre under a transparent heated dome. In the dome would be the water leisure centre, indoor leisure facilities, and other facilities such as restaurants, cafes, discos, bowling alleys, gardens, shops and beauty salons, all in a sub-tropical setting. Accommodation options have also been extended to include bungalows to house different numbers of guests, and also small hotels. Many activities are provided, such as evening shows, dancing or bingo, leisure activity courses, competitions, environmental education and children's entertainment. For these types of villages Center Parcs boast a 95% occupancy rate and 71% repeat visitors. Visitors generally come for short breaks, and include couples, singles and club groups, as well as families with children.

Corporate Entertainment

There is a demand for creativity in UK corporate entertainment, a business worth around £500 million a year and still growing. Main markets include the car, computer and insurance industries, and functions catered for include conferences, incentive weekends, training courses and customer hospitality. There are an increasing number of companies organizing corporate hospitality for their clients, and these aim to differentiate themselves from their competitors, often by offering ever more different, exotic and memorable events. Some examples are indoor kart racing (about £50 per person), a day out watching polo at an exclusive club, with four-course lunch and afternoon tea (about £250 per person), war games, activity weekends (such as golf, clay pigeon shooting) at country manor hotels, excursions to sporting events abroad, Caribbean cruises, and even elephant polo in Nepal.

Some companies are wary of the more exotic type of events. Successful people at the receiving end of business entertainment are often in their 40s or older and prefer holidays where they can choose whether to be active or not, rather than being forced to participate. Pro-am cricket and golf are cited as suitable activities of this type. On the other hand, winners of salespeoples' incentive weekends may be younger, fitter and more enthusiastic about unusual sporting activities. Sometimes partners or families are also invited on such trips.

The Over 50s Market

By the year 2000, more than half the population of Europe will be 50 or older, and the disposable incomes of many of these people are increasing. Services catering for this new market are slowly emerging. For instance, the Saga holiday company caters solely for this age group, organizing a wide range of holidays. The traditional stereotype of older people as less adventurous and less innovative is also being challenged. With people living longer and being more health and fitness conscious, they may choose more active holidays. However, more thought generally goes into their choice of holiday than with younger people – they make more comparisons, and service and quality are of prime importance.

Decision Time!

When the group next met, they had had a chance to look at all the information provided by the marketing consultant. The first big decision to be made was: were they going to go ahead with the original plan of a dedicated ski centre, or were they going to set up an all-year-round resort, with skiing as only one among a wide range of attractions? Only after that decision had been made could they continue their discussions with the consultant on development of a marketing strategy and marketing mix.

Questions

(1) Discuss the advantages and disadvantages of the two options: a dedicated ski centre or an all-year-round resort. Which should be chosen?

(2) Describe and discuss some of the most important stages pertaining to the development process of the Strathspey Centre.

(3) (a) What important factors should be considered by the Strathspey Centre in developing a marketing strategy?
   (b) What marketing strategies would you recommend to be implemented?
   (c) Prepare a marketing strategy statement for the Strathspey Centre introduction into the leisure market.

(4) Select a suitable market segmentation approach to be used by the Strathspey Centre and analyse the implications of its adoption.

(5) Prepare an advertising budget, based on the objective-and-task method, for the new Strathspey Centre and define the core elements of a suitable promotional strategy.

(6) What are the major factors affecting the choice of channels and the design of a distribution strategy?

Reference

Fache, Prof. Dr. W. (ed.) (1990), *Shortbreak Holidays*, Center Parcs, Rotterdam, Netherlands.

CASE 27

London Underground Ltd (LUL)

Marketing Mix Strategies

Luiz Moutinho

Cardiff Business School, University of Wales College of Cardiff

A Brief History

London Underground Limited (LUL) is a wholly owned subsidiary of London Regional Transport (LRT). The company was formed in 1985, but the organization dates back to 1863, when the world's first underground railway opened in London.

Today London Underground is a major business, with 2.7 million customers a day, nearly 500 trains, 250 stations, 21,000 staff and vast engineering assets.

Basic Management Structure

The provision of passenger services is the core activity. It is managed through nine general managers, each in charge of one of the underground's nine lines. These are run as individual business units, with a small head office support team.

Below the level of the line general manager's team, the management of the workforce is based on the concept that each member of staff should have a named boss to whom they will be directly accountable for their own performance, irrespective .of the shift being worked.

All other departments are structured to provide the necessary back-up to ensure the safe and efficient provision of passenger services to the company's customers.

Other Departments

London Underground needs a large engineering team to maintain and develop the railway. Each branch of engineering (civil, rolling stock, and so on) is headed by a specialist engineer who is responsible for setting standards. Other divisions provide the specialist resources for design work and the management of work programmes and projects.

Maintenance staff whose work relates to the fixed infrastructure of individual lines are being transferred from engineering to the local control of the Line General Manager.

Other specialized departments include Finance and Business Planning, Personnel, Communication, Safety, Quality and Development.

The Board

The Board has three major committees. All directors sit on the Executive Committee, chaired by the managing director; a former full-time director chairs the Finance Committee; and a safety specialist chairs the Safety Committee.

The Company's Mission

The company's mission is based on the following concepts:

- It is people who make up a company's personality and shape its beliefs and values.

- A company must have a shared purpose to which they can contribute.

The Board of LUL has agreed upon the following mission:

'To provide London with a safe, quick, reliable and value for money transport service of which we can all be proud.'

This stems from the thinking that 'we must be better than we are now'. The approach is based on a synergy effect, which is that 'the whole is greater than the sum of the parts'.

It is of primary importance that the mission is achieved with professionalism and integrity. In order for this to be ensured, all of the workforce must commit to the following four company values:

(1) Consider and respect each other.
(2) Care for their customers.
(3) Continually improve their safety, quality and efficiency.
(4) Contribute to their community and be environmentally friendly.

Company Goals

Company goals that are set to achieve the company's mission are as follows:

(1) Improve customer satisfaction.
(2) Improve service volume for customers.
(3) Improve service quality for customers.
(4) Improve safe services and environment for customers and employees.
(5) Improve financial performance and efficiency.
(6) Improve staff ability, willingness and utilization.
(7) Improve asset availability and return on investment.
(8) Improve relations with and performance of suppliers.

The goals are measured by performance indicators set each year (see Exhibit 27.1).

Implementation and Monitoring

The company goals will be achieved by implementation across all Directorates of a performance-based Company Management System (CMS). The CMS consists of a series of Company Directives which, when implemented, will support the achievement of company goals which will in turn move LUL closer towards meeting its company mission.

Every four weeks a performance report is published indicating performance against goals.

Business Policy

Five-Year Business Plan

The five-year business plan of the company has mainly operational effects, however the changes have implications for marketing, because there is an alteration in the nature of the product being sold.

The operational changes taking place are as follows:

- There will be a labour reduction over five years from 21,000 to 16,000.

- Cleaning has been contracted out. Savings have been achieved and high standards can be more effectively ensured.

- In the past there has been strict job demarcation, that is to say, one person doing one specific task. For example, in the booking office the clerk who was selling the tickets would not resolve other problems. Staff are now trained to undertake a range of activities.

- The number of grades of staff and different levels of pay are being reduced and simplified.

The marketing department gets its general directions for marketing strategy from the business plan.

Investment Programmes: Jubilee Line

The Jubilee Line extension will be a link from Central London to Docklands. This is a very important political project as the government is keen for Docklands to be well developed. A good transport system is required in order to encourage companies to move to Docklands. At the moment the service offered by the railway (overground system) to this area is not adequate because it closes quite early in the evenings and is closed at the weekends. The capacity is also very small.

Financial Position

Exhibit 27.2 presents a five-year summary of financial results, statistics and staff numbers, which should be studied with the following notes:

(1) Grant receivable from London Regional Transport is equivalent to the actual expenditure on renewals and benefit of past capital grants less any profit arising before charging depreciation and renewals.

(2) Definition of train miles includes all miles run by London Underground trains, including those run over British Rail lines.

(3) Assuming full loads with standing passengers in reasonable comfort. Under crush loads such as exist on most Underground lines during the height of the peak period travel, the trains carry up to 50% more passengers for short distances.

(4) Staff numbers for 1988/89, 1989/90 and 1991/92 reflect the reorganization which partly affected Passenger Services, Business Administration and transfer of London Regional Transport functions. Engineering staff numbers include 315 in 1991/92 (119 in 1990/91) in respect of Jubilee Line Extension and CrossRail. Miles operated per employee and staff per million passenger miles are based on the average number of staff employed.

(5) In the years 1986/87 and 1987/88 voluntary severance costs, which were then borne by London Regional Transport, were excluded. Unit costs in 1988/89, 1989/90, 1990/91 and 1991/92 have increased significantly reflecting additional safety work following the Fennell Report.

Exhibit 27.1   London Underground's Performance Indicators

Critical success factor	Key performance indicator
(1) Improve customer satisfaction	**Customer satisfaction** † 1. *Customer Satisfaction Index* (CSI) – unweighed average of Customer Satisfaction with 22 service quality attributes
(2) Improve service volume for our customers	**Service volume performance** † 2. *Trains in Customer Service* – percentage of scheduled number run throughout each peak 1 hour period † 3. Train mileage – percentage of scheduled train mileage in customer service † 4. *Escalators in Customer Service* – percentage of time in service throughout each peak 1 hour period † 5. *Lifts in Customer Service* – percentage of time in service throughout each peak 1 hour period
(3) Improve service quality for our customers	**Service quality performance** † 6. *Train service – headways* – percentage of planned headways achieved (high frequency services) † 7. *Train service – punctuality* – percentage of arrivals less than 2 minutes late (low frequency services) † 8. Train service – total number of all delays of over 20 minutes per period † 9. *Station service – station closures* – number due to staff absence/equipment failure per period † 10. *Station service* – percentage of stations with at least one ticket issuing facility available‡
(4) Provide safe services & environment for our customers & employees	**Service safety performance** † 11. *Customer Major Injuries* – number caused through accident per million customer journeys † 12. *Violent Crimes* – number of violent crimes against customers per million customer journeys † 13. Employee Lost Time Injuries – per 200,000 hours worked
(5) Improve our financial performance and efficiency	**Financial performance & efficiency** † 14. Operating contribution (gross margin) – income less operating costs§ † 15. Efficiency – average cost per loaded train mile (before depreciation and renewal)§
(6) Improve our ability, willingness & utilization	**People performance & work culture** † 16. Employee Satisfaction Index‖ † 17. Employee Attendance Rate (%)
(7) Improve asset availability and return on investment	**Asset performance** † 18. Projects over £1 million delivered to specification, within agreed time and cost tolerance (%) † 19. Asset Availability Index – weighted average of key asset availabilities
(8) Improve supplier relations & performance	**Supplier performance** † 20. External orders deliverd to specification, within agreed time and cost tolerance – %

Notes (a) Goals are to be achieved by year end of each financial year.
   (b) Goals in *Italic Type* are the externally published Company Goals included in our Customer Charter.
   (c) All prices at 1992/93 levels.
   (d) DTp Quality of Service Indicators provisionally agreed as 1 disaggregated, 2, 4, 5, 6, 9, 10 & 12.
   † Business goals.
   ‡ Replaced by 31 March 1993 with 'availability of ticket purchase facility with change given'.
   § Subject to confirmation.
   ‖ Employee Satisfaction Index established and goals validated by 31 March 1992 – LEG.

Exhibit 27.1 *continued*

92/93	93/94	Company goals 94/95	95/96
45	50	55	60
97.5	97.8	98.0	98.2
97.4	97.7	98.0	98.1
87	88	89	90
85	88	90	91
91	92	93	94
84	86	88	90
146	138	130	123
50	30	15	7.5
99.7	100	100	100
0.04	0.03	0.03	0.02
1.6	1.5	1.4	1.3
2.5	1.5	1.0	0.5
£3.6m	£98.6m	£159.3m	£214.2m
£18.94	£17.8	£17.13	£15.46
40	50	60	70
95	96	96	96
75	90	93	95
74	80	90	100
75	90	93	95

Exhibit 27.2   Five-Year Summary: Financial Results, Statistics and Staff Numbers

	1987/88 £m	1988/89 £m	1989/90 £m	1990/91 £m	1991/92 £m
FINANCIAL RESULTS					
Sales Revenue					
Traffic Income	400.8	431.6	461.9	530.6	558.9
Other Income	30.5	35.9	41.7	46.0	51.1
Total Income	431.3	467.5	503.6	576.6	610.0
Operating Expenditure					
Cost of Operations	336.1	378.4	462.2	560.3	581.6
Depreciation	63.5	74.9	81.9	101.5	106.5
Renewals	67.9	79.3	71.8	87.1	70.3
Cost of Ancillary Activities	7.0	7.5	11.3	14.9	18.2
Total Operating Expenditure	474.5	540.1	627.2	763.8	776.6
Loss before Grant	(43.2)	(72.6)	(123.6)	(187.2)	(166.6)
Grant and Benefits Receivable (Note 1)	43.2	72.6	123.6	187.2	166.6
Investment Expenditure	206.1	214.5	307.3	458.8	369.6
STATISTICS					
Traffic					
Passenger Journeys (millions)	798	815	765	775	751
Passenger Miles (millions)	3,888	3,910	3,738	3,830	3,663
Service Provided					
Train Miles (Note 2) (millions)	31.8	32.1	31.8	33.3	33.3
Place Miles (Note 3) (millions)	26,900	27,100	26,700	27,900	28,100
Route Miles	245	245	245	245	245
Operational Facilities (at the end of year)					
Stations	248	248	247	248	248
Depots and Workshops	17	18	18	17	17
Escalators	276	275	274	274	284
Passenger Lifts	71	70	70	70	72
Railway Cars	3,905	3,950	3,908	4,146	4,146
Staff Numbers (at the end of year) (Note 4)					
Passenger Services	12,705	11,762	13,080	12,641	11,622
Engineering	5,561	6,526	7,426	7,736	7,859
Police	346	368	412	457	461
Business Administration	380	989	1,261	1,253	1,242
Total Staff Employed	18,992	19,645	22,179	22,087	21,184

The Company Plan and Future of LUL

Long-term Planning

An improved service through better performance and increased efficiency was promised in LUL's company plan, announced on 26 November 1991. The plan describes a programme for radical change in pursuit of higher safety and performance standards, lower operating costs and better planned capital expenditure. It also:

- specifies clear performance targets based on research into customer expectations (described above);

- reaffirms the vision 'To be rated by customers as the best metro in the world' while aiming to be 'An Underground to be proud of';

- introduces a series of new business goals, covering overall customer satisfaction, passenger and staff injury rates, station opening hours, train service regularity, staff attendance and asset availability.

Restructuring of Marketing Department

Public relations and internal employee communications will be amalgamated with the advertising and publicity elements of marketing to form a Communication Directorate. This will also retain responsibility for design. Responsibility for market research and fares policy will be transferred to the Business Planning Unit. The existing secondary revenue and property development activities, currently within marketing, will be transferred to the Development Department. The Marketing Directorate, in its current form, will cease to exist.

The following customer orientation strategies are based on the psychological and consumer's perception research:

- Employee communication will work alongside media and public relations to ensure that staff and the public receive consistent messages.

- A Client Services Unit (CSU) will be created, responsible for delivering communication projects for its customers.

- Service delivery will be improved by regulating station stop times and ensuring on-time departure from terminal stations. Average waiting times will be reduced by 0.2 minute and journey times by 5%, giving a potential annual revenue increase of £30 million and reduced overcrowding.

- Rostering arrangements of station staff will be changed to ensure that staff availability is more closely matched to demand.

- A Passenger Services Support Group (PSSG) will develop a new system for producing timetables and duty schedules, reducing lead times for publication of notices, reducing staffing levels and providing a more flexible output for customers.

- Track quality and safety standards will be raised to improve passenger comfort, reducing rolling stock damage and day-to-day maintenance costs.

- LUL will replace off-peak services which are not cash generative with 'Underground buses' which are more capable of making money on small passenger numbers and might offer the '24 hour service' demanded by many customers.

'By 1995, London will have an Underground in which management and staff will be genuinely customer-driven, and services' quality, safety and efficiency will be markedly higher. It will then truly be an Underground to be proud of.'

Marketing Policy

Marketing policy had a slight change of emphasis in 1993. The Marketing Department developed an image campaign to emphasize the main benefit of using the Underground, which is the *speed* of the system.

This is a long-term policy designed to produce an overall image enhancement. At the same time short-term initiatives using tactical advertising in the local press were aimed at specific usage (that is, Christmas shopping, January sales and so on).

The primary problem confronting the Marketing Department is that of spare capacity. In the off-peak there is considerable spare capacity. Marketing policy targets maximizing revenue in the off-peak hours.

The Business Planning Unit provides the Marketing Department with data to help identify target markets. It mainly uses demographics and usage (shopping, leisure, and so on).

One of the most important measures of performance is the Customer Satisfaction Index. It covers 22 different attributes, such as cleanliness of stations, train service, friendliness of staff, and so on. An index is drawn up from these 22 factors. Stations are monitored and station staff's pay is linked to the index. Managers can achieve high pay levels if their index position is improving.

The index also indicates which are the most important factors to customers. It is essential to ensure that the hierarchy of factors perceived by the customers is used for planning as opposed to the ranking assigned by LUL's management. For example, headways (intervals) between trains had been perceived as the most important factor to LUL's management. To customers, however, this is not so important as long as the indicator board is working well and they know about these intervals. Customers attach greater value to other factors.

Marketing Orientation

Traditionally LUL was engineering focused. The company is trying to move from being engineering oriented to being customer oriented. For example, the ticket gates are very customer unfriendly and the ticket machines are difficult to operate. One of the Marketing Department's concerns is to communicate with customers about the operation of the ticket machines. The problem is that the engineers react to that saying 'we have produced the machines, what's the problem?' This means that they do not understand customer requirements very well.

The Marketing Department would like to participate more in pricing decisions, to apply marketing techniques such as discounting tickets, but the government controls pricing.

Competition

The main competitors are:

- Private cars
- Localness – Central London is perceived as dangerous because of terrorist actions so people prefer to do shopping and seek entertainment locally
- Buses
- British Rail
- Coach companies – which are becoming very popular

Marketing Budget

The marketing budget is £1.5 million, which is not enough. The total marketing budget for London Regional Transport (LRT) is £15 million. The Underground's budget is controlled by the government. LUL covers its operating expenses through ticket receipts, but for investment programmes it relies on government funds. Recently it had a severe budget cut from the government. Although the company has received money from the government to extend the Jubilee Line, other investment allocations have been reduced. This will affect LUL's services.

There are some priorities and good ideas that cannot be followed through because of the very tightly controlled and shrinking budget, which is not growing in line with inflation.

Marketing Research

The Market Research Department concentrates on five main areas of study.

(1) London Transport Household Survey (LTHS)

This research covers travel patterns and attitudes towards the Underground among London passengers. Of all trips made in London 12% are made on the Underground. Travelling by car comes first with a share of 49% and bus usage follows with 19%. This is shown in Exhibit 27.3.

Exhibit 27.3 *Proportion of London travellers using the Underground*

Mode of transport	% of all trips made in London
Car driver	49
Bus	19
Underground	12
Car passenger	10
British Rail	7
Other	3

Source: London Transport Household Survey.

(2) Underground Users Survey (UUS)

This entails research carried out among underground users giving demographic details and journey type. Exhibit 27.4 shows the percentage of trips made by all modes of transport and London Underground by journey purpose.

Londoners use the Underground for the same reasons that they use other modes of transport, but the proportions are different. It can be seen that work and school trips make up a much higher proportion of Underground trips than they do of all London trips. The second most common journey purpose in all London trips is shopping (18%) while in London Underground trips it is third with a share of 10%. Visiting friends and relatives comes second in London Underground trips with a share of 13%. Exhibit 27.5 presents a profile of the Underground's customers by journey purpose and by Underground line.

Exhibit 27.4 *Underground Users Survey*

Reasons for journey	All modes of transport (%)	London Underground (%)
Work/school	35	54
Shopping	18	10
Visiting friends and relatives	13	13
Entertainment	11	9
Personal business	7	7
Employer's business	4	4
Other	12	3

Sources: London Transport Household Survey; Underground Users Survey.

(3) Customer Satisfaction Index (CSI)

The purpose of this type of research is to measure satisfaction among Underground users. This is carried out by interviewing customers. As customers exit selected stations, they are asked for their thoughts about the standard of service they received on the journey they have just undertaken. They give performance rating scores for 22 different aspects of the service in a seven minute interview. These scores are aggregated to provide data on each Business Manager's area on a period-by-period basis.

(4) *Marketplace Performance (MPP)*

This is another system for measuring the quality of service to customers. MPP uses a market research method known as 'mystery shopping'. Trained customer service auditors travel around the Underground system in the same way as normal customers, but observing in great detail the standard of service being provided. They give performance rating scores for over 100 different aspects of the stations, trains and line services. These rating scores are collected for every station on a four-monthly basis, showing the rated standard of service at the time. A sample of the results of the period January–March 1991 is presented in Exhibit 27.6.

(5) *Ad Hoc Market Research Work*

Carrying out research for anyone who may need it within the company. A recently commissioned piece of psychological and consumer perception research emphasizing the psychological as opposed to the practical issues in order to highlight the motivations behind customer perceptions, produced the following findings:

(a) The underground experience is basically unpleasant, and this is not simply a question of comfort and practicality. This unpleasantness is psychological and centres around certain fears which people defend themselves against in a number of different ways.

(b) Airlessness, or stagnant air is a definite decay trigger, especially when it carries the smells of human waste products. Air conditioning, though not specifically requested, might well contribute to perceptions of a less decaying atmosphere.

(c) Practical issues on the platform were in general about the nature of information received, with customers noticing improvements and welcoming, for example, the dot matrix indicator boards and more specifically the TV video information at Baker Street. With auditory information the critical issue was, not surprisingly, that it was simply inaudible.

(d) During train arrival and departure, the main problem is one of survival for commuters, with fears including whether they will fall down the gap or be flattened by the surge of people. For the tourist and infrequent user, the critical issue at this point is adequacy of information en route.

(e) On the train itself, customers seemed to be complaining more about lack of information and cleanliness. The problem with crowding, though not pleasant, was slightly less panic-inducing than on the platform, but a minimum space to stand in was being requested. A strong plea was made to bring back guards, especially by women who felt unsafe on carriages.

Exhibit 27.5   Customer profile for each journey purpose (%)

	All trips (%)	To/From work/school (%)	VFR (%)
Male	55	56	49
Female	45	44	51
Under 25	35	36	36
25–34	36	37	37
35–44	12	14	5
45–65	11	12	7
45	6	1	16
AB	31	32	18
C1	43	43	43
C2	15	16	17
DE	12	8	22
5+ days per week	66	89	39
1–4 days per week	20	7	39
Less than once a week	13	4	22
All UK Res.:			
(proportion of sample)	(86)	(91)	(81)
Work/Study FT	85	95	66
P/T Worker	6	5	4
Other	10	0	30
Ticket Type:			
ODTCC (One Day Ticket – City Centre)	19	8	23
Weekly/Longer	51	71	31
Single/Rtn	23	19	29
Elderly/Disabled	5	1	15
Other	2	1	2
Time of Day:			
7–10am	22	34	5
10am–4pm	25	19	25
4–7pm	28	35	19
7–10pm	10	8	18
Saturday	10	3	18
Sunday	6	1	15

Source: Underground Users Survey

(f)   Changing platforms and the journey to the exit were essentially an issue of adequate routing. At the exit, people did not like the ticket barriers. While accepting them on the way down, many felt extremely unhappy about them on the way out. Where Kings Cross disaster fears were explicitly mentioned, it was the ticket barrier obstacle that often came up.

(g)   Some customers commented wistfully about the Paris Metro or an electronic security pass system. While realizing that the lack of flat rate fares presents a problem for LUL, they were keen to find a solution to what they perceived as the 'bottleneck' problem.

(h)   There was widely held mistrust of the system in a potential emergency. Tourists also said it was difficult to know which way the ticket went in.

Exhibit 27.5 *continued*

Social/Sporting (%)	Shopping (%)	Business (%)	Sightseeing (%)
63	36	60	58
37	64	40	42
43	37	24	28
37	25	31	44
8	12	15	10
6	8	22	10
6	18	7	8
29	27	41	50
50	41	36	33
11	15	12	8
10	17	11	13
42	39	41	35
38	37	30	31
20	24	29	34
(86)	(78)	(87)	(40)
85	64	75	74
4	9	7	6
11	27	18	19
36	39	31	54
24	24	28	17
30	21	34	23
5	16	6	5
4	1	1	1
1	5	14	14
14	37	49	35
22	16	20	21
25	2	9	8
20	33	5	13
18	7	2	18

Market Targeting and Segmentation

Market segments have been constructed in terms of behaviour variables and, more particularly, on the purpose of journey. Customer segment profiles have been developed and the more common customer groupings are as follows:

Commuters *(see Exhibit 27.7)*

- Regular and frequent users.
- Travel by Underground 5+ days per week.

Exhibit 27.6 MPP Average Scores by Line and Business Manager Areas (%)

Line	Line/BM areas	Station service			Train service: condition of seats
		Ease of seeing JP on platform (100 = best)	Ease of seeing where to exit	Level of graffiti in booking hall	
Bakerloo	line	51	76	77	56
Central	line	72	78	80	62
Central	East	73	81	82	—
Central	West	76	82	79	—
Central	Centre	64	67	76	—
Circle/ H&C	line	75	78	82	54
District	line	77	85	81	62
District	East	75	84	78	—
District	Centre	84	85	85	—
District	West	74	86	81	—
East London	line	70	85	87	75
Jubilee	line	75	83	76	69
Metropolitan	line	71	85	87	60
Metropolitan	City	68	83	87	—
Metropolitan	North	72	85	87	—
Northern	line	68	85	83	71
Northern	City & Sth.	65	85	85	—
Northern	N. East	67	84	82	—
Northern	N. West	74	85	83	—
Piccadilly	line	73	82	83	56
Piccadilly	North	69	80	76	—
Piccadilly	Centre	74	83	89	—
Piccadilly	West	76	84	85	—
Victoria	line	75	79	80	73

JP = Journey Planner.
Source: MPP, Jan–March 1991.

- 70% hold weekly or longer period Travelcards.

- Very Underground literate.

- Due to Travelcard, they made a high proportion of all discretionary trips on the Underground.

Their needs

- Regular service
- Maximum number of trains – frequent service

Exhibit 27.7 Profile of Joe Commuter

'I use the Underground every day to get to and from work. I've got a Travelcard so I'm not worried about the ticket machines, but I do like to be seen promptly at the ticket window when I need to renew it. I like to be dealt with efficiently and courteously when I'm trying to give London Underground hundreds of pounds of my money.

'My local station usually has a man checking the tickets. I like to see him there and awake and alert . . . and would it hurt so much if he were to smile sometimes?

'I usually don't have to wait too long for a train, perhaps 5 to 7 minutes. If it's 10 minutes or more, I know there's something wrong. I get annoyed when there is obviously something wrong and nobody says a word.

'I can take two routes to the office and I switch between them depending on the way the trains are running and if any stations are closed. I usually get my information from the radio, before leaving home. Why can't you give the useful, up-to-date information to me on the platform?

'I'm not greatly bothered by the train itself. It's sometimes a bit messy inside, but that's the other passengers for you. But sometimes it stops for no reason: that's bad enough when you're on the surface, but in the tunnels it's murder. The driver rarely tells you why he's stopped, sometimes I think it's just to annoy! I don't mind the crowding, either; at least, not usually. But if a couple of the earlier trains have been cancelled it gets really packed. I don't even mind standing for short trips, but standing in the middle, not knowing if you'll be able to get out before the doors shut because the crowd's so dense, that's horrible. That's why I swap between lines if I can.

'The station by my office is being modernized. It's been "being modernized" for 40 years, I exaggerate, but it has been going on a long time. I know it is for our safety and to help "us passengers", but I wish they'd tell us more about how long it will take! They also never tell you about alternative routes. If half a passageway is boarded up you need to know the shortcuts. I do, but there are always tourists and day-trippers milling about looking for the way out, and there are never any staff to guide them.

'I have to go up two escalators to get out. One of them has been out of order for six months: it's ridiculous. Can you imagine the escalator in Selfridges being out for more than six days? For all I know, the escalator is fine: it's just sitting behind its hoarding with no one working on it!

'On the way out we have to queue up and go through the ticket barriers. I'm used to them now, but I often get blocked while some tourist wonders why his off-peak Travelcard won't work yet. Mind you, once the thing ate my season ticket. It's hell letting go of hundreds of quids worth of ticket and just hoping it'll pop back out.

'In the evening, it's OK getting to the platform, but that's when the fun starts. They just keep packing hundreds of people in when there isn't room for them. There are never any members of staff there. If there were, at least you'd hope they could see what was happening. If a train is cancelled it gets really dangerous.

'If two are missing, you haven't got a hope. All the ones that come after that are full by the time they reach us, so you just stay on the platform forever. If this happens, I go back out and go to the pub. Why don't they tell us before we get down to the platform? There are lots like me who could do something else and not add to the crush on the platform.

'Oh, and I hate it when they call us "Customers". Customers have a choice, what choice do I have?'

Source: London Underground Ltd (LUL) – Market Research Department.

- Good information provision
- Escalator or lift service at their station

Their aspirations

- Not to be delayed
- More pro-active staff (so irregular travellers don't clog the flow)
- A seat

Shoppers (see Exhibit 27.8)

Shopping accounts for about 1 million underground trips each week.

- Shoppers tend to be female and live near an underground station.
- They do not hold period tickets and pay cash fares.

Their needs

- Good information provision
- Reasonable number of trains – frequent service (for time of day)
- Good ticket sales staff
- Visible staff presence

Their aspirations

- Help with baby buggy and shopping on fixed stairs and escalators
- More pro-active staff (don't have to ask for help)
- Information from operator on scheduled and unscheduled stops (where am I?)
- Cleanliness and 'hygiene' factors – public toilets

Visitors

Visiting friends or relatives is the second largest journey purpose among underground users.

- Many visitors are younger and have less disposable income.
- Many use the Underground for weekend trips.

Their needs

- Improved off-peak frequency
- Punctual train service – reliable service

Exhibit 27.8 Profile of Sally Shopper

Another of our regular, if less frequent customers we can call Sally Shopper. Sally is a young mother with a baby. Just listen to what she says:

'I use the tube about once a fortnight to go up to town, since my husband takes the car. I have to take the buggy, you see, because of the baby, so it's a real hassle. You never get any help.

'I use the ticket machines if I can, but I never have the right change and, if you're going up to town just after the rush hour, they always seem to want "exact fare only". Anyway, if you go to the window, at least you can speak to someone and maybe they'll tell you if the trains are alright. Otherwise, you can buy your ticket and be standing on the platform for half an hour before the Underground bother to say they've lost all their trains. With the little one, it's nice to have a loo to hand, but you never know if you'll miss a train while you're in there. There's no one to ask, only the cleaner sometimes, and they don't know what's happening to the service any more than you do. Anyway, the rest of it's so dirty, the loo wouldn't be nice and you feel it's safer to stay out on the platform, so other people can see you.

'If the trains are running they are usually fine, but they are so dirty. And there's such a step up into them, too. I like the maps, so you can work out where you're going, but they ought to tell you which station you're coming to next. I have to look out at every station and then it stops in the tunnel, the baby starts crying, and everything goes quiet. You wonder what's wrong.

'The worst bit is getting out at the other end. The escalators are always broken and there's no one there to help me with the buggy. Once I got one of the staff who was hanging around to help me up the stairs! But I usually ask another woman passenger. The gates are the worst. You just feel silly standing there, waiting for help, and then everyone looks at you when the alarm goes on when they do let you out. But you have to, I mean . . . imagine if a baby got caught in those jaws. Why can't they have one bigger gate for mums and people with luggage? And then there's finding the right exit to get up to the street.

'If I buy anything large I have to get a cab home, or take the bus. If not, I have to dodge the rush hour: I hate it and the baby hates it. So I'll either go earlier or stop and have tea and go later. I really only do that if I'm with someone, because you don't want to be on the Underground late, do you? It's not safe – is it?'

Source: London Underground Ltd (LUL) – Market Research Department.

- Visible staff or BT police presence
- Good lighting
- Guaranteed seat(s)

Their aspirations

- Public toilets
- Bus or minicab from station
- Cheaper off-peak tickets

Evening Entertainment

The perceived importance of the entertainment sub-market is out of proportion to its size.

- Many entertainment trips are made late at night and there is a fairly strong male bias in this group.
- Many are light users who only experience the Underground when travelling for this purpose.

Their needs

- Punctual train service – reliable service
- Good information provision
- Visible staff or BT police presence
- No threatening individuals or groups

Their aspirations

- More pro-active staff (don't have to ask to be helped)
- Local area information
- Minicab (or similar) home from station

Conclusion

The 'average' Underground customer is a young, adult male and in the upper social classes.

Several initiatives have been identified to meet customer needs and make the operating services more acceptable. These include line radio, Underground bus service, length of traffic day, new timetables, special customer programmes and station improvements.

Promotional Strategy

Communication Department

There are 80 people working in the communication department. The decision unit consists of three people, so there is flexibility and time-saving in decision-making.

Communication Strategy

Communication has a role to play within five of the LUL's business objectives which are as follows:

(1) *Attitude change* – to positively change the perceptions and attitudes towards the Underground.

(2) *Revenue generation* – to increase off-peak travel, thus generating net revenue by utilizing spare capacity.

(3) *Government investment* – to gain government commitment to sustain investment in the existing network and investment in new facilities.

(4) *Improved product* – to improve the efficiency and safety of product performance.

(5) *Improved staff performance* – to achieve excellence in the quality of service from staff.

The various target markets in which communications has a role to play are as follows:

(1) Commuters
   • Adults, aged 20–44 who live within Greater London

(2) Potential leisure travellers
   • Housewives, aged 25–44, part-time and non-working
   • Mothers with children or families (school holidays)
   • Couples, aged 20–34 (evenings and weekends)
   • Young adults and students, aged 18–21, single
   • UK visitors to London
   • Overseas visitors to London

(3) Opinion formers
   • MPs and government ministers
   • Political parties
   • Local authorities
   • Local councillors
   • Transport interest groups
   • Environmental pressure groups
   • Academics

(4) Employees
   • Both present and prospective

Advertising Strategy

Advertising plays a role in changing attitudes and generating revenue. The key targets are commuters and potential leisure travellers.

The main problem, according to research, is that although users are well able to appreciate the relative speed and efficiency of LUL as a mode of travel, these benefits tend to be overwhelmed by negative perceptions. These include bad word of mouth, media criticism, single bad experience, inherent fears of being underground and exaggerated concern about crime.

LUL believes that it must move from the defensive on to the offensive. This can be achieved by promoting a competitive product and giving people a reason to believe in the Underground to counter the negative climate.

The main message of LUL's advertising campaign is: 'In an ever more congested city, the Tube (because it travels underground) offers you the fastest way through to your destination'.

Acknowledgement

The author would like to thank former MBA students Panagelos Kanistras, Nikalars Kondylis, Ching Nei Ling and Atsumi Mizutani for collecting these data as part of a marketing assignment and for obtaining permission from London Underground Ltd (LUL) to transform them into a case study.

Questions

(1) Develop a brief S W O T (strengths, weaknesses, opportunities and threats) analysis of London Underground Ltd (LUL).

(2) Refer to Exhibit 27.2 and calculate the following corporate performance indicators:
   • average fare per passenger mile
   • average cost per passenger mile – including depreciation and renewal, excluding ancillary activity
   Comment on the uses of such indicators.

(3) Discuss some critical procedures that LUL could adopt in order to choose appropriate criteria for market segmentation and targeting. Summarize the key service benefits sought by the Joe Commuter and Sally Shopper market segments.

(4) Select two of the target audiences included in LUL's communication strategy:
   (a) classify them as primary, secondary and tertiary for each of the business objectives described; and
   (b) design appropriate messages and communication strategies for each group.

(5) Define the unique selling propositions (USPs) that LUL could utilize in its advertising copy strategy. Design a marketing communication strategy based on a core product benefit campaign targeted to all adults living in Greater London and, secondly, LUL staff. Emphasis should be placed on the tone of voice, communication needs and communication channels.

(6) Discuss some key issues pertaining to a suitable strategic agenda that could be implemented by LUL.

CASE 28
The Scottish Football League
Marketing Mix Strategies

Luiz Moutinho and Fiona Davies
Cardiff Business School, University of Wales College of Cardiff

Gerard J. Shepherd
Reidvale Housing Association Limited

History

The Scottish Football League (SFL) was formed at a meeting in Holton's Hotel, Glasgow, on 20 March 1890 with 10 clubs participating in the First Division, and in season 1893/94 a Second Division was formed also consisting of 10 clubs.

Although the two divisions set-up was now well established, automatic promotion and relegation, as in existence today, was not operative. Instead a voting procedure, adopted by the First Division clubs, decided the promotion–relegation debate.

The First World War saw the abandonment of the Second Division, which was not reinstated until the 1921/22 season, which also saw the introduction of automatic promotion and relegation.

Season 1923/24 saw the introduction of the Third Division. With clubs unable to complete their fixtures its existence was somewhat short lived, financial constraints enforcing its abandonment midway through season 1925/26. The two league set-up remained until the end of season 1938/39, when the Second World War intervened and the League was consequently suspended.

It was not until the 1946/47 season that the League was re-established in an 'A', 'B' and 'C' divisional format. The 'C' Division was subsequently absorbed into 'B' Division, resulting in a set-up which continued for about the next 20 years.

During the 1970s there had been frequent and lengthy discussions on restructuring Scottish League football to make it more competitive and therefore more attractive to the consumer. This restructuring finally materialized in 1975/76 with the now 38 clubs arranged into three divisions; a Premier, First and Second division consisting of 10, 14 and 14 clubs respectively. This format continued until season 1986/87 when a transitional 12, 12, 14, formation was adopted for two years with a return to the former system at the end of season 1987/88.

The League Cup was introduced in 1946/47 and except for the four seasons from 1977/78 to 1980/81, when it was organized on a straight knock-out basis, this competition has been structured in the form of mini leagues with the league winners then playing out the competition on a knock-out basis.

Both League Championship and League Cup come under the jurisdiction of the SFL which is run by a management committee of 12 members elected by the 38 clubs which up until 1986/87 recommended proposals to the clubs. Voting was on the basis of one vote per club with a two-thirds majority (that is, 26 clubs) required for a proposal to be carried.

The 10 Premier Division clubs on average account for 70% of total attendances yet on the basis of the one vote per club they have only 26% of the total vote. This was the basis of the threatening and very damaging crisis at the SFL the outcome of which was, *inter alia*, a revamped voting system whereby the Premier Division clubs have four votes per club, the First Division clubs having two votes and the Second Division one vote per club. The ramification of such a system is yet to be seen. Clearly the power base has shifted towards those clubs contributing more to the football scene but it remains to be seen whether the disconsolate clubs will remain loyal to the umbrella body – and what is it they say about absolute power?

Alterations, additions or amendments to the Constitution and Rules of the League can only be taken at an annual or special general meeting and require a two-thirds majority before they can be declared competent. Any notice by member clubs proposing alterations to the Rules of the League must be submitted to the Secretary not later than 31 March in each year in the case of the Annual General Meeting or 21 days in the case of a Special General Meeting.

The normal day-to-day duties of the League are vested in the administration headed by the Secretary, who is a paid official not permitted to vote at any meeting nor be connected with any League club. Some of the many duties undertaken by the administration include the compilation of League Championship and Cup matches and receiving all registration forms and contracts of service for players currently registered with the 38 member clubs.

The Product and its Price

Put simply the product is entertainment of the football variety packaged in two formats – League Championship and League Cup. Having lost 7 million spectators since 1945 the observer would quite rightly assert that league football was firmly encamped in the decline period of its product life cycle (PLC), as in the case of other entertainment products, such as the cinema. However, since about 1980 there has been a levelling of attendances at both league and cup matches, now around the 4 million figure. Indeed if the figures since 1980 are seen in isolation then attendances have perceptibly increased in successive years which may not indicate a resurgence but certainly a slowing down of the accelerating trend downwards. Although the fall off in sales has occurred throughout each division the Premier Division has fared less badly than the First and Second Divisions. This is perhaps just as well since the contribution made by the Premier Division accounts for some 70% of the total sales figure.

Marketing can be defined as a social process by which individuals and groups obtain what they need and want through creating and exchanging products of value with others. What needs are satisfied by the attendance at football matches? In the main it is those psychological human needs that are satisfied by allowing, for example, a vent for frustration and anger and an outlet for emotion and prejudices: the latter more apparent at some grounds than others. Being associated with success in these modern times will also hold much attraction for individuals whose self-ambition and fulfilment have not been, or have only partly been attained – leading one to perceive that the market for football is situated at the lower end of the social scale.

The cost of admission to SFL matches depends on a number of variables: where the customer wishes to view the match (terracing, enclosures, etc.); the class of fixture being played (Premier, First Division, etc.); and the individual's age group (adult, child or pensioner). Since about 1960 the price of admission has almost doubled in real terms and it is hardly surprising that the substantial increase in the cost of the product coincided with, or perhaps even contributed to, the marked decline in consumers of the product, particularly in a period of economic recession. These price increases may have been an attempt to increase revenue to compensate for rising costs but it appears that the football industry either misjudged or overlooked a basic economic principle. Where an industry (or company) is in competition with other outlets for consumers, which football is, the demand for its product will most probably be price elastic: that is, price increases will reduce quantity demanded by a relatively greater amount such that revenue from gate receipts will fall and subsequently reduce the benefit from price increases. Price flexibility was introduced at the beginning of the 1981/82 season when admission prices set by the SFL were 'recommended' only and clubs could vary the price on the basis of how they saw the attractiveness of the fixture: a realization that the laws of supply and demand could vary from fixture to fixture.

Marketing Environment

Senior grade football in Scotland is an industry where the companies (the clubs) are competing against other sports, leisure activities and various forms of light entertainment for consumers. Consequent on this mutual dependency of clubs on each other for public support, the football industry in Scotland might well be considered a business where the clubs are simply branches of a parent or holding group: the SFL with its head office in Glasgow. Just as traditional industries evolve, develop and change their organization and structure in response to environmental factors such as closures, liquidations and new entrants, so also has the Scottish Football industry during its existence.

Analysing further the environmental constraints within which it operates should enhance our understanding of the SFL, and go some way in explaining its current standing within the industry.

Economic

The demise of heavy engineering in the west of Scotland has contributed unquestionably to the fall in revenue experienced by the affiliated League clubs. Traditionally, the 'Saturday Sanny' was content and affluent enough to satisfy his demand for professional top grade football, a 'passion' which filled the coffers of football clubs in the calm days of 10 million supporters annually. This loss, understandably, has filtered through to would-be sponsors and endorsers.

Legal – Safety of Sports Grounds Act 1975

The most recent significant piece of legislation enacted has been the Criminal Justice (Scotland) Act which, *inter alia*, outlawed the drinking of alcohol to, from and at sporting stadia. The act was designed primarily to ameliorate the 'hooligan' problem at football grounds. In this respect it has been successful but at the same time revenues at the turnstile have been lost: a fact the League accepts as an acceptable cost of improving the image of the game.

Participation in sport

With the United Kingdom repeatedly being placed low down on variously compiled 'national health' league tables, successive governments have laid great store in participation as opposed to spectating. 'Fit for life' campaigns and the like, have seen the Scottish Football Association (SFA) enjoying an expansionary period with the growth in football participation, the corollary of which is that attendances at games has suffered: the lifeblood of the professional game.

Marketing Orientation

While not carrying out specific demographic research on its market, the SFL does extract data from social research papers (of which there are many) and also from the clubs themselves which they see as being more advantageously placed to carry out such work. Recent evidence of knowing the customer and supplying his needs has been the growth of 'executive' facilities, providing more than just a game of football. This area of growth is not seen as the panacea to football's malady but has helped to utilize overcapacity and at the same time ease the constant cash flow problem of the more enlightened clubs.

It has to be stressed that the SFL does not look to the executive market to reverse the decline of football but merely as a secondary source of revenue. It is towards the working class man and his family that the League angles its product, it is his money at the turnstiles, his 'boy' playing the game and his family spectating. This is where the market lies, not with the upper end of the market with 'quiche lorraine and side salad' thrown in. It is the 'punter' who in the past has provided the money and the talent for the long-term good of the game. The executive end of the market is only seen as marginal when compared with the income that can be derived from 30,000 or so fans turning out to watch.

Evidence of the SFL's thinking in terms of target market can be seen when we consider the sponsorship money being attracted: Fine Fare supermarkets, Mitre football products and Skol lager, all operating at the lower end of their respective markets. Further articulation of the marketing activities of the SFL can elicit its current marketing strategy.

Marketing Activities

Promotion

The SFL has on occasions allowed its product to be promoted in conjunction with another. A campaign whereby vouchers were enclosed with a particular brand of soap powder entitling the customer to attend a Premier Division League match of his/her choice is an example of the type of campaign periodically mounted. The pricing policy mentioned earlier is seen as another way of promoting a game where the fixture may prove less attractive than others.

Advertising

Football is seen as an ideal vehicle to promote/heighten awareness of a consumer product. A by-product and result of its broadly based consumer appeal is the ability of the League to negotiate deals whereby the 'coverage' of football is inextricably linked with some other product/service. Sponsorship as it is known provides the League with its second major source of revenue and it would be true to say that the SFL's deal is not in advertising, but in advertising space by promoting very actively this type of relationship. Glossy brochures advertise to potential customers the benefits from being sponsors of its variously packaged product.

At the corporate level, the SFL does very little in terms of advertising, content to let clubs themselves entice their audience.

Publicity

It is in this area of the communications mix that the SFL excels. The evidence is the average daily newspaper/tabloid dedicating some two to four pages of news coverage exclusively to the product. Its manipulation of the press and TV ensures a stimulation of demand by planting commercially significant items of news, via these media, for its public/customers at a negligible cost. Specific personnel within the organization are entrusted with the task of briefing or 'leaking' the propaganda, generally steeped in controversy and intrigue. The League's awareness of the nuances of and benefits from good public relations has resulted in a specially designed room equipped with external communication lines and the ubiquitous 'bar' (the negligible cost). By gearing itself for this type of activity the League could be said to be running a very slick and effective public relations department and benefiting from it as a result.

Financial Information

By far the main source of income for the SFL is the 'Pool Promoters Association' (PPA). Royalties accruing from the copyrights of the Scottish Football League's fixtures provide about £1.6 million per annum. This represents 25% of a total figure based on 2.25% of the 'net turnover' of the PPA. Contracts are entered into for periods of between 8 and 10 years, both parties seeing this as particularly advantageous in terms of stability and future planning. Sponsorship, the second major source of revenue, is split between several of the products, the main areas being:

(1) *League Championship* This has been sponsored by Fine Fare supermarkets to the sum of £250,000 per year (£750,000 for the three-year deal expiring May 1988).

(2) *League Cup* This has been sponsored by Skol Lager providing some £150,000. The SFL had this sponsorship involvement until 1982. A new three-year deal was then signed involving a total sum of £600,000.

(3) *Footballs and sportswear* Mitre sportswear contributed £50,000 per year for the endorsement of its products by the SFL, as well as 1,000 'free' footballs worth £65,000 (total £115,000).

(4) *Scottish Football League Review* A glossy compendium of facts and figures for the enthusiast published by the League and sponsored by the Clydesdale Bank Plc, contributing about £50,000 per year.

These inflows of cash are distributed to the member clubs at certain times of the year, after the running costs of the League (overheads, etc.) have been deducted. The basis of distribution, often a contentious issue, is such that the

Premier Division receives the lion's share. The exact details of the system are rather convoluted and serve no purpose within the marketing context. Suffice it to say that eight clubs in Scotland attract 69% of the total spectators to the game and that the basis of allocation is in no way reflective of this statistic.

From the Balance Sheet (Exhibit 28.1), the reader will observe that the 'Capital Account' sitting at £163,000 at 31 March 1985 is perhaps on the low side when you consider the size, complexity and responsibility of the body. This sum was designed for 'festivities' in their centenary year 1990, mainly because of the complex taxation implications. The policy of distributing all its revenues to the membership is short-term thinking at its worst and will in the long term serve no useful purpose in that the money is only going to bail out the less financially stable clubs. The laws of economic survival should be allowed to prevail, letting the more successful clubs thrive without the drain on resources by the lesser ones. The League, by securing 'reserves', would be able to plan strategically the way ahead.

The extent of the severe decline in public demand for the professional game threatened the complete collapse of the football industry in the late 1970s. Since then a levelling off has provided its administrators with a breathing space to allow

Exhibit 28.1   The Scottish Football League Balance Sheet 31 March 1985

		1984
	£	£
Current Assets		
Sundry Debtors	84,335	253,055
Stock	1,518	1,640
Bank – Current Account	89,559	23,423
Deposits – Money Market and Building Society	880,000	765,000
Cash in Hand	624	49
	1,056,036	1,043,167
Current Liabilities		
Monetary Awards	541,025	389,025
Sundry Creditors	410,737	570,735
Taxation	–	–
	951,762	959,760
Net Current Assets	104,274	83,407
Fixed Assets	74,450	64,548
Deferred Taxation	(15,267)	(5,287)
	£163,457	£142,668
Capital Account		
Balance at 1 April 1984	142,668	138,168
Surplus for year after taxation	20,789	4,500
Balance at 31 March 1985	£163,457	£142,668

The Financial Statements were approved by the Management Committee on 2 May 1985

DAVID LETHAM, President
JAMES FARRY, Secretary

a rethink and develop appropriate counter offensives before the game could again be sucked into the vortex of falling revenues and rising costs. That is unless a complete turnaround is achieved. Indeed the chequered history of the SFL makes its plight all the more galling in that large sums of money at one time flowed freely in and out of the game, and that their lack of policy and lack of foresight in marketing terms has contributed greatly to their present predicament. Indications are that the honing rather than abandonment of current thinking will hasten the reversal of trends already under way, auguring well for the future.

Questions

(1) How do you assess the process of setting the institutional goals and objectives of the Scottish Football League?

(2) Develop a SWOT (strengths, weaknesses, opportunities and threats) analysis of the Scottish Football League.

(3) What bases (approaches and variables) could the SFL utilize in order to segment the market?

(4) Describe the critical implications for designing a broad marketing strategy for the SFL.

(5) Develop a marketing mix programme that can contribute to the achievement of the SFL's goals and objectives.

(6) How should a manager evaluate and measure the effectiveness of sports marketing sponsorship?

The Scottish Football League – Case Study Update

Current League Structure

When the original case study was written, the league had 38 clubs arranged into Premier, First and Second Divisions with 10, 14 and 14 clubs respectively. A change to a 12, 12, 14 formation was then agreed. Suggestions were reportedly put forward in 1992 for the formation of a 'Super League', containing only the very top clubs out of the current Premier Division. However, only five Scottish clubs appeared to qualify, in terms of financial and on the pitch success, for such a league. Nothing has come of these proposals, but as from the 1994/95 season the Premier Division has been reduced in size to 10 clubs. Two additional clubs have joined the League, and a Third Division has been formed. The current format of the League is thus 40 clubs, divided into Premier, First, Second and Third Divisions of 10 clubs each.

SFL Sponsorship

The three-year deal with Fine Fare ended in May 1988. For the following three seasons (1988/89 up to 1991/92) the League Championship was sponsored by the DIY chain B & Q. This was a high-profile and active sponsorship; B & Q introduced many innovative support activities, as follows:

- *B & Q Fair Play League* – a league designed specifically to recognize fair play, and based on the disciplinary performances of the SFL clubs in League fixtures. A Waterford Crystal trophy was presented to the winners.

- *B & Q Super Skill Awards* – presented to players who had shown skill and craftsmanship in their game. Recipients received £100 worth of B & Q vouchers and a commemorative pennant. Overall season winners were presented with a Waterford Crystal decanter and matching glasses.

- *The B & Q Cup* – for Scotland's First and Second Division clubs only. B & Q ran an initial, one-off, Centenary Cup tournament for these two divisions in the 1990/91 season, and this was so successful that First and Second Division clubs unanimously supported the idea of continuing it as an annual cup competition. B & Q has agreed to continue to sponsor this competition.

- B & Q *Football Today Magazine*, published by the Scottish Braille Press.

- The B & Q Schoolboys Cup.

- *The B & Q (Schools) Soccer Skills Challenge* – an annual schools-based competition for under 15s, encouraging the development of young players.

- The B & Q North of Scotland Amateur Cup.

- The B & Q East of Scotland Amateur Cup.

- The B & Q Under 16 Amateur Cup.

B & Q sees its sponsorship of football, especially at the local and amateur level, as an opportunity for community involvement and as an investment, both in the present and for the future. Its activities are regularly covered by the sports media, gaining much publicity for the B & Q name. B & Q's chief executive, Jim Hodkinson, said in February 1992, 'We believe that we have given much to Scottish Football, and have enjoyed our sponsorship and the warm appreciation from fans and administrators alike. We have gained a great deal from our relationship with the League Championship and I know that the contribution we have made has been equally strong.'

B & Q's sponsorship of the League Championship ended in 1992, but its sponsorship of the B & Q Cup, *Football Today Magazine*, and its support for schools competition and the three amateur football cups continued. Also, recognition of fair play and of individual players was transferred to the B & Q Cup.

The current (1994) sponsor of the Scottish League Championship is Bell's Whisky, based at Perth in central Scotland. Its sponsorship is worth around £6 million over four years. Bell's feels that its association with the League will allow it to support the sport at all levels and across the whole country, and that both Bell's and football will benefit greatly. Bell's will also undertake additional activities, including Bell's Player and Manager of the Month/Year and Bell's Young Player of the Month/Year (for players aged 18–21).

The Scottish League Cup competition is now sponsored by Coca-Cola, which is investing about £3 million over four seasons. Scotland is an important market for Coca-Cola and Coca-Cola & Schweppes Beverages, the company's operating partner, has a major plant at East Kilbride, near Glasgow. Coca-Cola worldwide has sponsored a wide variety of sports, including football, baseball, cycling, stock-car racing and the Olympic Games. In Scotland over the past 20 years it has sponsored the European Special Olympics held in Strathclyde in 1990 and the Scottish Schools Golf Championships, and has supported the Scottish Schools Swimming Association.

Exhibit 28.2 details the various sponsorship agreements of the SFL.

Football – Marketing and Sponsorship

British football in the past has not been marketing-oriented. Many clubs believed that the most important factor in encouraging attendance at games was the team's performance, and paid little attention to the environment and facilities. However,

Exhibit 28.2 The Scottish Football League's Sponsorship Agreements

Company	Sponsorship	Commenced (season)	Duration	Worth (£m)
Bell's Whisky	League Championship	1994/95	4 years	6
Coca-Cola	League Cup	1994/95	4 years	3
Scottish Television	Broadcast of Bell's League Championship matches	1994/95	4 years	2.5+
BBC Scotland	Broadcast of Bell's League Championship and Coca-Cola Cup matches	1994/95	4 years	2
B & Q	B & Q Cup for 1st, 2nd, 3rd Division clubs	1991/92	4 years	0.4
Radio Clyde	Broadcast of League and Cup matches	1991/92	4 years	0.25
Mitre	Official supplier of footballs for League and Cup matches	1993/94	3 years	0.15
BBC Radio Scotland	Broadcast of League and Cup matches	1993/94	2 years	0.13
Scottish Brewers	Scottish Football League Review Book	1993/94	3 years	0.075
TWI	Sale of League and Cup matches to overseas broadcasters	1994/95	3 years	0.25

clubs are beginning to realize that the leisure industry is highly competitive, with football only one of a range of activities on which people may choose to spend their time and disposable income. The Taylor Report (1990), which followed the Hillsborough football ground disaster, revealed that many football grounds were unmodernized and often overcrowded, with inadequate facilities. Taylor called for a positive initiative from the football industry to upgrade grounds, making them 'seats only', to provide better facilities, and to reduce hooliganism.

Clubs have responded in different ways to this challenge. Millwall and Watford, for instance, aim to bring back football as family entertainment, as is seen in the United States. Watford has even opened a creche during matches to encourage the whole family to attend. Millwall is also home to one of the leading women's football teams in the country, the Millwall Lionesses, and this may attract more female interest in the club. (Women's football has seen a steady growth in popularity, with the first women's world championships being held in China in 1991.) Leeds United, Sunderland and Brentford are some of the clubs targeting local businesses for sponsorship. Sunderland tours trading estates with its promotional bus to attract local business people to sponsor the club, and dispenses gifts and corporate hospitality to encourage them to continue sponsorship. Leeds was one of the first clubs to become involved in corporate hospitality, installing executive boxes with armchairs, fridges, heating and a restaurant available, and also building a banqueting suite. Brentford's marketing and fund-raising activities have diversified into a two-day golf tournament, a supporters' tour of the United States and a telephone information service.

Even less well-known clubs in the lower divisions are able to find sponsors for their matches. Large TV audiences for football and the availability of demographic statistics showing who watches football, both live and on TV, have contributed to the increase in sponsorship for business names and logos on shirts and ground perimeter boards. Club shops can also be a source of revenue – Arsenal's World of Sport souvenir arcade sells merchandise bearing the team's crest, from small souvenirs up to leather baseball jackets and expensive jewellery. This merchandise is also sold by mail order.

Football sponsors in the United Kingdom currently include several alcohol companies, for example Bell's, Carlsberg, Skol, John Smiths and Federation Brewery, plus other large companies such as General Motors, Great Mills DIY and Endsleigh Insurance. However, despite a doubling of sponsorship revenues in the period 1987–91, the amounts of money raised by sponsorship are tiny compared with the commercial support given to the larger continental clubs – Juventus, for instance, is financed by Fiat, Inter Milan by Silvio Berlusconi and Leverkusen (West Germany) by the large chemicals company Bayer. British football may still not have overcome its image problems sufficiently to attract this level of sponsorship.

The 1994 World Cup, the world's biggest sporting event, was sponsored by MasterCard, which also sponsors the US national football team. MasterCard took every opportunity to get the most out of its sponsorship. A year before the tournament started, the company ran a series of seminars in the cities where World Cup games would be played, introducing businesses to the advantages of promoting MasterCard. It tied World Cup sponsorship into its existing Master Values Programme (its major point-of-sale promotion), used the soccer star Pele on mail promotions, distributed a World Cup Guide for visitors, and promoted Master-Card in association with travel agents, supermarkets, restaurants, cinemas and fast-food chains, in order to get maximum value from the thousands of international visitors who travelled to the United States for the tournament.

Sponsorship of football (or indeed any other sport) by companies may not always be, however, favoured by all their customers. Barclays Bank's recent sponsorship of the English Football League was discussed in a 1991 report in *Marketing Business*. Sponsorship involved the division of a lump sum, of the order of £1.5–2 million, among all the League clubs. In return, each club provided Barclays with facilities including advertising boards around their ground, a full-page advertisment in match programmes and 10 complimentary tickets for each Barclays League game. Barclays' chairman, John Quinton, believed firmly in the value of this sponsorship in promoting Barclays to people of all ages and sociological groups, young people in particular. Four Barclays' customers were also asked for their views on the sponsorship. In favour were cited the more respectable image gained by football by the association with Barclays, and the fact that large sums of money were needed to keep the sport of football alive, especially at club level. Against, the point was made that money given to football was money that could be used to give the bank's customers a better deal, for instance in terms of bank charges, although the response to this could be that sponsorship money comes out of the promotions budget, and if it was not spent on football it would go on some other promotional activity. It was also felt that the specific choice of football to sponsor could be seen as ignoring female customers.

The Finances of British Football Clubs

Despite increasing revenues from sponsorship, most British football clubs are still not profitable. Even some of the leading teams, with well developed fund raising strategies, do little more than break even, and their turnover is tiny compared with continental teams. For example, Arsenal's 1990/91 turnover was £6 million compared with the £100 million of the Italian club Juventus.

A few clubs have tried to raise revenues by floating their shares on the stock market, but the example of Tottenham Hotspur, the first club to do this, shows that this does not always solve financial problems. Its initial share issue in 1987 was four times over-subscribed, yet by 1991 the club was £13 million in debt, due to mismanaged diversification attempts and problems in stadium development.

Statistics from the English Football League show that the main financial problem is not revenue from gate receipts, but costs, mainly wages. Although attendances have fallen dramatically since the peak years of football after the war, they have not decreased as much as have cinema attendances. In 1948–49 41.3 million people attended league matches, while in 1989–90 the figure was 19.5 million. The rise in ticket prices has ensured that gate revenue has increased faster than inflation – from £5.48 million in 1963/64, to £38.73 million in 1980/81, to £84.71 million in 1989/90. However, the average wage for First Division players in 1991 was around £1,500 a week. The transfer market, valued at £55 million in 1989/90, can be both a source of revenue or of losses for clubs. In the English Football League (1989/90) it was found that First Division clubs paid out more than they received in transfer fees, to the benefit of the Third and Fourth Divisions who made overall gains in this market.

Further costs are being incurred by the implementation of the recommendations of the Taylor report, especially the introduction of all-seat stadiums. Some smaller clubs see a way round this by just closing the terracing of their grounds, as their current seating is sufficient for most lower division matches. However, they run the risk of then being unable to gain the revenue from big matches, if, for instance, they are drawn in a cup tie against a major club. Large clubs, on the other hand, may raise money by hiring their ground for use for other sports or mass events.

A further future source of finance could be the UK national lottery, which started in late 1994, and the proceeds of which will be distributed among charities, the arts and sport (through the Sports Council).

It is interesting to compare attitudes to the financing of football in Europe and in the United States. In Europe, each country has its own football league, typically with around half a dozen clubs which are more successful and also richer than the others. There are limits on the number of foreigners a club may have playing for it, so although there are some inter-country transfers, one rich club cannot buy up too many star players. There is a limited amount of revenue sharing, but this is not always appreciated by the richer participants. One of the reasons for the formation of the English Premier League was the desire of top clubs for a larger share of television money, and the reported wish of top Scottish clubs to form a Super League may have been similarly influenced. In the United States, however, the system is more egalitarian. Each football league has a company to sell merchandising rights. Successful clubs' merchandise may sell many times better than others', but each club gets an equal share of profits. National TV broadcasting payments are also shared equally. At any match, the visiting team takes 40% of the gate receipts. Finally, the 'draft' system, where top college players are recruited to the big teams, is set up to favour the less successful teams.

Sponsorship Decisions

How do companies decide which sport to sponsor, or indeed whether to sponsor sport at all? Most large companies will not have to go looking for sponsorship opportunities – they will be approached by agents working for individuals, teams and sports federations. But, to get the most out of their sponsorship, the sport and player or team they pick must match in some way the company's objectives. So, first, a player or team must be successful. Then there is the question of image. The sport and the personalities must match the image a company wishes to project. A sport may also give a company the chance to project some particular positive image to its market, for instance B & Q's sponsorship, mentioned above, of a fair play bonus scheme and of youth and local football, and the sports equipment company Adidas which works with FIFA to equip young footballers in developing countries.

An example of a major and successful sponsor of several sports is the Swedish car manufacturer Volvo. For many years it has had an association with professional tennis, which is extended to local US club tennis leagues and college coaches. Other sports sponsored by Volvo include golf and showjumping. All sponsored sports are carefully chosen to reflect the image Volvo wishes to achieve for itself, attracting players and spectators who belong to the company's demographically and psychographically segmented target market. In 1990, Volvo reckons that it gained £7 in media value for every £1 spent on tennis promotion and sponsorship – an excellent payback by any standards!

The Future

The possibility that the whole sports marketing industry could be heading for financial disaster, at least in the United States, was raised in *Marketing News* of 5 August 1991. The reasons given included:

- The ever-increasing cost of broadcasting, promoting, sponsoring and attending sports events.

- In contrast the lack of money among sports teams and broadcasters.

- The difficulty of quantifying returns on sponsorship (as with many promotional activities).

- Government monitoring of sports marketing activities, particularly in the areas of alcohol and tobacco advertising, and pressure from consumer groups in these areas.

Increasing costs of sponsorship mean that sponsors will look more closely at what they are getting from their sponsorship, and will demand better measurement of the benefits gained. Increasing costs of attendance, coupled with more and more TV coverage, may lead to a decrease in attendances – but if subscriptions to non-network channels also increase, due to rising broadcasting costs, this could lead to fans being priced out of the market completely and losing interest in a sport.

The massive number of TV channels in the United States undoubtedly plays a part in increasing competitiveness and raising costs, while it also means that viewers have so many choices of channel that each channel's audience share has decreased. This means that networks have had to consider new options in order to reduce costs, such as subcontracting to independent producers, networks putting on sports events themselves, covering them and possibly selling them on to others, and selling highlights of sponsored games.

The United Kingdom currently has a much smaller number of non-network channels than the United States, so there is not the same amount of competition. However, the costs of attending and broadcasting sports events are rising in the United Kingdom also. Whether the US industry is indeed heading for financial disaster, and whether the United Kingdom will follow the United States, remains to be seen.

Questions

(1) Why do you think the Scottish Football League's current sponsors – Bell's Whisky, Coca-Cola, B & Q and Mitre – have chosen to sponsor Scottish football?

(2) What would be the advantages and disadvantages to the Scottish Football League and the Scottish clubs of operating a revenue sharing scheme, similar to that described in United States football?